TRIAL OF MODERNITY

Trial of Modernity

Judicial Reform in Early Twentieth-Century China, 1901–1937

XIAOQUN XU

STANFORD UNIVERSITY PRESS
STANFORD, CALIFORNIA

Stanford University Press
Stanford, California

Some of the material in this book has appeared in print previously in different form: "Negotiating Western Models and Chinese Practices: Judicial Reform in the Late Qing 'New Policy,' 1901–1911" was originally published in *As China Meets the World: China's Changing Position in the International Community*, edited by Susanne Weigelin-Schwiedrzik, Agnes Schick-Chen, and Sascha Klotzbücher, ©2006, Verlag der Österreichischen Akademie der Wissenschaften. Reprinted with permission. "The Rule of Law Without Due Process: Punishing Robbers and Bandits in Early-Twentieth-Century China" was originally published in the journal *Modern China* (vol. 33, no. 2), ©2007, Sage Publications. Reprinted with permission.

Library of Congress Cataloging-in-Publication Data
Xu, Xiaoqun
Trial of modernity : judicial reform in early twentieth-century China, 1901–1937 / Xiaoqun Xu.
p. cm.
Includes bibliographical references and index.
ISBN 978-0-8047-5586-3 (cloth : alk. paper)
1. Justice, Administration of—China—History. 2. Law reform—China—History. I. Title.

KNN1572.X89 2008
340'.3095109041—dc22

2007049989

Typeset at Stanford University Press in 10/12.5 Palatino

For
My Parents

Contents

Map and Tables

Preface

This book grew out of a study on the issue of judicial independence in Republican China, which in turn arose from a study on the Chinese legal profession in that era. In the course of researching those issues, I noticed that there were virtually no studies on the Chinese judicial system in the Republican era. Most published scholarly works on Chinese laws and judicial practices focused either on the imperial era (221 BCE–1911 CE) or on the People's Republic of China (PRC) (1949–present), leaving the Republican period (1912–1949) largely unexplored. That "state of the art" in China studies prompted me to take up the research that has resulted in this book.

Between then and now, a few studies have appeared that shed some light on the subject. Books by Kathryn Bernhardt and Philip Huang on civil justice in China compared laws and judicial practices in the imperial era and the Republican era. Huang's book briefly sketched the development of judicial institutions from the late Qing to the early Republican period, as did my article on judicial independence in Republican China. Frank Dikötter studied the development of Chinese prisons during 1895–1949. Generally speaking, however, the evolution of the Chinese judiciary and judicial practices or the unfolding of the Chinese judicial reform in the early twentieth century has yet to be fully documented and analyzed, which in my view belongs to what may be called "basic research" in China studies. This book aims to fill that gap in China scholarship with an overview of the judicial reform during 1901–1937 and a closer examination of its results in Jiangsu province to understand how and why various reform initiatives issued from the central government were, or failed to be, carried out at the provincial and county levels.

This study is also worth pursuing because of its contemporary relevance. The project of striving for judicial modernity in Republican China and its ramifications offer clues to, and help an understanding of, the achievements and limitations in the similar project in post-Mao China, since many parallels between the two can be found. I hope this book will interest scholars of contemporary China and comparative law as well as historians of modern China and Chinese law.

The use of the word "modernity" in this book does not signify that I am oblivious to the criticisms of the discourse on modernity and of the dichotomy assumed between tradition and modernity. In fact, this study is a critical examination of the impact on China of the discourse on modernity (and the international power relations behind it). As will become clear to readers, I intend to show how Chinese reformers in the early twentieth century were caught up by the discourse on modernity (in various forms and vocabularies) and were compelled to act accordingly, and how the efforts to comply with the requirements for being modern led to paradoxical consequences and unsolvable issues in the judicial system and local society, and therefore to many trials and tribulations in the course of the reform, which is what the title "trial of modernity" refers to. Similarly, the term "judicial modernity" is shorthand for "a Western-style judiciary and judicial practices."

Regrettably, because of the space limit set by the press, I have to use many acronyms for institutions and titles mentioned in the text and to omit Chinese characters for some key words or phrases.

I cherish this opportunity to express my gratitude to the institutions and individuals that supported and helped me during the course of researching and writing this book. The initial archival research for the project was conducted during the 1998–1999 academic year, with the support of a National Endowment for the Humanities Fellowship for College Teachers. Without that crucial support, this project would not have been attempted at the time. I thank the NEH (and its readers of the applications) for offering the award to a project at its beginning phase, which strengthened my confidence in the worthiness of the project and my determination to complete it. The Professional Development Committee at Francis Marion University offered grants to support my follow-up research trips to China in the summers of 2000 and 2002. A

Dean's Office Summer Grant at College of Liberal Arts and Sciences of Christopher Newport University helped my final revisions of the manuscript.

The staff at the Number Two Historical Archives and the Jiangsu Provincial Archives rendered professional services. I wish to thank Ge Xia, Huang Zhan, and Liu Jingjing at the latter institution in particular for their assistance. The staff at the Pudong New District Archives, the Songjiang District Archives, and the Baoshan District Archives, and the Shanghai Municipal Library Modern Documents Section all contributed to this project more than they realize.

Bryna Goodman kindly agreed to read an earlier version of the manuscript. She offered helpful comments and suggestions for improving the manuscript, as did three anonymous readers for the press. Needless to say, I am alone responsible for any defects that may exist in the book.

I thank Muriel Bell, Kirsten Oster, and Joa Suorez of Stanford University Press for their work on this project, and Peter Dreyer for his copy-editing.

I am indebted to my son and wife, who tolerated my absences, due to this project, from many events and occasions normally important to a child and to a family. Finally, I dedicate this book to my parents, who encouraged me to major in history when I took a college entrance exam in China many years ago.

XIAOQUN XU
Yorktown, Virginia

Abbreviations

AC	Administrative Court
BP	Board of Punishment
CAD	Civil Affairs Department
CC	County Court
CCP	Chinese Communist Party
CFI	Court of First Instance
CGO	County Government Office
CJD	County Judicial Division
CJO	County Judicial Office
CSCG	Commission on Studying Constitutional Government
DC	District Court
DP	District Procuracy
FBHC	First Branch High Court
FD	Finance Department
GAC	Government Advisory Council
GMD	Guomindang (Kuomintang; Nationalist Party)
GP	General Procuracy
HC	High Court
HDJ	Heilongjiang Department of Justice
HP	High Procuracy
JC	Judicial Council
JD	Justice Department
JFP	Jiangsu First Prison
JHC	Jiangsu High Court

JHP	Jiangsu High Procuracy
JPJD	Jiangsu Provincial Justice Department
JSP	Jiangsu Second Prison
JTP	Jiangsu Third Prison
LCC	Law Codification Commission
LPRB	Law on Punishing Robbers and Bandits (1914)
MC	Military Commission
MF	Ministry of Finance
MJ	Ministry of Justice
ML	Ministry of Law
MLD	Martial Law Division
MPC	Military Police Command
NG	National Government
NGC	Nanjing Garrison Command
NRA	Nationalist Revolutionary Army
OPJI	Office of Preparation for Judicial Institutions
PC	Provisional Court
PGC	Provincial Government Commission
PNCC	Provisional New Criminal Code (1912)
PRPRB	Provisional Regulations on Punishing Robbers and Bandits (1927)
SC	Supreme Court
TPO	Trial and Prosecution Office

Republican Jiangsu

TRIAL OF MODERNITY

Introduction

> Right now a violent Japan is peddling its propaganda that China is a "nonmodern" state to the world in an attempt to deceive foreign powers and accomplish its design to dismember [China]; what our country needs is the aid of international public opinion, and what international public opinion will aid are "modern" states [*xiandai shi zhi guojia*]. The so-called modern state is defined not only by whether it is independent and unified, capable of protecting its own people and fulfilling international obligations, but also, as one of the main conditions, by whether it is a state of "the rule of law." If we destroy the rule of law ourselves, that would be no less than to provide evidence for Japan's international propaganda! The impact of this would go much further than just bringing [China's] national reputation down!
>
> —Shi Lianfang, *Falü pinglun* (Law Review [Beijing]), June 5, 1932[1]

Shi Lianfang's remarks reflected the logic of the modern world history underpinned by the rise of the West. Western conquest of and dominance in non-Western countries was accompanied and justified by a discourse on the backwardness of "uncivilized," "traditional," "premodern" conditions in those countries. In order to be free of colonial and semi-colonial shackles, a non-Western country had to demonstrate that it had become "modern" and was "ready" for self-determination. By the early 1930s, of course, Japan had long since achieved the status of being "modern" or sufficiently westernized and joined the imperialist club as an "honorary white" nation.[2] For obvious reasons, judicial modernity (that is, a Western-style judiciary and judicial practices) was one of the key markers by which a country was measured as modern or less than modern. Japan's judicial system and penal regime were among the first institutions to be reformed after the Meiji restoration, precisely because the previous Japanese methods of punishment were identified as barbaric and cited as justification for the unequal treaties signed between Japan and Western powers. Toward the end of the nineteenth century, after reforming its penal system and qualifying as a quasi-modern nation, Japan succeeded in getting the treaties revised.[3] In the early 1930s, in its attempt to colonize the Chinese mainland, Japan was deploying the same discourse as Western colonial powers did. Shi Lianfang's poignant comments pointed out the discursive power China had to deal with and the urgent task China faced of reforming its judiciary in order to make the country a modern nation-state and an equal member of international society.

Notably, in Chinese official discourse (official communications) on judicial reform in the New Policy decade (1901–1911) and the Beiyang era (1912–1927), reform-minded officials cited Western models by referring to "countries in the world" (*shijie geguo*), "countries in the East and the West" (*dongxi geguo*), "all countries" (*wanguo*), or simply "various countries" (*geguo*). By these terms, the officials meant the Western nations and Japan, which came to be identified with the world and thus universalized. Such an equation of the West (and Japan) with the world became a standard formula in the official discourse on reform, especially prior to the Nanjing decade (1927–1937). The equation revealed a particular conceptualization of the modern world that the Chinese had accepted owing to China's traumatic experiences since the Opium War: the modern world was a club, to which only countries that had modernized could belong. It was into this club that educated Chinese hoped China would qualify to enter through successful modernization. Although in the Nanjing decade, Guomindang (GMD) officials began to take some exception to the supposed universality of Western models, they continued to aspire to a modern Chinese judiciary as a ticket qualifying China to enter that club. In essence, the task was to transform traditional laws and judicial practices (*jiufa, jiulü*) into ones similar to their Western counterparts (*xinlü, xinzhi*) so that China would be considered "ready" for judicial sovereignty—the abolition of extraterritoriality. This was the international dimension of the underlying historical context of China's judicial reform in the early twentieth century.

The guiding principles of the judicial reform were the rule of law, judicial independence, and due process. To Chinese reformers, the rule of law would mean legal equality for all, with even government officials being held accountable to the law that was in force. Judicial independence was widely understood as (1) the judiciary being separate from state administration at all levels, and (2) judges adjudicating independently, free of interference by any authority.[4] Due process of law would ensure the rights of the accused and the impartial and fair resolution of civil disputes and criminal prosecution through established rules and open procedures.

Under those principles, from the final years of the Qing dynasty through the Nanjing decade, the reform agendas consistently included the establishment of the following: (1) a set of substantive and procedural laws that would separate criminal and civil proceedings, (2) a multi-level court system across the country that would allow for two appeals after the first trial, (3) a trained and disciplined corps of judicial officers such as procurators, judges, and prison administrators, (4) due process underpinned by criminal and civil procedural laws and checked by a regulated legal profession, and (5) humane punishments for crimes, with a reformed prison system in accordance with prevailing penal and criminological theories and practices in the West.

These reform goals and the principles behind them involved some fundamental reconceptualizations of the judicial functions of the state, as well as unprecedented measures of institutional construction and reforms that were part of modern state building. In traditional Chinese thought on statecraft, applying law and administering justice were considered the last resort in governance, implying a failure in moral suasion and virtuous rule on the part of the state; by the same token, resorting to litigation in civil matters or being charged and punished for crimes would mean a failure in moral rectitude and virtuous living on the part of ordinary people. By the time of the New Policy reforms, however, those notions of law and justice had changed to a new conception informed by Western models. Judicial institutions and processes were perceived as a necessary part of modern state functions and the appropriate venue for resolving disputes and punishing crimes. The typical Qing official mentality that took a negative view of all litigation and attributed case backlogs at yamens to people's litigiousness and pettifoggers' incitation no longer prevailed in the official discourse during 1901–1937.[5] Although legal scribes known as "litigation masters/sticks" continued to exist and case backlogs at all levels continued to be a fact of life and considered a serious problem, it was a problem now attributed, not to those who brought civil suits and caused criminal prosecutions, but to the inadequacy of the judiciary and the failings of judicial personnel. In a word, judicial modernity was considered the solution to all the problems in judicial process.

This book examines what judicial modernity actually meant to the Chinese state and society—to administrative officials and judicial officers at all levels, county magistrates and their staff, civil litigants and criminal defendants, and elite and nonelite people in local society. It looks into what intellectual and institutional innovations and adjustments were involved when reform initiatives were envisioned by the central government, how such agendas were received and responded to at the provincial and county levels, and how administrative and judicial institutions functioned and interacted with one another and with local society during the course of the reform. Other questions need to be asked. What impact did the reform have on local society? How far did it change social dynamics and power relations there? How did Chinese, elite and nonelite alike, make use of the increasingly accessible judicial system in their contests for resources or dominance? In short, the study explores what occurred when, in the course of the reform, the dynamics and logic of state institutions came to intersect and interact with those of local society, where the state efforts at modernizing—penetrating, regulating, and reforming—local society were manifested, resisted, and negotiated on a daily basis.[6]

It might be expected that the judicial reform, a daunting task in its own right under any circumstances, would encounter many problems and difficulties, and that it would inevitably have unintended consequences. Given the accumulated weight of official legal tradition (laws and judicial practices) and popular legal culture (litigation strategies and behavior), what was accomplished in the reform during 1901–1937 was remarkable, albeit falling well short of the goals set by the central government. In addition to documenting the strenuous efforts made by the reformers and their partial successes, however, this book also analyzes the reasons for the many defects and failures of the reform. The problems may easily be attributed to financial difficulties and resultant institutional inadequacies, which were often cited by contemporaries to account for the shortcomings of the reform. That is certainly a very important reason, and it is examined in some detail, but the financial woes do not tell the whole story. Although the reform achieved measurable progress under unfavorable conditions, including financial constraints, given the social environment of China at that time, the judicial modernity pushed by the central government created its own problems at the provincial and county levels, which had paradoxical consequences. To further conceptualize and contextualize the reform and its successes and failures, several analytical themes are outlined, as follows.

Judicial Modernization as Formalization

To capture the essence of what reformers tried to accomplish, one may define judicial modernity as formal justice, and judicial modernization as the formalization of legal institutions and procedures in accordance with uniform standards and modern techniques.

When the Qing dynasty (1644–1911) began to embark upon an ambitious project of modernization known as New Policy at the turn of the twentieth century, judicial reform was part of the project. One of the prominent features of a modern state that Chinese reformers accepted as necessary and pursued persistently was the rationalization and expansion of the state system and its functions. This was especially true of the judiciary, and the reform was to build institutions and lay down rules and procedures by which judicial functions would be performed in proper institutional settings.

To achieve judicial modernity, the reform focused on formalization, standardization, and bureaucratization. Ever-more-minute and elaborate rules and regulations were prescribed for institutions and procedures in the judiciary. All manner of norms and forms were spelled out in laws, ordinances, rules, regulations, directives, and orders, literally thousands of which were enacted, amended, issued, reiterated, repealed, and reinstated during 1901–1937. To be sure, in traditional China, the state bureaucracy also relied on rules and procedures. But at that time, the rules and procedures in adjudicating litigation and administering punishments were simpler, because the judicial functions of chief officials at the provincial level and below were not separate from the administrative ones. In contrast, the procedures, rules, norms, and forms that resulted from the reform greatly surpassed those of earlier times, being much more specific, comprehensive, and numerous. In the Republican era, for instance, litigants had to choose from among no fewer than fourteen kinds of judicial forms to fill out when they wanted to engage the state's judicial functions in any way. A fee was to be paid by litigants for each form they used, and each payment was to be documented, reported, and accounted for. Breaches in any of the formal rules were considered failures in achieving judicial modernity. And all rules and procedures were to be followed in formal institutional settings—courts, procuracies, prisons, and judicial administrative offices.

In short, the entire judicial reform can be viewed as a continuous effort to produce norms and forms and turn them into formal, *working* institutions and procedures at all levels of the judicial system, and the state system as a whole. Consequently, the project of achieving judicial modernity as performance of formality entailed a host of institutional and social ramifications in the history of early-twentieth-century Chinese judicial practices. These included continuous state expansion, massive paperwork within the state system, rising financial costs, and deviations from formalized practices, due to the limited effect of reform discourse and to local practices rooted in social environment—all this resulted in the ultimate paradox that the modernizing judicial system forever failed to reach the goals it set for itself.

Judicial Formalization and State Expansion

The formalization agenda had crucial implications for state expansion. First of all, it demanded centralization and uniformity in establishing and enforcing norms and forms. From the beginning, at the time of the New Policy, the Qing government aimed at centralization of state power, while allowing some incentives and expressions of provincial and local interests, in an attempt to "connect the country's territory, the people, and the state" (Chapter 1). The successive Republican governments largely inherited the centralization agenda, especially in the judicial field, but took provincial and local interests less into account, and thus faced more resistance from those interests. For reformers, centralization and uniformity were institutional prerequisites for an impartial and fair judiciary; indeed, without some uniform standards, there would have been no credible judicial system to enforce the rule of law, judicial independence, and due process. Centralization was therefore vigorously and persistently pursued in the judicial field throughout the Republican era.

Analysis of the institutional and procedural formalization as state expansion in Republican China involves the notion of "the reach of the state."[7] This book will show that during 1901–1937 the laws, rules, regulations, orders, and directives issued from the national capital reached and were followed within the judicial system at the provincial level and down to the county level where district courts and their branches were established. The matter was more complicated, and the patterns were diverse in counties where no courts were established and county magistrates performed judicial functions. In those places, the reform initiatives of the central government were followed to a larger degree in procedural formalization, though not consistently and universally, and to a much lesser degree in institutional formalization. The noncompliance in institutional formalization occurred, not because county officials would normally choose to ignore or shortchange the mandates from the central and provincial authorities, but because they lacked the necessary resources to carry out the mandates. In such cases, it would be inaccurate to conclude that the central government failed to "reach" the county level.

Theoretically, therefore, this study tries to convey a more complex understanding of the state in Republican China and its reach at the provincial and county levels than has hitherto been available.[8] The understanding requires a conceptualization of the state system and its reach in multiple dimensions and as *multiple hierarchies* that overlapped at lower levels. The judiciary was one of those dimensions and fields within the state system. The judicial field was composed of a hierarchy of judicial institutions at national, provincial, and county levels. At the same time, the judicial system was institutionally interacting with the administrative bureaucracy—another field of the state system with its own hierarchy, including counties at the lower level. Because the court system failed to be established in most counties, counties without courts were part of the hierarchy of the judicial field but were also part of the administrative field and subject to the provincial government. The administrative and judicial fields and their respective functions, therefore, overlapped and often conflicted at the county level. As the provincial governors were given powers to supervise judicial matters, the two fields further overlapped and interacted at the provincial level. Under those circumstances, the judiciary and its functions were subject to the influence of and interference from the administrative field. To complicate the matter further, in the Nanjing decade, an additional field—the GMD organization, with its own hierarchy—interacted with both the administrative and judicial fields. With different priorities and agendas, administrative officials (and GMD cadres) often acted in ways that distorted and subverted centralization, uniformity, and formalization in the judicial system, especially in places where formal courts were not established and county magistrates were under the stronger sway of the provincial government in judicial matters. As a result, the reach of the central government, the Ministry of Justice (MJ) in particular, manifested in different ways in different places, depending on the varying degree of the formalization of state judicial functions in those localities and the interaction between the judicial and administrative (and GMD) institutions.

To trace and understand the reach of the state in the course of the reform, this book addresses the tensions between the MJ and other agencies at the national capital, between the central government and provincial governments, between judicial officials and administrative officials at the provincial level, between provincial officials (judicial as well as administrative) and county officials, between county government offices and party organs at the county level, and between all the above and local people. As it turned out, the prominent theme in all those tensions was a constant contestation for financial resources. And our understanding of the said tensions is gained in the documents left behind by the formalization efforts.

Judicial Formalization and Documentation

In a sense, a drive for documentation or representation of policies being implemented and rules followed in a system or organization was a hallmark of modernity, or modern society. In a significant departure from the traditional practices, the reform mandated that every procedure and all institutional activities in the judiciary, from a case accepted for litigation or prosecution to its final resolution, were to be recorded, reported, categorized, and compiled in endless cycles of paperwork throughout the judicial system and beyond. These documents were material witnesses to a modernizing project, and they were literally part of that modernity in the making.

Although the interest of the central government in obtaining information from lower levels of the state system was nothing new, the scale and magnitude of paperwork resulting from the formalization agenda was unprecedented.[9] While the quantity of the information that the Republican state was collecting exceeded what the imperial state tried to get, a significant break between the two periods was in the nature and quality of the data that the state collected. The kind of information in which the Qing emperor was interested was essentially anecdotal (however vital it might have been to the emperor), whereas the Republican state wanted *statistical* and impersonal data about the state *system*. "From its inception," the sociologist Anthony Giddens observes, "the collation of official statistics has been constitutive of state power and of many other modes of social organization also. The coordinated administrative control achieved by modern governments is inseparable from the routine monitoring of 'official data' in which all contemporary states engage."[10] In this light, it is not surprising that as early as the New Policy decade, reform-minded officials spoke of "judicial statistics" and "prison statistics" as part of the judicial system to be established. Thus judicial modernity that included the formalization of data collection within the judiciary was a concrete aspect of modern state building in Republican China.

Besides a penchant for documenting, and accounting for, all institutional activities as a visible mark of being modern, the practical purpose of all paperwork was to inform the higher authorities about how the established norms and forms were followed or breached at lower levels. The norms and forms included the rules and procedures of making periodic reports to the higher authorities, as well as those of operating the judiciary. The MJ took great care to make sure all paperwork was in order and up to date. In 1917, when Minister of Justice Zhang Yaozeng found clerical errors in the reports on inmate deaths from the county jails in Wu and Huai'an in Jiangsu province, he brought each instance to the attention of the chief of the Jiangsu High Procuracy (JHP) and demanded elimination of such errors in the future.[11] In 1921, when the MJ found that the reports from the JHP did not indicate who was in charge of statistical documents collected in the province, it wanted an answer. When the JHP responded that three officials had successively been in charge of the task since February 1916, Minister of Justice Dong Kang immediately handed down disciplinary actions against these officials for having misfiled statistical documents (one of the three was simply fired, because his appointment did not have MJ approval), and the JHP chief was given a warning for failing to provide the statistics to the MJ in a timely fashion and to supervise his subordinates.[12] The ministry's attention to, or obsession with, complete and accurate data on the judiciary was driven by the need to know what transpired at the lower levels of the system. The MJ would routinely use the systemwide flow of documents to communicate reform initiatives to all officials and relied on the statistical data and written reports from below to monitor their implementation at the provincial and county levels. This was part and parcel of state expansion.

Judicial Formalization and Financial Costs

The project of judicial formalization was predicated on a rejection of the traditional notion of a minimalist state and an acceptance of an expansionist state, in terms of its functions and related expenditures. In a way similar to other New Policy projects (local self-government and new schools in particular), the formalization of judicial institutions and procedures entailed increasing financial costs that would not have been incurred with the traditional judicial practices. The costs included expenses at least on the following: training and selecting judges, procurators, court clerks, and prison officers through tests with specified standards; paying salaries to judicial personnel down to county jail guards at specified scales; building and operating courts, prisons, and detention houses with specified designs and standards; feeding prison and detention house inmates with specified rations; manufacturing, and enforcing the use of, formal complaint forms in a specified format; delivering court documents (summonses, warrants, court decisions, and sentences) to criminal defendants, civil litigants, and witnesses following specified procedures; escorting criminal defendants on appeals to higher jurisdictions for second or third trials within specified time limits; compiling and binding into books all reports, records, files, journals, and statistics of judicial activities and procedures in specified formats and at specified intervals; and so on and so forth. The word "specified" is repeated deliberately, since compliance with uniform standards in all institutional activities was what judicial modernity required, and it was pursued persistently by the central government, with rising financial costs.

The costs were not always justified by an increase in the efficiency and effectiveness of the state in performing judicial functions. Take documentation of judicial activities, for example. By the early 1930s, each formal court was to submit no fewer than 134 kinds of reports and journals annually, in addition to several dozen books and journals kept at the court. At the Jinhua District Court (DC) in Zhejiang province, a total of more than 180 kinds of reports and books were compiled. Deputy Minister of Justice Zheng Tianxi, who inspected the judiciary in Fujian and Zhejiang provinces in 1932, considered many of the reports, journals, and books "redundant, without scientific and statistical value."[13] Zheng was also of the opinion that procedural laws should suit the conditions of the economy, transportation, and the people's education level in a country, and that the Chinese procedural laws based on Western models might not be appropriate to China's conditions. The result was that redundant litigation procedures cost too much time and labor. He cited one example: a civil lawsuit with a target remedy of ¥450 was tried and closed after five months and the court prepared and printed more than 200 sheets of documents, costing the state more than ¥450.[14] Yet the costs of documenting and following procedures could not even begin to compare to those of building and operating a formal court system and a prison system.

In connection with the issue of cost-effectiveness, the formalization agenda also raised the issue of procedural/formal justice versus substantive justice. Simply put, the issue refers to the situation where in spite of, or even because of, a quest for procedural justice by following the established rules in proceedings, victims (and their loved ones) in criminal and civil litigations who had been injured in a variety of ways might not obtain justice in the sense of equity, restitution, compensation, and punishment of the wrongdoers. The issue may be deemed universal in all judicial systems and practices in all countries. The point here is that in the pursuit of judicial modernity, Chinese reformers did not even address the issue squarely; and only occasionally were some concerns voiced about it. In 1915, after the judicial retrenchment of 1913–1914, President of the Republic Yuan Shikai issued at least two directives scolding judicial officers for being overly concerned with procedures and much too indifferent toward the people's sufferings caused by case backlogs due to procedural technicalities.[15] "I have high regard for judges and great expectations of judicial independence. But [judicial] independence cannot be forced. I would have nothing to say if adjudication were fair, the people felt at ease with it, and the whole country happily accepted the role of the judiciary. It is putting the cart before the horse, however, if, in seeking judicial independence, we spend money only to benefit irresponsible officials, copy formalities [from foreign models] without officials understanding the principles, and leave the people boiling with resentment."[16]

Yuan Shikai may have been trying to justify the retrenchment of the court system, but what he said did reflect a sentiment shared by some judicial officials, especially those in the Nanjing decade such as Zheng Tianxi, cited above. Hong Lanyou, another judicial official, opined as late as 1937 that the civil and criminal procedural laws were not entirely suitable to China's societal needs, and that overelaborate procedural formalities burdened both the system and the people. Not only did ordinary people fail to understand the formalities, but judges considered them restrictive, unnecessary, and conducive to case backlogs:

> It often happens that a case goes through several trials, only to have more side issues spring up, or a case that could be decided in one word ends up dragging on for years. Since the civil procedural law stresses procedures, no matter the result of a trial, as long as procedures are found faulty, the case has to be sent back for retrial. So cunning and litigious types file lawsuits at both the court and the procurator's office to tie down the defendant, or file appeal after appeal to keep the case unresolved for a long time. People who have gone bankrupt owing to entanglement in litigation are everywhere, while judges are worn out and exhausted by dealing with procedures, detention houses are left overcrowded, and mountains of backlogged cases pile up—nothing hurts the people's livelihood more than this.[17]

Similarly, Ju Zheng, the head of the Judicial Council (*sifa yuan*) (JC), and another legal commentator believed that the three-trial system contributed to the dilatoriness of the judiciary.[18] It is important to note, however, that these criticisms did not categorically reject procedural formalization borrowed from the Western model; they merely questioned whether or not such procedural formalities suited China's social conditions at that time and best served substantive justice. And even such discussions were rare.

Financial costs and institutional inefficiency inherent in the formalization agenda were not uniquely Chinese and might be expected in modern judicial systems or bureaucratic organizations in any country. What is historically significant is that the requirements of being "modern" left Chinese reformers no choice but to stick to the formalization agenda; and with the exception of some GMD officials, cited above, no alternatives were seriously contemplated—anything less than the planned formalization was considered a failure. But for Republican China, where social and economic development was lacking and the state's priorities lay elsewhere, the enormous costs of institutional and procedural formalization in the judicial system were simply prohibitive. Consequently, the plan for establishing courts, procuracies, detention houses, and new prisons in all counties across the country was never realized. In a sense, the institutional formalization—a prerequisite for judicial modernity—was destined to fail given that it was not backed by the necessary resources.

Judicial Formalization and Deviations

Separate from building institutions, procedural formalization entailed a normalizing process. The norms and forms that were established by the reform legitimized desirable practices and behavior, and at the same time, practices that did not conform to the norms and forms became officially illegitimate, as irregularities, abuses, corruption, and miscarriage of justice in a spectrum from minor infractions to criminal acts. Yet, for reasons discussed below, acts contrary to the norms and forms were routinely committed and tolerated, while being routinely criticized and blamed in public discourse and official discourse for all sorts of problems in judicial process. Precisely due to more and more rules and regulations proscribing behavior that was commonplace in county government offices (CGO) across the country, practices that were officially chastised but practically accommodated multiplied. This accounts to a large degree for the criticisms of the Republican-era judiciary that one encounters in the sources.

The state itself also engaged in practices that did not align with the formalization agenda. Aside from the GMD practice of punishing politically defined offenses, even after the new criminal code and criminal procedural law had been enacted, the Republican state repeatedly resorted to special criminal laws to deal with robbery and banditry and other common crimes. Another example of informal practices was that the central and provincial governments allowed and encouraged petitions on judicial matters and individual lawsuits by people in all walks of life. These two informal practices were used as tools supplementary to the formal institutions and procedures, which were found inadequate even in places where county-level courts were established, and they were more widely used where formal institutions and procedures were absent. This fact points to the transitional nature of the Chinese judiciary, which was moving from a traditional pattern where fewer norms and forms existed to a "modern" pattern where, along with building institutions, it was imperative, albeit problematic, to design elaborate norms and forms and enforce compliance with them.

As far as procedural formalization was concerned, a profound paradox was that, on the one hand, where procedures were ignored or compromised, usually in low-level jurisdictions, the legal rights of litigants and defendants were infringed upon, that is, formal justice was not fully delivered; and on the other hand, where procedures were implemented and adhered to, they tended to contribute to trial delays and case backlogs, so that substantive justice was not fully served. In the end, both outcomes existed, and neither was satisfactory either to the state or to the people.

The Logic of Local Practices

Judicial modernity as performance of formality met with resistance in the form of various deviations from rules and procedures. Deviations at the county level especially undermined the reform agendas in no small measure. Irregularities, abuses, corruption, and injustice were familiar stories when it came to the behavior of local officials and county staff in late imperial and Republican China, and some such stories are recounted in this book. Instead of looking at such behavior as individuals' moral failures, it would be instructive to take a systemic view and analyze that behavior as a local and localized reaction to the impersonal national agenda of modernization that did not take into account varied local geographic, political, economic, and sociocultural conditions.

Since the project for judicial modernity was ultimately driven by external forces, as opposed to internal development, the intellectual outlook, political institutions, social structures, economic conditions, and cultural practices in local society were ill-prepared for the required transformation. High officials in the national capital, and perhaps in many provincial capitals as well, accepted notions about a modern judiciary as part of a modern state and the way it was supposed to function, and attempted to build institutions and formalize practices accordingly. Such understandings and commitments, however, were not equally shared across the country. Even in places where courts were set up and judicial officers were appointed, there were still irregularities, abuse, corruption, and miscarriages of justice. Those deviations from formalized rules were not entirely due to the shortage of judicial funding per se; they had to do with the overall economic conditions and survival strategies of all those involved. In a fundamental sense, therefore, there was a disjunction between the national agenda and local practices or a conflict between the logic and dynamics of a modernizing state and those of local society. The former were typically the impulses to seek formalization, standardization, and uniformity from the top down, while the latter, rooted in particularistic interests, were typically manifested in transgression, infraction, and informal degradation of officially sanctioned norms and forms.

When the logic and dynamics of the state and those of local society intersected in judicial processes, at least two social ramifications would emerge. First, by setting up formal procedures as norms, the reform agenda destabilized and delegitimized the customary informal process of dispute resolution that was shaped and defined by the sociopolitical environment of local society, that is, the local power structure and power relationships. Local power holders would try to resist the state agenda or, failing that, to adapt to the changing situation to turn it to their own advantage. In the wake of the 1911 Revolution, some local elites felt threatened by courts built in their locales that were independent of the local power structure, and others tried to control or influence judicial appointments at the county level. After the building of county-level courts was abandoned in 1913–1914, local elites reclaimed a larger social space and possessed a stronger political leverage to interfere, as they had done in the imperial era, with the judicial functions of the county magistrate and the trial officer (a new position created by the reform), who were outsiders to local society.

A noteworthy development during and after the New Policy decade was the proliferation of volunteer associations, either sanctioned by the state or declared by their founders as public bodies, representing the people or certain segments thereof, reflecting public opinion, and advancing the public good.[19] A variety of such local associations appeared at the county level and below after local self-government was proposed in the New Policy decade and pursued intermittently in the Republican era. Our archival sources show that in defense of local group and personal interests, organizations such as county assemblies, township assemblies, township associations, local militias, county chambers of commerce, and native-place associations often interacted with county magistrates, judicial institutions, and provincial and national governments on judicial matters and in individual cases.

The rise and active interaction with the state of such institutions in local society in the early twentieth century signaled the changing composition and strategy of local elites that were more than traditional gentry.[20] The term "local elites" includes complex social elements that did not always have the same interests in mind. The new elites were as powerful as the traditional type in local society but were often engaged in new lines of endeavor created by the New Policy projects, such as local self-government, Western-style schools, a new police force, the anti-opium campaign, and so on. Reflecting the new composition and social status of local elites in the Republican era, besides the familiar designations "gentry" and "gentry-merchant," newer terms were created by ordinary people and county magistrates to identify the new local elites. The terms included "outstanding elders and well-learned gentlemen" (*qiying shuoshi*), "powerful gentry-manager" (*quandong*), "evil gentry-manager" (*liedong*), "evil manager-litigation stick" (*liedong songgun*, and, of course, "local bully and evil gentry." The last term, not insignificantly, was used by ordinary people before the GMD state began to crack down on the local powerful in this category (see Chapter 3). These newer terms reflected sociopolitical changes in modern China in which the traditional gentry were joined and transformed by newer social elements and political institutions in local society. In the context of this study, certain local elites were called "outstanding elders and well-learned gentlemen" when the state wanted chambers of commerce to mediate commercial disputes, or when the state wanted to enlist local elites to donate money for and participate in prison reform at the county level. The other negative terms appear in reports from county magistrates and petitions from ordinary people that describe local elites who used their positions, connections, and powers to harm local people.

One of the ways local elites commonly exercised power was through the interaction of their organizations with the government authorities on judicial matters to advance or defend their interests. On quite a few occasions, such actions were denounced by the authorities as interference with judicial independence. But since judicial independence was never fully institutionalized, that is, most county magistrates as administrative officials continued to adjudicate litigation, local elites were not prepared to relinquish their role in the county judicial process, which became an increasingly important power arena because of its increasing accessibility, thanks to the reform. Critically, wherever the state mandated a new function but failed to perform to the standards it set for itself, societal forces would by default come to fill the space and perform the function in some way, shape, and form, which was often contrary to what the state agenda intended to bring about.

The second ramification of the intersection of the national and the local was that when the social environment, and the praxis rooted in it, did not change substantially, the new norms and forms that the state mandated to regulate judicial institutions and practices were not as functional and productive as they were designed to be. When old ways were yet to be completely replaced by new practices, there were many motivations and opportunities for social actors to undermine or deviate from the new practices. Old patterns of behavior and customs among county staff continued to operate with their own logic and dynamics, which made more sense to local actors than the official discourse on the reform. County functionaries did not hesitate to take advantage of their positions to benefit themselves by bending or violating official norms and forms, because to do so was reasonable from their perspective. The project of formalizing judicial institutions and practices tended to provide opportunities for abuse, undermining the effect of the reform. Thus each reform measure had its own downside. Supposedly new solutions to old problems only begot new problems of irregularities and rule-violations. For instance, the rule of avoidance in the appointment of adjudicating county magistrates, which was designed to minimize corruption, created a situation where the county magistrate had to rely on corrupt local clerks and runners in judicial proceedings, simply because as an outsider to local society, the magistrate did not speak the local dialect, and litigants did not speak Mandarin. Similarly, the procedures for delivering and copying judicial documents mandated by the formalization agenda became new avenues for county functionaries to squeeze money from litigants. Both county magistrates relying on local clerks and functionaries squeezing litigants—were officially proscribed but were routinely tolerated.

In short, judicial institutions and judicial officials at the national and provincial capitals operated above and almost apart from local society, which had little in common with the national agenda of judicial reform and functioned with its own logic and dynamics, grounded in its social environment. County magistrates and trial officers, and even district courts and their branches, tended to reckon with and yield to such logic and dynamics, while attempting to manage some semblance of carrying out the reform and delivering justice. The motivation, the vision, and the passion that drove the reform initiatives at the national level did not penetrate local society in any significant way, even though local actors learned to use the vocabulary and discourse of the reform and were more than ready to resort to judicial process in pursuit of their own interests. Thus a wide gap obtained between what was promoted as judicial reform at the national (and provincial) level and what was practiced as judicial process at the county level. While the achievements of the reform reflected the commitment of a modernizing state, its defects and failures may be understood at least in one dimension as symptoms of a structural incongruence between the logic of modern state building and that of local social environment, and the resulting institutional dysfunction.

Reform Discourse and Its Limits

In connection with the disjunction between the national and the local, this book pays due attention to how government officials and social actors appropriated the reform discourse and vocabulary in a variety of situations. The phrases often invoked during 1901–1937 were "the rule of law," "judicial independence," "protecting human rights," "legal sovereignty," "dignity of the judiciary," "authority-credibility of the judiciary," "maintain a code of conduct for officials," and so on. In addition, the goal repeatedly announced by the state of abolishing extraterritoriality was frequently cited to criticize perceived or real misconduct of judicial officers and miscarriage of justice. The fact that those vocabularies came into fashion as codes of positive moral values was a significant indication that the traditional notion of litigation as moral failure was no longer the orthodox one.

Yet why was it that although such vocabularies and discourses were invoked frequently, legal culture and litigation behavior did not change in local society, or why did the discourse not penetrate the mind of local actors, both litigants and county functionaries? For one thing, it would take more than reciting the words for people to understand, internalize, and practice what was invoked and for discourses to be turned into actual values and social practices and praxis. A crucial fact, however, was that almost all instances of invoking the vocabularies that were of political currency appeared either in official communications or in petitions and legal plaints written by lawyers and legal scribes for people involved in judicial process. In local society, especially in counties where no courts existed and therefore no lawyers could appear at county trials, legal scribes were indispensable, and more so in the Republican era than in the imperial era, precisely due to the reform that broadened access to judicial process. Not surprisingly, a scribe such as Cheng Wenhao of Liyang, Jiangsu province, was still active at the age of seventy-five.[21] In the late imperial era, the act of countering local elite power on the part of the weaker actors by bringing lawsuits beyond the local power arena took place with the aid of legal scribes.[22] This continued to be the case in the Republican era; and by that time, there was no longer any specific law to define and prosecute legal scribes as pettifoggers. The regulations on lawyers vaguely prohibited incitation to litigation, but this was difficult to enforce, because the proscribed behavior could not be easily defined or proven in court (see Chapter 7).

Legal scribes, then, along with lawyers, were able to play an important role in the judicial process and catch hold of what was fashionable and therefore persuasive in the political and legal discourses of the time and use it to increase their odds of winning for their clients and thus enhance their own marketability, notwithstanding the drag on them of traditional concepts and vocabularies, as shown in some of the complaints they wrote. That is to say, it was through the filter of scribes and lawyers that average Chinese citizens haphazardly learned the workings of the judicial institutions and procedures brought forth by the reform, at a time when the institutions were not established everywhere and the procedures were not always faithfully followed. Local people were far removed from what was driving the reform nationally, and hardly appreciative of what it should and would mean to them locally. All they saw was the same age-old litigation game for all to play, with some new rules added, such as filing lawsuits with official complaint forms for a fee that was state-mandated, or having a court decision notice or summons delivered to their homes, which was also state-mandated, for a fee that was often extralegal. The same outlook applied to county functionaries who copied criminal and civil complaints or delivered judicial documents—the new services meant opportunities for them to make money or make a living. Ideas about the rule of law, the people's rights, and so forth remained words invoked by litigants (or the scribes they hired) as discursive strategies in their litigation struggles, or by county magistrates and functionaries seeking to show themselves in conformity with state mandates, with very little bearing on how judicial functions were performed at the county level. This was an important aspect of the disjunction between the national agenda and local practices.

The Paradox of Judicial Modernity

A striking feature of the judicial reform during 1901–1937 was the continuity and consistency in the motivations and goals of the central government throughout the period, notwithstanding the peculiar ideological thrust and political agenda of the GMD. This was the case because the reform was part and parcel of a secular trajectory of modern state building in early-twentieth-century China. For all the setbacks and problems, the trajectory projected a general upward curve, tracing the tortuous and haphazard expansion of the Chinese state horizontally and vertically. This was especially true of the judicial system.

Did the institutional expansion of the Chinese state and the judicial system mean real development, in the sense of growing effectiveness and efficiency? Prasenjit Duara sees "state involution" at least in the area of revenue collection in the Republican era, while Julia Strauss identifies "strong institutions in weak polities" in the case of several national-level organizations under the GMD that grew in effectiveness, if not in efficiency, such as the Ministries of Foreign Affairs and of Finance, in addition to the formerly foreign-controlled Salt Administration.[23] This book documents a steady rise in the number of lawsuits and a growing capacity of the judiciary to handle them in the Republican era, which may be seen as a relative increase in the effectiveness, if not efficiency, of the modern Chinese state.

On the other hand, even the growth of institutional capacity was never adequate to meet the growing societal demand for more effective and efficient judicial performance by the state. The perennial case backlogs, which government officials and ordinary people alike deplored, were a widely cited indicator of the failure or inadequacy of the judiciary. Because the expansion of the judicial capacity to handle civil and criminal cases was in essence an expansion of the state, the problem of case backlogs was an issue, not only of delivering justice and ensuring social stability, but also of confirming the legitimacy of the state. Hence the serious concerns over the issue and strenuous efforts to wrestle with it on the part of the state. In the Republican era, every minister of justice, upon assuming the office, proclaimed his concerns over heavy case backlogs, deplorable prison conditions, and other unfulfilled reform goals. Such announcements were rhetorical exercises, to be sure, but they also reflected a real and deep anxiety over the disappointing statistics that seemed to discredit the judicial system and undermine the state's legitimacy.

That kind of anxiety need not, however, be taken as a truthful reflection of the conditions or the nature of what was happening. Societal demand for better judicial performance by the state was partly created and fostered, paradoxically, by the increasing accessibility to the judicial process as a result of the reform. Studies of Qing legal practices show that the Qing state discouraged litigation and encouraged informal resolution of disputes in the local community, while local disputants would try to break out of a local power arena dominated by their stronger opponents by taking cases to higher authorities.[24] In contrast, while the Republican state encouraged settlement of disputes outside the formal judicial process in order to reduce the burden on institutional and financial resources, the essence of the judicial reform was to broaden the access to formal judicial process and formalize it with new institutions and procedures. Inasmuch as people were more willing than before to resort to litigation, the newly established judicial system was financially hard pressed and tended to be overwhelmed, resulting in case backlogs in all jurisdictions.

In short, although case backlogs give the impression of systemic failure, this may not be historically accurate. In comparison with, say, the Indian judicial system in the 1970s, which one scholar has described as pathological, or the judicial system and process in Western societies today, the judiciary in Republican China would appear quite respectable.[25] Instead of taking case backlogs merely as an indication of the failure of the judiciary, one may regard them as a result of the state system being weighed down by its own commitment to judicial modernity, a commitment not supported by the necessary resources. This was the case because the ambitious, unrealistic goals were externally compelled or induced, not internally driven and prepared. In the final analysis, the paradox of modern state building in early-twentieth-century China was that while the state apparatus was expanding, it always fell short of what would be considered adequate in performing its functions as designed or desired, because the process itself would create more societal demands for ever more state functions and services, for which institutional and financial resources were always inadequate, especially given the overall developmental conditions in which China found itself.

PART I

Envisioning Reform from the Center

CHAPTER I

Western Models and Chinese Practices: The New Policy Decade

> We have now received Her Majesty's decree to devote ourselves fully to China's revitalization, to suppress vigorously the use of the terms "new" and "old," and to blend together the best of what is Chinese and what is foreign. . . . We therefore call upon the members of the Grand Council, the Grand Secretaries, the Six Boards and Nine Ministries, our Ministers abroad, and the Governors General and Governors of provinces to reflect carefully on our present sad state of affairs, and to scrutinize Chinese and Western governmental systems with regard to all dynastic regulations, national administration, official affairs, matters related to people's livelihood, modern schools, systems of examination, military organization, and financial administration. Duly weigh what should be kept and what abolished, what new methods should be adopted and what old ones retained. By every available means of knowledge and observation, seek out how to renew our national strength, how to produce men of real talent, how to expand state revenues, and how to revitalize the military.
>
> —Imperial edict, January 29, 1901[1]

The project of transforming China's laws and judicial practices into modern institutions and procedures was set in motion by the imperial edict quoted above, which led to what was known as the New Policy in 1901–1911 (the final years of the Qing dynasty).[2] The edict spoke against the terms "new" and "old," referring to the failed 1898 reform advocated by Kang Youwei in the name of "new laws." Nevertheless, the edict itself called for new methods from abroad to be considered and selectively adopted in changing the Chinese polity, hence the term "New Policy."

While the New Policy involved promoting industry, commerce, Western-style education, and local self-government, the centerpiece was a program for the gradual establishment of a constitutional monarchy. That a complete overhaul of the judiciary was part of the constitutional project was an understanding widely shared among high Qing officials, though they differed on the details. The judicial reform initiatives in 1901–1902 caught the attention of foreign powers. In the commercial treaties with China of 1902 and 1903, Great Britain, the United States, and Japan promised that given the Chinese government's desire to reform the judicial system "to bring it in accord with that of Western Nations," they would relinquish extraterritoriality "when the state of the Chinese laws, the arrangement for their administration, and other considerations" warranted such actions.[3] From then on, to abolish extraterritoriality was the most frequently cited rationale for the reform in Chinese official and public discourse: a modern judiciary tailored after Western models would deprive foreign powers of their justification for maintaining extraterritoriality.[4]

Even with the premise of building a modern judiciary after Western models, however, whether and to what degree China's traditional laws and judicial practices should be retained as "the best of what is Chinese" was not clear. During the New Policy decade, the issue of negotiating and reconciling Western models and Chinese practices was vigorously engaged and finally settled, with a general, if grudging, acceptance of Western models. The decade saw debates, negotiations, maneuvers, and compromises on reform agendas among high Qing officials, who cannot easily be categorized as reformers or conservatives; and the complexity and difficulty of the reform project could already be glimpsed at that early stage. This chapter seeks to illuminate how the political, institutional, and ideological issues were identified and approached, what progress was made, and what false starts, delays, and detours resulted. Where the judicial reform was concerned, the 1911 Revolution proved to be much less significant than the New Policy initiatives of 1901–1911. What was envisioned, proposed, and partially accomplished in fashioning a modern judiciary during the decade shaped the general direction in which the reform would continue in the Republican era.

The Institutional and Intellectual Setting

In June 1901, responding to the January imperial edict, Zhang Zhidong, governor-general of Hunan and Hubei, and Liu Kunyi, governor-general of Jiangxi, Jiangsu, and Anhui, jointly submitted three memorials on comprehensive reforms. One section of their second memorial dealt with "Moderation in Judicial and Penal Practices." The subject covered nine issues, including alleviating the burden that litigation imposed on the people, minimizing torture in trial, moderating punishments, and reforming prisons. The reform initiatives in the subsequent years essentially addressed, and expanded beyond, the issues first raised by Zhang and Liu in 1901.

In May 1902, at the recommendation of Zhang Zhidong, Liu Kunyi, and Yuan Shikai, governor of Zhili and commissioner of training the Army, the imperial court appointed Shen Jiaben and Wu Tingfang as commissioners of law codification in charge of revising existing Chinese laws in light of foreign models.[5] Shen and Wu were authorized to form and head a Law Compilation Commission (Falü bianzhuan guan), which was set up in 1904 and was renamed the Law Codification Commission (Xiuding falü guan) (LCC) in 1907.

Versed in Chinese traditional laws and informed by Western and Japanese models, Shen Jiaben was one of the most important individuals who contributed enormously to the development of a modern Chinese judiciary. A native of Gui'an, Zhejiang, and a *jinshi* degree holder, Shen became a deputy chairman of the Board of Punishment (BP) in 1901 and then the president of the Supreme Court (SC) in 1906, concurrently serving as commissioner of law codification. He served only on the LCC after 1907 and left the commission in 1910, when much of the drafting of laws was done, to become deputy chairman of the Government Advisory Council (Zizheng yuan) (GAC) and deputy minister of law in 1911.[6]

Wu Tingfang, too, played a crucial role in the initial stage of the judicial reform. Having received legal training in England and practiced law in Hong Kong, Wu served as minister of foreign affairs and in other capacities while working with Shen Jiaben until 1907. He was to become minister of justice in the Provisional Government of Sun Yat-sen in Nanjing during January–April 1912, helping to carry over the agenda of the late Qing judicial reform into the Republican era.[7]

Besides the LCC, a few other institutions were also instrumental. In 1906, the BP was refashioned into the Ministry of Law (ML), and the Court of Judicial Review (Dalisi) (CJR) became the Supreme Court (Dailiyuan). The first minister of law was Dai Hongci, who was succeeded by Ting-jie in 1909. Shen Jiaben served as the first president of the SC, and Zhang Renfu succeeded to the post in 1907. The ML and the SC often consulted with each other and jointly presented reform proposals and opinions to the imperial court in 1907–1911.

The Commission on Studying Constitutional Government (CSCG) (Xianzheng biancha guan), established in August 1907 and headed by Prince Yi-kuang, served as the gatekeeper for all reform proposals and counterproposals regarding the New Policy. It was the CSCG that proposed in 1907 to reorganize the LCC and make it an independent body in charge of drafting laws.[8] The CSCG reviewed and commented on all the proposals and opinions presented to the imperial court, including the laws and regulations drafted by the LCC, the ML, and the SC. During its existence, the CSCG proved to be open-minded and generally supportive of reform initiatives by the three other institutions.

Beyond those institutions, many high Qing officials appear to have understood rather well how constitutional government and the judiciary in the West worked and held views on how those systems might be adopted in China. The fact that Zhang Zhidong and Liu Kunyi initiated the reform suggested that they were informed of judicial and penal practices in the West and Japan and were capable of using them as models, however limited their visions may have been. Zhang's tenure as governor-general of Guangdong and Guangxi in 1884–1889 and his efforts at "self-strengthening" projects there exposed him to ideas borrowed from Western examples, mediated through his Western-educated staff members and Western experts hired for the projects.[9] During his tenure as governor-general in Guangdong and Guangxi, and then in Hunan and Hubei, Zhang's staff included 398 Chinese and 239 foreigners, the latter being from Japan, Germany, Britain, the United States, and other countries.[10] Although it remains to be documented, Zhang may have learned about Western legal practices during and after that period.

Zhang and Liu were not alone in being informed about Western practices. In 1907, Ze Gong, commissioner for reorganizing the governmental system, submitted a memorial arguing for an independent judiciary. In various countries, Ze observed, the judiciary and administration were not separate at first, but with the progress of civilization and the perfection of the legal system, it was recognized that to entrust judicial authority to administrative officials would only increase the power of those officials and multiply the people's grievances in return. Here, Ze connected separating the judiciary and the administration with making China a more civilized nation. More important, echoing similar utterances in the radical journals of the time, Ze articulated the notion of protecting human rights (*baohu renquan*) in official discourse probably for the first time.[11] "Revolutionary storms in various countries all stemmed from miscarriage of justice," he noted. "That is why all constitutional countries took as their priority the revision of laws to protect human rights. In order to use laws to protect human rights, they all established separate judicial institutions to gain the trust of the people, because only judicial institutions could follow the law and only the law could protect human rights." Ze did not fail to show that the purpose of constitutional and judicial reform was first of all to avoid revolution, but in his exposition of Western models, he made it clear that the prerequisite for protecting human rights was the rule of law, and the institutional prerequisite for the rule of law was judicial independence. Significantly, although the reform was compelled by international power relations, high Qing officials such as Ze Gong seem to have embraced the Western-derived notion of protecting human rights as a positive value, as opposed to miscarriage of justice; and no other officials challenged the idea either. Thus Ze introduced the vocabulary of human rights into the official discourse, where it would stay.

At the same time, in Ze's argument, the nationalistic agenda remained as strong as that of avoiding revolution. If China did not lay a foundation of judicial independence in preparing for constitutional government, extraterritoriality would never be abrogated. Ze did not seem to expect that abuse of power by officials would disappear merely due to a separation of judiciary and administration, but he argued that abuse of power by judicial officers in an independent judiciary would still be punished according to the law. "The point is that judicial independence is not to respect judicial officers, but to respect the law. No matter what the governmental system, [the goal of] respecting the law of the country was the same in all countries. Whether it can be achieved depends on whether judicial institutions are independent. This is the key to the preparation for constitutional government and must not be compromised even if other things might be."[12] By "all countries" Ze meant Western nations and Japan, which had become the embodiment of the modern world.

From 1907 on, high Qing officials, including those who opposed certain radical aspects of the reform (see below), routinely invoked the principles of separation of powers and judicial independence, as well as the notion of the people's rights, or human rights. The discourse hinted at a rich intellectual cross-fertilization between Chinese tradition and Western ideas at that time. On the surface, the Western vocabulary of human rights, if not the theories behind it, might have sounded deceptively familiar to the Qing court and high officials, being seemingly parallel to Chinese traditional thinking on statecraft about the people as the foundation of the state (*minben*). At the same time, a new conception of the role of the state also entered the discourse. In the words of Dai Hongci, the first minister of law, the essence of constitutional government was to divide state power into legislative, executive, and judicial branches "to protect the people's public and private rights." "Only then could the territory, the people, and the government of the country be connected together and solidified forever."[13] The idea that the territory, the people, and the government of the country should be connected and that the connection be solidified was not only a concrete example of envisioning China as a nation-state, but also a political formula that reform-minded intellectuals such as Liang Qichao, Yan Fu, and others were advocating around the turn of the twentieth century, which historians have identified as a version of statist nationalism.[14] Dai Hongci quite naturally appropriated the idea to justify the reform. The appearance of notions of the people's public and private rights in the Qing official discourse was refreshing and even revolutionary.

Memorials from high Qing officials show their familiarity with the Western origins of the idea of judicial independence. Li Jiaju, commissioner for studying constitutional government, located the origins of judicial independence in France. For him, judicial independence meant that adjudication was to be left to judges; the minister of justice should supervise judicial administration, but could not interfere with trials.[15] Zeng Wen, governor of Zhejiang, traced judicial independence to the theories of John Locke and Charles Montesquieu; and he argued that the separation of the administration and judiciary had also existed in ancient Zhou times before it was corrupted in Qin-Han times.[16] The efforts to find Chinese equivalents of Western judicial independence indicated the positive valuation of the principle among high Qing officials at the time.

These examples show that in the New Policy era, besides Shen and Wu, many high officials and non-official Chinese elites understood how justice and legal systems worked in the West. The background to this increasing, albeit haphazard, understanding was a growing body of translations by missionaries and Chinese scholars of Western and Japanese laws and legal histories, which created new vocabularies with which to express Western legal concepts. The new vocabularies almost all came from Japanese kanji writings, which were a convenient way for the Chinese to learn and use Western-derived legal concepts.[17] The term "public law" came from a work on international law written by the American missionary William A. P. Martin in the 1860s. Terms such as "sovereignty," "civil rights," "the people's rights" also came into fashion. Huang Zunxian's annotated translation of the Japanese criminal code, as part of *A History of Japanese State*, published in 1887, provided a whole set of legal terminology that was to be used in Chinese new criminal law and litigation law in the early twentieth century.[18] The period 1900–1911 also saw the publication of a large number of Western law books translated from Japanese and of several dictionaries of legal terminology based largely on kanji.[19]

Notably, Liang Qichao was among the first Chinese scholars who used the term "the rule of law" at the turn of the twentieth century. In an essay published in October 1910 in *Qingyi bao* (Pure Talk), a newspaper he edited in Japan, Liang described the important European idea that "all citizens are ruled by law, all are equal, and even monarchs cannot violate the national constitution decided by the public." He further said that "ruling the country with law is called the rule of law."[20] Although Liang's definition of the term was neither complete nor accurate, he helped start a discourse on the rule of law among educated Chinese. The official and public discourses on legal-judicial reform, conducted using newly acquired vocabularies and concepts from the West that reached China through Japan, thus informed each other as frame of reference in an evolving interaction, contributing significantly to the intellectual and political climate for the reform.

It is hardly surprising that in introducing Western legal concepts, Chinese reformers and legal scholars leaned heavily on the Japanese language, Japanese legal experts, and Japanese laws. The fact that Japan had successfully transformed itself into a modern nation accepted by Western powers persuaded the Chinese (from the Qing court to high officials to intellectuals) to take Japan as a copy of Western models, from which China could learn the original more easily. To cite one example, in a memorial dated June 11, 1907, Zhang Renjun, the head of the newly established SC, argued for combining Chinese and foreign legal traditions to devise the best legal system for China, noting that Japan was "especially the pioneer in East Asia," and that what Japan had accomplished was sufficient for the imperial court to select from and adopt.[21] That is why when Western legal notions and theories were translated and introduced into China, Japan came to serve as the "natural" transmitter, and the Japanese language as the bridge between Western concepts and the Chinese language. Such was the institutional and intellectual context in which the late Qing legal and judicial reform began.

Drafting Criminal and Civil Codes

Reforming Criminal Punishments

The reform started with the initiative to moderate criminal punishments, because cruel punishments and judicial torture were the focus of foreign criticisms. Under Qing law, criminal punishments fell into five general categories: (1) flogging with light bamboo canes (*chi*) or (2) heavy ones (*zhang*), (3) penal servitude of different forms (*tu*), (4) exile (*liu*), and (5) death (*si*), either by hanging (*jiao*) or by decapitation (*zhan*). Penal servitude usually involved transportation within the province and hard labor. The category of exile contained two subcategories—transportation to the frontier (*qian*), and transportation to and servitude in the army (*jun*). There were three subcategories of the death penalty, which provided for death by a thousand cuts (*lingchi*), displaying the head of the executed (*xiaoshou*), and mutilating the corpse (*lushi*) (to punish a guilty person who was already dead [this could also occur where the guilt was discovered after the person was dead]). Those three forms of punishment were of symbolic significance, differentiating the severity of offenses with different degrees of penalty.[22]

In December 1902, the governor of Shanxi, Zhao Erxun, proposed in a memorial that workhouses be established for criminals, and that confinement and servitude in these be substituted for *tu*, *liu*, and *jun* as punishment.[23] Zhao's proposal built upon the Zhang-Liu memorial of 1901 to focus on two categories of punishment—penal servitude and exile, while the concept of workhouses for criminals was obviously of foreign origin. When the proposal was referred to the BP, the latter modified it to the effect that while those condemned to *tu* would serve their terms in workhouses in the place where they had been sentenced, those condemned to *liu* and *jun* would have to serve them in workhouses elsewhere (thus retaining exile from one's hometown as part of the punishment). The imperial court approved the BP's opinion.[24] The historian Marinus Meijer is correct in noting that the BP wanted to keep exile as a category of punishment because of its symbolic usefulness in meting out penalties proportionate to varying degrees of offenses.[25] Nevertheless, Zhao's memorial launched the initiative to build workhouses for criminals, which became a standard item on the reform agenda through 1912, to be replaced by the agenda of institutionalizing prison work in the Republican era.

In April 1904, along the lines suggested by the Zhang-Liu memorial of 1901, Shen and Wu recommended the abolition of three cruel punishments—*lingchi*, *xiaoshou*, and *lushi*, along with the practices of tattooing criminals (*cizi*) and punishing family members and relatives of offenders (*lianzuo*), once again citing the goal of abolishing extraterritoriality.[26] The imperial court granted its approval.[27]

In another memorial, dated May 6, 1904, Shen and Wu addressed the use of torture in trials, corporal punishment, and problems in prisons, all issues raised in the Zhang-Liu memorial of 1901. The imperial court gave the nod to their proposals on those issues and ordered provincial officials to implement them. The Zhang-Liu memorial had proposed that short-term detention of a few days to several weeks be substituted for the punishment of flogging (*chi* and *zhang*). Shen and Wu reasoned that prohibiting torture in trials alone would not work, unless flogging as a category of punishment ceased; but detention of a few days to several weeks as a substitute for flogging would be too light a penalty to deter offenses. They recommended that fines—"a widespread Western practice"—be substituted for flogging and that those who could not afford the fine be confined to work in the workhouse for criminals, even though Shen and Wu were aware that only four provinces—Zhili, Henan, Shandong, and Yunnan—had reportedly built workhouses for criminals at the time, in spite of the imperial endorsement of Zhao Erxun's memorial in 1902.[28]

It should be noted that under the Qing criminal code, all categories of punishment—flogging (*chi, zhang*), penal servitude (*tu*), exile (*liu*), and even the death penalty (*jiao, zhan*)—could be commuted with a monetary payment called redemption (*zheshu, shoushu*). There were detailed tables setting out how much money was required for redeeming different kinds of punishment. The elderly (those aged seventy and older) and the disabled could redeem flogging and penal servitude with monetary payment on a separate scale. The law excluded certain serious offenses from redemption, but did not specify under what circumstances punishments for other offenses could be redeemed with payment, which was at the discretion of the officials in charge of judicial affairs.[29] In a sense, the Shen-Wu proposal for imposing fines as punishment was based on this precedent, but the practice was reworked conceptually to become a new category of punishment to replace the category of corporal punishment (flogging), a significant step in the direction of reforming penal practices.

In a separate memorial, Shen and Wu proposed that hard labor, rather than fines, be substituted for the flogging of robbers and thieves, because fines would not be a sufficient deterrent in such cases; one month of labor was to be substituted for 50 strokes with a heavy cane, two months for 60, and two more months for each additional 10 strokes, up to 100. In provinces where workhouses for criminals had not yet been established, convicts were to be held temporarily in prisons. At the same time, Shen and Wu noted that criminal codes in other countries did not apply capital punishment to the offenses of robbery and theft, and that they would consider the issue in drafting a new criminal code.[30] As it turned out, however, how to punish robbers would be a much thornier issue than they thought at this point (see Chapter 9).

Standardizing Judicial and Penal Practices

One important aspect of the reform was standardization of the varied legal and penal practices among different ethnic groups into a single judicial system and a single criminal code. Under Qing rule, the legal and penal treatment of Mongols and Manchu bannermen was different from that of Han civilians. Mongols had their own legal code, which predated the Qing dynasty and had evolved into its final form in 1789, while under Qing law, Manchu bannermen were given lighter or heavier punishments than Han civilians for the same offenses, and there was also special legal and penal treatment of other ethnic groups.[31] It was a logical conclusion in reformers' thinking that since the rule of law demanded the principle of legal equality, the different legal and penal treatment of ethnic groups within China should be abolished.[32]

The first step was taken in 1905 when the Board of Barbarian Management and the BP jointly initiated a move to reduce the difference between the penal treatment of Mongols and that of Han, which was approved by the imperial court. The abolition of barbaric punishments (referring to *lingchi*, *xiaoshou*, and *lushi*) was to be applied to the Mongolian Criminal Code, but those punishments in the Mongolian Code that were lighter than their equivalents in the Qing criminal code should be left as they were.[33]

On October 9, 1907, Empress Dowager Cixi personally issued a decree directing the Board of Rites and Shen Jiaben to review the existing laws to remove the differences between Manchu and Han as regards penal treatment. Praising Cixi's impartiality, Shen traced the original justification for maintaining the separate punishments for bannermen, calling it a measure of expediency. He pointed out that it was a misunderstanding to think the laws favored bannermen, since in some categories of offenses, bannermen received more severe punishments for the same offenses than non-bannermen. To standardize the judicial system, Shen proposed, all cases involving bannermen should be tried in the courts under the same law. He enclosed fifty articles in the existing law that he had deleted, revised, or collapsed together, changes that were approved by the imperial court.[34]

Drafting a New Criminal Code

The developments outlined above cleared the way for a systematic overhaul of China's criminal code in light of foreign models. Under the direction of Shen and Wu, the LCC extensively translated foreign law codes in preparation for revising Chinese laws. By 1904, the LCC had completed a large body of translations, and by 1907, it had translated a total of twenty-six foreign laws and legal works, and ten more projects were under way.[35]

What came out of the efforts to compare and choose between foreign models and Chinese laws was the completion of a draft criminal code in October 1907, with the help of the Japanese legal expert Okada Asataro. Under the code, punishments were limited to four types: the death penalty (by strangulation), imprisonment (term or life) (*tuxing*), detention (*juliu*) (under two months), and fines. All other forms of punishment were abolished. Thus, starting from the proposals for moderating punishments, the reform reached the point where exile and corporal punishment as penal categories were abolished, and incarceration became the primary form of punishment. The law greatly reduced the number of capital offenses and made strangulation in private (instead of public decapitation) the only form of capital punishment. It rejected application of the law by analogy (*bifu*), a practice where an act that was not explicitly proscribed by Qing law could be punished for offense by applying an analogical article in the law, and thus established an important legal principle—any act that was not prohibited by the law constituted no offense.[36] It set the age of criminal liability at sixteen and defined corrective education as appropriate for adult as well as juvenile offenders.[37]

The draft criminal code caused a major controversy among high officials, primarily over the issue of whether the traditionally harsher punishments for offenses against the imperial house, familial ascendants, and men (by women) should be upheld, to which the code said no.[38] A related issue was that the draft code decriminalized illicit sexual intercourse with unmarried women, which had been a punishable offense under Qing law. Zhang Zhidong, now a grand secretary, and Lao Naixuan, a member of the CSCG, among other high officials, vehemently opposed the draft code and criticized Shen for his "disregard" of the Confucian five relationships and traditional moral propriety (*lijiao*), protected by Qing law.[39]

The imperial court was uneasy about the radical nature of the draft criminal law as well. On February 16, 1909, an imperial edict urged provincial officials in charge of judicial affairs to respond to the draft criminal code. Another imperial edict the following day ordered that Shen Jiaben revise the draft code in light of the criticisms offered by Zhang Zhidong and others. It read in part: "Nowadays the whole world is connected and there are many international negotiations, so we must not stick to the old ways and fail to make changes to benefit the people. But we can only take [from foreign countries] what was good to remedy our shortcomings. None of the articles in our old law regarding social relationships must be lightly changed, so that the way of heaven and the [good] governance of the people may be preserved. The commissioner of law codification must base the spirit of revising the law on this principle."[40] The mixed message seemed to suggest that the imperial court and certain high officials were willing to accept legal and judicial reforms based on Western models for practical reasons, but that to their minds, the differential punishments of offenders depending on their relationships to the victims of crimes were what was good and essential in the Chinese legal tradition and should be preserved—the principle of legal equality was not so absolute or universal as to justify abandoning this tradition.

After the imperial court expressed its preference, memorials from provincial officials in response to the February 16 edict continued to criticize the draft criminal code along the lines of Zhang Zhidong's opinion.[41] Other objections were directed at setting the age of criminal liability too high, abolishing legal analogy in punishing crimes, and reducing harsher punishments. The governor of Henan, Wu Chongxi, argued that exile should not be abolished, analogy should be retained, and fines should not be a category of punishment, but be used as redemption for light punishments as before.[42]

On the other hand, at least one high official, the governor of Shangdong, Yuan Shuxun, voiced his full support for the draft criminal code as it was. China's criminal law would have to change, said Yuan, whether one wanted it to or not. "If we initiate the change, we may reap some benefits in the end; if we are forced to make the change, we may face a catastrophe endangering the whole Chinese people." Reflecting a sense of urgency to modernize China on its own initiative, Yuan said that if China did not revise its laws, it could neither survive in a world where great powers competed nor regulate its own people in the country. In Yuan's view, the only reason why the new code should not be put into effect just yet was the need for a police force and a reformed prison system first.[43] This opinion supported the draft code in principle, but held reservations for practical reasons; it should not be counted as one of those opposed to the draft criminal code, as Meijer would seem to suggest.[44]

At this juncture (probably in early 1910), Minister of Law Ting-jie presented the throne with "Provisional Regulations" to supplement the draft criminal code, which would satisfy conservatives and avoid abandoning the draft code entirely. The provisions revived most of what Shen Jiaben had stricken from the old law—the harsher punishments for offenses against the state, the imperial house, and familial ascendants, for robbery and kidnapping, and for illicit sexual intercourse with an unmarried woman.[45]

On January 25, 1911, the newly formed GAC informed the throne that it had discussed and adopted the general articles of the draft criminal code but not the specific articles. In response, the CSCG immediately requested the throne that in spite of the delay at the GAC, the entire code be issued to the provinces, so that officials could familiarize themselves with the law and prepare for its enactment in the near future.[46] An imperial edict thereupon ordered that the draft criminal code, along with the Provisional Regulations, be printed and issued to the provinces, with the age of criminal liability reduced from sixteen to twelve. This had been done by April 1911. The official enactment of the draft criminal code was scheduled for 1915.[47]

Separately, in 1907–1908, when the debate over the draft criminal code was raging, Shen Jiapen and his colleagues began revising the Law and Substatutes of Great Qing (Daqing lüli), with the imperial court's approval, to offer a compromise with the critics of the draft code and prepare a transition to the code. On February 29, 1908, Shen was able to present the imperial court with the revised law as the Current Criminal Law of Great Qing (Daqing xianxing xinglü). Not as radical as the draft criminal code in breaking with the past, this revised Qing code still incorporated some of the changes proposed over the previous years, such as abolishing exile, substituting fines for flogging, and applying the same law to Manchu and Han. Shen noted that when the draft criminal code was enacted as new law, the Current Criminal Law would be voided.[48] The law was referred to the CSCG, and the latter supported the revised law with minor additions (keeping exile and military servitude as punishments, per the former BP's opinion in 1902).[49] Under an imperial edict, the Current Criminal Law was printed and issued to provinces in early October 1909.[50] In other words, toward the end of the Qing dynasty, there were two versions of new or revised criminal code, in addition to the preexisting Law and Substatutes of Great Qing. It was the more radical version—the draft criminal code—that was adopted as the Provisional New Criminal Code after the founding of the Republic.

In the whole debate over the draft criminal code, even those officials who opposed the code did not object to the general thrust of the reform in simplifying and humanizing punishments and making incarceration the primary form of punishment. They questioned to what degree and how far that thrust should go. All memorials mentioned the necessity of the reform in order to cope with the changing world. The opponents of the draft criminal code were not prepared to abandon the most important aspects of the Chinese tradition in law and judicial practices that they believed to be the key to governing China. These Qing officials were aware of the international pressure on China to "civilize" its laws and judicial practices, but they did not believe that renouncing all things Chinese would serve the purpose of the reform—making China a viable nation in the modern world. Two examples will suffice here. The governor of Zhejiang, Zeng Wen, said that "if we were irresponsibly lenient toward all crimes just in order to admire [imitate] civilization [*tumu wenming*], then before the judicial sovereignty was regained the country would already irreparably disintegrate from within."[51] Another high official, from the newly established Ministry of Communications, noted that the loss of judicial sovereignty to foreign powers did indeed harm the governance of the country, but whether judicial sovereignty could be regained depended, not only on civilized laws, but also, and especially, on China being a substantive, powerful nation; it would be both diplomatically unhelpful and harmful to the governance of the country if the law became an ineffectual piece of paper.[52] The debate over the draft criminal code, therefore, was not between reformers and anti-foreign conservatives, but a difference in opinion on the issue of what combination of the Western and the Chinese would be best for China. The issue can only be understood in the historical context in which China was externally compelled to modernize in order to survive in the twentieth century.

Drafting a Civil Code

In traditional China, there was no conceptual and institutional separation between criminal and civil lawsuits, both being subsumed under the same law; and criminal offenses and civil matters were adjudicated by the county magistrate according to the law and local customs.[53] As a new criminal code was being drafted and debated, it was widely recognized that criminal and civil justice should be separate. In 1907, the newly established Ministry of Civil Affairs called for a civil code to be drafted. "Countries in the East and the West" had a separation between public and private laws, said the memorial; public law—a criminal code—dealt with the relationship between the state and the people, and private law—a civil code—with the relationship among the people. But Chinese laws did not separate criminal and civil cases, even though articles regarding civil matters were scattered through the laws. The Ministry of Civil Affairs requested that the imperial court order the commissioner for law codification to draft a civil code in light of Chinese social customs and foreign models and in consultation with the ministry. The request was approved.[54] Other officials also urged that a civil code be drafted as soon as possible.[55]

Toward the end of 1910, a civil code was drafted. After another eight months spent on revising the draft and adding interpretative notes, the LCC completed the draft civil code, in five books and thirty-seven chapters. The books on "Kinship" and "Inheritance" were to go through further revision in consultation with the Rites Commission (Lixue guan). The books on "General Principles," "Debts," and "Rights to Things" were presented to the imperial court on October 26, 1911, sixteen days after the Revolution that would bring down the Qing dynasty had broken out in Wuchang. The work was not wasted, however. The books on "General Principles," "Debts," and "Rights to Things" would be enacted shortly after the founding of the Republic.[56]

Establishing a Court System

Institutionalizing Judicial Independence

The official discourse noted earlier made it a foregone conclusion that a modern judiciary should be separated from administrative bureaucracy, and an independent court system be built as an essential condition for a constitutional government and the core of a modern judiciary. The institutionalization of judicial independence began when the imperial court decided in November 1906 to reorganize officialdom, including separating the functions of the CJR and the BP. By an imperial edict, the BP was changed into the ML, which no longer had a trial function and was only in charge of judicial administration. The CJR became the SC—the final appellate court in the country. (The annual budget of the SC was increased to 20,000 taels under Shen Jiapen, in contrast to the 600 taels that the CJR had received.)[57] Along with the SC, the General Procuracy (GP) was set up to function independently, although under the supervision of the ML.

The establishment of the ML and the SC in November 1906 was only the beginning of institutional formalization of the judiciary. In a memorial of December 1906 that won imperial approval, the SC argued for creating a system of four-level courts and three-level trials based on foreign models. The court system would consist of township trial bureaus (*xiang yanju*), district courts (*difang shenpanting*), provincial high courts (*gaodeng shenpanting*), and the SC. The trial bureaus would take up criminal cases entailing flogging and penal servitude and civil cases involving less than 200 taels. The appeal in such cases would go to a second trial at the district court and end in a third trial at the high court. Criminal cases entailing punishments of more than penal servitude and civil cases involving more than 200 taels would first be tried at the district court, and the appeals would go through a second trial at the high court and end with a third trial at the SC. At district courts and high courts, there would be procuracies (*jiancha ting*) responsible for prosecuting criminal cases.[58]

In a separate memorial on the institutional structure and responsibilities of the judiciary submitted in 1908, the ML discussed the separation of judicial administration and adjudication. Judicial administration was the function of the ML at the national level and of the justice departments at the provincial level, and judicial adjudication was the function of courts. The ML too argued for a four-level-court and three-trial system.[59] The system was appealing to reformers not only because it was based on foreign models but also because it mirrored Qing practices in a way and seemed a less dramatic change. Under Qing law, criminal cases entailing penal servitude and more severe punishments went through four levels of trial or review (county, prefecture, province, and imperial capital). The proposed system appeared to be a systematization and perfection of a familiar system. In reality, it would turn out to be a much more complicated and costly system to establish and operate.

In the meantime, relevant laws on organizing courts were being enacted. In December 1906, the ML issued the Law of Trial Functions of the Supreme Court, which actually covered not only the SC but also the high court, the district courts, and the city trial bureau in the capital city Beijing. In September 1907, the LCC presented the Law on Organizing Courts to the imperial court. The law was based on the model of "four-level courts and three-level trials," but the lowest court was now called the court of first instance (*chuji shenpan ting*). In presenting the law, Shen Jiaben pointed out certain aspects of it not found in all foreign legal systems, but that were pertinent to customs and conditions in China: (1) to limit expenditure, it provided for fewer judges at courts than was normally the case in other countries; (2) owing to a lack of judicial officers, it did not provide for circuit courts; (3) it did not provide for court vacations, which would inconvenience people; and (4) it provided for branches of the SC at high courts in remote provinces so as to avoid trial delays and save people from having to travel a long way to appeal their cases.[60] Clearly, Shen was aware of the conditions and constraints under which a modern Chinese judiciary was to be built. He was by no means blindly following foreign models, as his contemporary critics charged. The issues of access to courts and number of judges Shen mentioned here would be real problems, as we shall see.

The imperial court did not approve the Law on Organizing Courts until a few years later, on February 7, 1910, after the CSCG had made a few minor revisions. Approved at the same time were three related sets of regulations on examining and appointing judicial officers, on demarcating judicial districts, and on the competences of district courts and courts of first instance.[61] The law and the sets of regulations were not officially enacted before the fall of the Qing. But when matters of the court system and jurisdictions were discussed during 1907–1911, those documents were frequently invoked as the blueprint for a future system.

In the meantime, to allow a court system to take shape at the provincial and lower levels, the ML issued the Provisional Regulations on Establishing Courts at All Levels in December 1907. The regulations defined criminal and civil cases, the function of courts, litigation procedures, and the role of procuracies. The date of December 10, 1907, was set for courts of first instance and district courts to start functioning and taking up all criminal and civil cases.[62] This, however, did not happen. In August 1909, the ML issued three more documents: the Supplementary Articles to the Provisional Regulations on Establishing Courts of Various Levels, the General Principles of Organizing Courts and Procuracies at Provincial Capitals and Treaty Ports, and the Matters of Preparation for Courts of Various Levels at Provincial Capitals and Commercial Metropolises. In presenting these documents to the throne, the ML pointedly emphasized that provincial officials should not water down the structure and personnel of the courts to be established just to save funds, since these were already the bare minimum and since the courts were located in places where foreigners would be able to observe them.[63] Here the motivation to show foreign powers a functioning modern Chinese judiciary was obvious. The issue of resources to support the court system in provinces also emerged.

The capital city Beijing, the Tianjin prefecture, and the Fengtian prefecture were the locales where four-level courts were established the earliest. The rest of the country was unable to establish the system immediately.[64] Ze Gong had already suggested a plan for gradual establishment of a court system to avoid financial difficulty and shaky institutions in 1907. His plan called for a process of five three-year periods. Each period would see courts built in some provinces. At the end of fifteen years, a court system would have been set up across the country. Ze proposed that, given China's vast territory and underdeveloped transportation system, the SC and high courts should have branches at lower courts to take up appeal cases.[65]

In October 1908, the imperial court ordered all ministries, in accordance with a nine-year plan for establishing constitutional government, to submit their own nine-year plans in six months. In March 1909, the ML submitted its plan, a revision of an earlier plan called "an Overview of Year-by-Year Preparations." According to the plan, in 1908, the capital city Beijing should have the three levels of courts established, all with procuracies; in 1909, the Provisional Regulations on Establishing Courts at All Levels should be enacted; in 1910, courts in provincial capitals and treaty ports be set up without exception; in 1913, courts in prefectures and counties should be set up without exception, and the new criminal code should be enacted; and, finally, in 1915, courts of first instance should be established across the country.[66] The ML may have been trying to be conservative in making the plan, but in retrospect it was still more ambitious than Ze Gong's plan, and more ambitious than realistic. Although in 1909, what had been planned for 1908 and 1909 was completed in Beijing, the real difficulty would lie in establishing courts at the provincial and county levels in accordance with the schedules. It would seem that in 1909, the ML did not fully grasp the magnitude of the institutional and financial resources required to fully build such a court system as planned.

Guided by those goals, however, a court system, although not yet complete, had come into existence when the Qing dynasty fell. In 1912, a total of 345 courts had been established nationwide, including the SC in Beijing, high courts at the provincial level, district courts at major cities, and court of first instance at some county seats, each with their corresponding procuracies.[67]

Judicial Administration and Adjudication

The judicial formalization reached a milestone in February 1910, when the Law on Organizing Courts was finally adopted by the imperial court. In presenting the law to the throne, the CSCG pointed out that inasmuch as it demarcated the responsibilities of the ML and the SC, the two institutions should henceforth strictly adhere to their respective duties and not interfere with each other. All the matters of judicial administration should go to the ML, not be handled jointly by the SC. Cases tried and reviewed at the SC should not be sent to the ML for review. The only exception was that before the draft criminal code came into effect in 1915, the Autumn Assizes would continue to be processed by the ML.[68] Thus the trial function of the ML did not entirely end, because the Autumn Assizes continued.

In formalizing judicial institutions, a major concern of the ML was to standardize the judiciary. Standardization meant that judicial administration, the court system, and judicial process should be uniform and consistent throughout the country. As early as 1907, the ML proposed to adopt standard complaint forms across the country in order to "achieve judicial uniformity."[69] This aim became a running theme in the reform well into the Republican era.

For the ML, centralization was related to standardization or uniformity in the judicial system. Centralization required that all issues regarding judicial administration, judicial process, and legal interpretations in all provinces should be reported to and decided by the ministry. To take one example, in 1907, the governor-general of the northeastern provinces, Xu Shichang, reported to the imperial court on judicial affairs in his provinces. When the memorial was sent to the ML, the latter issued an opinion, co-signed by the SC, which endorsed the provincial justice department managing judicial administration in the northeastern provinces, while the courts tried cases, thus achieving judicial independence. The ML agreed with Xu's proposals that the criminal courts continue to handle the Autumn Assizes, and that a separate office be set up in the Justice Department to deal with penal confinement and the appointment of procurators. The opinion emphasized, however, that the ML should determine the competence and location of courts, appoint judges, and assign the duties of judicial officers, noting: "The ministry has the responsibility for managing the nation's judicial administration, and as provincial judicial administrative organs, departments of justice are its branches and should report to it. Although at this time of transition from the old to the new, they [i.e., the departments of justice] are also subject to governors and governors-general for the convenience of administration, they must be directly accountable to the ministry in order to have the effect of uniform judicial authority." Based on this argument, the ML disagreed with several proposals in Xu's memorial that would make the judiciary in the northeastern provinces different from that in other provinces, which "would be at great odds with the principle of uniformity" in the judiciary. The imperial court approved the ministry's opinion.[70] In short, from the early stage of the reform, a formalization agenda was articulated to include centralization, uniformity, and standardization.

Introducing Due Process

A key element in achieving the rule of law was due process in which the law was strictly applied and nothing extraneous to it was admitted. Reformers addressed the issue of institutionalizing due process when they strove to rectify two notorious traditional practices with regard to criminal suspects. One of them was torture during trials, which was widely criticized by foreigners (the other issue, summary execution of robbers and bandits, is discussed in detail in Chapter 9).

The 1901 Zhang-Liu memorial had condemned the practice of using torture in trials, which contradicted the spirit of governing the people with moral suasion. In foreign countries, Zhang and Liu noted, conviction was based on the testimony of witnesses, not confessions of the accused, because (1) judicial officers were in charge of trials, (2) few offenses called for capital punishment, and (3) prison life was not harsh. In China, because punishment for crimes was so harsh that conviction would have serious consequences, witnesses would not want to testify, and the accused would do anything to escape the punishment. The law provided that conviction could be imposed based on unambiguous testimonies, without a confession from the accused. But the convicted would always deny guilt on appeal and accuse the presiding official or the witnesses of taking bribes to frame him. Officials were therefore reluctant to close a case without a confession from the accused, which was why torture was used to a cruel degree to get confessions. Many people died in the process, yet on appeal the convicted would still deny guilt on grounds of having been induced to confess by torture. To solve the problem, Zhang and Liu proposed that, except in capital cases, which had to have confessions, in cases involving lesser punishments, if the witnesses were fair and trustworthy, testimonies to guilt were able to stand scrutiny, and superior officials had no doubts after questioning the convicted, then the conviction should stand as such, and any appeal to the central government should be rejected. This way, torture need not be used, and the innocent would not be burdened. In their 1904 response to the Zhang-Liu memorial, Shen and Wu fully agreed.[71] Zhang and Liu had actually raised the issue of due process and the rights of the accused, unwittingly articulating the dilemma inherent in the traditional criminal proceedings, but they failed to offer a solution to the problem. They did not, for example, spell out how one would determine that the conditions for conviction (witnesses were trustworthy, etc.) had been satisfied, and that confession was therefore not needed.

In May 1905, Imperial Censor Liu Pengnian opposed banning torture in most trials on the grounds that a procedural law was not available yet. One should not imitate foreign countries that did not use torture without studying the reasons, said Liu. In foreign countries, there were procedural laws. Before the defendant was arrested, police and detectives investigated. Lawyers and a jury were present at trials. From preliminary hearing to public sentence, a trial was based on testimony, not confession by the defendant. In China, the revision of the criminal law was just beginning, and a procedural law did not exist. If torture were allowed, but not used routinely, the accused would confess out of fear (of being tortured). If torture were suddenly prohibited, however, the accused would have nothing to fear and would refuse to confess, and the officials trying the case would have great difficulty getting a confession, which would cause cases to drag out and pile up.[72] It is instructive to note, once again, that Liu was familiar with criminal proceedings in the West, and that he argued against the abolition of torture in trials by saying that China lacked the conditions that prevailed in Western countries, including procedural laws.

When Shen and Wu were asked to respond to Liu's memorial, they offered a forceful refutation of Liu's argument as follows. First, the reform was being carried on for the purpose of ending extraterritoriality. To make Chinese laws on a par with foreign laws and to take the merit of foreign laws to remedy the defects of Chinese laws were the top priorities of the undertaking. And nothing distinguished Chinese law from foreign law more than torture in trial. Hence they (Shen and Wu) agreed with the Zhang-Liu memorial that torture not be used in non-capital cases. Torture was allowed as an expedient in capital cases precisely because ordinary people were not morally developed and judicial officials were not highly skilled. Second, as the existing statute stated clearly, officials trying cases "must obtain willing confession" (*wude shufu gongci*), and if the accused did not confess in cases entailing penal servitude or more severe punishment, the case could be reported, on the basis of testimony, to the emperor, who would make the final decision. "Willing confession," Shen and Wu argued, meant confession that was not obtained through torture, and "on the basis of testimony" meant that there was no need for a confession from the defendant. What they had proposed earlier (in response to the Zhang-Liu memorial) therefore simply reiterated the existing statute, with a little flexibility, and had nothing to do with copying foreign laws. Third, if it was argued that prohibiting torture would cause cases to drag out and pile up, had the use of torture prevented case backlogs in the past? Fourth, Shen and Wu characterized Liu's argument as concerns about ordinary people's lack of morals, but not about judicial officials' cruelty, which contradicted the universal truth (*gongli*). Moreover, normally, the meek would fear torture, and the tough would rather stand torture than confess, so that using torture inevitably led to decisions that erred in one direction or other (either the guilty got off or the innocent were wrongly convicted). Using Wu's experience as a judicial officer in Hong Kong, where British laws were applied to Chinese residents, Shen and Wu rejected the notion that the difference between foreigners and the Chinese in psychology and temperament warranted torture. Finally, Shen and Wu pointed out that prohibition of torture in trials was only the beginning, not the end, of the reform process, and that procedural laws would be drafted in light of similar laws in other countries. Their response won the approval of the imperial court.[73]

In essence, Liu's argument against the prohibition of torture was based on the premise that there was a need for it in order to obtain confessions in criminal cases, because China was different from foreign countries, even though the Zhang-Liu memorial had already cast doubts on that premise. By pointing to the absence of procedural laws, the argument logically did not rule out the possibility of abolishing torture when favorable conditions were present. On the surface, then, it was not entirely a traditionalist argument but a practical one, thus having some force of persuasion. But Shen and Wu's argument was more skillful and persuasive. First, they emphasized the importance of making Chinese judicial practices consistent with Western norms to end extraterritoriality, which both the imperial court and Chinese elites, including Liu, desired. Secondly, they undercut Liu's argument by asserting that (1) they were not borrowing from foreign laws, but proposing better enforcement of the existing Chinese law, (2) there was in any case not that much difference in temperament and psychology between Chinese and foreigners, and therefore (3) torture was of no use in serving justice. The point about enforcing an existing statute based on semantics seemed to be a stretch in interpreting Qing law. The phrase Shen and Wu quoted was not in the Law and Substatutes of Great Qing, and they probably were quoting from the Collection of Criminal Cases for Reference (Xing'an huilan) compiled by the BP in 1834, 1840, and 1886. An isolated phrase like *wude shufu gongci*, which might be found in thousands of cases in the collection, could not gainsay the overwhelming thrust in Qing law that sanctioned torture in trial.[74] For Shen and Wu, citing the phrase to make their argument was a tactical move to advance their strategic goal—to carry out the reform without delay. The end result of the Shen-Wu proposal on prohibiting torture in trials was that it was officially banned in most criminal cases, though it continued to be practiced by Qing officials in charge of judicial process as late as 1911 and well into the Republican era.[75] But the problem was identified at the early stage of the reform, and the practice was rendered illegal normatively.

As Shen and Wu noted in their debate with Liu, the draft criminal and civil procedural law being drafted in light of foreign models was completed by April 1906. It spelled out procedures for criminal and civil litigation, including legal representation by lawyers and jury trial.[76] When an imperial edict of May 11, 1907, asked provincial officials to comment on the draft law, however, the latter all cited the inconvenience of implementing the law and requested further study of the matter. Most provincial officials were uncomfortable with a law that would give offenders legal protection. But the governor-general of Hunan and Hubei, Zhang Zhidong, was particularly critical of the law for the principle it embodied of equality before the law, that is, denying the precedence of father over son, and husband over wife.[77] This criticism foretold the central point of the opposition to the draft criminal code later that year. When the imperial court ordered the ML to respond to the criticism, the latter asked for eight months to consider the matter. Then, in late September 1908, when the draft criminal code itself came under attack, the ML decided not to proceed with the procedural law until the draft criminal code was approved.[78]

After the debate on the draft criminal code abated and the Current Criminal Code was issued in 1909, the LCC began separately to draft a criminal procedural law and a civil procedural law. By January 1911, both laws had been completed, but they had not been enacted, presumably in deference to the concerns of provincial officials.[79] The CSCG proposed that before the criminal and civil procedural laws were put into effect, Shen should select the most important elements from the laws to draft a set of provisional regulations on litigation procedures to be used in tandem with the Law on Organizing Courts.[80] But the regulations were never produced, because Shen left the LCC in 1910. In the meantime, the ML finished drafting the Provisional Regulations on Criminal Litigation Fees and the Provisional Regulations on Civil Litigation Fees in January 1911.[81]

Reforming the Prison System

In traditional China (as in Europe until the eighteenth century), imprisonment was not a form of punishment for crimes, but an incidental condition in the adjudicating and punishing process. People were confined while *waiting* to be tried (and retried) as defendants, questioned as witnesses, or punished as convicts. Convicts had to wait to be punished because their conviction and punishments (usually harsher ones) had to be reviewed and approved by senior officials, and capital cases by the BP and ultimately by the emperor.[82] Normally, prisoners in capital cases were held in the inner jail, and those sentenced to lesser punishment in the outer jail, both of which were located within the compound of county, prefecture, and provincial governments and other trial agencies in the capital city Beijing. Suspects and witnesses in criminal cases awaiting trial were held in unofficial detention facilities under a variety of names, even though Qing law did not provide for this.

According to the Zhang-Liu memorial, jails and unofficial detention facilities in counties were crowded, filthy, disease-prone, and abuse-ridden, and the exhausted inmates often died as a result of torture, starvation, and disease. "Good people could not bear to see such places and would equate them with hell; foreigners in particular have criticized them relentlessly," the memorial noted. It proposed that provinces be ordered to raise funds to repair jails to make them roomy and clean, provide daily rations and make special provisions for summer and winter conditions, and prohibit mistreatment of inmates by jail guards and yamen runners, with severe punishment of any such abuses. Since unofficial detention facilities existed out of necessity, they should be institutionalized and regulated in the same way as jails, and the irregular types of unofficial detention facilities that went by names such as "runners' charges" (*chaidai*), "official shops" (*guandian*), "food stores" (*shipu*), and "shift rooms" (*banguan*) should be banned. In their 1904 response, Shen and Wu fully endorsed the proposal and proposed that upon completion of jail repairs in a province, governors and governors-general should send officials to inspect those facilities, punish those who failed to act, and report the situation to the BP.[83]

In connection with repairing jails, the Zhang-Liu memorial proposed appointing officials in charge of jails. The prefect (*tongzhi*) and assistant prefect (*tongpan*), who customarily took care of complaints from jail inmates, should be made explicitly responsible for jail matters. They should inspect county jails every month, and the jail at the seat of the prefecture every ten days, and report abuses and jail disrepair to governors and governors-general, as well as to the office of the provincial judicial commissioner. Concurring with the proposal, Shen and Wu further pointed out that a substatute of Qing law actually contained very specific provisions on how prisons should be managed. Citing the Law and Substatutes of Great Qing on the matter, they indicated that the way jails were run was in violation of the existing law.[84] To change the situation, Shen and Wu proposed, the prefect and assistant prefect should inspect prefecture and county jails monthly and submit a report on them every six months to the governor or governor-general, who should forward it to the BP at the end of the year.[85] Shen and Wu had no reason to believe that officials would follow the rules proposed any more seriously than they had followed the previous regulations. They probably knew that real prison reform had to be undertaken in a comprehensive way. If anything, their move was again tactical—to indicate that the prison reform they had in mind, in terms of prison administration, would not be a radical departure from the existing law, but its perfection and better enforcement.

As penal philosophy was changing and a draft criminal code was taking shape between 1901 and 1907, prison reform came to the fore as a pressing issue. In May 1907, Shen Jiaben submitted a memorial on the issue in which he observed:

> In Western constitutional countries, prison stands in a triangular relationship with the judiciary and the legislature. If there are comprehensive legal codes and wise and fair judges, but no proper prisons to carry out punishment, then [talk of] reforming [convicts] into better persons will be merely empty words. That is why all these countries have engaged in prison reform. They have also established the International Prison Association, held meetings at various countries' capitals once every few years, and sent delegates [to the meetings] to discuss prison reform matters, which have become almost a matter of international competition. As [we] are now vigorously carrying out the New Policy, prison [reform] is the most important undertaking among domestic matters and foreign affairs.

Shen made four proposals: (1) establish new prisons, (2) train prison officers, (3) enact prison regulations, and (4) compile prison statistics. In his ideal plan, every provincial capital and every treaty port should have a model prison, and prisons should be different from workhouses.[86]

Shen's plan was referred to the ML, which endorsed it and proposed in addition (1) that the money for building prisons at the county level be raised locally, and that centralization of the prison system be brought about by enacting uniform prison regulations; (2) that the Ministry of Education require that schools of law and government teach courses in penology to train prison personnel; and (3) that the ML instruct the provinces to report on conditions in prisons and collect prison statistics. The imperial court approved the ministry's proposals.[87]

The Qing government launched prison reform following Western models. When the International Penitentiary Congress was held in Russia in 1890, in France in 1895, in Belgium in 1900, and in Hungary in 1905, China's ambassadors to those countries attended the meetings as observers. In 1910, the Eighth International Prison Congress convened in Washington, D.C., and China was invited to participate. The Qing court sent Xu Qian, the chief of the Beijing High Procuracy, and Xu Shiying, a judge in the Fengtian High Court, along with Shen Qichang of the Ministry of Foreign Affairs and Luo Wengan of the ML, as China's delegates.[88] On their way to and while in the United States, they visited European and American prisons.[89] This direct exposure to the international prison reform movement and Western prisons greatly sensitized

Xu Qian and Xu Shiying to the problems in penal practices at home. In their report on the conference, they made a passionate call for prison reform to follow the international trend. The report was forwarded to the throne by the ML and won imperial endorsement, adding to the momentum for the reform initiative already under way.[90]

In that same year, a draft of the Prison Law of Great Qing was completed. Its main author was Ogawa Shigejiro, the leading figure in Japanese penal reform in the late nineteenth century.[91] The draft law laid out the fundamental principles for a modern prison system, based on the penal theory and practices prevailing in the West. It classified institutions of penal confinement into prisons (*jianyu*) (for imprisonment with labor), jails (*juliu chang*) (for imprisonment without labor), and detention houses (*liuzhi suo*) (for criminal defendants waiting for trial), and provided for juvenile quarters, male and female quarters, and single cells within institutions of penal confinement.[92] It embodied the principle of punishing and reforming convicts as the functions of incarceration by requiring work and moral education within prisons. It emphasized a humanitarian spirit of prison management, providing sanitation standards and medical care for the sick in penal institutions.[93] The draft law was not enacted before the Qing dynasty fell, but it offered a blueprint for prison regulations under the Republic.[94]

The judicial reform in the New Policy decade left a lasting legacy. It is almost astonishing in retrospect that while the whole project of the reform was triggered by a memorial from Zhang Zhidong and Liu Kunyi, it enjoyed broad support among many high Qing officials, as well as recognized reformers such as Shen Jiaben and Wu Tingfang. It is instructive to see that Shen and many high officials did not have training in or direct exposure to Western laws and legal institutions but nonetheless were knowledgeable about Western legal-judicial practices, which suggests a deeper level and wider scope than previously assumed of transnational circulation of ideas through translation projects by Chinese and foreigners alike. Even more revealing is that besides Shen and Wu, some high officials, such as Ze Gong, understood the importance of judicial independence, and others supported the principle of legal equality embodied in the draft criminal code, such as Yuan Shuxun, the governor of Shanxi (another provincial governor who had a better grasp of Western-derived legal principles was Cheng Dequan, the governor of Jiangsu, discussed in later chapters). A facile divide between conservatives and reformers among high officials in the late Qing era would not, therefore, withstand close scrutiny, and a more nuanced understanding of the New Policy decade is in order.

On the other hand, the willingness of many high officials to follow Western models to reform Chinese law and judicial practices had a limit, for both ideological and practical reasons. Opposition to the draft criminal code was one example, and the reluctance to abolish torture in trials (and summary execution) was another. In those cases of resistance to reform, Shen Jiapen and Wu Tingfang skillfully argued for reform by asserting that they were not just copying Western examples but trying to better enforce the intention of Chinese law or the Chinese legal tradition. Where they encountered the fiercest resistance, they were willing to take a step back, such as on the issue of the draft criminal code, in order not to jeopardize the entire project of the reform. Such strategies, along with a certain accommodation to them on the part of the imperial court and support from high officials such as Prince Yi-kuang, which proved crucial, made possible the progress that was made in transforming the Chinese judiciary in the short span of ten years. What was achieved and, more important, what were articulated as the principles of the reform in the New Policy decade laid the foundation for the continuation of the reform in the Republican era. At the same time, an underlying tension would persist between the Western models that were consciously emulated and Chinese practices subconsciously rooted in the native political, economic, and sociocultural environment.

CHAPTER 2

Judicial Modernity as Performance of Formality: The Beiyang Era

> The Taliyuan or Supreme Court, in Peking, was formally opened on the 17th instant [September 17—the report seemed to be sent before October 1]. Three appeal cases—viz. one case of smuggling opium, and two robbery cases—were listed. Five Justices sat on the bench, namely Messrs. Yao Chen, Pan Chang-hsu, Chang Hsiao-pin, Kao Chung, and Hsu Wei-chen. There were attorneys to prosecute as well as lawyers to defend the cases. The procedure of the Court was as follows: the Court Registrar read the cases that were to be reviewed. One of the presiding Judges stated the facts of each case, the decision of the lower Court, and the points to be settled by the Supreme Court. Then the prosecutors and the counsel for the respondents addressed the Court. Perfect order was maintained in the Court room.
>
> —*North China Herald* (Shanghai), October 5, 1912[1]

The significance of the New Policy initiatives was conclusively manifested in the fact that what was envisioned and partially accomplished of the judicial reform in the decade became the framework of the legal principles, the laws, and the judiciary in the Republican era. The Beiyang government was essentially developing, within that framework, more details in formalizing judicial institutions and procedures. Nevertheless, the working out of those details encountered difficulties and invited new challenges for which the state and society were ill-prepared. Paradoxically, the state set up institutional and procedural standards to which state agents were unable to measure up, and the reform created greater societal demands for judicial services that the state was hard pressed to supply adequately. An examination of how the Republican state was driven by Western models to move down that paradoxical path reveals what judicial modernity actually entailed in early-twentieth-century China.

Motivations and Strategies for Reform

Continuation of the New Policy Agenda

Upon the founding of the Republic of China in January 1912, Sun Yat-sen's Provisional Government enshrined the principle of judicial independence in the Provisional Constitution. Providing for separation of the administration, legislature, and judiciary, the document stipulated that judicial power was to be exercised by courts; judges were to adjudicate independently, without interference from administrative organs; and judges should neither be transferred nor their salaries be lowered during their tenure.[2] The short lifespan of Sun's government (January–March, 1912), however, did not allow for any substantive initiatives in judicial reform to take place. The task was passed onto the Yuan Shikai government (March 1912–June 1916) and the regimes that followed.

On March 11, 1912, upon assuming the office of provisional president, Yuan Shikai issued a presidential order that until laws of the Republic were promulgated, the draft criminal code of the Qing and other laws previously adopted would remain in force, minus articles contradictory to the republican form of government.[3] On April 30, the refurbished draft criminal code was enacted as the Provisional New Criminal Code (Zanxing xinxinglü) (PNCC).[4]

Yuan was not the first person to decide on adopting the draft criminal code of the New Policy years. Following the independence of Jiangsu from the Qing court in late October 1911, the provincial justice department (*tifa si*) under Zheng Yan issued an order to that effect on November 15, 1911. Noting the impracticability of making new laws in short order, he instructed all courts in Jiangsu to apply the draft criminal code of 1910 in criminal cases and to make decisions in civil cases in accordance with custom. The courts were also to follow the draft criminal and civil procedural laws of January 1911. In December 1911, the Jiangsu Provincial Assembly adopted a resolution to the same effect, but further specified that the three books of the draft civil code ("Kinship," "Debts," and "Inheritance") should be applied in civil litigation, and that civil cases that did not fall within the three areas be decided by considering provincial customs and foreign legal theories. Governor Cheng Dequan issued the resolution as a provincewide directive on December 17.[5] In other words, as early as late 1911, before Yuan Shikai or his advisers reached the same conclusion in March 1912, Jiangsu province had already taken the initiative and applied the draft criminal code. Obviously, to adopt the draft code was the only sensible and feasible approach to having a modern criminal code and a functioning judiciary in short order.

The rhetoric of the New Policy era was also appropriated and amplified in the official discourse, which mirrored similar expectations and languages in the print media. Although Qing officials such as Ze Gong spoke of protecting human rights as early as 1907, radical intellectuals attacked the Qing as a regime that violated human rights, and the Qing legal system was deemed deficient in protecting the people's rights.[6] When the Republic was founded, the popular expectation was that the new form of government would provide better protection of human rights. Using the same language, in a presidential order dated May 11, 1912, Yuan Shikai admonished all officials and military personnel not to confiscate people's properties arbitrarily. "The Republic is based on the rule of law, and the most important of civil rights is [the right to] property, which is the same under the law in [all] countries in the world." Yuan continued that if a person's property ought to be confiscated for breaking law, "the procurator is to prosecute and the judicial organ is to adjudicate and rule according to the law, but no one else should encroach on such procedures. For the purpose of restoring order and respecting human rights, this president issues the present decree and wishes that citizens enjoy happiness and keep the peace together."[7] The governor of Jiangsu, Cheng Dequan, duly transmitted the order to the Jiangsu High Procuracy (JHP) and other provincial government agencies.[8]

Yuan Shikai's order was probably aimed at the social turmoil in the wake of the 1911 Revolution, when properties of "the enemies of the revolution" were confiscated or looted by whomever in the name of the revolution, a situation that we shall turn to later. Whatever his motivation, the principle Yuan enunciated was unassailable; and his use of human rights vocabulary serves to indicate the degree to which such concepts as "the rule of law," "human rights," "the people's rights," and "civil rights" became key words in the official discourse, echoing a public discourse in the print media. Such rhetoric helped create a favorable intellectual climate for the reform, but it did not amount to actual reform. How committed Yuan and other high officials were to those ideas is another question. It may be safe to state that most high officials in the Republican era intellectually accepted these Western-derived ideas as positive moral values and enlightened political goals. They were not afraid to talk about them, when to do so cost nothing; but when it came to committing financial resources to building and operating the judiciary and enforcing laws, they would often as easily sacrifice such ideals for other priorities.

To its credit, the Yuan government continued the late Qing efforts at drafting laws in areas where none had existed. Besides the Legal System Bureau that was in charge of proposing, reviewing, and approving laws and ordinances, the Law Codification Commission (LCC)—a late Qing creation—was preserved.[9] Between 1912 and 1927, under Wang Chonghui, a J.D. from Yale University, and Dong Kang, a late Qing *jinshi* degree holder trained in law in Japan, the LCC compiled several dozen laws and ordinances. The laws included the amended criminal codes, four books of the civil code ("General Principles," "Kinship," "Inheritance," and "Rights to Things"), the civil and criminal procedural laws, securities law, corporation law, bankruptcy law, arbitration law, civil enforcement law, and others.[10] The crucial role the LCC played in the legal-judicial reform was widely recognized. Commenting in 1928 on the LCC, Liang Yunli, the secretary to the minister of justice in Nanjing, acknowledged that "China owes a debt to the Commission for most of the judicial reforms introduced since [the founding of] the Republic."[11]

The Champions for Judicial Reform

While the LCC continued to be an important institution for producing written laws, the Ministry of Justice (MJ) was the true engine that drove the reform in the institutional and procedural dimensions during the Beiyang era.[12] Significantly, throughout the period of 1912–1928, all but two of the successive ministers of justice in Beijing received legal training in Japan or the West.[13] To what extent those ministers' foreign exposure shaped their outlook and behavior as judicial officials can only be speculated, but they were apparently more sensitized than other occupational and social groups in early Republican China to the gap between traditional Chinese judicial practices and their Western counterparts, and were probably more motivated and committed to building a Chinese judiciary based on Western models. Their role in fashioning a modern Chinese judiciary should be recognized, as almost all of the reform measures in the Beiyang era were initiated by the MJ.

Moreover, as foreign observers pointed out, the subministerial government bureaucracy was even more important than the government ministers in early Republican China. "It has been the secretaries and the assistants, chiefly Chinese young men who have been educated in mission or government schools or abroad, who have kept the train[s] running in spite of the hordes of bandit soldiers and bandit generals who rode 'dead head' and disrupted traffic," *Millard's Review* (Shanghai) noted in 1918.[14] The same could be said of the personnel in judicial institutions in the national and provincial capitals. As the personnel below the level of deputy minister in the central government were not replaced as frequently as were ministers and deputy ministers, there was a large degree of continuity in the operation of the state apparatus, especially in the judiciary, throughout the Beiyang era.[15] The institutional insulation from political vagaries of the times, based on professional expertise, that Julia Strauss has analyzed in the Guomindang (GMD) Ministries of Finance and Foreign Affairs was also evident in the MJ and the judiciary as a whole in the Beiyang era.[16]

The MJ was able to play such a role partly thanks to the legitimacy of its reform agenda. Judicial officials were motivated to push for the reform by the goal, inherited from the New Policy era, of modernizing the Chinese judiciary in order to end extraterritoriality. Wang Chonghui, who presided over the LCC after a short stint as the first minister of justice, stated in 1918 that an objective of codifying laws was "to secure eventual cancellation of extraterritoriality." He expected that revision of the laws would be complete in five years, and that efforts would be made thereafter to abolish extraterritoriality.[17] When the SC president Dong Kang was interviewed in 1923, he expressed the view that extraterritoriality would be abolished one day and the Mixed Courts in Shanghai returned to the Chinese authorities.[18] Similar sentiments punctuated the official discourse of the time. "Everyone knows [extraterritoriality] harms our national prestige, and we are all trying very hard to get rid of [it], so [Chinese] society is watching the judicial reform closely, and nobody dares criticize the principle of judicial independence," Zhang Zongxiang, a former minister of justice (1914–1916), observed in 1923.[19] Even if this political and intellectual environment was limited to Beijing and perhaps some provincial capitals and treaty ports, it was an important condition for the reform to continue.

A Blueprint for a Modern Judiciary

Xu Shiying became minister of justice in July 1912. His career in the central government was associated with the reform that had started in the late Qing. Born in Qiupu, Anhui, in 1873, Xu obtained a *xiucai* degree at the age of thirteen and began his legal career in the BP in 1889 when he was sixteen. In 1908, he was appointed a judge at the Fengtian High Court (HC). In 1910, he joined the delegation to the International Prison Reform Congress held in the United States and saw firsthand how judicial systems and prisons operated in the West.

As minister of justice, Xu exhibited a high level of enthusiasm and energy in pursuing the reform. In December 1912, he circulated a long document entitled "A Plan for the Judiciary" among provincial governors and judicial officials.[20] This blueprint for a Chinese judiciary in terms of institutional infrastructure would be pursued in the Beiyang era and beyond, even though what was accomplished fell well short of the goals and far behind the timetable that Xu envisioned. A brief look at the main points of the plan provides a useful overview of the reform initiatives during 1912–1927.

The plan's rationale was stated at the outset: "Judicial independence is the key element of a constitutional state and the spirit of a country based on the rule of law; yet judicial independence can stand only after complete institutions are built." Xu expressed his resolve to spare no efforts to push forward the reform, so that "one day judicial independence could be practiced and extraterritoriality jettisoned." Under the plan, in 1914–1918, courts, procuracies, and prisons were to be established in all provinces except Mongolia, Tibet, and Qinghai. Each of China's more than 1,700 counties should have a district court (DC), with one or more courts of first instance (CFI). By 1918, over 2,000 courts should have been established. In counties where courts did not exist yet, three special trial officers (*zhuanshen yuan*) should be appointed so as to separate the judiciary from the administration and prepare for the establishment of courts. The plan was an expansion of what had been proposed in 1906–1907 by the SC and the ML.

One component of Xu's plan was to have a reformed prison system that would approximate what Xu had witnessed in America and Europe in 1910. Under his plan, Beijing should have a model prison in 1912 (which was being completed at the time). Provincial capitals and commercial metropolises should improve existing new prisons and build sixty more in 1913–1914. In 1915–1916, new prisons should be built for counties. Since it was impossible to build a new prison for every county, Xu proposed to build one prison for every six or seven counties, totaling over 240 prisons. Xu believed that it would be possible to raise the more than ¥24 million needed to build those prisons. Citing cases in "countries in the East and the West," he envisioned that two-thirds of the cost of operating new prisons would come from the work done by inmates behind bars. He noted the need to separate prisons from houses of detention and the need to train judicial officers and prison administrators.[21] Xu may have been overly optimistic, or even utterly unrealistic, but his plan conveyed the urgency he felt about the need to establish a modern Chinese judiciary.

In connection with Xu's blueprint, another document must be mentioned here. Liang Qichao, a well-known intellectual giant of the late Qing and early Republic, served as minister of justice after Xu Shiying from September 1913 to February 1914. He left a deep imprint on the reform when he submitted an opinion to Yuan Shikai at the time of his resignation, proposing ten measures to deal with the issues that arose from the reform at the time.[22] Yuan referred Liang's opinion to the 76-member Political Council convened from December 1913 to June 1914 to study policy issues, and after a panel of thirteen had reviewed Liang's proposals, the council reached a conclusion by April 24, 1914, and reported back to Yuan.[23]

Liang's proposals and the council's opinions would lead to several major policy decisions on the reform (addressed in the relevant chapters of this book). The most crucial consequences were the retrenchment of the court system (see below in this chapter), the adoption of the law on dealing with robbers and bandits (see Chapter 9), and the brief restoration of exile and flogging as punishments (see Chapter 8), all of which marked a serious regression from the earlier reform initiatives. In retrospect, however, it may be argued that those developments were largely forced by a depressing shortage of financial and human resources and other material conditions, and that Liang Qichao articulated such conditions realistically and provided an occasion for the Yuan government to step back from the reform goals that Xu Shiying had advocated. At the same time, Liang's other ideas were also translated into more positive government actions and regulations. Those included evaluating lawyers' qualifications, recruiting judges from administrative officials through special examinations, setting deadlines for closing cases, issuing a sentencing guide for the PNCC, and providing judicial funding by the national treasury. In a sense, the reform agendas of the Beiyang era were the results of negotiations and compromises between Xu's idealistic vision and Liang's pragmatic approach.

Reform as Institutional Formalization

Qualifications for Judicial Officers

Xu Shiying acted swiftly on some of the reform initiatives. Within a month in office, he proceeded to dismiss judicial officers at top posts in Beijing and installed their replacements. The list of new appointees shows what Xu was looking for and what he was able to get in terms of qualifications for those posts.[24] The common denominator of these men was their education in law in Japan or the West and their experience in China's law and judiciary. The dismissals and appointments were part of an effort to professionalize judicial personnel and standardize the credentials and qualifications for judicial posts. Xu urged heads of all high courts and procuracies to seek qualified, morally upright people to be judicial officers—what he called "the foundation of the judicial reform."[25]

The MJ began to require educational qualifications for judicial appointments at the district and provincial levels to enforce the relevant articles in the Law on Organizing Courts of 1910. Candidates who had three years' education in law were eligible to take a test and, if they passed, could be sent to district level as probationary judges/procurators. After two years' probation, they could take a second test to fill posts at district courts and procuracies. Candidates for posts at high courts and procuracies were required to have five years' experience either working as judges, procurators, or lawyers or teaching in schools of law and government; candidates for SC and GP posts were to have ten years' experience.[26] The regulations on educational qualifications were enforced, so that in 1925, among 955 judges and procurators in the country, 211 were graduates from law schools in foreign countries and 770 had received higher education in China.[27]

While educational credentials became the prerequisite for judicial appointments, the MJ was keen to recruit talents among those who had inadequate education but sufficient working experience. The MJ began to hold special tests to select judicial officers from such personnel.[28] In February 1914, Minister of Justice Liang Qichao proposed to institutionalize tests for officials who had handled judicial affairs in the Qing era without formal education in law; those who passed would enter a training institute for judges before being assigned to judicial posts.[29]

To ensure that judicial officers upheld professional ethics, institutions were set up to discipline wayward officials, among them the Committee on Disciplining Judicial Officers, the Committee on Disciplining Senior Civil Servants, and the Committee on Disciplining Ordinary Civil Servants. Starting in 1921, the regulations on prosecuting judicial officers for corruption were applicable to county magistrates and trial officers.[30] County magistrates were also under other disciplinary regulations against bribery, corruption, and dereliction of duty.

No Political Affiliation for Judges

The Law on Organizing Courts that the Republic inherited had a provision barring judges from belonging to political parties or being members of the Parliament or provincial and local assemblies. In December 1912, Xu Shiying instructed judges to quit their political parties to comply with the law.[31] Two weeks later, Xu ordered high courts and procuracies to report back on the matter.[32] In March 1913, when it was reported that judges in Guangxi province were all affiliated with political parties, Xu ordered the Guangxi HC to see to it that those judges severed their political ties.[33] In the meantime, the MJ published a list of all judges serving in various courts in Beijing, showing that they had either never joined or had withdrawn from political parties.[34] In March 1914, Yuan Shikai issued a presidential order to prohibit judges from joining political parties. He said that the judiciary was to protect the people's rights, and that judges should rise above personal and selfish opinions and uphold "the spirit of judicial independence."[35] In January 1915, the prohibition of party affiliation was extended to cover county magistrates who performed judicial functions and circuit administrators who supervised county judicial affairs.[36]

The efforts to keep the judiciary out of party politics were not without political benefits to Yuan Shikai. The abovementioned list shows that the judges in Beijing renounced the GMD and the Republican Party. Yuan's timing in weighing in on the issue in March 1914 is also suggestive of his political motives—it was a few months after the Second Revolution and the outlawing of the GMD by Yuan. For the same reason, the government prohibited military personnel and the police from political party affiliations in 1913.[37] For Xu Shiying and other reformers, however, requiring judges to quit political parties was a logical measure to ensure judicial independence, just as the requirement for educational qualifications was to ensure judicial competence. As late as 1920, the MJ transmitted a presidential order reiterating the prohibition both of judges' being affiliated to parties and of interference by administrative officials in judicial proceedings, "so as to safeguard judicial independence."[38]

The Court System and County Magistrates

The Law on Organizing Courts provided for a four-level court system: the SC, the high court, the district court, and the court of first instance, along with a three-trial process. The 1912 plan penned by Xu Shiying for a court system was based on this scheme. A court system was largely established in accordance with the scheme, but courts at the lowest two levels were set up only in selected areas in provinces.

How would judicial functions be performed in counties without courts? Under the 1913 Provisional Regulations on the Duties of County Trial Assistants, in a county without a court, an assistant trial officer (*bangshen yuan*) would adjudicate cases of first instance, with the county magistrate acting as procurator, which was designed to insulate the latter from adjudication, as the MJ expressly noted.[39] The county magistrate, one to three assistant trial officers, and one to three recordkeepers would constitute a county "trial and prosecution office" (TPO) (*shenjian suo*).[40]

Courts were not set up in all counties, because provincial governments were short of financial resources to do so. The situation in several counties in Jiangsu is illustrative. In 1912, Guanyun was authorized to have a TPO. The county magistrate proposed to set up a court and a procuracy and enclosed a budget. Governor Cheng Dequan shot down the idea by pointing to the lack of funds. The total county government outlay would take 90 percent of the taxes, based on a bumper harvest, but no one could count on a bumper harvest every year. The salaries proposed for court and procuracy personnel were too low and had to be raised to appoint qualified judges. The budget did not include a jail inmate ration fund. In short, the proposed budget of ¥5,000 was insufficient to cover all judicial expenses. How could a court and a procuracy be funded under such conditions?[41]

Situations in counties where courts and procuracies were established further bore out Cheng's point. In Jingjiang, a DC and a DP were set up in former garrison barracks that were in need of repair. Their operating funds were to come from the county government office (CGO), but the office would "borrow" the judicial funds. Having cut judicial personnel's salaries in half, the DC and the DP were still short of necessary funds to operate.[42] Similarly, the heads of the DC and DP in Liyang asked for a monthly budget of ¥833, which the CGO could not afford.[43] Local people and county magistrates might have regarded the DC and the DP in Jingjiang as extravagant, in that there were two judges, one procurator, four senior clerks, eight junior clerks, six secretaries, two coroners, six bailiffs, ten service staff, and thirteen judicial policemen—a total of fifty-two people, plus the court president and chief procurator.[44] Many counties did not have so complete a staff in 1912–1913, but the judicial formalization called for it, and county-level finance was unable to support it (see Chapter 5).

It was such a situation that led to Liang Qichao's proposal in February 1914 to change the four-level-court and three-trial system into a three-level-court and two-trial system so as to save resources and streamline and speed up the adjudication process. The Political Council that reviewed Liang's proposal held that the four-level-court system might be changed to three-level by doing away with the CFI, but that the three-trial process should be retained, with district courts (or adjudicating county magistrates where no district courts existed) trying cases of first instance.[45]

Liang's proposal was followed by telegrams to Yuan Shikai from governors in twenty provinces across the country who wanted to cut judicial organs in order to save money. Minister of Justice Zhang Zongxiang, who had succeeded Liang Qichao, tried to salvage as many established courts as possible by proposing to abolish the CFI and the TPO in some provinces but keep them in other places. Yuan Shikai again referred the matter to the Political Council, which in May 1914 reached a compromise between what provincial governors wanted and what the MJ wanted, that is, (1) to abolish the CFI everywhere but maintain established district and high courts, and (2) to make preparations to build branch high courts where needed. It also proposed that the newly restored circuit administrators (see Chapter 4) supervise county magistrates' handling of judicial affairs where DC or HC branches did not exist. This opinion became the policy.[46]

As the result, as many as 486 courts of first instance in the country were abolished, and more than 1,000 judicial personnel were laid off.[47] In 1914, all the TPO and the CFI and as many as 90 district courts were dismantled across the country.[48] What came out of the retrenchment was a system where the CGO would serve as the CFI for minor cases that would, on appeals, arrive at the DC for second trial and end in a third and final trial at the HC; and both the CGO and the DC would first try major cases that would go through the HC or their branches and end at the SC.[49] Thus some semblance of the four-level-court and three-trial system was maintained, but the institutional content changed.

It became obvious that a majority of county magistrates had to be given the power to perform judicial functions, as in the imperial era. This was institutionalized in 1914 with the Provisional Regulations on the County Magistrate Managing Judicial Affairs and the Provisional Regulations on the County Magistrate Disposing of Lawsuits.[50] Under the regulations, a trial officer (*chengshen yuan*) would replace the assistant trial officer, but he was no longer the only person to try cases; both he and the county magistrate would do so. The magistrate would appoint the trial officer, to be approved by the HC president.[51] The archival sources suggest that the HC approval was a formality for the most part and was routinely granted. The fact that the trial officer served at the county magistrate's pleasure and both would try cases erased any semblance of judicial independence at the county level.

The retreat from a major hallmark of judicial modernity—separation of the judiciary and administration—was hard for reformers to swallow. From 1914 through 1937, a key agenda of the reform would always be to change the situation and set up formal courts in all counties. In 1916, a national judicial conference convened by the MJ passed a resolution that in rural areas, county judicial offices (CJO) (*xian sifa gongshu*) be established, each with a trial officer adjudicating and the county magistrate acting as procurator. The regulations to that effect were issued in 1917.[52] But the necessary funding for the CJO was never included in the government budget, and in 1926, the plan still remained on paper.[53]

The Rule of Avoidance

In December 1913, Minister of Justice Liang Qichao submitted a report on the judicial reform to Yuan Shikai.[54] He suggested that a "rule of avoidance" be established in appointing judicial officers. Yuan Shikai responded favorably.[55] In January 1914, with Yuan's approval, Liang issued an order to lay down the rule as follows: (1) judges and procurators at the provincial level should not serve in their native provinces; (2) judges and procurators at district courts and procuracies should not be natives of the area their institutions served; and (3) judges and procurators at both the provincial and district levels who had close relatives serving in the same institution or immediately superior institutions should ask for transfers.[56] Two weeks later, the rule was fine-tuned to be applied to officers at branch HC and HP as well.[57] By February 1914, a first group of provincial judicial officers had been transferred out of their posts into the same positions in other provinces to comply with the rule.[58] Although Liang resigned the same month, the rule of avoidance would long survive his tenure as minister of justice. In 1919, the MJ took another step, ordering that if court clerks (*shuji guan*) had close relatives serving as superiors within the same institution, they should disclose the relationship and ask to be transferred.[59]

A somewhat different rule of avoidance was created for the legal profession. It was first suggested by the Jiangsu General Association of Lawyers, which proposed to the JHP chief Sun Runyu in July 1912 that former judges should not practice as lawyers in the same district where they had served within one year of leaving judgeship. Probably linking the role of lawyers with protecting the rights of the accused, not with unethical practices, Sun replied at the time that no such measure was necessary "to respect human rights and conform to legal principle."[60] Still, the issue did not go away. In 1915, the MJ decreed that lawyers who had served as judges, procurators, or clerks at courts and procuracies could not, within three years of leaving office, practice in the same area over which their former offices had jurisdiction. In 1916, the MJ revoked the rule without explanation.[61] In September 1918, however, the MJ reinstated the prohibition, noting that lawyers who had once served in courts or procuracies often used their connections to get inside information and advertised such to attract clients. The prohibition covered former clerks at courts and procuracies.[62] One month later, the rule was extended to cover lawyers who had formerly been court bailiffs (*chengfa li*).[63] At the inquiry of the Shanghai Bar

Association, the MJ clarified that the rule only applied to those who had served at the district level, not at the provincial level.[64] The rule of avoidance remained in force until early 1927, when the MJ in Beijing repealed it in response to a request from more than 200 judicial officers, only for it to be reinstated by the GMD government later (see Chapter 3).[65]

How seriously the rule of avoidance was followed may be glimpsed from one example. In May 1915, the Shanghai DC president, Yuan Zhongxiang, reported to the JHC that the ex-wife of Chen Zemin, a lawyer practicing in Shanghai who would appear in Yuan's courtroom, was his sister. He wanted to know whether this fact called for avoidance. The JHC inquired of the MJ, and the answer was yes. Chen Zemin had to transfer to the bar association in Jiangning to practice at the Jiangning DC. He would return to practice in Shanghai in 1916 with special permission from the JHC.[66]

The concept of the rule of avoidance was not new. In the imperial era, provincial governors, prefects, and county magistrates were all forbidden to serve in their native places. Insofar as those officials exercised judicial powers in the imperial era, even the application of the rule to judicial officers was not entirely new. On the other hand, however, in the Republican era only judicial officers, adjudicating county magistrates, and lawyers were subject to the rule of avoidance, while administrative officials in all other posts were not. This may properly be regarded as a measure specifically designed to help maintain the fairness and independence of the judicial process.

Centralizing the Prison System

From Xu Shiying's perspective, prison reform was to start with standardizing the names of penal institutions and separating new prisons from county jails. In August 1912, Xu ordered that the Beijing Model Prison be called the Beijing Prison.[67] In July 1913, Xu issued another order to standardize the names of penal institutions. All facilities for defendants attached to courts were to be called detention houses. All facilities for sentenced convicts, including former workhouses for criminals, would be called prisons. All provincial model prisons of the late Qing would be called prisons, with their location names. All old local jails would be called such-and-such old county jail (*xian jiujian*). All other names for penal institutions were abolished.[68] This order is significant, in that it not only standardized the names of penal institutions throughout the country, but conceptually classified three types of institutions. A detention house was different from a prison in functions, but a new prison was different from a county jail only due to the better facilities and management in the former.

Following the 1916 national judicial conference, the MJ directed all provinces to pay attention to four key issues in prison reform: (1) both building new prisons and reforming old jails were important, but the priority was to build one new prison for every group of counties (from several to more than ten); (2) new prisons should be located appropriately for the counties they would serve; (3) the new prison at a provincial capital should be called such-and-such province first prison, and other new prisons in the province were to be called the second, the third, and so forth; and (4) new prisons at provincial capitals should have a capacity for at least 500 inmates, and those at other locations a capacity for at least 300.[69] The directive was followed by the provinces with regard to names of new prisons, but the capacities of new prisons did not always conform to the standards set forth here.[70]

The prison reform in the Beiyang period resulted in some new prisons, though fewer than planned by Xu Shiying in 1912. In 1918, more than thirty new prisons were built, eleven of which were said to be well organized. In at least one modern prison, the Beijing First Prison, the system of one cell for each inmate both day and night was introduced in 1922. In 1926, there were twenty-seven new prisons nationwide, of which fourteen were reported to be well built and organized. In addition, there were eleven new branch prisons.[71]

A statutory framework regarding penal institutions was set up in the meantime. The Provisional Regulations on Detention Houses of February 1913 and the Regulations on Prisons of December 1913 (based on the Great Qing prison law) officially separated prisons and detention houses. A prison was a place for confining convicted and sentenced criminals. However, if necessary, detention houses could be used as prisons, and vice versa.[72] The prison regulations only applied to new prisons or detention houses, while the majority of penal institutions were old county jails, where confinement conditions were horrendous. The MJ did not expect conditions in county jails to change quickly, so it followed up the Regulations on Prisons with an order that county jails need *not* comply with parts of the regulations—22 out of the 103 articles—concerning single cells, prison work, moral instruction, education, clothing, periodic baths, sickroom, and so on.[73]

Reforming County Jails

For reformers in the Republican era, therefore, a major task of the prison reform was to improve county jails with better management and more humane conditions. The MJ persistently tried to learn about the conditions in county jails in order to regulate them more effectively. In March 1913, Xu Shiying issued a directive (Directive No. 67) to the provinces requiring counties to report on how old jails had been improved and what problems remained.[74] Successive ministers of justice repeatedly ordered jail overseers in all provinces to report on improvements in their jails and detention houses.[75] In 1922, Minister Zhang Yaozeng ordered that provincial HP investigate and make detailed reports on what had been achieved since the ministry's directive of 1916 on prison reform, and the JHP carried out the order.[76] Thus, by 1922, periodic inspections became a routine mechanism for the provincial authorities (and the central government) to learn about local conditions, and the practice would continue into the Nanjing decade.

In undertaking inspections of county jails and detention houses, the JHP did not just serve as a conduit for filing inspectors' reports to Beijing. It responded to the reports by issuing orders to the individual county magistrates in question demanding rectification of problems identified by inspectors. For their part, county magistrates and jail overseers either complied with the demand, explained why problems could not be fixed, or requested financial support for solving the problems. Indicative of the reach of the central government via the provincial institutions to the county level, those institutional interactions helped disseminate reform initiatives there.

The repeated requests from the MJ over the years for updates on conditions in county jails and houses of detention suggests the persistence of ghastly conditions in them. The specifics that the MJ wanted to know in 1921 included ten categories:

(1) The physical layout of the institution and sizes of doors and windows.

(2) The number of male and female defendants; whether they were held legally; whether they were held for a long period without trial; whether sentenced convicts who had served their time were still being held; and whether any had been released on parole.

(3) The number of inmates held in big and small cells respectively.

(4) The amount of food given to inmates, and whether there was embezzlement [of funds for food by staff].

(5) Whether inmates slept in shackles, and whether they had beds.

(6) Whether cells had sunlight and fresh air, whether there was anything unsanitary, and how sick inmates were treated.

(7) Whether prison work was done, and, if so, what kind, and how much was received from the sale of the products.

(8) How many staff worked at the facility and in what kinds of shifts; whether old practices such as having a "cell head" (*laotou*), "jail man" (*jinzu*), "companion woman" (*banpuo*), and "official go-between" (*guanmei*) still existed.

(9) Whether inmates had ever escaped, and, if so, how many times.

(10) Whether prison staff were equal to their jobs, and whether inmates were treated according to the law.[77]

The list shows the MJ's efforts at formalization and suggests the kind of problems known to have existed in county jails.

Reform as Procedural Formalization

A major thrust of the reform was to formalize judicial procedures consistent with judicial independence and the rule of law. Initially, when the PNCC was enacted, relevant provisions in the 1910 Provisional Regulations on Establishing Courts at All Levels were used as procedural law, as were portions of the draft criminal and civil procedure laws that covered the competence of courts at different levels.[78] Judicial procedures were gradually established through trial and error, with many ad hoc rules and regulations, and eventually with the enactment of procedural laws in 1921. This section traces the procedures that were formalized during the Beiyang era and provides an overview of how the judiciary was supposed to function.

The Reception of Lawsuits

If the workings of a modern judiciary were something new for judicial officers to get used to, they were even more confusing to ordinary people involved in lawsuits. Speaking of Chinese residents in Shanghai's International Settlement and their experience with Western-style judicial practices, the writer Yao Gonghe noted in 1917 that most Chinese knew nothing about them—"eight or nine out of ten average citizens would be stupefied by the question of what is a civil case and what is a criminal case."[79] That was precisely one of the problems encountered by the newly established court system. Whereas for ages there had been no conceptual separation between criminal and civil lawsuits, now litigants and legal scribes alike would have to separate the two and figure out which kind of lawsuit they should be launching in the first place, before filling out either criminal or civil complaint forms. Moreover, the two forms were not easily distinguishable to an illiterate or semi-literate person, and even to some legal scribes (given the frequency of mistakes). Criminal cases had first to go to procuracies and civil cases to courts, so when lawsuits were filed at the wrong places, they were rejected according to the law, to the litigants' great consternation. They bitterly complained that the new court system did not work for them.

In view of the situation, the Capital DP suggested in April 1914 to the MJ that when criminal and civil lawsuits were mixed up, the court and the procuracy should not just reject them, but notify each other and replace them with correct complaints for the litigants, unless the mistake was about wrong jurisdictions. The MJ adopted the idea and ordered all courts and procuracies to do the same.[80]

When a litigant filed a lawsuit at a procuracy or a court or the CGO, he or she had to pay a litigation fee, in the form of judicial stamps affixed on the complaint form, which was nonrefundable even if the lawsuit was rejected for mistakes. People often lost money for their errors, which was another source of widespread discontent with the judiciary. In order to avoid this situation as much as possible, the MJ ordered all courts to put upright and capable clerks in charge of receiving complaints; when litigants submitted wrong complaints, the clerks should explain the mistakes to them and tell them not to submit. If litigants insisted on submitting their complaints, then litigation fees should be collected according to the rules.[81] The measure did not appear to be helpful to litigants. In June 1915, the MJ circulated another directive that when courts and procuracies received a complaint, a court clerk or a procurator should review it to determine whether it was filed correctly; if not, the paid litigation fee and/or complaint fee should be refunded and the complaint returned with instructions, but an application fee of ¥0.50 was to be collected.[82] In August 1921, the MJ combined the abovementioned policies into the Measures of Reviewing and Accepting Civil and Criminal Complaints.[83] No criminal and civil lawsuits should be accepted unless written on official complaint forms. In October 1921, to enforce the order, the JHP issued a public notice on not accepting unofficial complaint forms.[84]

The MJ insisted on collecting litigation fees both because such fees were a source of revenue for the judiciary and because it wanted to discourage frivolous lawsuits.[85] In 1913, Liang Qichao pointed out that in the past, litigants had been charged fees only for first trials but not for the second and third trials upon appeals, which "both encouraged frivolous lawsuits and diminished the state revenue." He ordered that henceforth litigants be charged litigation fees for all appeals, and he also issued the first set of regulations on collecting civil litigation fees.[86]

Significantly, the MJ tried to strike a balance between collecting legitimate fees and providing access to judicial process for would-be litigants who could not afford the expense. In 1927, Minister of Justice Yao Zhen issued a new set of regulations on litigation fees, under which litigants who could not afford the fees could file civil lawsuits with guarantors, and the fees were to be paid either out of the remedy resulting from the lawsuit or by the guarantors.[87] In that same year, the MJ discovered a pattern: some courts and procuracies tried to obtain more judicial revenue by postponing the trials of criminal defendants who paid large sums of money as bail and by fining people who were financially unable to pay and should be punished by serving time instead. Noting that fines were punishment for crimes, not a ploy to increase state revenue, the MJ ordered all courts and procuracies to cease both practices and to keep a close eye on subordinate officers' behavior in the matter.[88] Given the financial woes in the judicial system (see Chapter 5), the ministry's consideration for litigants is remarkable but was probably ineffectual.

In short, the MJ tried very hard to formalize and standardize the way a lawsuit was to be filed and accepted, but the formalized rules created difficulties for litigants who were not well informed. There was a genuine concern on the part of the MJ and some other judicial officials to make the judiciary accessible to ordinary people. It attempted to balance the agenda to ensure access to the court system and the need to have legitimate judicial revenue collected in order to operate the system and to discourage frivolous lawsuits. All the best intentions were not fully met by the best results in the actual workings of the system for various reasons, as we shall see.

The Lawyer System

The principle of legal defense was accepted as early as 1907, when Shen Jiaben proposed the draft criminal and civil procedural law; and the 1910 Law on Organizing Courts assumed that lawyers would be present in judicial proceedings. In September 1912, the MJ issued Provisional Regulations on Lawyers, formally recognizing and regulating the legal profession for the first time. Several sets of rules and regulations on lawyers' qualifications, examination, ethics, obligations, supervision, and discipline were enacted thereafter.[89] In July 1915, the MJ issued a standard fee schedule to standardize lawyers' fees, which local bar associations had set for themselves, and prohibited lawyers from accepting gratuities over and above the officially sanctioned fees, called "public fees."[90] The MJ apparently stepped in because it wanted to bring down legal costs for litigants. Standardizing lawyers' fees would also make legal expenses predictable, in line with the formalization of the judiciary. The MJ soon learned that lawyers in various locales were ignoring the standard fee schedule and continued to charge their clients according to the local fee schedules set by their bar associations.[91] Recognizing that a national fee schedule did not make sense in light of the different living costs in various locales, the MJ repealed the 1915 regulations on lawyers' fees in October 1916 and allowed bar associations to set maximum fees according to local conditions and report fee schedules to the ministry for approval.[92] But, as some Chinese lawyers in Shanghai revealed, even the fee schedule set by the Shanghai Bar Association was little more than a piece of paper to which no one paid attention.[93] Conceivably, the situation may not have been limited to Shanghai. The MJ seemed to have resigned itself to the fact.

The most important aspect of the regulation of lawyers in connection with due process of law was that lawyers could only represent defendants or plaintiffs in formal courts, that is, they could not appear at trials conducted by county magistrates. This was implied in the Provisional Regulations on Lawyers, and the MJ made it explicit by a directive in early 1913.[94] When a county trial in Dantu, Jiangsu province, gave rise to the issue again in May 1914, the MJ reiterated the ban to all courts, procuracies, and county magistrates.[95] In response to another inquiry in April 1917, the MJ ruled that lawyers could not appear at county trials even in litigation between Chinese and foreigners.[96] The ministry's steadfast refusal to allow lawyers to appear at county trials under any circumstances was based on the rationale that the lawyer would be able to manipulate law and outwit a county magistrate who was not well trained in law, and that only in a court could the role of the lawyer be properly balanced by a legally trained judge. The result was that ordinary people in places where no courts existed could not avail themselves of legal representation, even though lawyers were allowed to write complaints for litigants.[97] Naturally, lawyers would not stay in a county where their practice was limited to writing complaints. The situation made the legal scribe an indispensable player in the county judicial process.

Trial Procedures

In June 1912, Minister of Justice Wang Chonghui reminded all courts and county offices that under the PNCC and Article 50 of the Provisional Constitution, criminal and civil trials should be open to the public, and no torture or physical abuse during trials would be tolerated; those who violated the rules would be prosecuted and punished according to Article 144 of the PNCC—by third-degree (three–five years) to fifth-degree (two–twelve months) prison terms—so as to "reform the judiciary and protect the people's rights."[98] The MJ issued the regulations on public attendance in courtrooms, requiring that a courtroom have seating space for the public to observe trials.[99] While the orders and regulations were not always followed everywhere, they rendered torture in trials illegal and made open trial a required practice.

The rights of litigants, especially defendants, were probably the most important issue that the MJ had to address. A traditional practice in dealing with civil litigation was to detain the defendant until trial. In 1912, the MJ prohibited detaining civil defendants unless there was evidence of their having committed crimes.[100] In November 1913, the MJ ordered that all courts, county magistrates, and trial officers follow Articles 46 and 47 of the PNCC when depriving defendants of civil rights and not resort to forfeit of civil rights without legal basis, so as to respect the law and civil rights and uphold the authority and credibility of the judiciary.[101] In May 1915, the MJ ordered that the texts of sentences at trials should be concise and easy to read, so that the ordinary people would be able to understand them.[102] In 1917, the MJ ordered that conviction and sentences in criminal cases be orally announced and then written up in public posters.[103] These orders manifested a strong spirit of making judicial procedures fair, transparent, and "user-friendly."

One of Liang Qichao's proposals in 1914 was to set deadlines for trying civil and criminal lawsuits so that cases would be closed quickly. The Political Council fully agreed with the idea.[104] In 1915, Regulations on Trial Deadlines for Criminal Prosecution were enacted. Investigation of a criminal case was to be done within ten days of detaining the defendant, a pretrial hearing was to be held within ten days of receiving the case file, and sentence was to be handed down within ten days of prosecuting (within twenty days in cases of homicide and robbery). Those rules applied to trials at all levels. High courts and the SC should finish trial review (see below) of a criminal case within ten days of receiving the case file. County magistrates should finish trying a criminal case within sixty days of receiving the case. County magistrates, judges, and procurators who violated the regulations were to be reported by superior officials for disciplinary action.[105] In 1918, the MJ revised the regulations to extend the deadlines to fifteen, twenty, and twenty-five days for investigation, hearing, and trial respectively.[106] In 1927, the MJ reiterated the time limits for criminal investigation and ordered procurators not to delay the process.[107] Another order required courts to forward files of appeal cases to the superior courts within five days of receiving notice.[108] These measures were designed to move lawsuits through the courts as efficiently as possible so as to prevent trial delays and case backlogs.

Backlogs plagued the Republican judiciary from the beginning. At the JHC in November 1912, of ninety-two civil cases received in previous months, only nineteen had been closed, and of thirty-eight civil cases received during the month, only five had been closed.[109] In 1913, Liang Qichao urged high courts to close backlogged cases. The JHC in turn ordered the DC and TPO to make monthly reports on the closing of backlogged cases and threatened judicial officers with disciplinary action for slacking.[110] In April 1915, Yuan Shikai ask the MJ to work out regulations to address case backlogs in civil litigation, criticizing judges who attributed backlogs to improper procedures and incomplete evidence for not caring about people's sufferings.[111] In 1917, Minister Zhang Yaozeng suspected that successive county magistrates deliberately hid case backlogs, because the number of cases often surged when the office of county magistrate changed hands.[112]

To reduce delays and backlogs, summary procedures for minor cases were introduced. In late 1913, with the MJ approval, the Capital DC and DP first experimented with a summary criminal chamber for minor cases to clear up the docket quickly. In three months, the summary chamber was able to dispose of more than a hundred cases a month. Other more serious cases also moved through regular courts more quickly as a result. In April 1914, the MJ decided to expand the practice across the country. Under the Provisional Regulations on District Court Summary Criminal Chambers, a summary chamber with one judge would try cases where evidence was clear, punishments would not exceed a fourth-degree prison term (12–35 months), and no pretrial hearing was required. The DP chief would decide whether a case belonged to the summary chamber. A procurator would prosecute a case within two days of receiving it. Trial would be conducted orally, with the proceedings recorded in writing. The judge would give sentence within two days of taking a case, but might have five days if authorized by the DC president. When the judge announced sentence, the defendant would be asked whether he or she wished to appeal, and if not, the case was closed.[113]

Similar procedures were set up for civil litigation too. In 1915, the MJ allowed summary chambers for both criminal and civil cases in district courts.[114] A separate summary procedure for minor civil lawsuits was formalized in 1920. Minor cases included lawsuits concerning ¥1,000 or less, rental disputes, hiring contract disputes, service charge disputes, property rights disputes, and real estate boundary disputes. Trial was conducted orally and recorded in writing.[115] Both criminal and civil summary procedures were standardized further in 1922, when the MJ issued the regulations on summary criminal courts and civil courts separately.[116]

One critical aspect of ensuring an impartial and transparent judicial process was the issue of who would actually control the trial proceedings. In September 1927, the MJ noted a long-standing fact that because judges and procurators often did not speak Mandarin, they had to let judicial policemen or court functionaries (*tingli*) speak on their behalf to litigants in local dialects, which tended to spawn irregularities and abuses by those underlings (see Chapter 6). The MJ ordered that henceforth judges and procurators who did not speak Mandarin were banned from dealing directly with litigants and could only handle work that did not involve talking to litigants.[117] Actually, the problem the MJ identified was worse at county trials than in formal courts. By controlling access to county trials, county functionaries such as judicial clerks and judicial policemen (often former runners and clerks of the

Qing era) were able to manipulate cases and squeeze illegal charges from litigants. The irony is that judges, procurators, and county magistrates who did not speak Mandarin were unlikely to speak the local dialects where they served either, due to the rule of avoidance. In other words, the rule of avoidance stood in the way of the prohibition of judges speaking through functionaries at trials. Since the system faced both a shortage of judges and case backlogs, the ban on judges and procurators who did not speak Mandarin presiding over trials was not taken seriously.

Another issue was that the PNCC provided judges with too broad a scope to impose punishments for offenses, which led to wide discrepancies in sentences for same offenses. In 1914, Liang Qichao proposed that a sentencing guide to the criminal code to assist judges in applying the law be compiled and issued as soon as possible.[118] But Liang was stepping down as minister of justice, and his successors were not keen on this issue. A sentencing guide for the PNCC was not mandated until 1920, when Dong Kang was minister of justice.[119]

Mediation Procedure

One way to reduce caseloads, and thus backlogs, was the time-honored practice of mediation to encourage settlement out of court. Traditionally, mediation was often conducted unofficially by elites in the local community.[120] In January 1914, the MJ and the Ministry of Industry and Commerce issued Regulations on Commercial Dispute Arbitration Offices, which officially empowered local chambers of commerce to mediate and arbitrate commercial disputes.[121] Perceiving similar merit in mediation and out-of-court settlement of other civil disputes to help reduce caseloads at courts, the MJ called for active mediation and settlement of civil disputes, but also cautioned against coercing litigants to settle.[122]

In July 1921, the MJ enacted Provisional Regulations on Civil Arbitration to formalize mediation and out-of-court settlement of civil disputes.[123] It explained that the regulations were designed to save the resources of the court system and reduce the number of civil lawsuits, but that it was essential to guard against any coercion in the process, which would give rise to more disputes.[124] Indeed, as the archives show, litigants would often claim that they had been coerced to accept unfair settlements.

Enforcement of Civil Decisions

The enforcement of court decisions in civil cases posed a much greater challenge to the judiciary than the trials themselves. In Chinese society, a culture of the rule of law barely existed, in that people did not have the habit of respecting the law and accepting the outcome of judicial proceedings. Local people's customary sense of fair play mandated that even if a court decision held a debtor accountable for his or her debt, the debtor was considered excused if she was poor and the creditor was rich, or if the court decision was perceived to be the result of some extralegal, unfair dealings of a more powerful party to a lawsuit. Of course, a powerful party to a lawsuit would also defy an unfavorable court decision, simply because no one could do anything about it. In endless variations on these themes, litigants tended to treat litigation as an economic, social, and political game, and an adverse court decision as one more hurdle to overcome, usually by defying the decision, delaying its execution, and wearing out the opponent by dragging out the case as long as possible. Philip Huang finds that in Qing civil justice, noncompliance by litigants with decisions of county trials was common.[125] Thomas Buoye also shows that in the eighteenth century, county magistrates generally tried cases involving property rights efficiently and fairly, but lacked the means to enforce their decisions when the losing side simply defied them, which often resulted in violence and even homicide.[126]

Similar defiance of court decisions was prevalent in the Republican era, and the MJ tried to tackle the problem through legal means. In early 1913, the Shanghai DC inquired of the MJ as to whether Article 42 of the Provisional Regulations on Establishing Courts at All Levels could be applied in civil litigation over properties. The article provided that if the losing party did not have property to compensate the winning party, the former might be forced to work in a workhouse for a period of one month to three years. The Shanghai DC asked for permission to detain the losing party in a civil suit in the spirit of this provision, because under the law, civil enforcement could not take place before the expiration of the appeal period, so that the losing party had enough time to hide and transfer properties. The MJ approved the request and ordered all courts to follow suit.[127]

In July 1913, the Capital DC proposed ways to enforce civil decisions. Articles 41, 42, and 79 of the Provisional Regulations on Establishing Courts at All Levels provided that necessary measures might be taken to seal, hold, and auction off properties of a losing party in civil litigation, but were vague about what measures were appropriate. In the DC's opinion, the property to be sealed should correspond in value to the remedy awarded by the court and the debtor's minimum standard of living should be maintained. If properties to be sealed included heavy items not easily movable, they should be entrusted to a specific agency. Auction of properties should be handled by a local chamber of commerce, supervised by court-appointed personnel. Since "Chinese people have a very thin notion of obeying the law," said the court, police officers should be present to enforce the judgment if anyone forcefully resisted sealing and holding properties for court-ordered remedy. The MJ agreed with the opinion and ordered that the suggested measures be followed by all courts as standard operating procedures to enforce civil decisions.[128] Two months later, the MJ added that a court clerk should be present when properties were sealed and held for civil remedy. It further formalized the procedure by issuing standard seals and registration and itemization forms for civil enforcement.[129]

Soon afterward, the Capital DC found that due to the absence of any provision as to who should conduct civil enforcement, bailiffs and clerks shirked their responsibilities, and the court could not hold anyone accountable. In response, the MJ issued Temporary Measures for Sealing and Holding Movable Properties: court clerks were to direct, and bailiffs to carry out, enforcement, and they were accountable for any financial loss resulting from dereliction of duty on their part. The measure also provided for a police presence at the scene of enforcement and an allowance of one-month's subsistence for the debtor.[130]

These measures remained in force until 1920, when the MJ issued Regulations on Enforcement of Civil Litigation, containing 138 articles. These required every district court to set up a civil enforcement office; under the order of the court president, judges and clerks of the office were to supervise the enforcing bailiffs.[131] County governments were to enforce civil decisions by reference to the regulations: the magistrate should do what was prescribed for the DC president, and the trial officer should do what was prescribed for the enforcing judge, and so forth.[132]

In 1927, the MJ issued an additional set of rules for civil enforcement. Courts were to select capable, amicable, and knowledgeable judges to be in charge of civil enforcement offices. Bailiffs were to carry out enforcement and should be either disciplined or rewarded for their performance. The remedy should be delivered to the creditor on the same day of enforcement, and at most no later than three days afterward. The debtor should not be detained without evidence of his seeking to hide or escape. Sealed properties of the debtor should be equivalent to, not larger than, the remedy awarded by the court.[133] All the regulations on civil enforcement indicate that the MJ tried to achieve a difficult balance among the interests of the debtor, the creditor, and the credibility of the judiciary and the law.

Trial Review

Trial review (*fupan*) was a peculiar procedure cross-bred by the Qing legal tradition and reform in the New Policy era. Traditionally, criminal cases that entailed exile or heavier punishments would be automatically reviewed by the higher authorities after county magistrates had tried them.[134] The reform agenda called for an appeal procedure to go with an independent court system, but not all courts at the county level were established. As a makeshift practice meant to be temporary, trial review was adopted as follows: the SC would review all capital cases tried by county magistrates and make its rulings in such cases known to the ML, and the latter would pass them on to the provinces to be carried out accordingly.[135]

Under the Republic, if a four-level-court and three-trial system had been fully established, trial review would have had no place in judicial process. But since courts did not exist in most counties, trial review did not officially cease. In August 1912, the MJ ordered that capital cases formerly sent to the SC be sent to the HC for trial review, because an additional level of review was necessary for capital cases tried by county magistrates.[136]

Two months later, the ministry issued Brief Provisional Regulations on Trial Review, which expanded the cases to be reviewed. Cases tried at the CGO that entailed the death penalty, life imprisonment, or prison terms of five years or more should all be sent to the HC for review if the defendant did not appeal.[137] Thus trial review was applicable not only to capital cases but also to most criminal cases tried at the CGO that were not appealed. In February 1913, the MJ clarified that only the HC, not the DC, should review cases tried at county offices.[138]

In 1914, the Brief Regulations were revised and renamed the Regulations on Trial Review (further revised in 1915 and 1918).[139] The 1912 regulations required trial review only for cases entailing five-year prison terms and above. To avoid the review procedure, county magistrates tended to give sentences just below five-year prison terms even for offenses that called for more severe punishments. So the 1914 regulations required almost all criminal cases tried at the CGO, including those entailing a fine of ¥200, to be sent for review. The new rules also stipulated that when defendants appealed inappropriately or withdrew their appeals, their cases should be reviewed.[140] County magistrates should send a case for review within five days of sentencing. Upon reviewing a case, the HC should take one of the three actions: (1) approve the sentence; (2) order retrial if the case was flawed in evidence, facts, or application of law; and (3) correct the sentence if it was too light or too heavy for the offense, but life terms and lesser punishments could not be changed to the death penalty. Retrial would take place either at the original CGO, or in a neighboring county or at a nearby district court or its branch, or at the HC, or by a judge appointed by the HC.[141]

Trial review was important to ordinary citizens, especially those who lacked legal and financial resources. With the procedure in place, there would have opportunities to correct cases that had been wrongfully prosecuted, tried, and sentenced at the CGO even if the defendants did not appeal. The practice was to remedy the fact that institutional and procedural formalization had not been completed at all levels.

The Appeal Process

Under the Provisional Regulations on Establishing Courts at All Levels, appeals in criminal cases went as follows. If a procurator decided not to prosecute a case, the plaintiff could appeal within seven days to the superior institution. If a judge decided not to prosecute a case after a pretrial hearing, the procurator could appeal within three days. After a trial, either the defendant or the procurator could appeal within ten days, but this was limited to sentences heavier than detention and fine. After a second trial, either party could appeal for a third trial, but limited to cases where the grounds for the appeal were that conviction and sentence contradicted the law. After the final decision, either party could file a special appeal to the SC, but limited to cases where grounds for the appeal were that the trial was illegal. Appeals in civil cases were simpler. Litigants could appeal to a second trial court within twenty days of a first trial. They could appeal for a third trial, if the remedy sought was more than ¥100, within twenty days of a second trial.[142]

The appeal of cases tried at the CGO was more problematic. Under the Provisional Regulations on County Magistrate Disposing Lawsuits, the DC or the HC were the appeal courts for county trials. In July 1914, the Anhui HP reported that district courts in the province did not have enough judges and staff, and counties were usually far away from district courts, causing difficulties in handling appeal cases. It requested permission to allow neighboring counties to serve as appeal courts for county trials. The MJ approved, as a temporary measure, allowing HP chiefs to designate a county as appeal court for a neighboring county in their provinces. By 1921, inasmuch as more branch high courts and district courts had been established, the MJ revisited the issue and instructed all provincial judicial institutions to investigate the conditions of transportation between counties and those courts, and designate district courts or branch high courts as appeal courts for county trials; only those counties that were indeed remote from any courts were allowed to continue the old practice.[143] Here the MJ was forced by conditions on the ground to deviate from the formalization agenda.

Lack of access to an appellate court on the part of litigants in counties remote from a high court was deemed a defect in judicial process. In December 1914, Han Guojun, governor of Anhui at the time, proposed that circuit administrators serve concurrently as presidents of branch high courts, to reduce the cost of establishing such courts. The Political Council disagreed: a circuit administrator was to supervise judicial affairs, and he should not be conducting trials he was supposed to supervise. In response, Yuan ordered that to allow people to have access to the appeal process during the transitional period, as a temporary measure, the circuit administrator should appoint two or three people to serve as an appellate organ for counties where no branch high courts were established; their competence was limited to minor cases; and such organs should be abolished as soon as HC branches were set up in their areas.[144]

The reform initiatives issued by the MJ during 1912–1927 were comprehensive in coverage and broad in scope—this chapter only touches on some of the most important ones. With the principles of the rule of law, judicial independence, and due process, and with institutional benchmarks such as building courts and prisons, the specific goals of the reform were to ensure that ordinary people had access to an independent court system; judicial personnel were ethical and competent; the judicial process was impartial, transparent, and efficient; criminals were punished according to the law, but not beyond the law; no innocent people were wrongfully punished or suffered in judicial process; and the judiciary was not overburdened by frivolous lawsuits and case backlogs.

To achieve all these goals, the central strategy for the MJ was to establish the judicial institutions and procedures informed by Western models wherever possible. This meant formalization. From the reformers' perspectives, only with formal, standard, and uniform rules and regulations could the judiciary function in a way consistent with the rule of law, judicial independence, and due process. A more detailed analysis of judicial finance is provided in Chapter 5, but it will already be evident here that the formalization of the judicial institutions and procedures would require huge resources, and that insufficient resources would force the ministry to compromise its agenda in trying to make a partially formalized system work.

Besides financial constraints, the MJ faced other formidable obstacles, ranging from a lack of legal knowledge among ordinary citizens, a lack of ethical norms and professional qualifications among lower-level judicial personnel, a constant tendency of administrative bureaucracy to interfere in judicial matters, friction among various judicial institutions within the system, and so forth. How all these difficulties came to pass at the provincial and county levels is explored in later chapters, after a look at the judicial reform under the GMD state during 1927–1937.

CHAPTER 3

Justice Under the Party-State: The Nanjing Decade

> "There does not exist in China today a system of independent Chinese courts free from extraneous influence," read the American [State Department] note in reply to China's request for the abolition of [extraterritoriality], "which is capable of doing justice between Chinese and foreign litigants." . . . [In light of] the reforms which have been and are being instituted by the Judicial Yuan of the Nationalist Government. . . . Is it not time, one wonders, . . . that America and the major powers granted recognition to the Herculean efforts that the government is making in this respect, by relinquishing the singular prerogatives granted to their nationals by the unequal treaties fostering extraterritoriality?
>
> —*China Weekly Review* (Shanghai), October 26, 1929[1]

During the Beiyang era, judicial reform was pursued based on the principles of the rule of law, judicial independence, and due process, and even on the notions of human rights and civil rights, albeit not clearly defined. Other than that, the Beiyang government lacked a political ideology. In contrast, when the Guomindang (GMD) rose to power in the late 1920s, it was armed with a party ideology or doctrine (*dangyi*) that included both the Three Principles of the People (national independence, democratic government, and people's livelihood) and the concept of a three-stage nationalist revolution: first, there would be military government, then, tutelage government, and, finally, an elected constitutional government. The establishment of the National Government (NG) in Nanjing under Chiang Kai-shek in 1927 was proclaimed as the transition from the military to the tutelage government. In this stage, the GMD would exercise state power on behalf of the people and rule the country through the party (*yidang zhiguo*).

This was obviously at odds with the principle of judicial independence. Whereas the reformers of the Beiyang era had struggled to modernize the judiciary by way of formalizing institutions and procedures, the GMD regime tried to find a balance between its monopoly of political power and continuation of the judicial reform in order for the regime to be accepted by Western powers as a legitimate modern state. Under the GMD party-state, judicial reform therefore unfolded in two major dimensions. One was the politicization of the judiciary as a weapon to be used against political foes, and the other was continuation of the reform initiatives started in the Beiyang era to elevate China's international standing and prepare for an end to extraterritoriality. A combination of the two agendas produced the peculiar judicial system and practices that in many respects pioneered what was to come under the Chinese Communist Party (CCP) before and after 1949.[2] From a larger historical perspective, however, although the GMD drive to politicize the judiciary was a negative, it was not the decisive factor that undermined the formalization agenda during 1927–1937. Ultimately, the GMD state was engaged in a transformative project inherited from the Beiyang government—modern state building. The problems it encountered were inherent in such a project and were aggravated by unfavorable circumstances, including the communist insurrection. The successes and failures of the GMD judicial reform may be better understood and evaluated from this larger perspective.

Politicization of the Judiciary

Partyizing the Judiciary: The Idea

The awkward phrase "partyizing the judiciary" translates the GMD catchphrase *danghua sifa*, an important concept in the GMD judicial reform. Xu Qian (1871–1940) was probably the first GMD official to advocate the notion. Xu's intellectual and political journey was an astonishing one, reflecting the rapid social and political changes China was going through in the late nineteenth and early twentieth centuries. A native of Hexian, Anhui, he obtained a *jinshi* degree in 1903 and then studied law and government in the Translation and Study Institute in

Beijing in 1904–1907. He joined the LCC for a while before being appointed the head of the Capital DC in 1908 and then of the Capital HP. In 1910, he was on the delegation with Xu Shiying to attend the Eighth International Prison Reform Congress. In April 1912, he became a deputy minister of justice, and four months later, he joined the GMD as a founding member. After the Second Revolution, Xu practiced law in Shanghai. Subsequently, he served several stints in the MJ in Beijing (1916, 1920, and 1922). He entered Sun Yat-sen's Nationalist Government in Guangzhou in July 1925 and was minister of justice and chairman of the Judicial Commission in Guangzhou from August to December 1926.[3]

In September 1926, with the success of the Northern Expedition expected, Xu presented a plan for reforming the judiciary nationwide. In the section on "Renewal of Judicial Institutions," Xu said that the Beiyang government prohibition of judges' party affiliation in the name of judicial independence was contrary to GMD doctrine. "If the political [organs] promote revolution and the judiciary opposes [it], then the judiciary will move in an opposite direction from the political program. For this reason, the judicial institutions must be controlled by the political [institutions]." In the section on "Renewal of Judicial Personnel," Xu proposed setting up institutes to train judges in politics and party doctrine, breed revolutionary new judges, and dismiss old-fashioned ones. He advised the abolition of the qualifications previously set for judges and the adoption of a special system to ensure the employment of revolutionary persons.[4]

In November 1926, the Judicial Reform Committee of the Nationalist Government in Guangzhou resolved that the ban on judges' joining political parties should be rescinded, and that only GMD members of good reputation with three years' legal experience be permitted to be judicial officers.[5] The emphasis placed on party membership, good reputation, and legal experience indicates that the committee did not totally disregard judges' legal knowledge and competence in favor of their political loyalty. The formula would suggest that GMD officials were not necessarily of one mind, and that the resolution might well have been a compromise among different opinions. Ideally, judicial personnel under the GMD should be politically reliable and professionally competent; but loyalty or at least conformity to GMD ideology was always the most desirable quality in GMD recruitment of judicial personnel. Xu's ideas were very similar to the later policies and practices of the CCP. Indeed,

Xu Qian was later wanted by Chiang Kai-shek's regime as a communist suspect for denouncing Chiang, and his judicial reform proposal was attacked as communist and Marxist.[6]

Partyizing the Judiciary: The Practice

Xu Qian's ideas were by no means eccentric to mainstream GMD ideology, however. The Nationalist Revolutionary Army (NRA) on the Northern Expedition under Chiang Kai-shek and the Nanjing government established in mid-1927 practiced exactly what Xu proposed with regard to reforming the judiciary along revolutionary lines. One example will show the revolutionary spirit and political approach to judicial issues on the part of some GMD officials. The Political Department of the 21st Division of the NRA wrote to the Wu DC in Jiangsu in early April 1927 saying that inasmuch as warlords, bureaucrats, local bullies, and evil gentry had used the judiciary as a tool to exploit the common people, and the mission of the tutelage government was to liberate oppressed compatriots from suffering, civil and criminal cases in which people had been imprisoned during the warlord era should be reexamined and the innocent released.[7] There is no evidence that the court complied, but the drive to politicize the judiciary was under way.

After the NRA arrived in Shanghai in March 1927, the GMD Jiangsu-Shanghai Command decided to take over the judiciary in Shanghai. The former DP chief Sun Shaokang would stay on, and Zheng Yuxiu would be the new president of the Shanghai DC.[8] Zheng was the first woman judge ever appointed in China. Her credentials included a law degree from the University of Paris, membership of the Chinese delegation to the Paris Peace Conference in 1919, and a law practice in Shanghai. Zheng assumed the post on March 24, 1927, and held it until November 1927.[9] Her appointment reflected the GMD's commitment to gender equality, also to be noted in the Regulations on Lawyers of 1927, which allowed female citizens to become lawyers for the first time in Chinese history.

The practice of appointing GMD officials to judicial posts became the rule. After Chiang Kai-shek secured Nanjing in April 1927, he appointed Zhang Jundu, the head of the NRA Court Martial Office, as the JHC president. After his appointment, Zhang was reported as saying that he would reform the judiciary in Jiangsu to conform to the rule of the party.[10] In the meantime, Chen Hexian, a former law professor and an adviser at the NRA headquarters, was appointed the head of the Jiangsu Provincial Justice Department (JPJD) with a mandate to make plans for judicial administration in all provinces secured by the NRA and to submit reform proposals to the Central Committee on the Legal System.[11] In an interview, Chen outlined his views on judicial reform. Like Xu Qian, he emphasized the necessity of establishing institutions to train judicial personnel. "Such training institutes will not be just for teaching lessons, as in schools; the purpose is to provide training in this party's ideology and thus lay a foundation for gradual judicial reform in the future." In the same breath, Chen criticized the idea of judicial independence and a judiciary that served the privileged. "The biggest evil [in the past] has been [for judicial officers] to hold fiefs and cultivate private factions in the name of judicial independence," he declared.[12] What Chen was referring to is unclear; perhaps he had in mind people like Lu Xingyuan, who was not following the party line and who was to be ousted in a move initiated by Chen (see below). In any case, categorizing judicial independence as an evil so casually reveals the mentality of GMD judicial experts like Chen, who did not grasp or care what judicial independence was really about.

The JPJD under Chen proceeded to scrap the ban on judges' having political party affiliations, set up an institute for training judicial officers in GMD doctrines, and urged GMD members to become judges.[13] In the same spirit, the new Ministry of Justice founded in Nanjing in July 1928 created the Training Institute for Judges, whose two hundred places were open only to GMD members who had graduated from schools of law and government after more than three years of study.[14] People who had the same background but were not party members could also apply provided they joined the party.[15] In 1935, in an effort to ease the shortage of judicial officers, Nanjing decided to train GMD headquarters staff at all levels to serve in the judiciary. They would take a test to enter the training institute and would be given preference for employment after being trained.[16]

It would have been practically impossible, however, to staff all judicial institutions, or, for that matter, all the government bureaucracies, with party members only. At a May 1927 meeting, the GMD Central Executive Council adopted several proposals from Bai Chongxi (1893–1966), commander of the Shanghai-Wusong garrison and a member of the GMD Jiangsu Provincial Political Council. One of the proposals was that except for departments of political affairs and party affairs, civilian bureaucracies should not limit their personnel to party members only, which would deprive the state of technical experts and create a culture where people would hunt for positions and personal gain by signing up for party membership. The resolution was transmitted through the National Government to the JPJD. Chen Hexian circulated the order to the JHP, with the instruction that the policy be applied there and in all county jails.[17]

The actual impact of the Training Institute for Judges was limited. From 1930 to 1935, the institute graduated 428 judges, 75 prison officers, and 61 court registrars.[18] By comparison, there were 2,382 judges and 1,071 procurators in the country in 1936.[19] Also revealing is the fact that in 1934, out of 248 employees in all positions in the MJ, only 104 were party members.[20] Despite the emphasis on partyizing the judicial system, there was a balance or compromise between the requirement of political allegiance and that of professional competence in appointing judicial officers and personnel, a phenomenon also seen in the Ministries of Finance and of Foreign Affairs in the same period.[21]

What partyizing the judiciary really meant for the GMD may be seen in the story of the Provisional Court (PC). Along with the French Concession, the International Settlement was one of the two concessions in Shanghai that were under foreign administration and independent of the Chinese authorities. Under an agreement between the foreign consular body in Shanghai and the Chinese provincial authorities in Jiangsu signed in August 1926, the International Settlement's Mixed Court, hitherto controlled by the Shanghai Municipal Council, became the Provisional Court, with a Chinese president and judges, in January 1927.[22] After the GMD established itself in Shanghai, Lu Xingyuan (1885–?), who held a Master's degree from Oxford and had once served in various judicial posts in Sun Yat-sen's government in Guangzhou, was appointed the PC president in May 1927.[23] At Lu's inaugural ceremony, Chen Dezheng (1893–?), an official of the GMD Municipal Party Headquarters in Shanghai, gave a speech. Chen praised Lu as a faithful follower and devoted disciple of Sun Yat-sen and went on to say: "Now that the Government has appointed him to this important post, we have no doubt whatever in our minds but that he will do his utmost to uphold the doctrine and the traditions of the Kuomintang [Guomindang] in the administration of justice according to the law."[24] Quoting Chen's speech, the editor of the *North China Daily News* observed: "We failed to see how Mr. Loo [Lu] can honestly use a law court to forward the interests of a party and at the same time administer what we call justice. We have no doubt that the Chinese see nothing incompatible in these two lines of endeavor."[25] The editor indeed captured the essence of the GMD approach to judicial reform.

What happened to Lu subsequently and to his successor was ironic but is equally revealing. Just five months later, Lu was fired from his post because he adhered to judicial independence and the rule of law and refused to hand over communist suspects arrested in the International Settlement to the Chinese military authorities.[26] He Shizhen (1894–?), an American-educated law expert and GMD member, upon succeeding Lu, pledged that he would abide by the decisions of the GMD and do his best to adhere to party principles.[27] He thought he could uphold judicial independence while being a good GMD member. Yet, after one year in the post, He resigned in August 1929, having found that his idea of judicial independence clashed with frequent interference from the GMD, and even from Chiang Kai-shek personally, in the cases handled by the court and in his duty as the court president.[28] He's resignation came a few months before the rendition agreement on the PC expired and a new agreement completely incorporated the court into the Chinese judicial system on April 1, 1930.[29]

The case of the PC was unique in a sense, because here the issue of judicial independence intersected with that of China's judicial sovereignty. Nevertheless, the underlying agenda of the GMD regime in trying to make the judiciary a political weapon is clear from the instances cited above. In short, the further development of a modern Chinese judiciary under the GMD became almost a party affair, and the system was politicized as much as possible.

Partyizing the Judiciary: The Justification

Official GMD discourse sought to justify party dominance of the state, including the judiciary. One of the earliest justifications for politicizing the judiciary appeared in 1927 when the JPJD scrapped the ban on judges' joining political parties. It was argued that judges were also citizens who had rights to participate in politics, and this right of citizens should not be forfeited just because one was a judge. Judicial independence was to be achieved by strict organization and fair operation of political institutions, not by prohibition of party affiliation.[30] The argument was rather weak, in that it precluded the possibility of citizens participating in politics without being political party members; but it made sense in view of the absence of electoral politics and the GMD-CCP conflict at that time.

In 1929, writing in the journal *Falü pinglun* (Law Review), Ge Guangyu (presumably a GMD official) urged that laws be partyized (*falü yi danghua*). He used the examples of European countries from Russia to France to Britain to argue that the principles of legislation in most countries change with political trends. "Our National Government rules the country through the party. All the political institutions are based on the Three Principles of the People and therefore all laws and regulations should be partyized. This is the principle of legislation that must be established."[31]

In an article published in 1930, Hu Hanmin (1879–1936), a veteran GMD leader, emphasized that the legislation based on the Three Principles was different from modern legislation in Europe and America. The latter was based on individualism and took individuals as the object of law, which was more backward than traditional Chinese law based on family. In contrast, the laws based on the Three Principles would ensure societal stability, economic development, and a balance of various social interests.[32] As noted in the Introduction, GMD officials were more ambivalent than their Beiyang counterparts had been about the Western models based on which judicial reform was envisioned and pursued, or even critical of them. They did not seem to consider Western legal principles universally valid or necessarily superior to Chinese principles, nor all Western judicial practices suitable to Chinese conditions. But Hu's point here was that since the GMD upheld the Three Principles and ruled the country for the sake of the society and the people, logically the party should make the laws.

Liang Yunli, a J.D. from the University of Washington and secretary to the minister of justice, explained the relationship between the GMD and the judicial system. Under the Law on the Procedure of Law-Making adopted by the GMD on March 11, 1928, the GMD Central Political Council had exclusive powers to make laws, which were then to be handed on to the National Government (NG) for promulgation and enforcement.[33]

Further theorizing about partyizing the judiciary was provided in 1934 by Ju Zheng (1875–1951), a GMD veteran who had once studied law in Japan. Ju held several important posts in the GMD and the government, including that of head of the Judicial Council (JC) (*sifa yuan*) and the SC in 1932. He became minister of justice in October 1934.[34] In a long article published in December 1934, "The Question of Partyizing the Judiciary," Ju explained what the process ought to entail. Whether to partyize the judiciary was no longer a question, Ju declared; the question was how. This did not mean that all high positions in the judicial system should be given to party members, that unqualified party members should become judicial officers, or that party-member judicial officers be able to decide cases in disregard of all laws. Partyizing the judiciary required that judges apply party doctrines to adjudication and that judges be selected from among those who understood and would carry out party doctrines. Judges were not required to have party membership, but to have social consciousness of the Three Principles. "In a nutshell, partyizing the judiciary is not to make a judiciary of party members [*sifa dangrenhua*], but to make a judiciary of party doctrines [*sifa dangyihua*]."[35]

Every society, nation, and epoch had its particular worldview, upon which a certain uniform sense of justice was formed, Ju explained, and such a sense in turn provided the central principle of a nation's laws.[36] GMD doctrine represented the worldview, sense of justice, and central principle of law at the present time in China. Judges should apply GMD doctrine to (1) supply what the law failed to address; (2) concretely resolve practical problems where the law was too abstract to deal with them; (3) revitalize aspects of the law that had become ossified; and (4) void law that obviously contradicted the realities of social life.[37] Ju's article was probably the most serious intellectual effort at reconciling two contradictory principles: party dominance and judicial independence. Illustrating what Ju Zheng meant by "a judiciary of party doctrine," the MJ and the JC issued regulations in November 1928 and January 1929, respectively, mandating that all officials and staff in the two institutions should study party doctrine.[38]

Political Crimes and Punishment

Discounting offenses against emperors or imperial houses, it may be argued that prior to 1927 Chinese law had never contained a category of crimes that was politically defined in terms of political party lines and ideologies. The GMD state founded in 1927 began to create categories of political crimes for the first time in Chinese history—the crimes of being "counterrevolutionaries" or "local bullies and evil gentry," something the CCP would later adopt as well. The essence of classifying a group of people as political offenders was for the state to go beyond regular laws, the court system, and due process to eliminate or "reform" people thus categorized. Such an effort contradicted and undermined the agenda of formalizing judicial institutions and procedures.

The well-known category of "local bullies and evil gentry" sprang from the political rhetoric that accompanied the Nationalist Revolution of 1924–1927 and in response to a popular movement inspired by such rhetoric. In May 1927, for instance, the county magistrate of Wuxi, Jiangsu, reported to the JHC president that many common people had come forward to file cases against "local bullies and evil gentry," but that he did not know how to prosecute such cases, since there were no precedents, no provisions in the criminal code, and no standards by which to define "local bullies and evil gentry." The JHC president Zhang Jundu replied that there was no way to punish local bullies and evil gentry as such yet, but that if there was evidence of criminal offenses, the CGO should prosecute them under the criminal code.[39]

There was, however, a strong demand from local activists for suppressing local bullies and evil gentry in various provinces, so much so that in May 1927, the provincial government in Anhui, a province under GMD control, proceeded to adopt Provincial Regulations on Punishing Local Bullies and Evil Gentry, to be applied in the province. The regulations lumped together several categories of politically defined offenses, including taking advantage of intellectual, political, and economic privileges to oppose revolution or engage in counterrevolutionary propaganda, conspiring with bandits to ravage local areas, oppressing the common people (such as physically hurting or killing people; infringing on others' rights, property, and reputation; forcing marriage on women), inciting litigation to swindle and extort people, and so on.[40]

But the measure in Anhui could not be considered enforceable in court, and it only added to the legal confusion. In June 1927, Zhang Dingyi, a journalist from Zhengjiang, Jiangsu, submitted a petition to the JPJD asking it to answer twelve questions on five issues: (1) how to define "local bullies and evil gentry"; (2) what constituted false accusation; (3) who could arrest local bullies and evil gentry; (4) what constituted counterrevolutionary propaganda; and (5) whether a case would still stand if the plaintiff did not show up at the trial. Chen Hexian chose not to answer those questions, saying that his office was not the SC, and that it was not proper for him to provide legal interpretations.[41] Similar incidents and confusions must have arisen in other provinces as well.

It was in this political atmosphere that the NG issued Regulations on Punishing Local Bullies and Evil Gentry and established Special Provisional Criminal Courts (SPCC) to try the offenses in August 1927.[42] "Local bullies and evil gentry" were not defined, but the following acts were to be punished severely: dominating the countryside and oppressing common people; forcing women to marry against their will; depriving debtors of personal liberty; profiting from usury; providing for opium-smoking and gambling; inciting and scheming lawsuits; controlling public offices and embezzling public funds; and so on. Thus "local bullies and evil gentry" were defined by what the offenders did, not by what they were. A lot of the rich, the powerful, and the resourceful in local society readily fell into the category, setting the stage for local power struggles waged in the name of opposing local bullies and evil gentry.[43] Such local struggles eventually forced the GMD to scale back the rhetoric on this issue for fear of undermining local social order and power structures, the stability of which was regarded as crucial for the consolidation of the GMD party-state.[44]

Soon after the category of local bullies and evil gentry was created, a separate category of people was criminalized as "counterrevolutionary," which had earlier been included in the category of local bullies and evil gentry by the Anhui provincial government. In March 1928, Nanjing enacted the Provisional Law on Punishing Counterrevolutionary Crimes. Offenses under the law were tried by two levels of special criminal courts—local courts in the provinces and a central court in Nanjing—with severe punishments.[45]

The two special laws were justified as necessary. "The fact that neither offense was provided for in the criminal law," Liang Yunli argued, "rendered the establishment of special criminal courts necessary." Liang said that "the former [law against counterrevolutionaries] is directed against all kinds of offenses inimical to the Kuomintang [Guomindang] and the Nationalist Government, while the latter is against the exploitation and oppression of the people by local miscreants and bad gentry, offenses of the latter category being very frequent in the interior."[46] The assertion was not false. As we shall see in later chapters, the kinds of activities mentioned in the Law on Punishing Local Bullies and Evil Gentry were a lived reality in local society, which was often beyond the reach of law and justice or state control.[47] Liang promised that "these laws were intended to be provisional only in order to meet the present revolutionary situation."[48] In November 1928, the GMD Central Political Council decided to abolish the special criminal courts, but not the special laws. Thereafter, counterrevolutionaries would be tried at the HC and local bullies and evil gentry at the DC.[49]

In December 1929, the Provisional Law on Jury Trial in Counterrevolutionary Cases was issued. Under the law, accused counterrevolutionaries were to be tried by a jury composed of GMD members selected by local party organs. Conviction was to be determined by a simple majority. The law was officially abolished in March 1931 when the Emergency Law came into effect.[50] But in late 1932, GMD juries were still being selected for the trial of alleged communists in the third branch of the JHC in Shanghai's French Concession.[51]

According to a JC report, in 1929, the judiciary prosecuted 72 defendants (including two women) under the law against local bullies and evil gentry, and 897 (including thirty women) under the law against counterrevolutionaries.[52] These numbers only reflected cases tried by regular courts and did not include those handled by the military authorities. Under a special order from the NG dated December 10, 1929, all cases of CCP suspects arrested in Shanghai were to be processed by the Shanghai-Wusong Garrison Command; less serious cases would go to regular courts for trial, and serious cases would be tried by military courts.[53] Actually, the practice of the military authorities arresting and executing communist suspects with or without trial long predated the order.

In January 1931, superseding the laws on punishing counterrevolutionaries and local bullies and evil gentry, Nanjing enacted the Emergency Law on Crimes against the Republic which provided for the death penalty and heavy prison terms (fifteen years to life) for offenses against the NG, the GMD, or party doctrine. The offenses included organizing activities against the state—they were not defined, so this could be stretched to cover anything and everything that the GMD party-state deemed objectionable—and printing and distributing publications in violation of the Three Principles.[54] The enforcement of the Emergency Law may be glimpsed in one report: in fiscal year 1933 (July 1, 1933–June 30, 1934) the JHC tried ninety-one defendants prosecuted under the law and convicted fifty-nine of them.[55]

The cases that were prosecuted in courts under the counterrevolutionary law and the emergency law did not appear to be a large number, because the offenders in those cases were communists (and other political dissidents) arrested in the GMD-controlled urban areas or senior officers of the Red Army captured in battles. The rank and file of the Red Army and communist guerrillas were mostly subject to summary execution by the military and security forces without trial upon capture. In 1930, for example, local gentry in Taixing, Jiangsu, organized a Provisional Relief Association Office to work with the government troops and local security forces fighting communist guerrillas. Some villagers were executed as communist suspects, which caused local people to sue Wang Zonghao, a member of gentry who played the key role in this, for indiscriminately killing innocent people.[56]

The GMD party-state operated a host of special penal institutions to incarcerate and secretly execute communists and political dissidents outside normal judicial procedures. These included military prisons run by the military authorities, concentration camps and labor camps controlled by civilian and military secret services, "institutes for repentance" (*fanxing yuan*) run by the MJ, and detention centers run by military police or security and garrison forces.[57] The GMD regime kept its political assassinations and the imprisonment, torture, and execution of left-wing and communist writers secret, because such practices went beyond even the special laws against political offenses and amounted to state lawlessness, notwithstanding the context of judicial formalization.

Change and Continuity in Judicial Reform

Criminal and Civil Codes and Procedural Laws

As Yuan Shikai had done in 1912, the NG decreed on August 11, 1927, that all substantive and procedural laws and other regulations previously in force should be applied for the time being, with the exception of those that were incompatible with GMD doctrine or the laws newly enacted by the NG.[58]

In March 1928, the NG promulgated a new criminal code, based on the revised criminal code of 1918 prepared by the LCC under Wang Chonghui, which was to replace the PNCC as China's criminal code as of September 1928.[59] In August 1928, it followed this with a criminal procedure law, largely based on the 1922 version compiled by the LCC.[60]

Nanjing did not miss the opportunity to celebrate the new law for a public relations effect. In its work report of 1929, the MJ identified thirteen differences between the criminal code of 1928 and the PNCC, all pointing to a thrust of moderating punishments and limiting judges' discretion in imposing harsher sentences. One of the changes, for example, was that even a fine could be suspended under the new code, which was not the case under the PNCC.[61]

Liang Yunli publicized some of the characteristics of the 1928 criminal code in the *China Weekly Review*. According to Liang, four cardinal principles guided the making of the code: (1) it was informed by the recent trends in codifying criminal law in foreign countries and the new theories of criminology and penology; (2) it was made "agreeable to the juristic attitude of the Chinese people"; (3) it was "bent upon enforcing the fundamental principles of the Kuomintang [Guomindang] Party"; and (4) it was framed in light of the changed and changing social conditions and specified appropriate punishments for new forms of crime.[62]

It is noteworthy that it was in the *China Weekly Review*, a well-known Shanghai English-language publication, that Liang chose to laud the new criminal code's modernity—which, as it happened, was distinctly Chinese—to foreign readers. While the first guiding principle indicated the role of Western models in order to satisfy foreign powers for purposes of getting them to relinquish extraterritoriality, the remaining three principles alluded to making modern laws and judicial practices suitable to Chinese conditions, something GMD officials spoke about frequently, stressing Chinese traditions and conditions as the basis on which to make laws, in addition to Western precedents.

In citing the second guiding principle—the need to make the law compatible with "the juristic attitude of the Chinese people"—Liang adopted a discursive strategy that Wang Chonghui had also deployed in creating the blueprint for the 1928 code. The strong influence of European Continental law, as opposed to Anglo-American law, in the revised criminal code he worked on was "the result of mature deliberation," Wang had claimed in 1918. "Anglo-American law emphasizes the individual at the expense of the family, whilst continental law inherits something of the old *familia*. The family being the unit of Chinese society, anything which weakens the existence and power of that institution must be as [un]acceptable in principles as it would be unworkable in practice."[63] Wang chose to make a connection between a major Western legal tradition and Chinese tradition, as Liang did in 1928. But it is unmistakable that in the Nanjing decade the emphasis on Chinese characteristics in judicial-legal practices appeared more prominent in the official discourse than before.

The 1928 criminal law was further amended, and a revised criminal code went into effect in July 1935.[64] For the most part, the 1935 criminal code was similar to the 1928 version, but where it differed was noteworthy. Under the new code, taking concubines was illegal. Married men who took concubines and were sued by their wives could be convicted of adultery and punished under the law (which was not, however. retroactively applied). This was a further application of the gender equality principle. Paying a fine for certain offenses in lieu of a prison term of less than six months was allowed, apparently in order to reduce the prison population.[65] The French legal scholar Jean Escarra went so far as to call the 1935 criminal code "a remarkable scientific work, based on profound studies of criminology and comparative law."[66] Whether or not the new criminal code (both the 1928 and 1935 versions) was indeed progressive and more in tune with Western models, it (and the criminal procedure law) did not suffice for the GMD party-state, which resorted to the special laws mentioned earlier to deal with political crimes and certain violent crimes (see Chapter 9).

The Civil Code

Book I of the GMD civil code (General Principles) was enacted in May 1929 and went into effect in October of that year, and Books II (Obligations), III (Rights to Things), IV (Kinship), and V (Inheritance) were enacted in 1929–1930. The civil procedure law was promulgated in two installments in February 1930 and February 1931.[67] The enactment of substantive and procedural civil laws, after criminal laws, marked the culminating achievements by a generation of legal reformers since the New Policy years.

The historians Kathryn Bernhardt and Philip Huang have analyzed the significance and implications of the civil code and civil procedure law, and it would be redundant to reproduce their insights here.[68] But to contextualize the development, it is useful to note how the civil code was evaluated at that time. First, commentators applauded the fact that the civil code provided that where the law was clear, it should be applied; where the law was silent, local custom should be taken into consideration; and where neither was available, judges should be guided by legal principles.[69] Secondly, the civil code emphasized the interest of the community and public bodies rather than individual interests."The public interest should always have our prior consideration."[70] Whether a local custom was good or bad depended on whether it harmed the public interest. "Individual activities are to be restricted when they could be harmful to the group," another commentator wrote, even though "the property of individuals [is] protected just as firmly as before."[71] Thirdly, the principle of gender equality embodied in the civil code was highlighted. On these points, the code reflected GMD ideology. The MJ also singled out several aspects of the civil procedural law as positive changes. One of them was that under the law, if litigants filed lawsuits at wrong jurisdictions, courts were obligated to transfer such cases to the proper jurisdictions without the litigants' having to request it.[72] This provision represented a determined attempt to address a long-standing problem in the judiciary that various regulations and directives from the MJ had failed to solve in the Beiyang era (see Chapter 2).

In seeking to reduce civil litigation by introducing civil mediation and arbitration, the GMD continued another Beiyang practice. The Law on Civil Mediation of 1930 provided for a civil mediation office to be set up in the court of first instance. A judge was to be the chief mediator, and each party to a civil dispute was to recommend one mediator, who could not be either a lawyer or a judicial officer. The mediation period was to be seven days, unless the two parties agreed to extend it.[73] This represented the formalization of mediation in civil disputes, which would weaken, but not eliminate, the role of local elites in unofficial mediation.

Judicial Administration and the Courts

The genesis of judicial administration under the GMD party-state can be traced to July 1, 1925, when the Nationalist Government was established in Guangzhou under Sun Yat-sen. At the time, the Judicial Administrative Commission was the body assigned the task. In November 1926, after the Nationalist Government moved to Wuhan, the MJ was established. In July 1927, after Chiang Kai-shek founded the National Government in Nanjing, the MJ was reestablished. In November 1928, it was reorganized as the Ministry of Judicial Administration (referred to as the MJ in this book), along with the formation of the JC.[74]

As one of the five branches of the central government envisioned by Sun Yat-sen, the JC was an institutional change under the GMD. The council was to propose legislation in judicial matters to the Legislative Council; to issue orders in matters such as amnesty or commuting sentences; to explain laws and regulations; and to supervise and correct illegal acts of government agencies or dereliction of duty by officials. Under the council were the Administrative Court (AC), the SC, and the MJ (during January 1932–October 1934, the MJ was placed under the Executive Council). In the Nanjing decade, the JC was under the chairmanship of Wang Chonghui (November 1928–December 1931), Wu Chaoshu (December 1931–May 1932), and Ju Zheng (May 1932–June 1948).[75] But in practice it was the MJ, not the JC, that oversaw the judiciary as a whole, including reviewing criminal and civil cases and having legal or factual errors corrected.[76]

Not formally established until June 1933, the AC was a revival of a similar court (*pingzheng yuan*) of the Beiyang era. It allowed citizens to sue government officials for violating their rights after they had exhausted petitioning for redress to the superior offices of the defendants. The redress sought by plaintiffs was the revocation of the illegal or improper acts of officials and, where restoration was impossible, monetary compensation. If officials were guilty of criminal acts, they were handed over to the ordinary criminal courts after the proceedings at the AC.[77] By 1936, the AC processed 404 cases and found government actions illegal and had them nullified in 43 cases.[78] Whereas the similar court in the Beiyang era had had the power to take disciplinary action against delinquent officials, the new court did not possess that power,[79] which was vested in the Central Committee on Disciplinary Punishment of Civil Servants (formed in 1932) and its provincial committees.

The SC originated in the Nationalist Government in Guangzhou in 1925. After the government moved to Wuhan, the SC assumed the new name Zuigao fayuan, in place of Dali yuan, in March 1927. It moved to Nanjing in October 1927 and came under the newly formed JC in November 1928. Initially, the SC had two civil chambers and one criminal chamber. More chambers were added later, resulting by March 1931 in four civil and four criminal chambers, with five judges each.[80] Another civil and three criminal chambers were added in 1933. In that year, the SC accepted a total of 8,559 civil cases and disposed of 8,823 (including old cases), and accepted 5,786 criminal cases and disposed of 5,852.[81]

Another institutional change made by the GMD was the abolition of procuracies. In the early 1920s, there were debates over whether procuracies were necessary. Critics argued that the institution was redundant and costly, that it made litigation procedures complicated for litigants, that the equal status of a court and a procuracy caused friction between the two, and that the funding for procuracies could have been used to build more courts.[82] In May 1927, as the head of the JPJD, Chen Hexian proposed that procuracies be abolished and procurators attached to courts (and that the court system be changed to a two-level system).[83] In February 1928, Nanjing formally abolished procuracies. Procurators would continue to function, but they became officers attached to courts.[84] The SC had a procurators' section (Jiancha shu).[85] The change would seem to have made practical sense, but debates continued over the usefulness of procurators.[86]

Under the GMD, courts were called *fayuan* (court of law), instead of *shenpan ting* (court of trial), the name coined in the New Policy decade and used in the Beiyang era. The GMD spared no efforts to show its determination to establish a complete court system in the country. In December 1928, the *North China Herald* quoted the JC chairman, Wang Chonghui, as saying that the system where county magistrates functioned as judicial officials "impaired the integrity and independence of the judiciary and must be abolished," and that in its place, DC would be established throughout the country.[87] According to a plan that the MJ unveiled in 1929, in the span of six years for which the tutelage government was supposed to last (1930–1935), the new courts would include 657 CC; 1,631 DC with detention houses; 42 HC branches with detention houses; and four SC branches.[88] Another version of the plan provided for 1,597 CC to be upgraded to DC in 1930–1933 and for DC in all 1,782 counties in the country by 1935.[89] Given the limited resources available to the judiciary and what it would cost to establish all those courts, one is not convinced that the GMD state took the plan seriously as feasible. The plan was probably designed more to sway public opinion in the West in an effort to end extraterritoriality than to be implemented. However, at least the editor of the *China Weekly Review* was impressed by the plan (see the epigraph to this chapter).

The plan already implied that the four-level court system would not be maintained for long, since all CC would become DC. In October 1932, Nanjing issued the new Law on Organizing Courts, to be effective in July 1935, which provided a three-level court system: the DC, the HC, and the SC, with a three-trial process.[90] The new court system was to be adopted in the country in two phases—fifteen provinces in July 1935 and the rest in July 1936.[91]

But courts were never built on the scale Nanjing planned. By early 1929, two HC, three HC branches, 29 DC, 87 DC branches, and 101 CC, totaling 222 new courts, with detention houses, had been added.[92] In 1934, the JC counted an increase of 35 HC branches, 56 DC, and 46 DC branches, plus 105 CC upgraded to DC and 23 to branch DC.[93] By 1937, another 44 HC branches and 197 DC had been added, so that there were 23 HC, 83 HC branches, 298 DC—a total of 404 DC or HC.[94]

The goal of every county having a court (CC or DC) by 1935 was never reached. Of 75 counties in Zhejiang province in 1927, only 11 had courts or their branches.[95] By 1934, some 43 counties in the province had no courts.[96] Zhejiang, like Jiangsu, was one of the economically more developed and politically more stable provinces under the GMD state. Poorer provinces could only fare worse. Guizhou, a province with 81 counties, prior to 1934, had only one HC, one DC, one detention house, and one new prison; in 1934, two HC branches and two DC were added; and by 1936, another DC had been added, with thirteen county judicial divisions (see below) planned for 1937.[97]

Nationwide, 1,046 to 1,054 counties (depending on sources) saw county magistrates performing judicial functions.[98] "Where the *Hsien* [county] courts cannot be established on account of financial difficulty," Liang Yunli explained in 1928, "the judicial function will be principally vested in the Trial Officer sitting as the judge, while the *Hsien* magistrate will serve as procurator. In this way, the administrative officer, i.e. the *Hsien* magistrate, will be prevented from interfering with the judgment of judicial matters."[99] This design was not matched by the reality, however. Not every county had a trial officer to begin with, and where there was a trial officer, the county magistrate tried cases as well.

A work report of JC in 1934 admitted that it was impossible to set up DC in all counties to replace adjudicating county magistrates, and that the task at hand was to gradually reduce abuses arising from the situation.[100] To remedy the situation somewhat, county judicial divisions (CJD) (*xian sifa chu*), similar to the county judicial offices of the Beiyang era, began to appear in 1936. A trial officer appointed by the HC would adjudicate, and the county magistrate acted as procurator in criminal cases and administered judicial affairs generally.[101] The Supplement Regulations on Conducting Litigation at County Judicial Divisions of June 1936 and the Measures on Lawyers Carrying out Duties at County Judicial Divisions of September 1936 allowed lawyers to appear in trials at the CJD, but only when the county magistrate appeared as procurator.[102] The CJD was to serve as a transition from adjudicating county magistrates to independent courts, but in late 1936, the CJD existed in only 384 counties.[103]

In 1934, the entire court system had a total of 12,349 judicial officers and staff, including 1,295 court presidents, procurators, and judges; 649 probationary procurators and judges; 79 apprentice judges and procurators; 1,709 clerks; and 1,278 probationary and apprentice clerks; the rest were interpreters, secretaries, forensic doctors, coroners, bailiffs, and judicial policemen.[104] In counties where no courts existed, a total of 5,719 judicial personnel were reported for 1934, including 37 judicial commissioners, 1,096 trial officers, 1,091 clerks, 1,764 bailiffs, and 758 coroners.[105] With the expansion of the court system, the number of cases handled by all courts increased dramatically. Whereas all courts handled 52,322 criminal and 64,667 civil cases in 1930, the numbers almost doubled in 1935 to 111,843 criminal and 120,646 civil cases, not including county trials.[106]

Other Judicial Rules and Regulations

As late as 1936 lawyers were still barred from representing litigants and defendants at county trials, and even former lawyers who had left law practice could not serve as legal consultants or set up consulting firms in counties where county magistrates adjudicated. As the result, in most counties, litigants had access to one legal service only—they could have lawyers write complaints for them, which was allowed by laws and regulations, to the annoyance of county magistrates.[107]

On the other hand, the state continued to ask lawyers to provide volunteer service at courts for defendants who could not afford to hire lawyers. In the 1920s, informal arrangements were made between the Shanghai Bar Association and the courts in Shanghai for such services, but the result was not satisfactory to all concerned.[108] In the Nanjing decade, the JHC continued to call on local bar associations to provide public defenders (*gongshe bianhuren*), but sometimes designated lawyers failed to show up at trials for various reasons, causing trial delays. In 1934, the JHC decided to appoint four permanent public defenders, who would be paid ¥40 for transportation a month, half of which was from judicial revenue at the JHC and the other half from the bar association. The MJ approved the measure, but pointedly changed the name "public defender" to "designated defender" (*yueding bianhuren*), because the government did not pay those lawyers a salary.[109]

Since county magistrates continued to adjudicate, the practice of trial review was maintained. In September 1928, the MJ issued Provisional Regulations on Trial Review, which differed from the latest Beiyang regulations on trial review in several aspects: (1) only criminal cases where convicts received third-degree prison terms or fines of ¥500 and up need be reviewed; (2) trial review decisions were final and not to be appealed; (3) prison terms would start the day after the appeal period expired; and (4) those sentenced to detention or to a fine were allowed to be released on bail.[110] In 1936, the MJ issued a set of regulations requiring that the CJD forward criminal cases for trial review.[111] That is to say, the MJ regarded the CJD as essentially closer to an adjudicating county magistrate than to a formal court.

One new development in judicial procedures was that a civil defendant who resisted civil enforcement or refused to honor a civil decision would be detained, which was called "civil detention" (*minshi guanshou*). Yet the regulations provided, and the MJ stressed, that a civil detainee could be held no more than three months, even if he did not find a guarantor or come up with payment to fulfill the court decision by then.[112] Perhaps due to the fact that some defendants would rather sit out the three months than make payments, courts often held civil detainees beyond three months, as happened at the Jiangdu DC Detention House in October 1931.[113] At the same time, some courts and county magistrates gave up on enforcing civil decisions and detaining defaulters, contributing to case backlogs (see Chapters 4 and 6 below). Admitting that the inability to enforce civil decisions damaged the courts' authority and credibility and litigants' interests, Zheng Tianxi blamed the problem on the absence of a bankruptcy law and a property registration system.[114] As we shall see, there were more reasons than that.

Regulating Judicial Personnel

Besides the political training mentioned earlier, the GMD paid attention to the professional training of judicial personnel. The regulation of the legal profession also continued along the same lines as in the Beiyang era, with a strong dose of party supervision and control.[115] Membership of the National Bar Association both reflected the size of the legal profession and showed steady growth—6,969 in 1932; 7,651 in 1933; 8,397 in 1934;[116] 10,249 in 1935; and no fewer than 10,400 in 1936.[117]

The government held various tests to select candidates for judgeship. In 1929–1936, a total of 585 candidates for judicial offices were selected through tests.[118] The Training Institute for Judges graduated three classes of probationary judges—a total of 438 (172 in 1930, 141 in 1932, and 125 in 1934), plus 75 prison officers in 1933 and 61 court clerks in 1935.[119] Another source reported a total of 1,191 judges selected through tests (and further training) in 1926–1936.[120]

The GMD government revived the rule of avoidance for judicial officers and lawyers. As early as June 1927, the fifteenth meeting of the Jiangsu Provincial Government Commission (PGC) resolved to recommend to the NG a proposal from the secretary Zhao He that judges should avoid serving at courts in their native places. The NG responded that the issue would be studied by the MJ when it was founded.[121] In February 1929, the MJ issued a directive prohibiting any lawyer who was a former judge or procurator from practicing in the same district where he had served within one year of leaving the office. In December 1931, the restriction was expanded to cover former court clerks and interpreters.[122] In 1933, the restriction period was extended to three years.[123] In February 1932, the MJ announced that a judge could not serve in a court where the superior officer was a close relative or from the same native place.[124] Another measure in January 1932 prohibited former lawyers from serving as judges in the same district where they had practiced. The MJ also ordered that judges and lawyers should not socialize with each other, and that judges should not socialize with local people.[125] Most of those policies on avoidance revived Beiyang-era practices, testimony to the enduring notion that avoidance was a positive measure of good governance, to which the GMD also subscribed.

In the Nanjing decade, the career path of judicial officers was as follows. After passing a first test, candidates were assigned to courts as apprentice judges or procurators. After two years of training on the job, they took a second test and, if they passed, became probationary judges or procurators. The time needed for promotion from probationary status to full judge or procurator was not set. Because the promotion involved a pay raise from ¥120–180 (as allowance) to ¥200–400 (as formal salary), the judicial authorities stalled many judicial officers in probationary status, some for as long as ten years, in order to cut costs.[126]

This had implications for formalization. In the 1930s, as more courts were set up, with fewer judges, probationary judges routinely adjudicated cases along with judges. In February 1935, Minister of Justice Wang Yongbin ordered that probationary judges at the HC no longer adjudicate appeals, because they did not have enough experience to judge serious cases and were not high enough in stature to make the trial of appeal cases credible.[127] When the JHC president Zhu Shusheng circulated the order in the province, the branch HC presidents complained that the new policy would simply make the task of clearing up case backlogs impossible and cause further backlogs. After intense negotiations with the HC branches and the MJ, Zhu Shusheng finally decided to promote probationary judges to judgeship, with increased costs borne by those courts, something the MJ readily approved.[128] For further formalization, in 1936, the MJ ordered that from fiscal year 1937 on, all probationary judicial officers should be given full appointments in three years.[129]

Prison Reform in the Nanjing Decade

Initiatives and Problems

Although prison reform remained part of the judicial reform, only ten new prisons were built between 1927 and 1930. The 1929 reform plan included a "Working Guide for Improving the Prison System." The period 1930–1935 was to see the construction of 47 juvenile prisons, 205 regular prisons, 22 prisons for recidivists, and 21 prisons for the insane and the sick.[130] Other sources indicate that a total of 215 new prisons were to be built during the period, with varying capacities from 1,000, 700, 500, to 300 inmates each.[131] Even if those prisons had been built as planned, the goal of one new prison for each county would not have been met. The plan, of course, was not for actual implementation, as noted earlier, and the total number of new prisons actually built fell far short of the plan. The period 1928–1937 saw 30 prisons, 75 detention houses, and 10 institutes for repentance (for political prisoners) built, resulting in a penal system of 60 new prisons, 11 new branch prisons, 101 new detention houses, with old jails in most of nearly 1,800 counties.[132]

Besides the innovations in incarcerating political prisoners, Nanjing issued a host of laws, regulations, and ministerial directives on the prison system and its management. Most were based on Beiyang precedents, and some were updated with recent penal theories from the West, including a grade system, provided for the first time in the Draft Prison Law of 1935.[133]

In the mid-1930s, the GMD invented three new practices, all designed to alleviate prison crowding and reduce the cost of inmate rations. The first was a plan to move prison inmates to remote areas to reclaim wasteland, provided for in 1934 by a set of regulations.[134] The plan was not easy to implement for logistical reasons. No reclamation was conducted until 1941, when the MJ set up a first penal reclamation area in Sichuan province.[135]

The second plan, unveiled in July 1935, was that provided they showed remorse, prison inmates who were common criminals could be released on parole after serving one-third or at least six months of their terms. This was more generous than what the criminal code provided for—serving half of the term or a minimum of twelve months before an inmate could be released on bail or parole. This measure was explicitly designed to reduce the prison population and was in addition to the 1920 regulations on releasing prisoners on bail.[136]

The third initiative was to draft inmates into the armed forces, launched one month after the Sino-Japanese War broke out in July 1937. Prison inmates could volunteer for military service, excluding those who were guilty of treason; smoked opium; were aged fifty or older; were physically unfit; were serving terms of ten years or more; or were recidivists. Those who served as high-risk shock troops were considered on parole; the military service of others counted as part of their prison terms. Inmates doing military service were regarded as regular servicemen.[137] Within a year, over 3,330 inmates had enlisted.[138] By January 1946, the number of inmates in the armed forces exceeded 38,000.[139] While the impact of this practice on the Chinese military is unknown, it seems to have led to only a minimal reduction in the prison population.

What difference did the GMD prison reform make in prison management? Conditions in some new prisons in the Nanjing decade are described in an article written in 1931 by Ching-yeuh Yen, a Chinese member of the Howard League for Penal Reform in England. (County jails are examined more closely in Chapter 8.) Yen voluntarily entered the Beijing First Prison to learn about conditions there and reported what he had experienced to the Tenth International Penal and Penitentiary Congress in Prague in 1930. "I told the audience what a horrible feeling I had in the prison, although I was specially well treated in every aspect." Yen also visited other prisons in North and Northeastern China. At a prison in Datong, a mid-sized city in Shanxi province, he found that the ration budget for 222 inmates was only ¥15 per month, and that 68 men without clothing on their upper bodies (in winter) were crowded into a 20' × 12' cell, in which more than 100 men had been held the previous year. In Taiyuan, the provincial capital of Shanxi, the prison physician did not even know that some prisoners had died in the cells of the detention house (presumably attached to the DC or HC). "In the Mukden [the provincial capital of Liaoning] First Prison the officers did not feel strange at all, when there were several death reports every day in the prison of about 2,000 population. . . . It was a rare occasion when there was only one death a day."[140]

The Anti-Drug Campaign and Crisis in the Prison System

The conditions in new prisons were deplorable because prison reform or judicial reform as a whole was not a top priority for the GMD state. In fact, the reform was often affected adversely by other state agendas.

A case in point is the dire situation in the prison system caused by a vigorous anti-drug campaign launched in 1933 and stepped up in 1935.[141] On April 1, 1935, in Wuchang, where Chiang Kai-shek was staying as the Military Commission (MC) chairman—he would become "drug tsar" (*jingyan zongjian*) in June—issued Opium and Narcotics Prohibition Implementing Measures. These were followed in October 1935 by draconian regulations punishing narcotics and opium offenses, under which the minimum jail term for opium-smokers was six months; that for sellers, three years; for narcotics users, seven years; and the penalty for sellers of narcotics (other than opium) was death.[142]

Conceived as a political and financial rather than a judicial matter, the anti-drug campaign was headed by the MC and enforced primarily by the military and security apparatus and secondarily by the administrative offices and the judiciary, which contradicted the agenda of formalizing the state's judicial functions. In addition to the regular courts and county government offices, agencies such as the Nanjing Garrison Command (NGC) and the Military Police Command (MPC) were processing large numbers of drug offenders arrested by their forces, leading to serious complications not experienced before.

In December 1935, the head of the NGC, Gu Zhenglun, wrote to the MC, pointing out three problem areas faced by the anti-drug campaign. (1) There was a lack of prison space to house sentenced drug offenders. In the Jiangning DC alone, over 6,140 drug cases were tried and over 8,500 drug offenders sentenced in 1934, and the NGC had been sentencing more than 300 drug offenders a month since the new prohibition measures were issued in April. (2) As more and more offenders were incarcerated, the increasing cost of inmate rations was a serious matter. The NGC and MPC had only limited confinement space, and none for female inmates, who had to be sent to the Jiangsu First Prison (JFP). The Central Military Prison already refused to take in more drug offenders because of a shortage of inmate rations. Other prisons might do the same. (3) With the increasing drug cases, plus cases of serious political crimes transferred from all the provinces to Nanjing, the NGC did not have enough military trial officers.[143]

The MC referred Gu's message to the Department of Military Administration (DMA), which responded that inmate rations for drug offenders should be paid according to actual expenditure; two military trial officers could be appointed temporarily to try drug cases; and the prisons holding female inmates should be given additional funds, but should not refuse to take in inmates. The DMA stressed that the anti-drug campaign had originally been a local matter; the military had taken it over because previous anti-drug measures were ineffective, but the burden of feeding drug offense inmates should still be shouldered by local and provincial governments. All prisons and jails in the judicial system should take in such inmates, no matter where those offenders were tried. The opinion, endorsed by the MC, became an order issued by the JC, via the MJ, to all provincial high courts.[144]

The order merely lifted the problem from the shoulders of the military and security apparatus and dumped it into the lap of the judiciary, which ran the prison system. With the order from the JC, when the military and security apparatus sent all drug offenders and political/military prisoners to prison, they would not care whether the system was able to absorb such a large number of inmates. Thus the prison system designed mainly to handle common criminals was pressed to a breaking point.

What happened at the JFP in Nanjing is a revealing example. In September 1935, the JFP governor, Niu Chuanqi, sent a message to the Martial Law Division (MLD) of the NGC, pleading that it stop sending female offenders to the JFP. By converting sickrooms into female cells, the prison could house a total of 116 female inmates, but the number of female inmates had consistently been above 200 in recent years, because all military prisoners were serving long terms. As a result, overcrowding had become intolerable, and managing the prison extremely difficult, while female inmates kept arriving. Niu requested that the number of female military prisoners be limited to 80, per the ration budget provided by the DMA for them.[145]

The MLD referred the matter to the NGC, with an argument that since there was no other place to hold female prisoners in Nanjing, the JFP had to take female inmates so that the MLD would be able to process cases involving women. It asked the NGC to telegraph Chiang Kai-shek to have the MJ order the JFP to cooperate. The NGC did that. Chiang endorsed the MLD's argument and sent the matter to the MJ. Minister Wang Yongbin passed it to the JHC, saying that what the MC had requested should be done—JFP was to accept female inmates. The JHC referred the whole matter back to Niu.[146]

In April 1936, an exasperated Niu telegraphed the JHC to report the dire situation in the prison's female quarters. As of April 12, the number of female convicts had risen to 230, while more were arriving, for whom there was simply no longer any space. Niu enclosed the data: of 142 female inmates from the NGC, 104 were drug offenders and 30 were military and political prisoners (13 "red bandits" and 17 convicted of "harming the Republic"). Of the 142 women, 90 were serving terms of from more than five years to life. Despite the support of the acting president of the JHC, Zhu Shusheng, the NGC and the MC were unmoved. Their unyielding position was again transmitted back to Niu by the MJ and the JHC.

On May 28, Niu told the JHC that the number of female inmates at the JFP had reached 262, and he was unable to follow the order. Niu proposed that more prison cells be built or civilian houses be rented immediately. Zhu Shusheng asked Niu to send a bird's-eye-view drawing of the prison, "to help verification and consideration." As the drawing Niu sent on June 23 shows, the JFP had three male quarters and one female quarter, and all were overcrowded. The south quarter was designed for 208 men but was holding 484. The west and east quarters, each designed for 240, were each holding 290 men. The north (female) quarter was designed for 82, but had 305 women in it, plus seven children. Under the prison regulations, the female and male quarters of a prison were to be strictly separated, and therefore even if there had been space in the male quarters, female inmates could not have been housed there.

By June, the MLD finally conceded that what Niu said was true. Maintaining that it could not stop sending offenders to the prison while the anti-drug campaign was going on, the office suggested that the MJ ready other facilities to house drug offenders. The NGC endorsed the opinion. Responding to the messages from Niu and the NGC, Wang Yongbin told the JHC to rent civilian houses to hold female drug offenders. In early July 1936, the MC too came to grips with the situation in the JFP and endorsed the idea of renting civilian houses as confinement facilities.[147] Thus after ten months of bureaucratic tug-of-war, a stopgap solution was finally agreed upon, but the solution, albeit out of necessity, seriously compromised the prison regulations and the efforts at judicial formalization. It is not clear whether or how many civilian houses were actually rented for confining female drug offenders. In fact, the inmate population in the JFP continued to be several times over the designed capacity, and around 80 percent of female inmates and around 65 percent of male inmates were drug offenders.[148]

The crisis at the JFP was the tip of an iceberg about the situation in the prison system at the time. The agenda of formalizing the judiciary often conflicted with other agendas, and funding for judicial formalization was often sidelined, or the money was used for purposes unrelated to building and operating the judiciary, such as incarcerating and feeding drug offenders. Historians consider the GMD anti-opium campaign to have been a ploy to monopolize the sale of opium and collect special taxes on it, while making a halfhearted effort at eliminating drugs, which had little real effect.[149] As we have seen, substantial resources were spent on arresting, trying, incarcerating, and feeding drug offenders, which any profit from monopolizing opium sales might not have been able to offset. But the critical point is that the profit that the anti-drug enforcement agencies did obtain was not shared with the judicial system, which was exactly why the system, including prisons, especially felt the pinch. In short, for whatever motives, the anti-drug campaign undermined the judicial reform and formalization agenda.

Judicial reform under the GMD party-state showed both a radical departure from and substantial continuity with the Beiyang era. The politicization of the judiciary was the most obvious departure that contradicted the guiding principles of the reform. From the GMD perspective, there was no contradiction as such, because even the rule of law, judicial independence, and due process were to serve the purpose of "ruling the country through the party." On the other hand, besides dealing with political offenses and some violent crimes, the GMD state continued to formalize judicial institutions and procedures in general. The promulgation of the civil and criminal codes and procedural laws was an important milestone in the endeavor. Other rules and regulations dealing with the court system, judicial personnel, judicial procedures, and prison management moved in the same direction, toward uniformity, formalization, standardization, and bureaucratization. The GMD state ran into the same kinds of difficulties as the Beiyang government in its formalization agenda. Forced to allow extrajudicial institutions and personnel to conduct judicial affairs and informal, nonstandard, and irregular practices to persist in the judicial system, the GMD state compromised the judicial formalization that it was supposed to accomplish. Like its Beiyang predecessor, the GMD state suffered from financial constraints; and unlike its predecessor, it had other commitments and priorities, from fighting the communist insurgency and political enemies to prohibiting opium and narcotics, that diverted precious institutional and financial resources from the judicial reform. In a word, the GMD party-state was simultaneously taking on and overwhelmed by the task of modern state building under unfavorable conditions, both of which were reflected in the performance of the GMD judicial system.

PART II

Provincial Setting and Financial Constraints

CHAPTER 4

Provincial Institutions and Judicial Reform in Jiangsu

> Owing to the lack of control of the central government and the failure to execute its will throughout the provinces, the new statutes, especially as to procedure, have in many cases been disregarded. . . . It must be admitted that some of the evidence on this point comes from persons who are interested in the maintenance of extraterritoriality in China, and their statements must be taken with due allowance for partisanship. Nevertheless there is sufficient testimony of this sort to raise a serious question as to whether the Chinese administration of justice is, or will be in the near future, of such a quality to warrant the relinquishment of extraterritorial rights. The burden of proof is upon China.
>
> —Benjamin H. Williams, *China Weekly Review* (Shanghai), August 19, 1922[1]

The comment that in Republican China, the central government had little control over the provinces is familiar. It is only partially true, however. If one conceives of the state system in multiple dimensions and as multiple hierarchies, a somewhat different picture emerges. The archival sources and printed government documents available to this study suggest that during 1901–1937 in the judicial field—one of the dimensions of the state system—a chain of command extended from the national capital through the provincial judicial institutions down to the county level, especially where district courts and their branches existed.[2] In terms of procedural formalization, all laws, rules, regulations, orders, and directives issued from the central government were followed, at least in Jiangsu, even though individual deviations from legal rules by a judge or a county magistrate would occur, which might be common in any state system. One is aware of deviations from rules and regulations in judicial procedures, precisely because the norms and forms were established or publicized at the county level, and their violations were reported and actions were taken to rectify them, even if such actions would not prevent deviations. As for instances of noncompliance in institutional formalization, such as below-standard conditions in county jails, they usually resulted from a lack of resources, not from willful violation of national standards. While research remains to be done to learn whether and to what degree this generalization holds true of other provinces, Jiangsu will serve as a case to bear it out in this book.

Jiangsu has been chosen because it was one of the politically more stable and economically more developed provinces, especially during the Nanjing decade. An examination of how the judiciary functioned at the provincial and county levels in Jiangsu will illuminate how the reform impacted judicial practices and local society, and what factors prevented it from being more successful than it was. This chapter outlines the political and social terrain in the province, discusses the provincial judicial administration, and presents the institutional outcomes of the reform—the rise in the supply of and demand for judicial services—that indicate the reach of the state in Jiangsu and the successes and limitations of the reform. This survey prepares the ground for a closer look at county judicial processes in Part III.

Political and Social Topography

Historical and Economic Geography

Prior to the founding of the Ming dynasty (1368–1644), the territory of what was to become Jiangsu province was divided into different administrative formations. Not until the Ming did an administrative formation called "Nanjing province" come into being, containing today's Jiangsu, Anhui, Shanghai, and parts of Henan and Jiangxi. In 1645, the Qing changed Nanjing province into Jiangnan province, with Jiangning (later the city of Nanjing) as the capital. Two administrative commissioners (*buzheng shi*) posted in Jiangning jointly oversaw fourteen prefectures, four greater counties (*zhili zhou*), and ninety-seven counties.

In 1661, the Qing divided the administration of Jiangnan between the two commissioners: one, in Jiangning, was responsible for nineteen prefectures (mostly north of the Yangzi River), while the other, in Suzhou, was in charge of five prefectures—Jiangning, Suzhou, Songjiang, Changzhou, and Zhengjiang.[3] In 1665, an adjustment was made of the prefectures under Jiangnan's two commissioners. The change divided Jiangnan into two parts, which would become Jiangsu and Anhui provinces. The final separation of the two was completed in 1760.[4] The changes in Jiangsu's provincial boundary over the ages reflected the efforts of the central government to rationalize the administration of China's many provinces, with their wide-ranging ecological, economic, and sociocultural diversities. The Qing took great care to mix less developed and more developed areas to achieve a certain balance. The division of Jiangnan into Anhui and Jiangsu followed that principle. Instead of separating them along the Yangzi River, an otherwise "natural" option, the Qing created the two provinces in such a way that both had more developed areas south of the Yangzi River and less developed areas north of the river.[5]

Consequently, Jiangsu remained a very diverse piece of territory. Using William Skinner's model, the historian Bradley Geisert has noted that Republican Jiangsu straddled two economic macroregions. The northern half of the province belongs to the North China Region, and the southern half lies within the Lower Yangzi Region. The northern part shared physiographic and sociological features with other provinces in the North China Region, including "dusty yellow soil, dry climate, and treeless expanses," an "alternating cycle of frequent drought and flood," "dry-farming methods," widespread banditry, and armed violence, the last two often being survival strategies of poor peasants. Another consequence of northern Jiangsu being an economic backwater was that elites there were fewer, more powerful, faced less competition, and were more likely to reside in the countryside than their counterparts in southern Jiangsu.[6] In contrast, southern Jiangsu, like the rest of the Jiangnan (south of the Yangzi River), featured abundant and dependable rainfall, wet rice cultivation, diversified economic activities, more commercialization and urbanization, and the dominance of gentry-merchants as local elites.[7] Geisert's analysis is relevant to our study of how judicial reform would unfold in the particular sociopolitical ecologies of various counties in Jiangsu.

Provincial Administration

When Jiangnan province was formally separated into Anhui and Jiangsu in 1760, governors-general and provincial governors evolved from commissioners on assignment from Beijing to resident chief provincial administrators. The governor-general of Jiangsu, Anhui, and Jiangxi and the governor of Jiangsu were the top officials overseeing civilian and military affairs in the province. Administrative and judicial commissioners, their deputies, attended to the day-to-day business of governance.[8]

In 1907, during the New Policy reform, the Qing court issued Uniform Rules of Provincial Officialdom, formally making provinces the highest administrative units under the central government. The regulations stipulated the component offices of the provincial government and their functions. Under the provincial governor or the governor-general (a provincial governor was not posted in a province where a governor-general was resident) were departments of administration, education, and justice, plus divisions of industry and police. In addition, ten sections were in charge of official appointments, civil affairs, revenue, agriculture, industry, and commerce, the postal service, military affairs, and so forth. Jiangsu was among the five provinces to implement the regulations first in a pilot trial.[9]

After the founding of the Republic in 1912, the administrative hierarchy below the central government was based on a two-tier system—provinces and counties—for the most time. In 1913, the Yuan Shikai government reestablished one more layer between a province and its counties, the circuit (*dao*). The sixty counties in Jiangsu were grouped into five circuits—Jinling, Huhai, Suchang, Huaiyang, and Xuhai—each with a circuit administrator (*daoyin*). Circuits existed until 1924.

Immediately following the 1911 Revolution, the chief administrative official of Jiangsu was the military governor (*dujun*). Cheng Dequan, the Qing provincial governor (*xunfu*) of Jiangsu, assumed that position during the Revolution, and was officially reappointed by Yuan Shikai in April 1912. Under the military governor, six departments administered military, financial, foreign, internal, transportation, and judicial affairs. In January 1913, the Yuan government ordered the separation of military and civil administration at the provincial level. The civilian governor (*minzheng zhang*) became the chief administrator, and the military governor managed military affairs only. Not all provinces followed the rule, but Jiangsu did.

In May 1914, Yuan Shikai issued Regulations on Provincial Officialdom. The title of provincial head was changed to "pacifying governor" (*xun'an shi*), which implied a military role. In July 1916, after Yuan's death, the title of provincial head was changed to "provincial governor" (*shengzhang*). Under the provincial governor were four departments—administration, finance, education, and industry. The administrative department was in charge of a wide range of tasks, with a staff of 237 people, while the staff in three other departments totaled 233. In 1918, under an order from the Ministry of the Interior, a division of police affairs was set up in the provincial government, with a staff of 92, plus 60 interns from various counties.[10]

During 1913–1925, a military governor under different names was always posted along with the civilian governor. In December 1925, the warlord Sun Chuanfang, self-proclaimed General Commander of the Joint Army of Five Provinces (Fujian, Zhejiang, Jiangsu, Anhui, and Jiangxi), appointed a provincial governor for Jiangsu. He did not change the administrative structure and functions, merely superimposing himself on top of the provincial government.

After the GMD established the National Government in Nanjing in 1927, the seat of the Jiangsu provincial government moved to Zhengjiang (former Dantu) in February 1928.[11] Under the Provincial Government Commission were the departments of civil affairs, finance, economic development, and education, along with a secretariat.[12] A provincial justice department existed for about six months (May–November) in 1927.

Subprovincial Administration

During the Beiyang era, Jiangsu had sixty counties. In 1928 Waisha was carved out of Chongming to become another county, called Qidong.[13] Although circuits were abolished in 1924, in March 1933, a new institutional layer between the province and counties was created by the Jiangsu provincial government under Chen Guofu to strengthen local security and administrative efficiency, the subprovincial district (*qu*). Initially, there were thirteen such districts, each consisting of from three to seven counties, and the head of the district, called the special administrative supervisor, was in charge of monitoring the performance of county magistrates and coordinating joint security efforts of the counties, among other things. Each subprovincial district office had a monthly budget of ¥2,280. In counties where subprovincial district offices were located, the supervisors served concurrently as county magistrates. In December 1933, in an effort to save expenses, the number of subprovincial districts was reduced to nine, each comprising from four to nine counties. The supervisor no longer served concurrently as magistrate, but as the commander of all local security forces in the district.[14] Unlike the circuit administrator of the Beiyang era, however, the supervisor did not oversee judicial affairs per se.

More significantly, the GMD state reached a level below the county for the first time in Jiangsu in terms of institutional framework. A county was composed of wards (also called *qu*), towns (*zhen*), and townships (*xiang*). The heads of wards, but not those of towns and townships, were appointed by the Civil Affairs Department (CAD). They could be dismissed for incompetence at the request of county magistrates.[15] Piloted by Yan Xishan in Shanxi province as early as 1917, the ward system as an institutional extension of the state into subcounty level in the 1930s was a new attempt at reconciling state control and local self-government, an objective that had eluded the state since the late Qing.[16] Under published plans for local self-government, all the counties, wards, towns, and townships were to move toward self-government at some point, but this did not actually occur in any significant way.[17] As for the implication of the new structure for judicial matters in local society, each ward had a mediation committee to mediate civil disputes. Referring to the committees, a writer observed that "while the intention of setting up such organizations is good, in every county they often led to fraud and extortion."[18] Part III of this book provides a better background of how this happened.

The Relationship Between the Administration and the Judiciary

The Provincial Governor and Judicial Reform

In early 1907, in the context of reorganizing the bureaucracy, the Qing court asked for input from provincial officials on the issue of provincial judicial administration. The ML proposed to separate administrative and judicial functions at the provincial level, with the high court controlling judicial matters completely. An alternative approach was to allow the provincial governor or governor-general to control everything, including administrative and judicial matters, with a judicial department attending to judicial matters and supervising the high court—essentially a continuation of the old system plus a high court. A majority of the provincial officials who responded to the Qing court were in favor of the second approach.[19]

On July 7, 1907, an imperial edict ordered that the provincial department of justice change its name from *ancha si* to *tifa si* and that a separate trial court be established. The order seems to have mainly been in response to proposals from provincial officials, but setting up a high court at the provincial level was nevertheless a significant step. The edict instructed that the Northeastern provinces should experiment with the system first, and Zhili and Jiangsu should select areas to do the same as well; other provinces should have the system established within fifteen years.[20] As of March 1909, however, departments of justice were not established in many provinces, impeding the establishment of provincial courts and procuracies to be supervised by such departments.[21]

In Jiangsu, the Justice Department (*tifa si*) (JD) was established in 1910, with general affairs, criminal and civil, and penitentiary sections. The estimated operating cost of the department was 24,000 taels a year, which was said to be well within the budget.[22] Serious criminal cases and important judicial administrative issues would be jointly discussed by the three sections and the decisions were to be forwarded to the department head or the provincial governor for approval.[23]

The 1907 edict did not change the tradition whereby the provincial governor supervised judicial administration and reviewed capital cases. In February 1911, the governor of Jiangsu, Cheng Dequan, in a meeting with the JD chief, Zheng Yan, told the latter to make sure that no officers and staff at the JHC and district courts visited pleasure quarters, socialized with questionable characters, or used their positions to extort money from people. Zheng took the oral instructions seriously and issued an order to that effect to all district court presidents.[24] Obviously, at that point, Cheng regarded the courts and judicial personnel in the province as part of his responsibility, and Zheng did not find the governor's concerns out of place.

With the founding of the Republic, it was widely assumed that judicial reform should and would continue, but how to separate administrative and judicial institutions at the provincial level was not clear. By default, the governor would continue presiding over all governmental institutions. After Yuan Shikai issued an amnesty in May 1912, counties in Jiangsu sent the files of criminal defendants to be pardoned to Cheng Dequan for approval. Cheng demanded that the Songjiang DC resubmit the files with complete information.[25] Neither the JHC nor even the JD entered the picture at all in this matter.

The Governor and Judicial Appointments, 1912

The governor and the JD took a firm hand in appointing judicial officers, a critical issue in the establishment of a judiciary after the 1911 Revolution. Judges and procurators at county-level courts were appointed by the JD with Cheng's approval or recommended by the JD first.[26] In managing judicial matters in the province, the governor had to deal with the popular activism and political turmoil unleashed by the 1911 Revolution. The impact of the Revolution on the judiciary may be seen in a request to the governor from the JD dated March 1912 that the DC president and the DP chief in Suzhou be awarded merit points for keeping their institutions operational during the turmoil of the 1911 Revolution.[27] In other words, paralysis of the court system at the time of the Revolution was a common occurrence, so that keeping the judicial institutions operational stood out as worthy of commendation.

Critically, local elites were motivated to welcome the establishment of judicial institutions in their locales to protect their interests, but only if they could control the appointment of officers at those institutions. In the new political culture created by the New Policy and the 1911 Revolution, local elites were emboldened to contest with the provincial government for the power of judicial appointment at the county level. In early February 1912, the Rugao county magistrate, Sha Yuanbing, and a military commander there, Zhou Lian, reported to the governor that when the head of the court in Rugao was dismissed, they had had the chief procurator Zhang Xiang assume the post, and the county assembly was going to elect a chief procurator to replace Zhang. Zhuang Yunkuan, the acting governor in Cheng Dequan's absence,[28] replied that the judiciary should be a uniform system; all judges and procurators should be appointed by the governor; and local assemblies had no authority to elect those officers—"the assembly is a legislative body without power to elect judges." Zhuang appointed the new head of the court in Rugao, which voided the action of Sha and Zhou.[29] In Yangzhou, the county assembly authorized setting up a court and a procuracy and elected a court president and a procurator, but the two men departed to take positions elsewhere. In March 1912, the magistrate recommended two former judges to the governor for the two positions in Yangzhou. Zhuang Yunkuan replied that both administrative and judicial officials were to be appointed by the governor, not to be nominated by local officials. Zhuang allowed the nominees to fill additional positions in Yangzhou after having the JD appoint the court president and the chief procurator.[30] These examples illustrate a pattern immediately after the 1911 Revolution in which local elites (the county assembly here) lost no time in trying to control the appointment of judicial officers at the county level; and the provincial government was vigilant in guarding its prerogatives and was able to maintain its control in this respect.

One variation of the pattern was local elites trying, in the name of "the people," to oust provincial government–appointed judicial officers whom they did not like. In April 1912, Cheng Dequan issued a public notice observing that after courts were organized in Jiangsu, there were frequent petitions from local people, often in the name of voluntary associations, attacking judges and demanding their dismissal. All judicial officers were, however, selected based on their professional credentials, expected to carry out their duties according to the law, supervised by superior offices, and counterbalanced by the lawyer system. If there were wrongful prosecutions or trials, the victims could appeal to superior judicial organs. There was no room for third parties to intervene with vague accusations using terms such as "not compatible with local opinion" or "dereliction of duty." From then on, the provincial governor would not accept any petitions from voluntary associations or third parties intervening in judicial appointments, "so as to respect [judges'] personal dignity [*renge*] and protect the authority of law [*faquan*]."[31] Cheng thus guarded his power of judicial appointment against local interference that he considered improper from either a traditional or modern point of view.

The governor's public notice did not stop local organizations from trying to interfere in judicial appointments, however. Local elites tried to control judicial organs in local society in disregard of the principle of the separation of powers—ironically, while invoking it. They acted as if a local assembly (elected by a process they controlled) were a sovereign body, entitled to do anything, including electing or appointing judicial officers. That was something the governor had to set straight whenever it came up. In May 1912, the provisional county assembly in Tongshan petitioned Cheng, accusing the DC president and the DP chief there of disregarding local finance, opposing a reduction of their salaries, and spending public funds carelessly. They described the DC president as following the old habit of bringing in private assistants, and the two judicial officers as lacking legal knowledge and training. Asking for their dismissal, the assembly informed the governor that it had elected two replacements and urged him to approve their choices to make the "system of separation of the three powers" work. In his reply to the assembly, Cheng mocked its rhetoric about separation of powers and pointed out that the assembly was only a local legislative body, with no authority to elect judicial officers, since the judiciary was a function of the administration. "Under what law does the action of the assembly not contradict the principle of separation of the three powers?" he asked. "Since this governor is responsible for supervising administrative affairs in the province, he has to seriously advise the assembly to study calmly what its functions should be."[32] In other words, while the administration and judiciary were not separate at this point, Cheng deemed it preposterous to have a local legislative body interfere with judicial appointments in the name of separation of powers.

Local elites reacted with anxiety to the establishment of the judiciary in counties, because the new institutions were an expansion of the state system at the county level and a new seat of power installed from outside that might interfere with their power and status in local society. A magistrate would have to rely on local elites' cooperation to perform his administrative duties, and it would therefore be easier for local elites to manipulate and pressure him with respect to litigation. In contrast, a court and a procuracy that were independent of local society would conjure up very different local power play scenarios in local elites' minds. Furthermore, the financial cost of building and operating a county-level judiciary would ultimately have to be borne by local society, where local elites might have other priorities. Having to pay for a new institution that might hurt their interests doubled local elites' pain.

One example will serve to illustrate the situation. On September 16, 1912, a joint petition reached Cheng Dequan from the county assembly, the county education society, and the branch chamber of commerce in Suining, a county in northern Jiangsu. Two days, later a similar petition arrived, which was signed by twenty-three assembly members and township managers (*xiangdong*) from various townships in the county in the name of the Association of Cities and Townships (*shixiang lianhehui*). The petitions criticized the DC president, Chen Tongshou, and the DP chief, Mei Yinjie. They said that Suining was a poor county and that the CGO tried to save its resources by cutting the salaries of county employees. In preparation for establishing the DC and the DP before the arrival of Chen and Mei, the magistrate and the county assembly had selected Yang Yiqi as the preparation officer (*choubei yuan*) and allocated 500,000 copper coins as judicial funds. But after Chen and Mei assumed their posts, they spent more than 400,000 coins on top of the 500,000 coins allocated, and refused to allow Yang Yiqi to look into their accounts. "The people of Suining have suffered exploitation by [the judicial organs] before enjoying any benefits from them." When confronted by the county assembly, Chen and Mei were uncooperative, saying that the judiciary was independent of local officials and the judicial funds were allocated by the provincial government, to which alone they would be accountable. The petitioners also charged that Chen and Mei had hired as judicial staff either people from their native places or bad characters in local society, some of whom had previously been fired by the CGO. "Although there is separation of [the] three powers under the Republican government, the people are sovereign, after all. Anything that benefits the people should be accepted, and anything that harms the people should be opposed," the second petition argued. "Only institutions accepted [by the people] can be established, whatever they are, and those opposed [by the people] should be abolished."[33] By exercising a discourse of the people's rights and popular sovereignty, the local elites claimed to represent the people and opposed the newly established judicial organs in the county because "the people" could not control them.

The opposition to Chen and Mei must have been very vocal and strong, so that the two men felt it necessary to state their case to the governor. In a letter to Cheng Dequan, they reported that the DC and the DP had started operation on September 16, 1912, and that a local gentry-pettifogger (*donggun*) named Yang Yiqi who had used to control all litigation (*baolan cisong*) in the county was afraid of losing his business and, having managed to get himself installed as the preparation officer, had instigated a campaign to discredit the DC and the DP.

In response to both the petitions and the Chen-Mei letter, Cheng issued a long order to the county assembly head in Suining. He refuted the point that Chen and Mei exploited the local people, since the judicial funds were taken from the regular taxes to be forwarded to the province and had nothing to do with local finance. The court president and the chief procurator had the power to hire personnel based on qualifications, and where the hired were from was irrelevant and was not restricted by the law. If, as Chen and Mei reported, Yang Yiqi wrote letters naming his personal friends to be hired as judicial personnel, it was probably illegal. The county assembly's attempt to look into the accounts of the judicial organs decided by the provincial assembly was also illegal, since the judiciary was an agency of the central government, not of the local administration. Chen and Mei were correct in insisting that they were accountable only to the provincial authorities.[34] It is highly instructive that at this particular juncture, it was the governor who, while controlling the provincial judicial administration, defended the principle of judicial independence at the county level. Even in the wake of the 1911 Revolution, in the early months of the Republic, the provincial government (and, by extension, the central government) prevailed in this matter over county-level elite groups, even if its power was contested.

Local elites were also anxious about the new courts at the county level because they feared such institutions might empower nonelite people in local society. Because a court judge would be more independent of local elites than a magistrate, local elites sensed the possibility that nonelite people might use the court to redress the injustice they suffered from powerful locals. In May 1912, the Jiangdu magistrate sent the governor a petition signed by sixty "citizens" from townships around the county seat, Yangzhou. Following the 1911 Revolution, went the petition, law and order had broken down in Yangzhou. Vagrants and local ruffians (*youmin digun*) conspired with local bandits and caused frequent disturbances. Under an order from the government, townships had organized militias that rounded up and executed bandits, thus pacifying local society, which was a temporary measure born out of necessity at the time. Since the court had been set up in Yangzhou, evil gentry-managers and pettifoggers (*liedong songgun*) had been soliciting the families of the executed bandits to file lawsuits, causing great concerns and anxieties in local society. The petitioners requested that the governor order such cases to be dismissed and, when there were doubts, to have the cases verified by local self-government organizations and by the public, so that human lives would be respected and local public security maintained. Cheng Dequan responded that the magistrate might post a public notice warning against making false accusations and have such cases handled by the court according to the law.[35] Clearly, those who were in a position to organize local militias were local elites who had properties to protect from "bandits"; and they were now concerned that the families of those put to death as bandits would use the new court to settle old scores. It may be surmised without a stretch of imagination that the local elites put enough pressure on the magistrate in the name of local security to make the latter to act on their behalf. The reply from the governor, however, essentially rejected the request to allow so-called local self-government bodies, which were most likely controlled by the same local elites who had earlier organized militias, to interfere in cases that were brought to the court. The anxiety perhaps would also explain why the county assembly in Yangzhou tried to control judicial appointments there in March 1912, as mentioned earlier.

The above cases point to the reach of the state, not only in terms of the relationship between provinces and the central government, but also that between counties and the provincial government. The evidence shows that in the immediate aftermath of the 1911 Revolution, the Jiangsu provincial government controlled judicial appointments at the county level and kept courts in counties independent of local elite power. In places where courts and procuracies survived the retrenchment of 1913–1914, this relationship between formal judicial institutions at the county level and local elites would continue through 1937.

The Governor and Judicial Independence, 1912

One aspect of the conflict between the provincial government and county-level institutions and local elites was that despite the reform, local people continued to regard the governor as the arbiter when they felt the judiciary failed to deliver justice. What is striking is that Governor Cheng steadfastly insisted on judicial independence and refused to step into individual cases. In April 1912, a certain Ren Liansheng in Shanghai wrote to Cheng to lodge what he called an administrative lawsuit. The intended target was the chief of the Jiading DP, who had decided not to prosecute a case in which Ren accused a local headman (*dibao*) of seducing his wife. Cheng told the petitioner that he should appeal his case to a superior court and had no cause to bring an administrative lawsuit against the procurator.[36] That Ren used the concept of "administrative lawsuit" to petition the governor is interesting. Ren probably knew that he could appeal but did not feel he would win his case at the high court. Perhaps he also knew that the governor would not be in a position to interfere with the case, but an administrative lawsuit might involve the governor. However, Cheng's strong sense of judicial independence upset his calculation.

Another case that reached the governor involved a charity establishment called the Funeral Service Bureau (*daizang ju*) in Jiangning. In 1908, the bureau bought the user right (*dian*) for a house as rental property from Li Changqing to use the income to defray the cost of the bureau's operation.[37] In July 1912, with a tenant about to rent the house, Xu Bingnan, the owner of a teahouse across the street, forcibly occupied the premises, saying that since the house was public property (this probably meant that it was for charity), anyone could use it, and refused to move out. The bureau sued Xu at the CFI, and Xu was ordered to move out within twenty days. Xu appealed, claiming that a certain Dai Weitao had borrowed money from him using the property as a collateral. He named two witnesses to the transaction, but one of the witnesses denied any knowledge of it. The DP held that Dai's having borrowed money from Xu, even if true, had no bearing on the bureau's user right. When the case reached the DC for second trial, however, the judge decided that both the bureau and Xu held effective user rights, and the property should be auctioned off to reimburse the bureau and pay the debt to Xu. Four members of the funeral bureau's board of directors then wrote to Cheng Dequan asking for justice, saying that they had no more funds to pursue the case in court any further. In all legal propriety, Cheng replied that they would have to do it according the law. "They must understand that as the judiciary is now independent, this governor absolutely cannot intervene [in such cases] from outside the law."[38] With clarity and fortitude Cheng once again upheld the principle of judicial independence, in the sense that judges should adjudicate without interference from administrative officials. Although the outcome might not necessarily serve perceived substantive justice in a given case, it was for a court to decide the right and wrong of the matter, if the judicial process was to remain consistent and impartial. Cheng was able to see the larger picture.

To summarize, in the months following the 1911 Revolution, Cheng Dequan and Zhuang Yunkuan exhibited to a remarkable degree their adherence to the principle of the rule of law and judicial independence in the face of either local elite opposition or appeals from ordinary people for help. In doing so, they played a constructive role in judicial reform in early Republican Jiangsu. If it may be argued that their power of judicial appointment contradicted judicial independence, it was not their personal decision but the institutional role that they were supposed to play at a time when the demarcation between the power of the provincial government and that of the judicial administration at the provincial level was not clearly defined. But that was to change.

Judicial Administration, 1912–1927

By July 1912, the chain of command in the judicial system was finally established. The JD was abolished in April 1912, and by default the JHC and the JHP became the top provincial judicial authorities—the approach favored by the ML in 1907. In August, the MJ requested and received the permission from Yuan Shikai to change the names of court presidents and chief procurators from *tingcheng* to *tingzhang* and *jiancha zhang* respectively to "fit the republican system." The change was carried out in Jiangsu.[39]

In January 1913, on orders from Minister of Justice Xu Shiying, provinces set up offices of preparation for judicial institutions (*sifa choubei chu*) (OPJI), which were to plan for gradual establishment of courts and new prisons in the provinces.[40] Xu urged all high courts and procuracies to work with the OPJI to pursue their projects without delay.[41] After Xu resigned and Liang Qichao succeeded him as minister of justice in September 1913, Yuan Shikai ordered the dissolution of the OPJI in all provinces except Xinjiang, where no high court was established.[42] Thereafter, the HC was not only a trial organ with criminal and civil chambers, but also the judicial administration authority in a province. The HP was not only to investigate and prosecute criminal cases, but also to oversee all institutions of penal confinement at the provincial and county levels.

Under the Regulations on Provincial Officialdom issued by Yuan Shikai in 1914, however, the provincial governor was "specially authorized by the government to supervise judicial administration" and had "the power to have judicial funds accounted for and evaluate judicial officials." The high court president was "to report all appointments, dismissals, rewards, and disciplining of county trial officers and jail overseers to the governor for forwarding to the Ministry of Justice." And the governor could dismiss any judicial officers found to be corrupt.[43] The Regulations on the Purview of High Courts reiterated these points and provided that the HC should submit financial documents to the governor as well as to the MJ.[44]

Similar supervisory power was given to circuit administrators under the Regulations on Circuit Officialdom.[45] When "specially authorized by the provincial governor," the administrator was to supervise judicial affairs in counties within the circuit. The HC president could ask the administrator to investigate and verify judicial matters in those counties. If a circuit administrator was not equal to the task, he could be disciplined and dismissed at any time by the provincial governor, and the HC president could ask the governor for disciplinary action against an administrator.[46] In July 1914, Governor Han Guojun issued an order to authorize all five circuit administrators in the province to supervise judicial affairs, in accordance with the regulations and with a separate order from Yuan Shikai.[47]

The provision for the governor to supervise judicial administration did not square with the principle of judicial independence and the ongoing agenda of separating administration and judiciary. In June 1914, Minister of Justice Zhang Zongxiang sent a request to Yuan, asking him to grant special authorization to provincial governors as spelled out in the regulations, so that the said supervisory power would not automatically be the purview of any provincial governors. Zhang argued that "judicial administration should be uniform across the country and directly supervised by the MJ, but given the situation in the country where local order was just restored and the jurisdictions of the provincial and central governments have not been delineated, this supervisory power over judicial administration might as well be entrusted to provincial governors to assist where the central government is unable to attend to [matters]."[48] In April 1917, Minister of Justice Zhang Yaozeng again asked President Li Yuanhong to grant special authorization to provincial governors to supervise judicial administration. He challenged the governor's power to dismiss corrupt judicial officers, arguing that that power contradicted the 1912 Provisional Constitution and the Law on Disciplining Judicial Officers. His proposal that governors not have the power to dismiss judicial officers was approved.[49] The two ministers tried to make sure that provincial governors' supervisory power over judicial affairs was specially authorized case by case, not an intrinsic power of provincial governorship. Besides the fact that they acted in the interest of judicial independence, this was an example of the national-level judicial authorities contesting the power of provincial governors—a contest between the judicial and administrative fields within the state system, rather than between the central and provincial governments.

The provincial governors and circuit administrators did exercise their supervisory power. On July 11, 1914, Governor Han Guojun asked the JHC president, Cai Yuankang, for a list and the credentials of trial officers appointed by the court to counties. Within three days, Cai sent the files on nine appointed trial officers to the governor. Within weeks, Cai also sent a list of trial officers to Yin Hongshou, the administrator of Suchang Circuit, under whose jurisdiction the trial officers in question would serve. This action was in accordance with the regulations under which the administrator would evaluate the judicial performance of county magistrates, trial officers, and jail overseers.[50]

Judicial Administration, 1927–1937

As noted in Chapter 3, the initial provincial authority in Jiangsu was the short-lived Jiangsu Provincial Justice Department (JPJD) that functioned during May–July 1927. Then the office transferred its mandate to the Ministry of Justice upon the latter's establishment in July 1927.[51] Under the Law on Organizing Provincial Governments of October 1927, the JHC would take over the functions of the JPJD (and those of the former JHP when it was abolished in 1928). Thus, in the Nanjing decade, the JHC became both a trial organ and the highest judicial administration authority in the province, without supervision from the provincial government head.

One area where the power of the provincial administration affected the judiciary, though indirectly, was the appointment by the CAD of county magistrates and public security bureau chiefs, since most county magistrates performed judicial functions and public security chiefs would arrest robbers, bandits, and any criminals including political offenders. The head of the CAD had a decisive say in the matter of county-level appointments.[52]

Provincial governments would often issue administrative orders to address problems in county judicial processes. In June 1929, having heard of torture being used by county magistrates or public security forces, the PGC ordered all county magistrates to see to it that "in order to maintain the law of the land and protect human rights," torture was strictly prohibited in criminal proceedings.[53] Two months later the PGC received a report from Wujiang that the Water and Land Police Corps there routinely used extremely cruel torture in robbery cases. In response, the PGC issued another order to all counties to reiterate the previous order.[54] Such actions may be considered administrative measures, but they had a bearing on county-level justice. Whether those orders were effective is doubtful.

Reform in Jiangsu: Institutions and Regulations

Courts and County Magistrates

Jiangsu was one of those provinces where the reform showed results from the beginning. In December 1910, the JHC was set up in Suzhou, and a month later, district courts were established in ten counties.[55] Each court had criminal and civil chambers, complete with a general managing section and a secretary's office.[56] In addition to a district court, Jiangning also had two CFI and their procuracies no later than May 1911.[57] Wujin saw a DC and a CFI and their procuracies built in September 1911.[58] Some of the DC had jurisdictions over more than one county, because under the Provisional Regulations on Delineating Judicial Jurisdictions of 1910, the DC at the seat of prefecture had authority over the entire prefecture.[59] In January 1911, the JD ordered that to function effectively, the Jiangning DC should have jurisdiction over two counties rather than all seven in the prefecture and the Suzhou DC should have jurisdiction over three counties rather than all eleven in the prefecture. The rest of the counties in those prefectures should be under the judicial powers of county magistrates, as before.[60]

The founding of the Republic in 1912 spurred a new wave of court-building in Jiangsu. In April 1912, the Jiangsu Provisional Provincial Assembly reviewed a proposal from the JD calling for one HC, one HC branch, twelve DC, and sixty-seven CFI to be established. The assembly revised the proposal in more ambitious terms by replacing CFI with DC in all those counties and adding another HC branch, each with a procuracy. The revised proposal was issued as the Provisional Law on Organizing Courts and Procuracies in Jiangsu.[61] This plan, no less ambitious than the one Xu Shiying had envisioned for the country in 1913, became the blueprint for creating judicial organs in Jiangsu until the retrenchment of 1913–1914.

What did happen in 1912 and early 1913 was impressive. District courts were built in twelve counties. The Jiangsu First Branch HC was set up in Jiangning, with jurisdiction over twenty-one DC. The Second

Branch HC was set up in Huaiyin, with jurisdiction over twelve DC. All this was in accordance with the provincial assembly's plan, down to the locations and jurisdictions of the two HC branches.[62] Instead of DC, some counties only had trial and prosecution offices (TPO). On the other hand, some counties had not only DC, but also CFI or branch DC, above the provincial assembly's plan.[63] Until their abolition in May 1914, there were eight CFI with procuracies under the Shanghai DC.[64]

The new courts were staffed by judicial officers who mostly met the qualifications mandated by the central government. Tables 4.1 and 4.2 provide a sample of judicial officers and staff at the Jingjiang DC and DP, and at the Jiangning DP. Note that most of those who served at the Jingjiang DC and DP were natives of Jingjiang and from the same two or three schools and training institutes of law and government. Similarly, most of those who served at the Jiangning DP were from the few same schools, even though they hailed from different provinces. It seems that at the time, native place ties and schoolmate ties were as strong as before. It is conceivable that when one graduate from a school of law and government was employed at an institution, he would bring his schoolmates and/or fellow natives to the same institution to be hired. The local gentry's complaints and anxiety in this regard mentioned earlier would seem to have been well founded. But the key factor here is that all or most of those people were qualified, or as qualified as could be found at the time, in terms of their training and educational background, which set them apart in one important dimension from county functionaries in the imperial and Republican era.

In short, within a year, an independent court system had largely been established in Jiangsu. The important initiatives that the Jiangsu provincial assembly took should be duly recognized. The achievement may be attributed to a consensus on the necessity of such a court system among provincial elites, and to an enthusiasm shared by reformers in the central government and at the provincial level in Jiangsu. In the end, however, the financial reality would dash the high hopes of the reformers and render the achievement in Jiangsu short-lived.

Some signs of financial stress had already appeared in 1912. The ambitious construction of a new court system pushed by the provincial assembly came so rapidly that many counties were ill-prepared for it. In a letter dated July 11, 1912, the newly appointed DC president and the DP chief in Gourong informed Cheng Dequan that because of lack

TABLE 4.1

Personnel Roll of the Jingjiang District Court, December 1911

Position	Name	Native	Education	Note
President	Shang Wenwei			
Judge	Liu Chengjun	Jingjiang	Zhejiang School of Law and Government	
same	Xie Dingrong	Jiangyin	Jiangnan Institute of Adjudication	
same	Zhu Chunian	Jiangyin	School of Law and Government	Former legal assistant
same	Luo Yongqing	Jingjiang	Liangjiang School of Law and Government	Former lawyer
Ch. Registrar	Tong Yupei	same	same	Not graduate
Registrar	Zhu Bingjia	same		
same	Luo Dingxin	same	Liangjiang Normal School	
Recordkeeper	Fan Xunru	same		
same	Zhu Dazhang	same		
same	Tang Kexiu	same		
same	Sheng Deyu	same		
Procuracy				
Ch. Procurator	Luo Fengyin			
Procurator	Wu Rangli	Suzhou	Liangjiang School of Law and Government	Former lawyer
same	Shi Jiuchi	Changzhou	Jiangnan School of Law and Government	Former lawyer
Ch. Registrar	Xu Jinzhang	Jingjiang	Liangjiang School of Law and Government	Did not graduate
Registrar	Chen Xin	same		
Recordkeeper	Zheng Shijie	same	Police School	
same	Liu Wenxue	same		
Prison Head	Qu Yidian	same	Training Institute of Law and Government	

SOURCE: JGFD, RS-7.

of funds, they could not fill the positions of two judges and two procurators mandated by the provincial assembly, and that their institutions were set up in a temple, several *li* away from the county jail, which was still under the care of a former Qing jailer.[65] From the letter, one can sense a gap between the feverish enthusiasm among many and the sobering reality of inadequate resources. It comes as no great surprise that many of the judicial organs established at the county level proved to be financially unsustainable.

The retrenchment that started in 1913 resulted in the dismantling of all CFI and many DC in Jiangsu. In forty-one counties, DC and DP were closed down and TPO were set up instead, while the Second Branch

TABLE 4.2

Personnel Roll of the Jiangning District Procuracy, August 1912

Position	Name	Native	Age	Education
Ch. Procurator	Liu Huan		35	U. of Law and Government, Japan
Procurator	Li Shiqiu	Anhui	33	Liangjiang School of Law and Government
same	Zhou Guangyon	Jiangsu	36	Beijing School of Law and Government
same	Zhao Hanlun	same	31	U. of Law and Government, Japan
same	Wu Xueyou	Anhui	42	Jiangnan Institute of Adjudication
Ch. Registrar	Zhou Yuexiang	Zhejiang	36	Liangjiang School of Law and Government
Registrar	Zhang Zonglin	Anhui	35	same
Recordkeeper	Sun Yi	Jiangsu	32	Jiangnan Institute of Adjudication
same	Shi Shiyong	same	29	same
same	Shi Yongnan	Hubei	36	same
Secretary	Yang Jinlai	Zhejiang	37	same
same	Zhu Zhinong	same	36	same
same	Lai Gan	Jiangxi	33	same
same	Bao Dian	Jiangsu	48	Jiangnan Institute of Law and Government
same	Teng Jinxiu	Jiangxi	35	Liangjiang School of Law and Government
same	Weng Zemin	same	30	Jiangxi Dialect School
same	Peng Zhuofu	Anhui	56	Jiangnan Institute of Law and Government
Med. Officer	Wang Renshu		42	same
Jud. Po. Chief	Huang Jiaji	Hunan	27	Shanghai Police School

SOURCE: JGFD, RS-6.

HC was moved to Huai'an. A total of eighty-six CFI were abolished.[66] In the province, only eleven DC survived. Shanghai was allowed to maintain two CFI besides the DC. In all other counties, TPO replaced courts.[67]

The worst was yet to come. In 1914, with the reduction of judicial funding from the central government, a further cutback took place. The First and Second Branch HC, the two CFI in Shanghai, most DC, and all TPO were dismantled.[68] Only three courts survived in the whole province—the JHC and the Shanghai DC and the Jiangning DC. The other fifty-eight counties reverted to the practice of county magistrates performing judicial functions.[69]

In 1916, on orders from the MJ, the Shanghai DC and the Jiangning DC set up summary criminal chambers; summary civil chambers were to be added later. In late 1917, the First Branch HC (with a branch DC) was restored in Huaiyin, which would hear appeal cases from twenty-one counties in the northern and northwestern part of Jiangsu. After the MJ issued the Regulations on County Judicial Offices in 1917, no such offices were established in Jiangsu.[70] Not until 1922 and later were a few DC reestablished in Jiangsu. The Wu DC was built in July 1922. The Dantu DC was restored in late 1922.[71]

In 1924, the JHC had two civil chambers, each with a presiding judge and two judges, and one criminal chamber, with a presiding judge and four judges. The court had a staff of fifty-nine.[72] The JHP, under a chief procurator, consisted of the general managing section, penitentiary section, and records section, with a total staff of forty-six, including nineteen judicial policemen.[73]

The First Branch HC in Huaiyin, the Wu DC, the Shanghai DC, and the Jiangning DC were similarly staffed with varying numbers of personnel. The First Branch HC had one civil and one criminal chamber. The Jiangning DC, with a total of six judges and six probationary judges, had one civil and one criminal chamber, and a civil enforcement office. The Wu DC, with a total of six judges and five probationary judges, had one civil and one criminal chamber, one summary civil and one summary criminal chamber, and a civil enforcement office. The Shanghai DC, with a total of nine judges and ten probationary judges, had two civil chambers and one criminal chamber, one summary civil and one summary criminal chamber, and a civil enforcement office.[74]

After the GMD took over Jiangsu in 1927, no courts were built in Jiangsu before 1930.[75] New courts began to appear in the early 1930s. When the Provisional Court in Shanghai's International Settlement and the Mixed Court in the French Concession were integrated into the Chinese judiciary in April 1930, they became the First Special DC and the Second Special DC respectively.[76] In 1930–1934, three new DC were set up in Wuxi, Tongshan, and Tai; and a branch DC in Jiangdu and three county courts (CC) in Wujin, Nantong, and Songjiang were upgraded to DC.[77] In 1934, the Second Branch HC was set up inside the First Special DC, and the Third Branch inside the Second Special DC; the Fourth Branch was established in Tongshan and the Fifth in Zhengjiang.[78] Thus by 1935, there were five HC branches and ten DC in Jiangsu.[79]

Under the 1935 Law on Organizing Courts, Jiangsu would have a three-level-court and three-trial system. By 1937, with new DC added in Rugao, Dongtai, Huaiyin, Xinghua, Liyang, and Yixing, the number of DC reached eighteen (not including the two special DC in Shanghai); and except for Gaochun, which had a CJD, the remaining forty-two counties continued to see county magistrates performing judicial functions.[80] For a quick review, counties where county magistrates adjudicated litigation numbered fifty-eight after 1914, fifty-six after 1922, 46 after 1934, and forty-two in 1937.

By the mid 1930s, the personnel in all courts had increased. Table 4.3 shows the judicial personnel in provincial-level institutions in Jiangsu. Compiled in January 1935, the roll may not have been complete, with minor omissions. Juxtaposed with the increased number of cases handled by courts (see next section), one may conclude that the court system in the Nanjing decade became relatively more effective and efficient than before.

The Supply of and Demand for Judicial Functions

What difference did the formalization of judicial institutions and procedures make in the lives of ordinary citizens and in the functioning of the judiciary? One answer is that by setting up formal courts and uniform procedures, the reform increased the supply of state judicial functions or services, but also created an even greater societal demand for such functions or services, with a never-filled gap between the supply and the demand, in the form of case backlogs. In this section, an analysis is offered on the basis of provincewide statistical data to illustrate the issue; other effects of the reform in local society are explored in Part III.

Courts in Action

One measure of the effect of the reform is to see how many cases the court system in Jiangsu processed in the Beiyang era and the Nanjing decade and what changes took place between the two periods. Table 4.4 shows the total number of cases received and tried at the JHC, the Jiangning DC, and the Shanghai DC in fiscal years 1914–1917. In 1916, the case disposal rates at the three courts were 91.6 percent, 97.4 percent, and 97.7 percent respectively, or an average of 96.2 percent. Another source shows that in fiscal year 1917, three procurators at the JHP

TABLE 4.3

Judicial Personnel in Jiangsu Provincial Institutions, 1934

Institution	Head	Judge	Probationary judge	Apprentice judge	Clerk	Probationary clerk	Apprentice clerk	Record keeper	Warden	Total
High Court	1	19			32	6	15	41		114
1st Branch HC	1	3	9		7	3	4		1	28
4th Branch HC	1	3			6	2	3			15
Jiangning DC	1	10	4	4	15	4	3			41
Shanghai DC	1	18	10		29	7	4		2	71
Wu DC	1	5	7	2	8	5	2		1	31
Zhengjiang DC	1	5	1	1	11	2	1		1	23
Jiangdu Branch DC	1	1	4	1	2	2	3		1	15
Wuxi Branch DC	1	1	4	1	1	4	4		1	17
Wujin CC	1		2		1	2	3		1	10
Nantong CC	1		3		1	2	3		1	11
Songjiang CC	1		2		1	1	1		1	7

	Head	Procurator	Probationary procurator	Apprentice procurator	Clerk	Probationary clerk	Apprentice clerk	Record keeper	Coroner	
HC Procurator Office	1	5			9	2	6	10		33
1st BHC Pr. Office	1	1	1		4	1	1			9
4th BHC Pr. Office	1	1	1		4	1	1			9
Jiangning DC Pr. Off.	1	6	4	1	6	4	2	3	1	28
Shanghai DC Pr. Off.	1	6	7		8	4	1		3	30
Wu DC Pr. Office	1	3	2		5	2	1		2	16
Zhengjiang DC Pr. Off.	1	3	1		6	2			1	14
Jiangdu BDC Pr. Off.	1		3		1	1	2		1	9
Wuxi BDC Pr. Office	1		3		1	1	2		1	9
Wujin CC Pr. Office	1		1		1	1	1		1	6
Nantong CC Pr. Off.	1		1		1	1	1		1	6
Songjiang CC Pr. Off.	1		1		1	1				4

	Head	Section chief	Warden	Probation-ary warden	Teacher	Medical staff	
1st Prison	1	3		5	2	2	13
2nd Prison	1	3	3	4	2	2	15
3rd Prison	1	3		3	2	3	12
4th Prison	1	3		2	1	1	8
3rd Branch Prison	1			5	1	3	10
Tem. Detention Center	1			2		1	4
TOTAL							618

SOURCE: JGFD, RS-596.

TABLE 4.4
All Cases Processed at High and District Courts in Jiangsu, 1914–1917

	High Court	Jiangning District Court	Shanghai District Court	Total
		1914		
Civil	981	863	1,179	3,023
Criminal	557	991	4,837	6,385
TOTAL	1,538	1,854	6,016	9,408
Unclosed	203	69	54	326
		1915		
Civil	1,205	1,368	2,324	4,897
Criminal	947	1,179	2,682	4,808
TOTAL	2,152	2,547	5,006	9,705
Unclosed	90	163	14	267
		1916		
Civil	1,075	1,287	2,179	4,541
Criminal	943	971	2,028	3,942
TOTAL	2,018	2,258	4,207	8,483
Unclosed	169	63	96	328
		1917		
Civil	1,190	1,250	2,249	4,689
Criminal	840	940	2,187	3,967
TOTAL	2,030	2,190	4,436	8,656
Unclosed	181	61	29	271

SOURCE: ZG, 1918, no. 955.

handled 2,492 cases, including 614 prosecutions, 153 appeals and complaints, and 334 trial reviews.[81] On the other hand, as shown in Table 4.5, for fiscal year 1923, the JHC processed a total of 3,117 civil and criminal cases, most of which were appeals, trial reviews, and complaints. The court was able to dispose of 87.9 percent of the cases, leaving 12.1 percent of cases unclosed, a slight drop in the case disposal rate from 1916. Of all appeals, trial reviews, and complaints, decisions of lower courts and county trials were voided or changed in over one quarter (26.1 percent) of cases (not shown in the table). If the judicial judgment of the JHC judges may be trusted, the rate of correct decisions by lower court judges and county magistrates was 73.9 percent.

In comparison with the 1920s, the statistics from the 1930s shown in Table 4.6 indicate that (1) there was a great increase in the number

TABLE 4.5
All Cases Processed at the JHC and Its Branch, 1923

Civil	Total	Reject	Change	Settle	Other	Unclosed
High Court	1,350	697	279	33	176	165
2nd Trial	492	193	114	32	69	84
3rd Trial	529	329	114	1	18	67
Complaint	273	175	51		35	12
Other	56				54	2
First Branch High	301	166	62	13	28	32
2nd Trial	122	46	30	11	12	23
3rd Trial	95	63	14	2	10	6
Complaint	52	35	12		3	2
Other	32	22	6		3	1
Criminal	Total	Reject	Change	Withdraw	Other	Unclosed
High Court	1,074		349			94
2nd Trial	7	2	4			1
3rd Trial	629	172	341	33		83
Complaint	139	123	4	1	1	10
	Total	Approve	Change	Sent Back	Retrial	Unclosed
Tri. Review	299	65	66	123	11	344
	Total	Reject	Change	Withdraw	Other	Unclosed
First Branch High	392		123			87
3rd Trial	180	41	78	6		55
Complaint	69	49	7	8		5
	Total	Approve	Change	Sent Back		Unclosed
Tri. Review	143	34	38	44		27
GRAND TOTAL	3,117		813			378

SOURCE: JZN, 294–305.

of cases handled by the JHC; (2) the rate of wrong decisions of lower courts and county trials remained around one-quarter (24.1 percent); and (3) 12.7 percent of all cases received were unclosed, also comparable to the 1920s, even though the total number of cases handled showed a 168.5 percent rise, from 3,117 to 8,370 (the former number did, and the latter number did not, include cases handled at its branch courts, which means the increase should be greater if the cases at branch courts were included for the 1930s). In short, from 1923 to 1933, both the capacity of the JHC and the willingness of litigants to bring lawsuits to the court grew significantly.

Similarly, as shown in the Table 4.7, in 1923, the three DC in Jiangsu handled 12,835 cases a year, with a high disposal rate of 95.8 percent. At

TABLE 4.6

All Cases Processed at the JHC, 1933

Civil	Old	New	Total	Reject	Change	Settle	Withdraw	Other	Unclosed
2nd Trial	380	1,783	2,162	1,057	268	183	151	123	363
3rd Trial	60	551	611	423	93		13	19	63
Retrial	7	38	45						7
Complaint	20	981	1,001	686	191		10	96	17
Criminal	**Old**	**New**	**Total**	**Reject**	**Change**		**Withdraw**	**Other**	**Unclosed**
2nd Trial	445	2,419	2,864	729	1,318		245	79	493
3rd Trial	14	150	164	84	64		3		13
	Old	**New**	**Total**	**Conviction**	**Acquittal**		**No jurisdiction**	**Other**	**Unclosed**
1st Trial	38	57	95	61	26		2	2	4
	Old	**New**	**Total**	**Reject**	**Change**	**Sent back**	**Approve**	**Other**	**Unclosed**
Tri. Review	89		1,279		115	408	646	20	90
Complaint	7	273	244	187	35			13	9
GRAND TOTAL	928	7,442	8,370		2,020				1,059

SOURCE: JGFD, TJ-1713. "Old"—cases left from the previous year. "New"—cases received in the current year. "Settle"—litigants settled their suits without trial. "Withdraw"—appellants withdrew their appeals. "Change"—decisions in the lower court trial were voided or changed. "Sent back"—trial review cases were sent back to counties for retrial.

TABLE 4.7

All Cases Processed at District Courts in Jiangsu, 1923

Civil	1st Trial	2nd Trial	Complaint	Enforce	Other	Total	Unclosed
Jiangning	742	834	107	555	9	2,247	179
Wu	106	164	23	19	13	325	54
Shanghai	2,064	653	79	987	1,528	5,328	155
1st Branch Attached		355	87		45	487	67
TOTAL	2,912	2,006	296	1,561	1,595	8,387	455
Criminal	**1st Trial**	**2nd Trial**	**Complaint**	**Hearing**	**Other**	**Total**	**Unclosed**
Jiangning	1,472	38	2	23	118	1,653	20
Wu	408	25	1	48	40	422	31
Shanghai	1,952	33	12	118	114	2,321	30
1st Branch Attached		34	12		6	52	5
TOTAL	3,832	130	27	189	278	4,448	86
GRAND TOTAL	6,744	2,136	323	1,750	1,873	12,835	541

SOURCE: JZN, 285–286, 291–292. Note: The First Branch HC in Huaiyin had a DC attached and it heard appeal and complaint cases only.

TABLE 4.8

First Trials at District/County Courts and Counties in Jiangsu, 1934

Civil	Total	Unclosed	Civil	Total	Unclosed
Shanghai 1st Special DC	8,896	1,232	52 CGO	11,078	1,659
Shanghai 2nd Special DC	3,513	242			
Jiangning DC	1,328	132			
Shanghai DC	5,550	475			
Wu DC	965	80			
Wuxi Branch DC	638	71			
Zhengjiang DC	444	18			
Jiangdu Branch DC	707	38			
Wujin CC	346	28			
Nantong CC	477	27			
Songjiang CC	353	15			
TOTAL	23,217	2,358			
Criminal	**Total**	**Unclosed**	**Criminal**	**Total**	**Unclosed**
Shanghai 1st Special DC	8,170	33	52 CGO	17,025	2,284
Shanghai 2nd Special DC	5,245	38			
Jiangning DC	8,558	146			
Shanghai DC	7,670	191			
Wu DC	1,375	23			
Wuxi Branch DC	895	22			
Zhengjiang DC	569	10			
Jiangdu Branch DC	610	29			
Wujin CC	540	26			
Nantong CC	699	56			
Songjiang CC	275	12			
TOTAL	34,606	586			
GRAND TOTAL	57,823	2,944		28,103	3,943
PERCENTAGE	100%	5%		100%	14%

SOURCE: Sifayuan, 1936, 81, 207, 264, 654.

the same time, out of 2,302 appeals and complaints heard at those district courts, decisions by county magistrates were voided or changed in 591 cases, or about a quarter (25.7 percent) (not shown in the table).

In comparison with 1923, the statistics from 1934 in Table 4.8 show a dramatic rise in the number of cases processed by DC, branch DC, and CC. A high disposal rate of 95 percent, similar to that of the early 1920s, was achieved. Considering the absolute increase in the caseload from 12,835 to 57,823, or from 7,649 to 13,220 for the Shanghai DC alone (note that the numbers for 1934 were for first trial cases only, not including appeals and complaints), and considering the financial constraints under which those courts were operating, the achievement was remarkable.[82]

Another government source showed that in fiscal year 1934, the total number of cases accepted in all courts in Jiangsu was more than 84,000, with over 83,800 closed, and those accepted in all county offices numbered more than 51,700, with over 52,800 closed, including 1,100 cases accepted in previous years. On average, a judge at the JHC or a branch HC would handle 38 civil and 40 criminal cases a month; a judge at a DC would handle over 40 civil and more than 130 criminal cases (including some summary proceedings) a month.[83]

Case Backlogs

While the judicial capacity of the state grew dramatically, criminal and civil cases multiplied even faster, outpacing the system's capacity and resulting in case backlogs in all courts and county government offices. At the Wu DC, for example, 224 cases were pending in the month of May 1927. Of 72 cases of civil enforcement, one was being transferred to the procuracy because criminal acts were involved; in one, the properties in question were under investigation; and the rest were cases in which properties were in the process of being auctioned off or the proceeds thereof being handed over to creditors. Of 51 pending criminal cases, a witness had not responded to a summons in one; the defendants could not be located in four; and the rest were scheduled to be tried. Of 152 open civil cases (mostly appeal cases from county trials), two had been settled out of court; litigants had not paid fees in seven; lawsuits had been withdrawn in thirteen; case files had not been received from counties in twenty-three; and the rest were scheduled to be tried.[84] The unclosed cases had larger legal and social implications, examined in Chapter 6.

Like its Beiyang predecessor, the MJ in Nanjing considered case backlogs a serious issue, reflecting the judiciary's failure, and tried to rectify the situation. In November 1932, the SC borrowed judges from high courts to form a provisional chamber to process backlogged cases. The JHC contributed two judges, who were later officially appointed to the SC. The positions they vacated in the JHC were filled by judges transferred from district courts. Then in July 1933, under an order from the MJ, the JHC also formed a provisional chamber by transferring judges from district courts to dispose of backlogged cases. The provisional chamber was supposed to exist for six months, but by February 1934, there were still over 490 civil cases and over 430 criminal cases unclosed. The JHC requested an extension of another six months, which the MJ approved.[85]

The efforts to clear up case backlogs seemed futile or perpetual, because new cases continued to pile up faster than old cases were disposed of. As First Branch HC President Sheng Shibie testified, the number of new cases at his court rose steadily. Between January and October 1934, over 2,700 criminal and civil cases were received, 44.4 percent more than the same period in 1933. In April 1934, the case backlogs stood at 500, and the JHC sent four probationary judges to help dispose of them. Although those judges spared no efforts and disposed 900 cases more than the number in 1933, backlogs remained at more than 500, because new cases continued to flow in.[86] This example at one court gives a sense of the magnitude of the problem in the entire judicial system.

The problem of case backlogs, however, should not blind us to the achievements of the reform and the growing capacity of the judiciary. In fact, the rise of the societal demand for judicial services may be considered one of the positive results of the reform, because the reform broadened access to judicial process and therefore encouraged litigation.

The Prison System

Prison reform fared worse than building and operating the court system. As the capacity of the judicial system grew, even in counties where county magistrates adjudicated, the number of defendants waiting for trial and convicts serving time rose correspondingly. The demand for prison space and for rations to feed inmates constantly strained the judicial system, while the construction of new prisons and the improvement of conditions in county jails moved very slowly. Nevertheless, what was accomplished in prison reform would point to the same conclusions about the formalization agenda and the reach of the state as did the development of the court system.

Right after the 1911 Revolution, county jails remained under the authority of county magistrates. In late 1911, the Jiangsu Provisional Provincial Assembly resolved that prison affairs should be administered by judicial institutions and each county jail should have a warder, a head guard, and several guards. Cheng Dequan issued a directive asking all counties to keep on jailers and jail guards of the Qing era to maintain jails until district courts and procuracies were established. But in several counties, the new courts and procuracies refused to take over county jails, because judicial officers did not want to be responsible for funding the jails. Acting Governor Zhuang Yunkuan ordered county magistrates to take care of the expenses of maintaining county jails until new legislation on the issue was enacted by the Provincial Assembly.[87] With the retrenchment of the court system in 1913–1914 and the Prison Regulations of 1913, the county jail came under the jail overseer appointed by the magistrate and confirmed by the JHC, while the JHP would administer provincial prisons and detention houses.

During the Beiyang era, Jiangsu had seven new provincial prisons built over time. Jiangnan Model Prison in Nanjing had been built during the New Policy decade; its name was changed to the Jiangsu First Prison (JFP) in March 1917. It had 28 single cells and 68 communal cells, including 6 for female inmates. With a designed capacity for 752 inmates, it held 621 male and 38 female prisoners in 1924. Jiangsu Second Prison (JSP) in Chaohejing town, Shanghai county, had 18 single cells and 74 communal cells for male prisoners (for 520 people), and 20 communal cells for females (for 104). In 1924, it held 449 male inmates and 93 females. Jiangsu Third Prison (JTP) in Wu had 96 communal cells and 31 single cells (all for male prisoners), a capacity for 532 inmates; and in 1924, it housed 462 inmates. The branch of the JFP in Jiangning had 12 communal cells for 150 male inmates, but in 1924, it held 182 men. The branch of the JSP in the Chinese city in Shanghai had eight communal cells for 200 people. In 1924, it held 249 men. The branch of the JTP was in Suzhou. With a capacity for 530 (30 for female), it held 413 inmates in 1924.[88] Jiangsu Fourth Prison in Nantong was built from the scratch with donations from local gentry in 1919.[89] It had 48 cells for 240 males and nine cells for 40 females. In 1928, the prison held 244 men and more than 10 women.[90] Besides these new prisons, the JHC and three DC in Jiangning, Shanghai, and Wu had detention houses, each holding between over 100 and more than 300 defendants.[91]

The new prisons and detention houses only constituted a small part of the prison system in Jiangsu. The majority of convicts and defendants were held in old county jails and detention houses in fifty-seven of the sixty counties in the province. In 1924, the Jiangsu provincial prisons held 3,778 inmates, including 211 women, and county jails held 7,332 inmates altogether, including 389 women—a total of 11,110 inmates in the penal system in Jiangsu.[92]

Confronted with inadequate prison space, the Jiangsu provincial government and the JHC and the JHP tried to implement the call from Beijing to build more new prisons. In the early 1920s, they had a plan: to build ten new prisons and four branches to replace old county jails.

Each new prison would hold prisoners from surrounding counties (two to seven). Old jails would then become detention houses, which could also hold short-term convicts, so that new prisons would not be overcrowded. The plan seems to have followed Xu Shiying's plan of 1913 and was quite ambitious.[93]

The plan did not materialize. Official statistics show that no prisons were built in Jiangsu before 1929.[94] Not until 1935 were Jiangsu Fifth Prison in Wuxi (for 600 inmates) and a new branch prison in Jiangpu (for 200 inmates) built. Jiangsu Sixth Prison in Zhengjiang and Jiangsu Seventh Prison in Donghai were under construction at the time.[95] In 1936, the Seventh Prison was completed, but the old county jail still held inmates.[96] In 1935, the provincial prisons held over 9,920 inmates—520 more than the designed capacity, and all county jails housed over 15,100 inmates—3,500 more than the capacity.[97] Thus the prison system held a total number of 25,020 inmates, more than double the 1924 number, while prison space had only increased by a designed capacity for 800 inmates (the Fifth Prison and the branch prison in Jiangpu) by 1935.[98]

Answering a survey conducted by the Guangdong School of Law in August 1935, the JHC indicated that the prison system in Jiangsu held about 20,070 inmates at the time, half being convicts and the other half defendants (the figure was untruthful, belied by the statistics cited above). The court said that the prison finance depended on the budget, decided by the number of inmates. Each inmate was given ¥0.10 per day for rations and ¥2.00 per year for clothing and bedding. The provincial treasury spent ¥1,276,196 a year to fund the prison system.[99] These numbers reveal that the National Government underfunded the prison system by pretending that there were fewer inmates than there actually were, while its anti-drug campaign threw an unprecedentedly large number of inmates into the prison system precisely at that time (see Chapter 3).

In April 1937, prompted by a petition criticizing county jails sent by a resident in Zhengjiang to the Judicial Council, the MJ ordered the JHC president, Zhu Shusheng, to report on how county jails were being reformed and rebuilt in Jiangsu. Zhu's report showed that the number of new prisons had grown to eight. The plan for rebuilding and remodeling county jails was being carried out as follows: (1) new county prisons (*xian jianyu*) had been built in Wuxi and Donghai and were under construction in Tongshan and Zhengjiang; (2) remodeling of old jails had been completed in Jiangpu, Luhe, Feng, Xiao, and Changshu; (3)

remodeling of jails had been planned in Chuansha, Qidong, Guanyun, and Xinghua but not yet started; (4) remodeling of jails was not needed in nine counties, and was under preparation in eleven others; and (5) jails in the remaining twenty-four counties would be improved over a five-year period from 1937 to 1941. Unsatisfied with the pace at which the county jail reform was being pursued, the MJ pushed for a three-year (instead of five-year) schedule for item (5), but Zhu did not budge, citing a lack of financial resources. The MJ finally accepted Zhu's plan.[100] The implementation of the plan was, of course, interrupted by the Sino-Japanese War, which broke out in July 1937.

The above survey of judicial reform in Jiangsu serves as an example of how the reform was implemented at the provincial level and provides an institutional context in which to examine the same at the county level, along with a context of local society. Some attention has been paid to the agency and initiatives of the provincial judicial and administrative institutions and their interaction, and their responses to the reform agenda issued from the national capital. We see that the agenda of institutional and procedural formalization and the reach of the state were intertwined, and that both made important progress to a much larger degree than has been recognized in the scholarship on Republican China. Cheng Dequan, the first governor of Jiangsu in the Republican era, and the JHC from the Beiyang era to the Nanjing decade deserve credit for carrying out the reform initiatives and for what was achieved in 1912–1937, the limitations of the reform notwithstanding.

With the provincial-level reform examined, one begins to appreciate the achievements, difficulties, and unfinished tasks of the reform in Jiangsu (and probably to varying degrees in other provinces), but a better understanding has to include a sense of what was taking place at the county level. Besides the institutional framework at the provincial level, the financial constraints under which the judiciary had to work constituted an even more crucial context for the county judicial process. How county judicial functions were performed, how county jails were managed, and how the reform initiatives were implemented and undermined at the county level may be explained more clearly after a comprehensive examination of judicial finance at the national, provincial, and county levels.

CHAPTER 5

Judicial Finance: Nation, Province, and County

> Needless to say, without sufficient funding, the reform and reorganization of the judiciary cannot be expected to achieve results. In recent years, judicial funds have not always been delivered on time in the provinces. In some provinces, funds are several months in arrears, and in others, notices of payments are issued without actual money being given. It has been found during this inspection tour that in order to keep functioning, various courts in many provinces, being hard pressed for funds, have to use the judicial revenue that is supposed to be forwarded to the ministry, and even to borrow money under litigation held by courts. Court officials are constantly busy seeking funding, externally damaging the authority of the judiciary and internally failing to fulfill their duty of planning and supervising court operations. Court staffs are not motivated to work diligently, since owing to shortage of funds, their salaries are reduced or withheld, affecting their personal livelihoods.
>
> —Deputy Minister of Justice Zheng Tianxi, *Zhonghua faxue zazhi* (Journal of Chinese Legal Studies), January 1933[1]

The judicial reform in the Republican era cannot be fully understood without considering judicial finance. If the reform agendas were the proverbial half cup of water—to be regarded as "either woefully inadequate or strikingly effective,"[2] a look into the financial conditions under which the judicial system operated and the reform agendas were pursued will illuminate why the system was inadequate and why it might be considered rather effective under the circumstances. After all, formalizing the judiciary would cost a great deal of money. Equally important, the behavior of county judicial personnel needs to be explained in the context of scarce resources in local society and the survival strategies of local actors, among other things. This chapter provides an overview of judicial finance at the national, provincial, and county levels and analyzes the institutional logic of financial strains in the state system.

Two preliminary points may be made at the outset. First, the Republican state had rather limited capability to obtain revenue—it was unable to collect taxes cost-effectively.[3] In the Nanjing decade, the central, provincial, and local governments collected taxes consistently at below 10 percent of gross domestic product.[4] This was no more than what the Qing dynasty had collected as state revenue in the late nineteenth century.[5] Secondly, in 1912–1937, the state's national revenue was largely spent, in order of priority, on (1) military expenditures—maintaining armies and fighting civil wars, (2) foreign indemnities and foreign and domestic debt service, and (3) modernization projects in education, public security, government administration, and judicial functions. In other words, judicial funding was given a permanent back seat in government spending throughout the period. These two facts are the context in which the judicial reform and its funding will be examined.

A National Overview

The issue of finance had critical implications for the central government's reach at the provincial level. If a province faced financial strains and had to use its own resources to carry out projects mandated by the national capital, it would be less motivated to respond to such projects and would do so less effectively. In the New Policy decade, the time-honored decentralization of state finance under the Qing entailed that each province had to provide funding from its own revenues for the reform initiatives.[6] The belated attempt at a finance reform in 1909 led to few institutional changes by 1911, with little impact on how the New Policy reforms were financed.[7] Projects related to new schools and local self-government were often taken up by local elites and financed by local levies, which enraged the populace and contributed to the downfall of the Qing dynasty.[8] But the establishment of a modern judiciary, which was a function of the state by definition, was financed by provincial treasuries. In larger provinces, annual judicial funds alone amounted to more than one million taels in the New Policy years.[9] Provinces scrambled to find resources to finance various reform projects mandated by the imperial court; some appropriated funds from the salt tax, and others from customs duties, where those resources were available. The New Policy reform as a whole did not have a coherent and uniform financial underpinning.

Judicial Funding, 1912–1927

After the founding of the Republic, Beijing made plans to centralize provincial revenues on which to base a national budget. For that purpose, provincial departments of national taxation (*guoshui ting*) were set up.[10] These offices were designed to be agencies of the Ministry of Finance (MF) in the provinces, but in the end, they failed to serve that purpose and fell under the control of provincial governments, eventually becoming provincial finance departments (*caizheng ting*).[11]

The agenda of centralizing provincial revenues impacted provinces where the salt tax and customs duties had formerly been available as revenue sources. In 1913, the MJ asked the MF to allow provinces to continue allocating judicial funds from their own revenues, including the salt tax and customs duties. The MF responded that since the founding of the Republic, the salt tax and customs duties had been earmarked to service foreign debts, which concerned the credibility of the central government. Judicial funding could not come from those two sources anymore, but provincial governors could appropriate judicial funds from provincial revenues other than the salt tax and customs duties. The MJ communicated this message to the provinces.[12] Thus, the salt tax and customs duties became off-limits to provincial finance.

The MF's message indicates how the judicial system was funded in the Beiyang era. That is, the central government would come up with a national budget that included funding for judicial institutions in both the provinces and the national capital. Under the budget, provincial governments would withhold their shares from what they forwarded to Beijing as national revenue. By 1921, if not earlier, it had become accepted that no provinces forwarded any tax revenue to Beijing; they all withheld their revenue for provincial expenditures.[13] The reach of the central government at the provincial level was thus virtually nonexistent with respect to revenue collection. This is one of the major reasons why the central government of the Beiyang era was and is usually regarded as ineffective by contemporaries and historians.

What was the share of judicial funding in the national budget? Under the ordinary account of annual outlay of the 1916 budget, judicial funding amounted to ¥7,665,772, with ¥6,371,583 for all provinces, ¥324,000 for the MJ, ¥219,912 for the SC, and ¥742,764 for other institutions under the MJ. Under the extraordinary account of annual outlay, the judiciary had an additional amount of ¥45,572, of which ¥40,000 was for the MJ, the SC, and other judicial organs in Beijing.[14] Judicial funding accounted for about 1.63 percent of the projected total annual outlay for 1916 (¥1,519,436,000), behind educational expenditure (¥12,837,307, or 2.72 percent of the total).[15]

The projected judicial funding in the 1916 budget pointed to a decline in appropriation for the judiciary. Incomplete statistics show that judicial funding dropped from ¥10,348,535 in 1911 and ¥15,042,137 in 1913 to ¥7,258,459 in 1914 and ¥7,711,344 in 1916.[16] The steep drop reflected and explains the retrenchment of the court system in 1913–1914. Even the MJ was forced to reduce its staff. Under the July 1912 Regulations on Officialdom, the ministry was to have 123 positions, but in 1914, it actually had 94 officials and staff, plus 84 service crew, with a monthly expense of ¥21,636 in salaries, wages, and meal allowances (or an annual expense of ¥259,632).[17] The budget for the MJ in 1916 (¥324,000) was hardly an increase, considering operating costs beyond salaries, wages, and meal allowances.

Judicial Revenue

Provincial judicial funds came from regular tax revenues and were supplemented by judicial revenue—various fees paid by litigants and fines and confiscations from criminal convicts. The central government counted judicial revenue as a major source of judicial funding. In 1913, the MF required, with the endorsement of the MJ, that all provincial judicial organs make quarterly reports on their judicial revenue, including complaint form fees, litigation fees, fines, confiscated properties, and revenue from prison work, so that the MF could audit them.[18] It was the responsibility of the MJ to collect the information, however. The archival sources indicate that the MJ kept a close eye on this financial resource. The reporting of and accounting for judicial revenue constituted a large part of the paperwork that moved from the CGO and DC (and their branches), through the HC, to the MJ, along with other documents. This was at once part of the formalization scheme and a reflection of the real need to make every financial resource available to fund the system.

How much did the state collect from litigants as judicial fees? After 1912, the scale of judicial fees in the 1909 Provisional Regulations on Establishing Courts at All Levels was applied. In 1920, the MJ issued a new set of regulations on complaint forms and on litigation fees, and

TABLE 5.1

Judicial Fee Schedule Issued by the Ministry of Justice, 1921

(unit: ¥)

Action/Target of remedy	Fees	Action	Rate	Fees
Civil Litigation				
Under 10	0.3	Copying document	100 characters	0.1
10–24.99	0.6	Delivering document		0.1–0.5
25–49.99	1.5	Call for witness	1 person	0.5
50–74.99	2.2	Call for appraiser	1 person	0.5–5
75–99.99	3			
100–199.99	6			
200–299.99	8			
300–399.99	10			
400–499.99	12			
500–599.99	14			
600–699.99	16			
700–799.99	18			
800–899.99	20			
900–999.99	22			
1,000–1,999	25			
2,000–3,999	32			
4,000–5,999	42			
6,000–7,999	55			
8,000–9,999	70			
Above 10,000 add	3 per 1,000			
Civil Appeal				
Add	60%			
Civil Enforcement				
Under 25	0.3			
25–49.99	0.5			
50–99.99	1			
250–499	1.8			
500–999	2.5			
Above 1,000 add	1.5 per 1,000			

SOURCE: ZG, 1921, no. 1802.

it further revised them in 1921. The new regulations specified fourteen types of forms: (1) civil and (2) criminal complaints (*su*), (3) civil and (4) criminal defenses (*biansu*), (5) civil and (6) criminal appeals (*shangsu*), (7) civil and (8) criminal delegations (*weiren*), (9) limitations (*xian*), (10) submissions (*jiao*), (11) receipts (*ling*), (12) bail guarantees (*bao*), (13) affidavits (*jie*), and (14) out-of-court civil settlements (*hejie*), each costing ¥0.10–0.30.[19] Under the regulations, fees were collected for conducting trials, enforcing civil decisions, copying court documents, and delivering documents. Fees were classified on more scales than the 1909 regulations, as shown in Table 5.1.

The 1921 regulations on fees reduced the litigation fees set in 1909, and the more detailed scales (smaller increments) also helped reduce payments by litigants. Moreover, with guarantors attesting to their financial conditions, litigants who could not afford those fees were allowed to apply for reduction or waiver of relevant fees.[20] Thus there was an express agenda to assure that poor people had access to judicial process.

But, starting in 1914, the shortage of judicial funds forced the MJ to allow courts and county offices to add a surcharge of up to 50 percent to complaint form fees and litigation fees to help cover judicial expenses, which contradicted the intent of reducing litigation fees. The surcharge became so financially important to the judiciary that when the 1920 regulations reduced the rate of civil litigation fees, the First Branch HC in Jiangsu asked the JHC whether the 40 percent surcharge instituted earlier would still apply, and JHC President Zhu Xianwen replied yes, without consulting the MJ.[21]

The MJ policies, therefore, manifested two impulses: a concern to lessen the financial burden on litigants to broaden access to judicial process and a desire to find additional resources to fund the judicial system to allow it to operate. In 1920, the MJ told all courts to set up complaint-writing offices to standardize the practice of copying the complaints that litigants wrote onto official complaint forms for a fee. But the rate of the fee—8 copper coins per 300 characters—was much lower than the rate that courts in Jiangsu were using—16 copper coins per 100 characters. According to Zhu Xianwen, the rate change would mean a loss of ¥200 a month at the Shanghai DC alone. Zhu informed the MJ that while complaint-writing offices would be set up as ordered, the courts in Jiangsu would continue to use the old rate so as not to cause financial woes. The MJ did not object.[22] This may be viewed as an instance where the MJ was flexible and responsive to the provincial-level institutions within the judicial field, rather than as one of the ministry "losing control" over the provincial institutions.

How judicial revenue should be shared among institutions was a bone of contention. Not until May 1914 did the MF and MJ agree on a scheme. In a message to President Yuan Shikai asking for permission, they stated that to rationalize judicial revenue to help support the judiciary, a special account for the revenue was to be set up separately from the national budget, to be reincorporated into the budget when the processing of the revenue was reorganized and standardized. The scheme would operate as follows: (1) litigation fees would be collected through selling special print tax stamps; (2) fines and confiscations at HC and DC would be forwarded to the MJ, and those at CGO would supplement judicial funding in counties; and (3) complaint form fees would be collected through selling official complaint forms issued by the MJ. Half of the complaint form fees would be sent to the ministry and half would be kept by courts and county offices. The proposal was approved by Yuan.[23] This became the official scheme for appropriating judicial revenue. If the MJ managed to keep judicial revenue within the judicial system and centralized part of the revenue at its disposal, the significance of such a gain was only relative to the small share of judicial funding in the national budget to begin with.

The MJ demanded that provincial judicial organs use the ministry-issued complaint forms and forward the fees from selling the forms as the 1914 scheme required. When some provinces did not forward the fees two months after the scheme was formulated, the MJ suspected that the provinces were using locally produced complaint forms and pocketing the fees. On July 23, 1914, the MJ issued a directive that all judicial institutions in the provinces remit complaint form fees according to a rolling schedule. The MJ expressly prohibited high courts and procuracies from manufacturing their own complaint forms.[24] The ministry was trying to standardize complaint forms and control judicial revenue at the provincial level at the same time.

Judicial revenue proved to be so crucial in judicial finance that it came to be included in national budgets. The 1916 budget put ¥1,305,004 of judicial revenue in the category of "provincial revenues" and ¥35,410 of "Ministry of Justice revenues" in the category of "central institutions revenues." In other words, the financial planners in Beijing expected a total of ¥1,340,414 from judicial revenue, or 17.38 percent of the annual judicial funding (¥7,711,344), in the national budget.[25] As the May 1914 message from the MF and MJ would suggest, the processing of judicial revenue was deemed reorganized and standardized, and it was therefore incorporated into the budget by 1916.

In June 1920, the MJ further changed the way judicial revenue was allocated. In a joint proposal with the MF to the president of the Republic, the MJ stated that it would set up a special account, into which all judicial revenue would go, to fund construction of new courts and prisons; and expenses now covered by judicial revenue should be covered by regular provincial budgets.[26] With presidential approval, the MJ officially issued the new regulations on judicial revenue. It changed the 1914 arrangement as follows: (1) all litigation fees, fines, confiscations, and complaint form fees would be sent monthly by the HC to the MJ; and (2) registration fees (for property registration), income from prison work, and other revenues would be retained by courts, procuracies, and county offices, but how the funds were spent should be reported to the HC and the MJ.[27] By the new measure, the MJ cut itself a larger share of judicial revenue than under the 1914 scheme, but in practice the ministry did not always receive the judicial revenue it expected.

Analytically, the issue of who should get what share of judicial revenue may be viewed as a horizontal contention between the judicial and administrative sides of the state system, rather than a vertical contention between the provincial and central governments. The MJ tried to use judicial revenue to support expanding and formalizing the judiciary and make provincial administrative budgets finance the operation of the existing judicial functions. From this point of view, even if high courts failed to forward judicial revenue to the MJ, as long as the money was spent on the judiciary, it was acceptable to the MJ. In fact, the financial need for the judiciary to operate was such that supporting the existing functions was always a more pressing issue than building new courts and prisons. Very little, if any, judicial revenue was actually used for building new institutions, and therefore forwarding judicial revenue for that purpose was largely moot.

Judicial Funding, 1928–1937

Following many years of proposals and discussions, going back to 1912, a national conference in 1928 finally separated China's national finance (*zhongyang caizheng*) from provincial finance (*difang caizheng*). Henceforth, the central government would finance judicial institutions in the national capital, and provincial governments were responsible for funding the judiciary in their jurisdictions, while the MJ would continue to oversee accounting for judicial revenue from the provinces.

A direct result of the change was that the actual spending by the central government on judicial institutions in the capital increased. Table 5.2 shows that judicial expenditure more than quadrupled in a decade. But the funds allocated for the judiciary in the capital did not address the needs of judicial functions in the provinces. When Nanjing launched initiatives and issued orders regarding the judicial reform, funds necessary for the initiatives were for provincial governments

TABLE 5.2
Judicial and Total Expenditure by the Central Government, 1928–1937

Year	Judicial expenditure	Percentage of	Total expenditure
1928	913,844	0.20%	405,151,000
1929	1,362,245	0.20%	582,308,000
1930	1,853,376	0.20%	773,761,000
1931	2,182,485	0.30%	747,734,000
1932	2,493,228	0.40%	705,215,000
1933	2,676,359	0.30%	811,709,000
1934	2,963,910	0.30%	1,069,354,000
1935	2,834,805		
1936	3,240,898		
1937	4,315,894		

SOURCE: Jia Dehuai, 1941, 229, 235. Another source gives somewhat lower numbers as judicial expenditure for 1934–1936 (Sifayuan, 1936, 78; 1938b, 507)

to worry about. In a sense, this was a return to the Qing practice of provinces financing not only regular state functions with their own resources but also reform projects mandated by the central government, with similar institutional and social implications. Jiangsu can serve as an example of how provincial judicial finance fared in the Beiyang era and the Nanjing decade.

Judicial Finance in Jiangsu

Judicial Funding in the Beiyang Era

"Provincial judicial finance" refers, first of all, to the judicial funds a province was entitled to withhold from the national tax revenue under the national budget, and its distribution among the courts, procuracies, and county offices performing judicial functions, and, secondly, to the judicial revenue generated by those institutions. The provincial budget allocated judicial funds to courts and procuracies, but not to county offices, whose judicial functions were paid for out of county general funds, that is, what counties were allowed to withhold from tax revenues destined for the provincial treasury.

In the New Policy decade, Jiangsu carried out the reform with its own resources. In January 1911, in order to establish trial courts in Jiangsu, certain counties were merged with neighboring counties so as to save the expense of operating county governments and paying the salaries of magistrates. In all, twelve counties were abolished and more than 100,000 taels of silver were saved to help fund the new courts.[28] A training institute for coroners was set up in 1909, but it was closed down after 1911, when the funding had been exhausted.[29]

After the 1911 Revolution, the Provincial Assembly decided that counties could withhold 5 percent of their land tax as judicial funds, but many counties argued that land tax revenue varied among counties; for counties that did not have much land tax to collect, 5 percent of it would be too little to cover judicial expenses. In response, the assembly stated in 1912 that the provincial government would allocate judicial funds for all counties; counties that had little tax revenue would be given more funds and those that had more tax revenue should forward their surplus, after covering expenses, to the provincial government.[30] This scheme did not work, and poorer counties would always be worse off in funding their judicial functions.

A sharp drop in judicial funding in the national budget in 1913–1914 seriously impacted Jiangsu, where judicial funds were cut by three-quarters. District courts and CFI in Wujin, Taicang, Songjiang, Jiangdu, Nantong, Huai'an, and Tongshan were dismantled in April 1914, but the reduced judicial funds were still not sufficient to finance the JHC, the First Branch HC, and provincial prisons. Scrambling for funds, the JHC and JHP asked the governor for permission to appropriate litigation fees and complaint form fees collected in counties to help support the provincial judicial institutions, but this proposal was undercut when the MJ and MF decreed in May 1914 that counties and judicial institutions had to pay half of the complaint form fees they received into a special national account.[31]

Like the central government, the provincial governor expected judicial revenue to supply a larger share of judicial expenses. In 1914, Governor Han Guojun reduced judicial funds for 1915 from ¥240,000 to ¥180,000, expecting the gap to be filled by judicial revenue. However, the judicial revenue collected in 1914 amounted to only ¥10,000. In early 1915, some counties asked for permission to use the surplus from inmate ration funds at county jails to help cover judicial expenses, while others asked for additional funding. Qi Yaolin, the new governor, approved the use of the inmate ration fund surplus, if such a surplus existed.[32] But in some county jails, the inmate population rose unexpectedly, causing a deficit rather than a surplus. The JHC president Cai

TABLE 5.3

Judicial Expenditures in Jiangsu, 1921

(unit: ¥)

High Court	69,557
1st Branch High Court	38,560
Jiangning District Court	32,876
Shanghai District Court	61,004
Wuxian District Court	24,936*
Dantu District Court	24,936*
JHP	42,624
1st Branch JHP	21,979
Jiangning District Procuracy	32,724
Shanghai District Procuracy	37,921
Wuxian District Procuracy	24,552*
Fifty-six County Offices	278,381
TOTAL	690,050

SOURCE: KSJ, 165–173, 234.
*Budgeted expenditure.

Yuankang informed Qi Yaolin that whereas the county jail in Jiangdu was allocated rations for 30 inmates, it actually held more than 120 inmates, and that most counties were feeling the financial pinch and asking for additional funding. Cai stated that he could not advocate additional funding, for fear of a deficit in the provincial budget. But Qi decided that from January 1916 on, general funds for all counties would be increased by 10 percent, or more than ¥87,000 for the year, to help cover judicial expenses in counties.[33] This was a rare instance where the provincial governor responded to financial strains at the county level. From then on, 10 percent of county general funds became the normal share for judicial functions.

In the years after 1916, judicial finance in Jiangsu seems to have improved somewhat, partly due to the surcharge imposed on various judicial fees instituted in counties that year. Table 5.3 shows the budgets (marked by *) or actual expenditures for all courts, procuracies, and counties in Jiangsu in 1921. This leads us to an examination of judicial revenue in the province.

Judicial Revenue in Jiangsu

Judicial institutions and county offices in Jiangsu generated a steadily rising amount of judicial revenue, which helped fund judicial functions. It was not uncommon for appeal cases to be rejected by the

TABLE 5.4

Judicial Revenue from Courts in Jiangsu, 1917–1922

(unit: ¥)

	Fiscal year					
	1917	1918	1919	1920	1921	1922
High Court	6,111	9,764	8,848	12,445	20,869	29,523
1st Branch HC	1,086	3,362	4,598	5,391	6,765	10,440
Shanghai DC	19,916	25,529	33,811	34,124	43,658	56,006
Jiangning DC	6,724	7,894	8,530	8,046	13,576	16,237
Wuxian DC						17,946
Dantu DC						5,959
TOTAL	33,837	46,549	55,787	60,006	84,868	136,111

SOURCE: JGFD, GZ-90.

JHC because the necessary judicial stamps had not been affixed to the complaint form.[34] Such enforcement contributed to the rise of judicial revenue. For July 1914, the JHC reported ¥3,956 in litigation fees from the First Branch HC, the two DC in Jiangning and Shanghai, and all counties.[35] Assuming that the number was typical for a month, the annual total would have been ¥47,472. Another set of data shows the judicial revenue collected at the JHC, the First Branch HC, and four district courts during 1917–1922, as seen in Table 5.4.

An important finding here is that judicial revenue made up an increasingly larger share of judicial funding in the province. A comparison of Table 5.3 and Table 5.4 reveals that for 1921, the judicial revenue collected at the JHC constituted 30 percent of the judicial expenses there; 41.3 percent at the Jiangning DC; 71.6 percent at the Shanghai DC, and so forth. The increase in judicial revenue at the JHC was due in part to surcharges on litigation fees (added in 1919) and on fees for copying court documents and for lawyers' registration (1920), and in part to the imposition of fees for filling out complaint forms and delivering court documents (1921).[36]

How much of the judicial revenue was spent in the province and by whom? In 1919, 1920, and 1921, the JHC, the First Branch HC, the DC in Jiangning, Shanghai, and Wu, and fifty-seven county offices generated an average annual revenue of ¥95,778.[37] Of that amount, each year, the courts retained ¥71,139 (74.3 percent), of which ¥24,999 was formally allocated by the FD and the remaining ¥46,140 was retained and directly spent by those institutions.[38] In the same three-year period, the DP in those jurisdictions collected an average annual revenue of ¥94,630 from fines, complaint form fees, prison work, and confiscations (in that order). With MJ approval, the DP retained an average of ¥72,931 (77.1 percent) of the revenue each year.[39] Thus those DC and DP retained about three-quarters of the reported judicial revenue generated in the province, while the rest, plus an unknown amount of unreported or underreported judicial revenue, was retained by and spent in counties.

To conclude, judicial revenue was helpful in supporting the operation of the existing courts, but insufficient in itself to completely relieve the financial strains on the judicial system, let alone for building new courts and prisons as the MJ and MF envisioned.

The Provincial Treasury and Judicial Revenue

Provincial judicial finance was one of the arenas where the competition for financial resources between the judicial and administrative fields within the state system took place. As early as 1913, Minister of Justice Liang Qichao observed that whereas provincial governors were able to take from provincial revenues whatever they needed, judicial institutions, as a separate system, were unable to get the necessary funds.[40] Provincial governors consistently tended to neglect or sacrifice judicial funding whenever money was tight. The MJ sent a telegram to all provincial governors pleading for cooperation in judicial funding in their provinces in the wake of the 1925 May 30th Incident (the British-controlled police killing Chinese students in Shanghai's International Settlement), which it used to highlight the necessity of abolishing extraterritoriality and the imperative of developing the judiciary. The telegram urged governors to instruct the provincial finance departments to deliver funds for the judiciary in a timely fashion.[41] Highlighting the critical importance of the provincial government in financing judicial functions in a province, the plea suggests that such cooperation was often absent.

Besides the proper allocation and timely delivery of funds for the judiciary by the provincial treasury, the handling of judicial revenue was also an issue that reflected the judicial-administrative tension. When financially stressed, provincial governments were tempted to count judicial revenue toward the provincial judicial funds that should normally have come from the provincial budget, thus undermining the funding for the judiciary. The following episode shows how and why that happened.

In 1923, the Jiangsu provincial government faced a deficit of more than ¥13.3 million that had piled up over the years and was in addition to more than ¥2.68 million in the red in the 1923 budget. In January 1924, a finance reorganization committee appointed by Governor Han Guojun proposed to reduce expenses in the remaining months of the fiscal year (to July 1, 1924) and vigorously collect the remaining tax revenue for the year. The committee called for a saving of ¥1,717,834 by reducing the budget of all institutions. The cut in judicial funding was ¥60,000, to be offset by judicial revenue. The amount was a fraction in the total projected savings, but a great deal of money for the judiciary to lose. When informed of the decision, the JHC's president, Zhu Xianwen, and the JHP's chief, Zhou Yike, immediately petitioned Han, begging to disagree. The judiciary in Jiangsu was funded under the budget of 1919, but over the years the cost of operating the system had risen considerably due to inflation and the increases in caseloads and the prison population. Judicial revenue was always used to help cover judicial expenses, since the annual expenses of the judiciary amounted to ¥500,000, while the provincial treasury only provided ¥301,230. There was no way to generate another ¥60,000 of judicial revenue to offset the new cut.

When informed of the situation in Jiangsu, the MJ made the same point and requested Han Guojun to reconsider the decision. But Han refused to budge and asked the ministry to understand the province's financial difficulties. In April, the MJ agreed to share the burden—it would take a cut of ¥30,000 in judicial revenue from the province. Having won the concession, however, Han continued to insist that another ¥30,000 still had to come from the provincial judiciary. In the end, Zhu and Zhou decided that the ¥30,000 that the MJ relinquished would be borne by the JHC, the First Branch HC, and the four DC (¥15,000) and by the DP (¥15,000). The other ¥30,000 of the reduction would be realized by a cut of ¥20,000 from a total of ¥79,670 in county judicial funds (10 percent of the county general funds) and by a cut of ¥10,000 from a total of ¥30,000 in county detention house funds (separate from judicial funds). Counties were supposed to offset the cut by vigorously collecting judicial revenue to the last penny.[42] It appears that the provincial government expected the judicial system to be able to economize and absorb a cut of ¥60,000 a year. Similarly, the JHC expected counties to be able to dig up underreported and undercollected judicial revenue or just function with reduced funds, even though it knew, and argued with the governor and the FD, that with reduced funds, the quality of services the judiciary provided would suffer, alluding, of course, to case backlogs, prison overcrowding, irregularities, and abuses.

As this illustrates, the competition for resources took place mainly between the judicial and administrative fields, rather than between the central and provincial levels, of the state system; moreover, the structure of judicial finance was such that by institutional logic, counties would be the losers in the competition for funds, because the bottom layer of the state system—counties—was expected to be able to squeeze money directly from citizens. Part III of this book will show that, in addition to ordinary taxpayers, civil litigants, criminal defendants, and county jail inmates would ultimately pay the price.

The Nanjing Decade

Although the GMD government separated national and provincial finances in 1928, Jiangsu did not have a provincial budget until 1933, when Chen Guofu became the chairman of the provincial government. Chen attributed the earlier situation to various agencies pursuing misguided financial self-sufficiency, which only caused provincial finance as a whole to run out of control.[43] With that in mind, let us take a look at the judicial expenditure in Jiangsu in 1931–1936, shown in Table 5.5.

The table indicates a gradual increase in provincial judicial expenditure in Jiangsu in the 1930s, but it was much slower than the rise of the total expenditure by the provincial government in the same period. Compared with the judicial funding from the central government to the provinces in 1916 (a total of ¥6,377,155 for all twenty-six provinces and an average of ¥245,275 each), judicial funding in Jiangsu in the Nanjing

TABLE 5.5

Provincial Judicial Expenditure in Jiangsu, 1931–1936

(unit: ¥)

Year	Judicial Expenditure	Percentage of	Total expenditure
1931	1,214,471	5.94%	20,453,810
1932	1,220,628	5.24%	23,284,719
1933	1,923,141	6.99%	27,507,939
1934	1,967,765	8.45%	23,298,995
1935	2,413,347	5.60%	43,093,054
1936	1,812,185	3.89%	46,539,677

SOURCE: Shi Yangcheng, 1946, 322–338. Another source of the 1930s vantage point shows higher numbers in judicial expenses and lower numbers in total outlay for 1933, 1934, 1935, and 1936 (Chen Guofu, 1983, caizheng, 3–4). The numbers I cite here were compiled in the 1940s and are based on the National Government Yearbooks and the National Government Statistics Monthly.

TABLE 5.6

Revenue from Judicial Institutions in Jiangsu, 1931–1933

(unit: ¥)

	Fiscal year		
	1931	1932	1933
HC	78,922	99,883	69,446
1st Branch HC	8,989	6,569	8,740
Jiangning DC	47,895	70,373	94,596
Shanghai DC	107,872	169,803	201,728
Wu DC	31,923	37,347	41,898
Zhengjiang DC	22,067	22,748	24,409
Jiangdu CC	17,121	30,045	29,492
Wujin CC	15,716	17,895	18,285
Nantong CC	14,052	18,065	20,971
Wuxi CC	15,476	26,504	27,927
Songjiang CC	9,586	13,825	13,990
Fifty-two CGO	120,769	138,820	156,888
1st Prison	895	8,443	8,766
2nd Prison	5,033	10,676	13,494
3rd Prison	2,228	2,711	2,268
4th Prison	2,025	2,148	1,843
3rd Branch Prison	1,510	1,639	1,471
Temp. Detention Center	399	246	643
Wujin C. Prison	201	135	289
Wuxi C. Prison	235	657	953
Huaiyin C. Prison	46	32	49
Haimen C. Prison	38	68	91
Jiading C. Prison		14	26
Xinghua C. Prison		71	80
Changshu C. Prison			23
Taicang C. Prison			104
Chongming C. Prison			257
TOTAL	502,998	678,717	738,729

SOURCE: JGFD, TJ-1418. Another source indicates that in fiscal year 1933, the Shanghai DC spent ¥198,460 (MDWH, 2-1456).

decade increased over 1916. But these numbers did not reflect the actual expenditure on the judiciary in the province, because they did not include the judicial revenue generated in the province, much of which was retained there. In 1934, the MJ allowed ¥3,548,138 of judicial revenue to be retained by judicial institutions in all provinces, which was called "state subsidies to local judicial expenses."[44]

Despite the increase, however, judicial funding in the Nanjing de-

TABLE 5.7

Judicial Expenditure and Funding Sources in Jiangsu, 1931–1933

(unit: ¥)

Sources of funding/year	1931	1932	1933
Provincial Treasury	1,274,060 (59.6%)	1,517,985 (65.9%)	1,530,757 (65.3%)
Judicial Revenue	428,945 (20.1%)	515,083 (22.4%)	544,392 (23.2%)
Shifting Payment	433,026 (20.3%)	271,449 (11.7%)	268,243 (11.5%)
TOTAL	2,136.031 (100%)	2,304,517 (100%)	2,343,392 (100%)

SOURCE: JGFD, TJ-1418.

cade still fell short of what was needed to achieve the goal of the judicial reform. To grasp provincial judicial finance further, one may compare the above statistics with those in Table 5.6, based on archival sources, showing the raw data of judicial revenue in Jiangsu in 1931–1933. Besides the regular annual revenue shown in the table, there were local donations in the category of "one-time annual revenue," which amounted to ¥26,819 in 1931, ¥8,046 in 1932, and ¥24,329 in 1933.[45]

The archives corroborate what was reported in the national statistics—a steady increase in judicial revenue in the 1930s. This reflected an expansion of the capacities of the judicial institutions and county offices processing all cases, especially civil litigation, which generated more revenue than criminal prosecutions. To see that side of judicial finance, we turn to judicial expenses, as shown in Table 5.7.

Three things should be noted here. First, comparing Table 5.7 with Table 5.6, we notice that spent judicial revenue (¥428,945) was 85.3 percent of the total judicial revenue (¥502,998) in Jiangsu in 1931, 75.9 percent in 1932, and 73.7 percent in 1933. In other words, only the much smaller remainders were forwarded to the Ministry of Justice. In fact, in the Nanjing decade, the portion of judicial revenue required to be sent to the MJ was officially reduced. By 1935, only one-third of complaint form fees and one-quarter of judicial fees with judicial stamps (trial, enforcement, delivery, copying, registration, fines, petition, etc.) were sent to the MJ to cover the cost of manufacturing complaint forms and judicial stamps. Confiscations, complaint-writing fees, and prison work income were retained directly by courts and counties.[46]

Second, the category of "shifting payments" (*nuo dian*) means that there was a gap between what was funded and what was needed, which was patched up by resorting to other funds or raising new funds somehow. This portion of expenses was typically spent by the CGO on county detention houses where the number of defendants rose unexpectedly. The shifting payments amounted to ¥98,973 in 1931, ¥77,695 in 1932, and ¥48,907 in 1933.[47] To put this in perspective, the number for 1931 would mean an average monthly amount of ¥158.61 for each of fifty-two counties.

Finally, Table 5.6 does, and Table 5.7 does not, include the local donations. That such funds were accounted for at all is noteworthy, given the prevailing impression of chaos and corruption in county-level governance at that time, though it is not known whether any similar donations ever went unaccounted for.

To conclude, judicial expenses in Jiangsu increased in the Nanjing decade over the Beiyang era. It is unclear whether this was due to the separation of national and provincial finances or due to the fact that Jiangsu was now the political center of the country. As for the contention for resources between the judicial and administrative fields within the state system, it did not end with the establishment of the National Government in Nanjing.

County Judicial Finance

No Separate Judicial Funds

County governments faced two issues in judicial finance. First, prior to 1934, there was no independent county budget in Jiangsu. Counties took whatever the provincial FD allowed them to withhold from taxes destined for the provincial treasury. Inevitably, counties always got the short end of the stick.[48] As contemporary critics noted, counties lacked resources to carry out initiatives mandated by the central and provincial governments, relied on surcharges on regular taxes, had no means to initiate programs beneficial to local society, and engaged in accounting irregularities.[49]

Second, there were no judicial funds separate from general funds in counties. In 1922, among the twenty-one provinces that drew up provincial budgets, only seven had some delineation between judicial funds and general funds at the county level. Jiangsu did not separate the two kinds of funds and did not include judicial revenue in its budgets.[50] The

TABLE 5.8

Provincial Expenses on Judicial Functions of Fifty-eight Counties, 1917–1922

(unit: ¥)

Fiscal year	1917	1918	1919	1920	1921	1922
Special Grade County	1	1	1	1	2	2
Salary	1,920	1,920	1,920	3,394	3,320 + 2,046	101 + 1,920
Operation	1,920	1,920	1,920	1,100	2,061 + 1,893	101 + 1,920
Detention House	5,760	5,760	5,760	5,891	4,867 + 2,555	324 + 2,427
TOTAL	9,600	9,600	9,600	10,385	10,248 + 6,494	526 + 6,267
1st Grade Counties	8	8	8	10	10	10
Salary	11,136	11,136	11,136	17,756	18,764	17,826
Operation	9,024	9,024	9,024	10,933	14,976	14,227
Detention House	21,504	21,504	21,504	20,865	24,589	23,130
TOTAL	41,664	41,664	41,664	49,554	58,329	55,183
2nd Grade Counties	14	14	14	13	15	15
Salary	18,480	18,480	18,480	20,720	24,657	25,080
Operation	15,792	15,792	15,792	8,682	11,882	12,188
Detention House	21,504	21,504	21,504	21,529	25,827	28,029
TOTAL	55,776	55,776	55,776	50,931	62,366	65,297
3rd Grade Counties	16	16	16	15	14	14
Salary	13,440	13,440	13,440	19,944	13,031	13,324
Operation	10,368	10,368	10,368	7,339	7,920	8,072
Detention House	15,360	15,360	15,360	16,360	17,560	18,612
TOTAL	39,168	39,168	39,168	43,643	38,511	40,008
4th Grade Counties	19	19	19	19	18	18
Salary	15,504	15,504	15,504	11,839	11,523	12,025
Operation	11,856	11,856	11,856	11,355	13,138	13,112
Detention House	10,944	10,944	10,944	22,353	24,157	25,061
TOTAL	38,304	38,304	38,304	45,547	48,818	50,198
GRAND TOTAL	184,512	184,512	184,512	200,060	224,766	217,479

SOURCES: JGFD, GZ-90. Note: The special grade county in 1917–1920 was Wu; Wujin was upgraded to that status in 1921. The DC and the DP were set up in Wu in July 1922, and in Dantu in January 1922, which explains the drop in funding for the two counties in that year.

absence of judicial funds in county finance probably resulted from the practice of magistrates performing judicial functions, which tended to suppress the need to separate judicial funds from administrative funds. Separately accounting for judicial funds would have uncomfortably exposed the inadequacy of county revenues overall, creating "inflexibility" for the magistrate in spending money to perform his functions.[51]

Since counties did not have judicial budgets, their judicial expenses depended mainly on the general funds from the FD under a provincial budget. Table 5.8 shows the provincial budget for the judicial functions of fifty-eight counties during 1917–1922.

The numbers for 1917–1919 in Table 5.8 are from the provincial budget and do not reflect the actual judicial spending in counties, because counties had to find ways to fill the gap between the provincial funds and the actual needs at their locales, but those "fillers" were not shown.[52] From 1916 on, counties were to take 10 percent out of general funds for judicial expenses, so the numbers for 1920–1922 reflected the actual payout from the provincial treasury but not the actual expenses in counties. In 1917–1922, the salaries of county judicial staff took a much smaller share of county judicial funds than the county-level courts and procuracies in 1912–1913 did, which helps explain why few courts were established in counties and why county judicial personnel tried to collect irregular fees to supplement their income.

Judicial Revenue in Counties

All counties resorted to judicial revenue to help support their judicial functions. Before surcharge on litigation fees was instituted, judicial revenue was very limited.[53] After a 40 percent surcharge on litigation fees was instituted in July 1914, county judicial revenue increased. In July–November 1914, thirty-five counties in Jiangsu collected ¥7,235 in complaint form fees, averaging ¥41 a month for each county. In the same period, thirty-three counties collected fines worth ¥29,274, or ¥177 a county per month.[54] County reports on complaint form fees indicate that all surcharges on the fees were retained by counties, and that only 50 percent of complaint form fees *before* the surcharge went to the Ministry of Justice (*yingjie yuanjia wucheng*).[55]

Besides the MJ, the provincial government also made policies concerning judicial revenue. In 1920, the governor ordered that counties forward all litigation fees to the FD (the JHC could use that fund with the governor's approval). Counties were to retain judicial revenue other than litigation fees.[56] Table 5.9 shows the judicial revenue that all counties retained in 1917–1922.

The data from 1917–1919 show that only a smaller percentage of the revenue came from litigation fees—projected to be 34.4 percent in the 1917 provincial budget, but actually only 21 percent in 1920, 18.5 percent in 1921, and 10.3 percent in 1922—and the bulk of the revenue came from surcharges on fees and from fines and confiscations. Besides

TABLE 5.9

Judicial Revenue Retained by All Counties, 1917–1922

(unit: ¥)

Fiscal year	1917	1918	1919	1920	1921	1922
Litigation fees	32,000	32,000	32,000	32,884	31,667	15,833
Surcharges, fines, and confiscations	60,970	60,970	60,970	123,501	139,608	138,426
TOTAL from all counties	92,970	92,970	92,970	156,385	171,275	154, 259

SOURCE: JGFD, GZ-90.

these, counties retained other fees and surcharges that did not enter the provincial books. Those included fees and surcharges for enforcing civil judgments and copying and delivering documents, not to mention irregular charges collected and pocketed by county functionaries. Conceivably, those unreported revenues would have been the sources, at least in part, of the "shifting payments" the magistrate had to come up with when necessary.

Squeezing County Funds

As noted earlier, thanks to institutional logic, when there were financial strains in the province, counties were the first to be squeezed. In 1924, Governor Han Guojun reduced the funds for county detention houses by ¥20,000, to be made up for by counties through more vigorous collection of judicial revenue—in his view, there was more that could be collected, either as judicial revenue or under whatever other title. Han ordered that from 1925 on, counties north of the Yangzi River provide half of the county detention house funds out of their own resources. When those counties complained, the JHP was inclined to allow them to use the "national treasury subsidy" that was in the coffer of the provincial treasury, but Han objected. Not surprisingly, fiscal year 1925 ended with deficits in forty-eight counties.[57]

In August 1926, the JHP chief, Zhou Yike, concluded, like Han, that counties did not vigorously collect and truthfully report judicial revenue. He decided that from 1926 on, 5 percent of county general funds (¥40,200) and the national treasury subsidy (¥20,000) for county detention houses would be distributed among counties; after that, any shortfall in the funds would have to be made up by counties out of their own resources, including judicial revenue. The twenty-five counties on the former Huaiyang and Xuhai circuits—the poorer northern part of the province—would be responsible for half of their detention house funds, and the thirty-one counties on the former Jinling, Suchang, and Huhai circuits would be responsible for 70 percent of their funds. Chen Taoyi, the new governor, approved the plan.[58]

The decision alarmed magistrates. Eight magistrates on the former Xuhai circuit jointly petitioned Zhou Yike. Out of all litigation in their counties, which suffered from poverty and rampant banditry, civil cases amounted to fewer than 10 percent; 20 percent were homicide cases; and 70 percent, banditry cases. Inmates in county detention houses were mostly banditry suspects, who were difficult to convict and could not be lightly released, for fear of harm to local security, but had to be fed. In Tongshan, running the detention house cost ¥6,000 a year, and there was no way to get half of it (¥3,000) from fines. The chiefs made a point that under the code of conduct for officials, they were unable to squeeze defendants so as to maximize judicial revenue. These petitions did not move Zhou, however.[59] The county judicial funds for 1926, separate from the county detention house funds, showed a total deficit of ¥96,600 in forty-four counties after provincial funds and judicial revenue were spent (because of the turmoil caused by the Northern Expedition, twelve counties did not report).[60]

In short, a pattern emerges from the sources that whenever finance was tight, the provincial authorities, either administrative or judicial or both, would shortchange counties, on the assumption that they would be able to dig up unreported or undercollected revenues or simply squeeze litigants and taxpayers in general more vigorously to make ends meet. In this configuration, the contention for resources was between the administrative and judicial fields of the state system, as well as between the provincial authorities and county governments, since judicial and administrative functions were performed by the same institutions in those counties.

The Nanjing Decade

As noted earlier, Nanjing separated national and provincial finances in 1928, but there was still no independent county budget. In an effort to distinguish county finance from provincial finance, the national finance conference of 1934 adopted the Standard Principles of Dividing

Revenue and Expenditure Between Provinces and Counties. But the broad principles established at the national level had only a limited impact at the provincial and county levels. As provinces were allowed to design specific formulas to divide financial resources between province and counties, the actual situation of provincial and county finances varied from province to province.[61]

Counties in Jiangsu did not have budgets prior to 1934, each spending whatever it could acquire as revenue.[62] In 1934, the FD in Jiangsu began to draw up a budget for all counties, in the spirit of the Standard Principles. At the same time, the provincial government proceeded with another mandate from the conference to abolish local levies and surcharges. A total of 632 kinds of levies in all counties were abolished in five steps during 1934–1936, amounting to ¥1,243,026 a year. County governments would directly collect all legal taxes and fees, and any form of tax farming was banned.[63]

Judicial funds in the post-1934 county budget were insignificant. The judicial revenue that counties collected accounted for 67 percent of judicial expenses in 1935.[64] At the same time, county detention house funds came separately from the provincial judicial funds.[65] Beyond the regular fund for county judicial functions, the provincial authorities would not provide extra money for any county that went into deficit. When the Songjiang magistrate, Jin Qingzhang, requested permission to use surplus detention house funds to cover judicial expenses in August 1929, the JHC responded by asking that he find ways to solve the problem on his own. Jin wrote back, noting that to tell a magistrate to cope with the deficit on his own amounted to asking him to donate his personal money; while the honest might be willing to do so, the cunning would resort to irregularities, both harming the judicial reform and contravening the code of conduct for officials.[66] Jin stated the obvious, which the JHC president probably knew as well: to ask a magistrate to find resources on his own to perform his official duties was to ask him to squeeze litigants and taxpayers any way he could, in the form of irregular levies and surcharges, which were to be abolished in the 1930s (one cannot but suspect that abolished levies would come back in new guises).

How did counties manage to make ends meet and perform their judicial functions, given the persistent underfunding, shortfalls, and accounting abuses? The glimpses of county judicial functions provided in the archives create a picture of irregularities, instability, and ad hoc and patched-together services. On the one hand, counties continued to collect the officially mandated fees and the surcharges as judicial revenue.[67] On the other hand, counties did tend to underreport judicial revenue. Many counties failed to use the ministry-issued complaint forms. Ni Yaokui, an assistant accountant at the JHC during the Nanjing decade, recalled that in 1928–1929, many counties used blank paper as complaint forms, with a stamped line reading: "Official complaint forms not arrived yet." No judicial stamps were affixed to the unofficial complaints, in violation of the official rules.[68] The fees litigants paid for such irregular forms at the price of official forms would then disappear into the county coffers without being accounted for. Such unreported cash could be appropriated by the magistrate or used to cope with a cost overrun, or both. Given the financial circumstances under which a magistrate had to operate, one can see why the chief would have been motivated to build unreported cash funds, even if he did not intend to profit personally.

Other counties managed their judicial finances by disregarding the formalization agenda. A 1932 report from Wujiang, a relatively wealthy county near Suzhou, gives an example. The regular county judicial fund was ¥380, and after paying the salaries of judicial personnel, only a couple of dozen yuan would be left for all other expenses. The county's judicial functions were largely funded out of judicial revenue. This much was legal. But to cut expenses, the county would have the county public security force deliver criminal summonses and county administrative police deliver documents in civil cases. At one time, the magistrate used more than ¥3,000 of bail money to offset the overrun in the cost of inmate rations in the county jail and detention house.[69] Although this was necessary, it violated various formalization regulations. Yet, knowing the financial conditions in counties, the JHC president who read the report did not raise any issue. One can only guess what other more egregiously irregular measures were taken to finance judicial functions in counties.

The anti-drug campaign started in 1935 brought county offices and district courts some additional revenue, namely, fines imposed on drug offenders. At the CGO, 80 percent of fines were retained as a reward to drug enforcement personnel and 20 percent as judicial revenue (at the DC, 70–80 percent and 30–20 percent). While the DC had to report how the fines were spent, the CGO did not.[70] As we saw in Chapter 3, however, the additional revenue from drug fines was easily outstripped by the mounting cost of incarcerating and feeding drug offenders in county jails (and provincial prisons).

The Financial Burden of the Appeals Process

As the judicial reform broadened access to the courts and more people were willing to bring lawsuits, the CGO faced some new costs that would not have been incurred otherwise. The issue of escorting criminal defendants on appeals to the HC is a revealing example of the unintended financial consequences at the county level of the reform agenda.

In the Beiyang era, when a county had to deliver a criminal defendant for trial at the HC, it would send the defendant to a neighboring county en route to the court. The neighboring county would then send the defendant to the next county further along, and so forth. The cost of escorting the defendant was borne by the counties involved. This was essentially a continuation of the Qing practice.[71] In the Nanjing decade, with a steady increase in appeal cases, such occasions became more frequent, translating into a heavy financial burden on counties.

In November 1932, the Jiangdu magistrate complained to the provincial government chairman, Gu Zhutong, that whereas counties with adjudicating magistrates might be able to handle the task of escorting defendants to the HC, for counties such as Jiangdu (where a DC was set up in early 1932), the practice created a big problem. The county had no judicial police trained to deal with criminal defendants, no detention house to secure them, and no funds to cover the cost of transporting and feeding them. He requested that all counties deliver defendants directly to the JHC, and that magistrates who did not perform judicial functions not process such defendants. In response, Gu instructed the JHC that counties that did not administer judicial affairs be exempted from accepting defendants in transit. A few days later, Gu issued an order to the effect that the exemption did not apply to deserted soldiers or vagabonds being sent back—all counties were responsible for these.[72] The policy was not consistently applied, however, for practical reasons. If a county was located far away from the JHC, it would bankrupt it to escort defendants to the HC entirely at its own expense. That was why the JHC intervened on behalf of the Lishui magistrate when he objected to the Liyang magistrate's refusing to accept a criminal defendant in transit from his county in March 1933.[73]

TABLE 5.10

Actual Expenses in Forty-three County Jails in 1922

(unit: ¥)

County	Wages	Admin.	Ration	Total	Note
Dantu	1,080	435	3,676	5,191	
Wuxi	972	445	8,341	9,758	
Kunshan	1,176		3,302	4,478	
Fengxian	672	240	2,770	3,682	
Wujiang	1,474	271	4,372	6,117	
Chuansha	696	111	1,288	2,095	
Taicang	1,117	384	2,936	4,437	
Yixing	639	240	2,530	3,409	
Baoying	752	502	1,898	3,152	
Baoshan	685	360	2,526	3,571	¥472 raised by the overseer not included in the total.
Gaochun	648	36	245	929	
Dongtai	540	240	2,202	2,982	
Luhe	600	180	612	1,392	
Nanhui	672	240	2,383	3,295	
Jiading	850	227	2,697	3,774	Of the total, ¥297 from chief and overseer.
Changshu	990	120	4,608	5,718	
Tai	1,020	240	1,701	2,961	
Jiangyin	744	324	2,387	3,455	
Jintan	516	168	949	1,633	
Wujin	1,944	638	6,755	9,337	The HC found expenses on wages too much.
Dangshan	624	156	3,321	4,101	
Gourong	648	84	1,396	2,128	
Tongshan	540	240	3,487	4,267	
Taixing	996	240	3,784	5,020	Of salary, ¥456 from chief and overseer.
Feng	540	144	1,278	1,962	
Huaiyin	672	408	1,874	2,954	Overseer ¥36/m; 5 guards ¥3/m each.
Lishui	504	180	1,216	1,900	
Chongming	866	474	3,369	4,709	
Jiangpu	588	960	1,220	2,768	
Songjiang	972	780	3,878	5,630	Overseer ¥30/m; 7 guards ¥7/m each; 1 helper, ¥2/m.
Yangshong	540	144	586	1,270	
Haimen	672	240	1,619	2,531	
Huai'an	672	240	3,753	4,665	
Funing	540	144	1,398	2,082	
Suining	684		1,951	2,635	
Lianshui	670	240	2,264	3,174	
Rugao	924	360	4,376	5,660	
Suqian	540	144	800	1,484	
Shuyang	540	180	955	1,675	
Siyang	684		1,977	2,661	Additional funds provided by magistrate used for salary.
Jiangdu	936	384	4,782	6,102	Overseer ¥30/m; ¥48/m for guards
Ganyu	684		1,173	1,857	Overseer ¥30/m; 3 guards ¥7/m; 1 female guard ¥6/m.
Liyang	936	240	2,066	3,242	Overseer ¥30/m; 6 guards ¥7/m; 1 female guard ¥6/m.
TOTAL				155,843	

SOURCE: MDWH, 2-1338.

The underlying cause of the problem was, of course, the scarcity of funds in counties. From April 1932 to August 1932, Pi county had to escort more than thirty defendants, costing more than ¥370. From August 1932 to March 1933, it escorted another fifty or so defendants, costing more than ¥640. The magistrate borrowed the money from local reserves, but had no way to pay it back. In April 1933, the magistrate asked that the JHC come up with a comprehensive way to solve the problem. The JHC replied that the county would have to work it out on its own.[74] The unspoken message was that the magistrate would have to impose fees, levies, and surcharges on the people of Pi county to do so.

An Anatomy of Prison Finance

The largest chunk of whatever resources judicial institutions and county offices acquired went to keeping defendants and convicts behind bars. The financial woes that plagued the reform were most conspicuously manifested in prison finance. A look into the financial conditions of county jails and provincial prisons throws additional light on judicial finance in Republican Jiangsu.

The Salaries of Prison Staff

We start with an examination of county jail staff salaries shown in Table 5.10. In 1922, the monthly salaries of most jail overseers were around ¥30 (very few received ¥36), and those of jail guards were in the range of ¥3–7. In 1923, most jail guards had a wage of ¥5–7. In some counties, the monthly wages of guards were as low as ¥4, which an inspector believed was too low and would cause guards to resort to irregularities.[75]

Certain practices were irregular under the central government regulations, but were necessary for counties to perform their functions. In 1923, the Danyang magistrate forwarded a request from Jail Overseer Peng Shiqi to the JHP. According to Peng, with five guards and more than 100 inmates, his jail needed people to run errands to buy food and night watchmen for security. Peng planned to spend ¥12 a month to hire two people, using the surplus from the inmate ration fund. The JHP chief, Zhou Yike, rejected the request, suggesting that county police be stationed at the jail to help with security and inmates be used for errands, since they were supposed to work anyway.[76]

Zhou's position on the inmate ration surplus was not consistent. When the jail overseer at Wujiang informed Zhou of his plan to use the surplus from inmate ration funds to cover other expenses, Zhou did not object and only told the overseer not to use the surplus from the previous year.[77] Not surprisingly, many county jails did hire night watchmen, cooks, errand runners, and other helpers out of necessity, but in violation of the regulations. When a jail overseer found it necessary to hire more staff, he would first try to request more funds to cover additional hiring; and failing that, he would hire more guards by reducing wages for each so as to stay within the existing budget. Such situations occurred as late as 1935.[78]

JHC officials appeared to have been halfhearted in insisting on the established rules of running county jails, because they knew the financial difficulties there. If any counties chose not to report what they were doing, they could do anything with whatever funds were available to them. The provincial authorities knew about irregular practices through inspectors who visited those jails. The authorities did not endorse those practices explicitly, but they did not explicitly prohibit them either, as long as counties managed to make ends meet on their own. Only when counties chose to ask for permission to do certain things did red tape get in the way, because the provincial officials did not want to be held responsible for rule-breaking at the county level. In a sense, the jail overseer and the magistrate faced a situation quite similar to that in the imperial era, when the county magistrate had had to find ways to pay for private assistants necessary for him to carry out his official duties. Given the situation, it is notable that counties requested permission from the JHC and JHP to use funds intended for use at the county level—county judicial revenue and provincial inmate ration funds. The fact adds complexity to our understanding of how far and how effectively the state's reach penetrated county-level institutions.

By the 1930s, the monthly wages of county jail guards had risen somewhat over the 1920s. The head guard of the detention house in Yixing was paid ¥24, and four guards were paid ¥8–12 each (a female guard, ¥8). At the county jail, the head guard was paid ¥16, and eight guards were paid ¥8–12 each.[79] An inspector who visited Fengxian in 1935 reported that the county jail head guard was paid ¥19; guards, ¥7–9; and detention house guards, ¥7–11. By contrast, twenty-three policemen in that county who served as judicial police were paid ¥6, and two police chiefs, ¥10. With such low wages, the inspector observed, it would be difficult to prevent those policemen from extorting money from people.[80]

Significantly, the monthly payment to guards and other helpers in a county jail was officially called a "meal allowance for work" (*gongshi*), rather than a salary (*xinfeng*), which the jail overseer received. In theory, a guard's monthly pay of ¥7 or ¥8 or ¥10 was supposed to support him on the job, not his family, which justified the low rate. In reality, of course, the guard relied on the full-time job to support himself *and* his family, if he had one. Hence the inspectors' worry that guards would commit irregularities due to their low pay.

Inmate Rations

Of all the expenses of running an institution of confinement, the largest portion was spent on feeding inmates. The need for money to feed inmates was both a perennial problem with which all jail overseers wrestled and a source of embezzlement that tempted some of them.

The provincial authorities that decided the ration budget tended to underestimate the number of inmates in counties and refused to face the consequences when they went over the budget. In 1914, Wujiang was given an inmate ration fund for 270 people, but the jail there (designed for 150) held more than 300. The inmates complained about their rations at ¥1.60 per person-month. In October 1914, the jail overseer, Yu Jiaxiang, petitioned the JHP chief, Xu Shengjin, for permission to use county criminal fines to add ¥0.20 per person-month to the ration. Xu replied that if the overseer explained the financial situation to inmates and had cooks serve the full amount of the available ration, inmates would accept the fact in the end.[81] Xu seems to have implied that rations were not fully served in the jail—that the ration fund was being embezzled. That might or might not have been true, but Xu conveniently dumped the problem back on the jail overseer. In the end, Magistrate Zhou used criminal fines to help provide rations for inmates above the 270-person quota and asked the JHP for approval after the fact. The JHP chief Xu gave the approval, but he stood firmly against raising the inmate ration budget by ¥0.20, despite the rising grain price cited by Zhou and Yu.[82] In light of the provincial judicial finances examined earlier, one can see why Xu would not or could not open this door and why the provincial government underbudgeted inmate rations to begin with.

Although funds at the county level were supposed to have designated uses per the formalization agenda, in reality the magistrate and the jail overseer had to juggle around whatever money was at their disposal to cover various expenses. Using fines (judicial revenue) to cover inmate ration overruns was a common practice. But when those sentenced to pay fines had no means to pay and had to be imprisoned, it meant more inmates but fewer fines to be used to help feed them, as the Dantu county magistrate complained to the JHP.[83] Another type of juggling the money was in the opposite direction—to use the surplus from inmate rations to help cover staff wages and operational expenses. But when the number of inmates rose drastically, ration costs would increase and affect the wages and operational expenses, as the Wujiang jail overseer told the JHP in 1923.[84]

An important question is whether jail overseers (and magistrates) tried to acquire more funds to maximize the opportunity for embezzlement, as popular descriptions of jail officials would have one believe. The archival sources and prison staff memoirs suggest complex situations and varied responses along a spectrum. Some jail overseers did embezzle ration funds, but others had to use ration funds to cover other expenses that the provincial budget failed to cover, and still others had to use their own money to cover unforeseen expenses to keep the jail running.

Miao Wengui worked in the Jiangsu prison system in the Republican era. At the Jiangsu Second Prison in 1921–1926, he rose from apprentice guard to chief warder, and he then worked as a county jail overseer at Jiading, Jinshan, Tongshan, and Kunshan in 1926–1945. As Miao recalled, it was difficult for the CGO to obtain funds from the FD, and for the jail overseer to get funds from the magistrate. Since the latter could earn interest on unspent operating funds and pocket it, he would delay the delivery of jail funds to the overseer as long as possible. Moreover, the budget for county jail operation was out of touch with the reality to begin with. The monthly allocation for lighting was ¥30, but operating and maintaining a generator ran up a monthly bill of ¥100. If the overseer made a request for additional funds, it was either rejected or ignored. "In short, the operational funds at new prisons and old jails were unreasonable, and it was impossible not to have deficit. If the jail overseer wanted to keep his rice bowl, he had to cheat on inmate rations to make up the shortfall, and the superior knew and allowed it. If one wanted to request an increase in funds based on the actual needs, he would not only get nowhere but also be deemed an annoyance."[85]

Miao's account is corroborated by the archival sources. Songjiang had a court of first instance and a procuracy between 1912 and 1914. The budget for 1914 allocated inmate rations for 100 people to the county jail, but in January 1914, it held over 120 inmates and counting. The overseer, Zhou Enxu, asked the JHP chief, Xu Shengjin, for additional funds. Xu instructed Zhou to draw on criminal fines at the local procuracy. But the local procurator did not cooperate. Forced to write again to Xu, Zhou requested that the governor order the magistrate to provide funds each month based on actual needs. Xu obliged and wrote to Governor Han Guojun. Han responded that the county general funds were provided by the national budget and could not be changed at will; and the JHP should manage fines in all counties in a comprehensive plan to put the money where it was needed most. Han neglected the reality that there was no accounting for county judicial revenue, and that it would be impossible for the JHP chief to force one county to spend its money on another county's problem. Knowing the reality, Xu neither went back to Han nor tried to tap other counties' fines. He ordered the procuracy in Songjiang to use complaint form fees to help cover inmate rations. But Zhou Enxu could not get any money from the procuracy. He resigned in April 1914. By then he had spent ¥108 of his own money in order to feed inmates.[86] Zhou was not the only jail overseer to have spent his own money in order to run the jails without major incidents such as riots, brawls, or deaths. Similar cases were reported elsewhere.[87] Such cases should balance tales of jail overseers engaging in corruption and embezzlement, which also took place.

One variable that would affect prison finance but lay beyond the control of county officials or the provincial authorities was the grain price. During the 1910s–1930s, the grain price fluctuation in Jiangsu may be inferred from that in Shanghai, which manifested a moderate and steady rise from the 1910s to the mid-1920s and then a leveling-off through 1937.[88] In October 1917, Jiangsu First Prison bought 113 piculs of rice for ¥407.32 (less than ¥4 per picul).[89] Rice was no longer available at such a low price by the 1920s. In 1920, magistrates of thirteen counties jointly sent a petition from their jail overseers asking for an increase in inmate rations to keep up with rising grain price to the governor, the FD, and the JHP chief.[90] The provincial authorities seem to have responded. In 1921, the budget for inmate rations was raised to ¥0.06 per person-day.[91] In 1923, all county jails were operating with ¥0.07 per person-day for inmate rations.[92] This was another instance where the provincial government responded to the financial reality at the county level.

By the early 1920s, the JHP had devised a practice for all county jails to follow: in the fall, when grain price was low, the magistrate would loan money to the county jail to buy grain for inmate rations for the whole year. The loan would be paid back in monthly installments from the inmate ration fund. The scheme made economic sense for county judicial finance. But it could be undermined by the vagaries of the provincial government. In 1923, the FD demanded that the tax in the county be delivered ahead of the tax collection time, and the county was ordered to borrow from banks. When grain was harvested and tax collected in the fall, the revenue went to repaying these loans, plus high interest, leaving the county coffers empty. The magistrate only managed to gather ¥800 to buy grain for inmate rations, instead of the regular amount of ¥2,000.[93] Here the provincial government exacerbated county-level financial woes.

The problem of inmate ration overruns plagued most counties in the 1920s to varying degrees. To give a sense of its prevalence, the statistics for fiscal year 1926 may be cited as an example. The overrun in Jiangsu totaled ¥93,170 among forty-seven counties in different months—an average of ¥1,982.34 per county.[94]

Improved County Jail Finance

Prison finance improved from 1929 to the early 1930s, for two reasons. First, compared to the national budget in the Beiyang era, the provincial budget in the Nanjing decade allocated more funds for inmate rations at a higher rate. In May 1932, the MJ ordered all provincial HC to see to it that the inmate ration standard—¥0.10 per person-day—was met in all institutions of confinement.[95] With largely stable grain prices in the 1920s–1930s, the increase in inmate rations to ¥3 per person-month in county jails and provincial prisons was significant. When the grain price shot up occasionally, as it did in 1931, the ration was even allowed temporarily to increase to ¥3.3 a month, to be reduced back to ¥3 when the price returned to normal.[96]

Secondly, overcrowding in county jails was not as serious as in the 1920s, and in some counties there was no crowding at all, as was the case in Feng, Qidong, Nanhui, and Haimen in late 1933.[97] Many county jails saw a surplus of inmate ration funds rather than shortfalls. Xiao saw a surplus as early as 1929.[98] Surpluses from inmate rations continued to be reported from counties in the province in the early 1930s.[99]

In short, the early 1930s were a relatively good time in finance for county jails in Jiangsu, before they were again plagued by overcrowding and financial woes in the mid-1930s due to the anti-drug campaign. This suggests that county jails could be run on a sound financial basis and highlights the negative impact of state agendas other than the judicial reform on financial conditions in the prison system.

Problems at Provincial Prisons

The provincial prisons did not experience the good time that county jails did in the early 1930s, however. From 1929 on, owing to an increasing prison population, provincial prisons frequently faced inmate ration overruns. In April–December 1929, the overrun in the First, Second, Third Prisons, the Third Prison Branch, and the Wujiang DC Detention House totaled ¥29,848. In January–September 1930, those institutions, plus the Shanghai DC, the Jiangning DC and the Temporary Detention Center (TDC, founded in April 1930), had a ration overrun of ¥67,829. The JHC reported the extra costs to the MJ, and the latter told the provincial government to deliver the needed funds to the JHC.[100]

But it became an impossible task for the prisons to obtain allocated funds from the FD and other official sources. As early as 1929, Niu Chuanqi of the JFP reported that the FD was routinely late by half a month in delivering the monthly budget, so that the prison had to scramble to cover more than ¥2,000 in the first half of every month.[101] In July 1934, the JHC issued a directive to the provincial prisons demanding a return of funds it had lent them over the years. The JFP owed ¥16,000; Jiangsu Second Prison (JSP), ¥7,100; Jiangsu Third Prison (JTP), ¥8,500; Jiangsu Fourth Prison, ¥3,500; the Third Prison Branch and JHC Detention House, ¥10,500; and the TDC, ¥4,300.[102] None of those institutions were able to pay back the money, because the FD and other agencies owed them funds. The JSP in Caohejing held more than 3,200 inmates at its peak, and at least 2,500 to 2,600 in the early 1930s, with the cost of inmate rations and operating expenses reaching ¥300–400 per day. Each month, the budgeted funds would not arrive until the following month or even later. At the end of July 1934, the FD owed the prison more than ¥30,000 from June and ¥19,000 yuan from July. The Department of Military Administration owed the prison over ¥1,900, due in February (for military prisoners' rations).[103] Similar stories were reported from the JFP and the JTP.[104]

Moreover, the provincial prisons and detention houses experienced inmate ration overruns simultaneously with arrears in budgeted funds. In April 1935, the JTP and the JHC Detention House spent ¥4,710 on inmate rations (¥1,110 over the budget); the JFP, ¥4,497 (¥1,497 over); and the Shanghai DC Detention House, ¥1,800 (¥604 over). Only the Zhengjiang DC Detention House and the TDC stayed within their budgets of ¥600 and ¥1,500 respectively.[105]

The immediate cause seems to have been that the FD was routinely behind schedule in delivering budgeted funds. In 1934, noting the tendency of provincial treasuries not to provide funds to the judiciary on time, Deputy Minister of Justice Zheng Tianxi advised the judicial organs to spend less money than budgeted.[106] Zhu Gemin, who served as county jail overseer at several counties in Jiangsu in 1921–1944, recalled that the FD would often issue payment papers without making actual cash available, causing great difficulty for new prisons; as for county jails, magistrates had to find ways on their own to keep jails running.[107] To the extent that it was true, the situation again manifested a tension between the judicial and administrative fields in the state system.

In the meantime, some prison governors may have been guilty of embezzlement and graft. Ni Yaokui worked as an assistant accountant at the JHC in the 1930s and had sources of information in various prisons. Ni recalled that Ding Lei, governor of the TDC, Zheng Zhen, governor of the JTP, and Kong Xianglin, chief warder of the JHC Detention House, would borrow money from the JHC, in amounts of ¥5,000, ¥6,000, and up to more than ¥10,000, to invest and do business, and did so under the pretext that the funds from the FD were in arrears.[108] Ni's story is credible, since it is corroborated by the archival sources cited above. Another trick those prison officials used, Ni said, was to buy rice for inmate rations when it was cheap and store it; then, when the grain price went up, they had the merchants write them receipts for the rice at the going rate and pocketed the difference.[109] This was a perversion of the practice that the JHP set up in the early 1920s to help county jails save costs on inmate rations.

Even if Ni's story is true, however, there is no doubt that the judicial system in general and the prison system in particular did face a financial problem. First, human nature, and the social ecology and political pathology of Republican China in particular, meant that some degree of financial leakage in the form of embezzlement and graft had to be taken into account in running the state system, including the judiciary at the provincial and county levels. Second, even if graft and embezzlement had been absent, the total judicial funds would still have been insufficient for the judicial system, including the prison system, to perform its functions up to the standards of the reform agenda under the prevailing rules and regulations.

This analysis of judicial finance in the Republican era reveals two important points. First, a recurring phenomenon was the tension between the central-provincial authorities and the county-level institutions in the arrangement of judicial finance. The way in which the judiciary at all levels was financed, through negotiations and compromises among the central, provincial, and county governments, speaks to the issue of the reach of the state in an ambiguous and complex fashion. In view of the fact that the central-provincial authorities, both administrative and judicial, often squeezed county governments financially, we may conclude that the state controlled county government. But if we recognize that the central-provincial authorities squeezed the county institutions because they believed there were under- or unreported and under- or uncollected revenues at the county level that the CGO could be forced to tap into, we may conclude that the reach of the central government was limited. The two scenarios are not mutually exclusive.

Second, the examination of the financial side of the reform exposes a structural incongruence between the agenda of institutional-procedural formalization and the practice of revenue collection and resource allocation, which remained quite informal and irregular. It appears that the agenda of formalizing judicial institutions and procedures was much easier to formulate on paper than to fund, because it involved revenue collection and resource allocation at all levels and in different fields of the state system, which depended upon another set of institutional and procedural formalization in modern state-building. The failure in the latter area, along with a dearth of overall resources to begin with, turned out to be an important factor in undermining the judicial reform, albeit hardly the only one. Part III of this book looks at how other factors in local society framed the way judicial functions were performed at the county level during the reform.

PART III

The County Judicial Process

CHAPTER 6

The Social Context of County Judicial Functions

> According to Chinese law, no district magistrate can execute a criminal before getting sanction from the capital. But I have recently learned of a case where the magistrate, new to his post, has shot a man without even reporting to the provincial Law Courts. He seems, too, to be in a hurry to get rich by oppressing people in his district. In this he is ably assisted by his subordinates (mostly local men) who are as scoundrelly a lot of men as one could expect them to be. *In theory,* the old style of yamen runners have been abolished; but *in fact,* they are just called by a new name, "judicial police" (司法警察). And I am afraid that this is true of the province generally, probably of China as a whole. To attempt to administer justice by keeping to the letter of the law is hopeless so long as these scoundrels are employed by the magistrates. I have known of magistrates who have tried to deal justly but have been constantly frustrated by their subordinates, especially the 差 and 差头, *alias* 司法警察 ("yamen runners" to use the old term).
>
> —A correspondent of the *North China Herald* (Shanghai), writing from Guiyang, Guizhou province, November 3, 1917[1]

To a large degree, what the *North China Herald* correspondent observed in Guiyang was indeed true of many places in China at the time. But the story told by the correspondent provides no insights into the workings of the county judiciary. Why, for example, did the county magistrate have to employ "scoundrels"? What drove the Republican reincarnation of "yamen runners" to prey on litigants at the CGO? To answer these questions, it is necessary to view the county judiciary within the context of an interaction between the reform initiatives issued from the central and provincial capitals and the county-level responses rooted in the local sociopolitical environment. This chapter explores the county judiciary in Jiangsu from several angles. We first look at the making and unmaking of courts in counties in 1911–1914 to show local elites' demands for and anxieties over county-level courts, the financial reasons for such courts to be dismantled, and the provincial governor's position on the rule of law and judicial independence. We then examine how county judicial functions were performed, in what kind of sociopolitical environment, and what roles the county magistrate and county personnel played in the process. Finally, we explore the reasons for perennial case backlogs at the county level.

The (Un)Making of County-level Courts, 1911–1914

Local Demand for County Courts, 1911–1912

Although local elites in many counties in Jiangsu must have already heard about the judicial reform initiatives launched in the New Policy decade, the founding of the Republic proved to be a great catalyst spurring an upsurge of interest in and indeed demand for the rule of law and judicial independence. Studies have documented that widespread popular unrest existed in Jiangsu and elsewhere prior to the 1911 Revolution, and that a large part of the unrest took the form of local resistance to New Policy initiatives that led to higher taxes and greater local elite power but no perceived benefits to the common people.[2] Where judicial reform was concerned, the archival sources present a complex picture. Local elites were often eager to see formal courts established in their counties, but anxious to control such institutions. Some county magistrates embraced the project of building county-level courts as a way to avoid handling lawsuits, while for different reasons, others did not want to see such courts established. A brief look at the making and unmaking of courts in counties in the early years of the Republic provides a useful baseline and a background against which to explore how the county magistrate performed judicial functions in the Republican era.

On November 30, 1911, Yan Shimeng, a member of the local gentry in Chongming who served as a member of the advisory bureau (*ziyi ju*) and deputy chairman of the self-government assembly (*zizhi yihui*) there, arrived at the Civil Affairs Department (CAD) in Nanjing to report on the lawlessness in his county in the wake of Jiangsu's independence from the Qing government. He requested that Magistrate Wang Shaozeng concurrently be made the presiding judge at the court in Chongming because Wang enjoyed local trust—apparently, Wang was trusted by local elites like Yan himself.

The CAD and the Justice Department (JD) endorsed the idea, and Governor Cheng Dequan approved the appointment. Under the Provisional Guidelines on Officialdom issued by the provincial government, Cheng reasoned, each county was to have a presiding judge and a chief procurator, so as to separate judicial and administrative authorities; but Chongming was different from other counties, because it was isolated off the coast, with many potential bandits. What the local gentry requested was an expedient to pacify the locale, which should be allowed.[3] In other words, Cheng knew that the appointment was at odds with the principle of judicial independence but approved it for reasons of expediency.

In his request, Yan Shimeng described how local people had stormed his home and those of other elites:

> The doors, windows, walls, and furniture in my home were all savagely destroyed. Bandits Lin Qinglang, Xu Yougen, Huang Xingqing and the female bandit Lu Xiaofeng and wife of Zhu Bolang looted at the same time. I lost more than 1,600 silver yuan, and more than 200,000 copper coins, more than 300 garments. Books, calligraphy, paintings, antiques, and other items accumulated through generations were all gone in a day, which was verified by Magistrate Wang. Before this disaster, I was concentrating on securing the community and hoping to prevent civil strife. I did not do anything to secure my own home and property for fear of causing panic. That is why my loss was enormous. After leaving my home, the bandits went on to vandalize the homes of [the] gentry Huang Housheng, Lu Mengxiong, Zhang Ziying, Huang Liehou. I have heard that in recent days the homes of all those in charge of new schools and self-government assembly and those known to be wealthy in Ruqiao town, Miao town, Houjia town, Dachun town, Xinhe town, and Shou'an market have been robbed and vandalized and even set afire. At the moment, the whole county lies in smithereens, and one does not know where it is going to end.[4]

The description clearly shows the popular resentment against the gentry-managers who presided over and benefited from the New Policy projects. Yan hoped to get someone he and other gentry-managers could trust appointed judge in Chongming, and to have the court deal with the lawlessness that threatened their personal lives and properties and local society in general.

Similar efforts were seen in Jiangyin. Right after the local version of the 1911 Revolution was over on October 22, 1911, local elites in the county decided to set up a court and a procuracy to handle criminal and civil lawsuits. They reported their initiatives to the provincial governor and managed to have their choices, Zhao Zengxiang and Chen Yurui, appointed as presiding judge and chief procurator respectively. In March 1912, Zhao, Chen, and Magistrate Liu Jinghuan wrote to the acting governor, Zhuang Yunkuan, and the JD chief, Zheng Yan, proposing that the court and procuracy be turned into district-level institutions, with a CFI and its procuracy attached, so that appeal cases could be handled locally. They claimed to be speaking on behalf of "local gentry in town and countryside." Zhuang replied that the idea was good but impractical, given the shortage of judicial funds.[5] In contrast to the cases cited in Chapter 4, local elites in Chongming and Jiangyin were able to have their choices appointed as judicial officers in their counties because they did not claim a right to elect or appoint judicial officers, but simply recommended their candidates to the provincial government.

Menghe in Wujin was a town twenty-eight miles northwest of the county seat, Changzhou. In the Qing era, it was a military post under a fourth degree-rank military officer (*dusi*) and a security officer (*xunjian*). After the 1911 Revolution, the military post was abolished and the security officer fled, causing a collapse of law and order. Local gentry raised a militia to secure peace, but the members were peasants, who had to go back to the fields in the spring. In February 1912, local gentry wrote to the provincial governor asking for a CFI in Menghe, saying that in the absence of judicial authorities, local ruffians and roaming bandits were brazen and robberies were frequent. Local gentry were hesitant to get tough with the ruffians due to local human relationships (*xiangqing*). As in Jiangyin, the local elites in Menghe wanted to establish order through authorized local judicial organs, which they hoped to control. But again the acting governor was unable to oblige for lack of funds.[6]

In addition to local elites, a county magistrate might well also want a court to be set up in his county, which for one thing would spare him the thankless task of handling lawsuits and dealing with interference in litigation by local elites. There was a TPO in Guanyun. After taking office as county magistrate, Shen Zhangshou wanted a court and a procuracy in the county. He explained what a difficult task an adjudicating county magistrate had. The magistrate's administrative duties and judicial functions were mutually contradictory, Shen said. On the one hand, he had to work with local gentry to conduct elections, supervise self-government, pacify the countryside, develop industry and education, and obtain donations to pay off county debts; on the other hand, in admitting lawsuits, holding pretrial hearings, searching for evidence, presiding over trials and sentencing, and enforcing civil judgments, he had to confront them; and it was impossible to do both at the same time. Furthermore, the local people were uninformed about the Republican system and judicial procedures. Litigants launched lawsuits the way they had done in the Qing era, such as appealing their cases right after filing their lawsuits, failing to pay litigation fees for civil cases, asking for mediation in criminal cases, and so on. If he were to accommodate those actions, he would be violating the law, and if he were to insist on following the law, he would arouse local opinion against him. And there were simply too many tasks for the magistrate to handle. Even with an assistant trial officer, he would have to handle serious cases and get involved even in routine cases, besides administrative matters. It was not that he was seeking an easy job, but that judicial independence was an important goal, and he took it as the premise of his job that the Republic was founded on the separation of the three powers. Shen's rhetoric about judicial independence may have been an excuse, but what he said about the negative effects of a county magistrate performing judicial functions was true. This was probably old news to Governor Cheng Dequan, however, and he rejected Shen's proposal, citing financial difficulties.[7]

While some county magistrates wanted to have a court and a procuracy in their locales, others did not, for reasons of their own. Gourong was scheduled to have a court and a procuracy, but the county magistrate, Xu Wenjun, suggested to the governor in early 1912 that it would be very difficult to set up a court in Gourong, and an assistant trial officer might be appointed first (which would mean a TPO). His proposal was rejected. In April 1912, four commanding officers of the military units stationed in Gourong and four "citizens"—apparently local gentry—sent a petition to the governor, criticizing Xu for obstructing the establishment of a court. In response, the governor again ordered Xu to proceed with setting up the court without delay.[8] Military officers and local gentry jointly petitioning the governor was a curious combination, and it is not known what transpired in Gourong, though it would appear that the county magistrate was not doing what the local elites wanted him to do and a local power struggle was afoot in the process of establishing the court. In any case, Xu left office by September 1913, which probably means that he lost the struggle and could not or did not want to take responsibility anymore.[9]

The history of county-level courts and procuracies in Jiangsu during 1911–1914 is told here to make several points. First of all, local elites had motivations to demand formal judicial organs in their counties. In a sense, the judicial reform was a continuation of the New Policy initiatives, which local elites had identified with and benefited from. The post-1911 Revolution local disorder only convinced local elites of the threat of lawlessness by the common people, which the new judicial organs would help contain. For precisely this reason, however, they sought to control appointments to those judicial organs (see also Chapter 4). Secondly, the attitudes and motivations of county magistrates varied with regard to the emerging county-level courts and procuracies. Some wanted to see courts established in their counties to spare them from having to perform judicial and administrative functions at the same time; but others did not, perceiving such courts as a burden on local resources, for example, or that local elites would simply take them over. Thirdly, the elite enthusiasm of 1911–1912 for setting up county-level courts and procuracies did not result in such institutions in all counties, due to lack of funds. It is no surprise, therefore, that most of the courts and procuracies set up in counties in 1911–1912 were dismantled in 1913–1914. In the end, the societal demand for county judicial functions and the financial inability of the state to support formal courts at the county level left only one option open—to continue the practice of county magistrates handling judicial affairs.

The County Magistrate and Judicial Staff

The County Magistrate and His Environment

To understand the behavior of county magistrates in administering justice, one should consider, first, the kind of people who became county magistrates and the sociopolitical environment in which they functioned. In the Beiyang era, the regulations on testing and appointing county magistrates ensured that a magistrate would be an educated and experienced man, verified by an elaborate process of tests (two written and one oral).[10] Similar rules prevailed in the Nanjing decade.[11] As noted in Chapters 2 and 3, the rule of avoidance for judicial officers and prohibition of judicial officers from having political party affiliations applied to adjudicating county magistrates and trial officers. Under the GMD party-state, the ban on political party affiliation was abolished, but the rule of avoidance remained. Thus the educational qualification, the rule of avoidance, and non-party affiliation (for the Beiyang era) determined what kind of people would become county magistrates.

In the period of 1912–1937, some county magistrates in Jiangsu held Qing civil service degrees, others had been educated in modern schools and colleges in China or abroad, and still others had been county magistrates or clerks under the Qing or were former mid-level bureaucrats or GMD cadres. In 1923, out of a total of sixty county magistrates in Jiangsu, sixteen were *jinshi* or *juren* degree holders; eight were graduates of Japanese law schools or departments; thirty-one were former officials exempted from examination; and the rest had passed examinations for county magistrates. The average age of the sixty magistrates was 46, the oldest being 64 and the youngest, 31.[12] While all the magistrates were educated men, this did not guarantee that they understood and were committed to the principles that drove the judicial reform; those who had served under the Qing might have been adversely affected by their old experiences in administering county-level justice.

The rule of avoidance was largely followed, but during times of political chaos, local elites would install (*tuiju*) a native person as the county magistrate, who would be replaced by a non-native appointee when political order was restored. After the 1911 Revolution, the first magistrate of Shanghai county was a native, Wu Xin, who was said to be the most effective magistrate.[13] In Dantu, a native, Yang Bangyan, was installed by local elites as the county magistrate twice—in the wake of the 1911 Revolution and the 1913 Second Revolution respectively.[14] The rule of avoidance made it possible that many county magistrates hailed from other provinces, as far away as Hebei and Liaoning in the north and northeast and Guizhou and Sichuan in the southwest; but most magistrates were from other counties within Jiangsu. Sometimes, magistrates were appointed due to their connections, aside from their credentials. Yuan Xiluo was appointed the county magistrate of Taicang in 1928 partly because he was a member of the Revolutionary Alliance to which Niu Yongjian, the Provincial Government chairman, also belonged, and because Miao Bing, the CAD chief, had been a student of the Nanjing Middle School, where Yuan had been the principal. Similarly, Wen Chongxin became the county magistrate of Taicang in 1934 when his former schoolmate in America, Yu Jingtang, was the CAD chief.[15]

A striking fact in the data on county magistrates in early Republican Jiangsu is that almost all magistrates served only a very short period in one post before being fired or transferred. Many served less than a year, some for one or two years, and only a few for more than three years. Statistically, each of the eleven randomly selected counties had on average about 24 magistrates succeeding one after another during 1912–1937, magistrates holding their posts for an average of twelve and a half months; times of political volatility, such as 1911–1912, 1913, and 1927, saw the most frequent turnover of county magistrates.[16] Another source reveals that in 1912–1923, the sixty counties in Jiangsu saw 612 magistrates filling and leaving offices (many were recycling from county to county); on average, 10 magistrates (10.2 numerically) had served in each county in the twelve-year period.[17] The average tenure of each county magistrate was just over a year, shorter than that in the late imperial era, when a county magistrate would typically serve three years or less.[18] Between 1912 and 1927, Shanghai county saw as many as 16 magistrates, and within the month of January 1925, four came and went.[19] The high rate of turnover in the CGO was a common phenomenon in Jiangsu and perhaps across the country in the early Republican era.

Sources suggest that most county magistrates were dismissed or transferred from or resigned their posts because they were opposed by local elites for various reasons—most often for alleged corruption and embezzlement, but sometimes for policies that were unpopular with local elites, or because of conflicts with local GMD cadres.[20] If a magistrate was unpopular for social and political reasons, he could be conveniently accused by his opponents of being corrupt or abusing power. Cao Yinfu was appointed the magistrate of Pei county in March 1928. Cao appears to have intended to reform the county governance by dismissing former county clerks and appointing educated young people; he also declared his hostility to "local bullies and evil gentry" by posting public notices to that effect and by arresting a village head (*weidong*). His agenda alarmed local gentry, who organized a campaign and raised funds to lobby the provincial government to depose Cao, which they succeeded in doing by early 1929.[21] On the other hand, Zhang Zuo-chen, the magistrate of the Suqian county, who accommodated local gentry and was guilty of corruption along the way during 1931–1933, was finally dismissed because local GMD cadres opposed his doings and insisted on his removal. When Zhang was fired, he tried to flee the county without accounting for funds, and county party cadres chased him down aboard a train and brought him back to town. He was not allowed to leave until his family had sent the county government ¥3,000 he had allegedly embezzled.[22] The two cases suggest a complex scene of local power struggles in the relationship between the county magistrate and local elites, whose compositions and internal cohesion varied over space and evolved over time.

Thus the relationship between the county magistrate as an outsider, on the one hand, and local gentry-managers or party cadres, or some other configuration of power players, on the other, was the most important variable in the sociopolitical environment in which the county magistrate performed his administrative and judicial functions. The provincial government understood the importance of the magistrate cooperating with local elites to the normal functioning of a county government, such as collecting taxes and maintaining local peace, as well as delivering justice. That is why whenever local power holders in a county at a given moment, either gentry or GMD cadres, pushed hard making a case against a county magistrate, whether it was legitimate or not, the provincial government tended to transfer or dismiss that magistrate to defuse the local tensions, hoping that the next appointment would work out better.

Knowing all this, the report by Shen Zhangshou of Guanyun in 1912 cited earlier makes compelling sense, as does what critics at the time had to say about the practice of the county magistrate handling judicial affairs: "As an administrative official, the county magistrate is restricted by superior officials from the above and surrounded by local bullies and evil gentry in local society, so it is really impractical to expect that he can adjudicate, like judicial officers constrained by laws, with impartiality and integrity based on the spirit of independence."[23]

As late as 1931, an inspector from the JHC made a similar observation when he visited Yancheng. In carrying out his administrative duties and soliciting donations, the county magistrate relied upon local gentry, who would seek to intervene in lawsuits and threaten noncooperation if they did not get their way. Beholden by the need for the local gentry's cooperation, the magistrate would try to accommodate such lobbying as much as possible. This state of affairs could not be rectified until an independent court was established, the inspector noted.[24]

The environment in which the county magistrate had to function was such that it was in a sense a filtering system based on individuals' moral scruples; those who could not live with a certain level of corruption and injustice in county governance would be screened out, either resigning of their own accord or being forced out. As late as 1936, a returned student, who had been educated in the United States and specialized in civil engineering, after failing to find a job suitable to his training, accepted a position as county magistrate in Jiangsu that was offered to him because of his uncle's connections in the provincial capital. Within a year, he had resigned the office, and a friend found him a wounded man who looked ten years older than his age. "Although poor, I have always been honest; and although ambitious, I have always despised the art of flattery," the one-time county magistrate confided to his friend. He tried his best to run a clean and honest government by doing away with all the corrupt and evil practices prevailing in most of the city governments in China. As a result, he encountered hostility all around him: his superiors were unsupportive, because he did not curry favor with them; local gentry were unsympathetic to his attempt at reforms, "because they were determined to preserve their evil influences over city administration"; and his subordinates refused to cooperate, because the reform would "cut off the sources of their illegitimate gains." He was left isolated and was looked upon as a fool. Worn out by the constant struggle between his conscience and the temptation to go along with corruption and profit from it himself, he had finally decided to resign.[25] In short, when corruption was the local norm, anyone who tried not to be corrupt was seen as abnormal and could not survive. One is able to appreciate the poignancy of the story after seeing all the elements in the sociopolitical environment in which the CGO operated, especially in judicial affairs.

Although the environment in which the county magistrate worked was quite similar to that of the imperial era, the establishment of provincial high courts (and some district courts), along with the practice of county magistrates performing judicial functions, had some new institutional implications for the county magistrate that had not existed before. Previously, the magistrate had been responsible for anything that happened on his watch, including mishandling of lawsuits, but his judicial functions were only part of his overall job performance, and he was evaluated as an administrator by superior administrative officials, who also had judicial functions and therefore understood what it was like for administrators to handle lawsuits. In contrast, the county magistrate in the Republican era had to perform all functions, including judicial ones, as before, but he was now not only accountable to his administrative superiors—the provincial governor (and circuit administrator in 1913–1924)—for his judicial and administrative functions. He was also subject to one more line of supervision, namely, the provincial judicial officials, who were mindful of judicial rules and regulations. Thus the county magistrate was accountable for negligence or misdeeds in judicial matters separate from his administrative role. And he was more likely than his predecessor in the imperial era to be found wanting as a county magistrate, because his judicial workload became heavier than before and because he was supposed to abide by more elaborate judicial norms and forms established by the reform. He had to be prepared to respond to the inquiries and investigations by the provincial judicial institutions and face disciplinary actions against him for such incidents as mishandled cases or escaped prisoners.[26] All these requirements and mechanisms resulting from the institutional and procedural formalization were new and "modern," but the environment in which the county magistrate operated remained traditional. Such a situation had profound implications for the behavior of the county magistrate when he dealt with judicial affairs.

Trial Officers and Judicial Staff

A second important variable that affected how county judicial functions were performed was the county judicial staff, the most important of whom was the trial officer. Under the 1919 regulations on examining county trial officers, the trial officer had to meet certain educational qualifications, verified by examinations.[27] If a county had more than 900 criminal and civil cases a year, it was entitled to have two trial officers to assist the county magistrate; if it had between 600 and 900 cases a year, it was to have one trial officer; and if it had fewer than 300 cases a year, no trial officer was funded, but the county magistrate could hire one at the county's own expense. In all these cases, it was the county magistrate who would recommend the trial officer to be formally appointed by the HC. As it often happened, the county magistrate would have a personal friend or even a relative appointed as the trial officer, even if the county was not entitled to have one and had to fund the position from county resources; if a nomination was not approved by the HC for lack of credentials, the county magistrate would have the person handle lawsuits in the name of "temporary appointment."[28] When a trial officer picked by a county magistrate committed abuses and irregularities, it was rare for the magistrate not to defend the officer. The practice of the county magistrate nominating the trial officer tended to encourage abuses and irregularities and their cover-ups in the county judicial process.

To address the problem, in September 1922, the JHC issued two sets of regulations to standardize and formalize the appointment of trial officers. Under the regulations, a trial officer nominated by a county magistrate would be interviewed by the HC president and pass a test offered by the court before being appointed. Previously appointed trial officers would go through vetting of their credentials according to the regulations.[29] By November 1922, as many as thirty-eight trial officers had been selected through such tests in Jiangsu.[30] One provision in the regulations, consistent with the MJ standing order since 1919, was that when a county magistrate left his post, the trial officer should stay on the job, not to be replaced without cause.[31] This provision would prove to be troublesome to some county magistrates, who found trial officers not of their choosing uncooperative or obnoxious. The testing of trial officers continued in the Nanjing decade. In 1928, the JHC selected sixteen trial officers through tests; twenty-one in 1929; and nineteen in 1931.[32] In short, the appointment of trial officers became formalized after 1922, but this did not ensure that handling of lawsuits by the trial officer would be fair and just.

Other judicial personnel in the CGO included judicial clerks (*shuji yuan*), record-keepers (*lushi*), complaint-writing clerks (*shanzhuang yuan*), bailiffs (*chengfa li*), coroners (*jianyan li*), judicial policemen (*sifa jingcha*), and jail overseers (*guanyu yuan*) and jail guards (*kanshou*). Although their titles were new, these people performed jobs that were not substantively different from what their predecessors had done in the imperial era, except the requirement of more paperwork, which they often failed to fulfill. The number of the judicial staff varied from county to county. Table 6.1 shows the judicial staff in the CGO in Jiangdu, a first-grade county in 1923, which was probably typical of most counties of the same grade. A second- or third-grade county would have had a somewhat smaller staff.

TABLE 6.1

Judicial Staff of Jiangdu County, Jiangsu, 1923

Position	Name	Age	Native	Education	Experience	Apt. date
County magistrate	Cao Yuanding	47	Wuxi	Jinshi	County magistrate	1923
Trial Officer	He Yan	45	Zhejiang P.	Law school	Trial officer	
Clerk	Li Yi	39	Same	Shengyuan	Staff	
Same	Tao Rong	30	Jiangning	Law school	Staff	
Prob. clerk	Cao Wenhong	35	Jiangdu		Legal assistant	1917
Same	Xu Shaopeng	41	Same	Law institute	Clerk	1912
Record kpr	Zhou Baohua	32	Same	Private school	Staff	1919
Same	Wang Fengzhao	30	Same		Staff	1918
Same	Xu Liangcai	24	Same	Elementary school		1919
Probationary record kpr	Zhang Yushu	42	Same			1914
Same	Liu Gancheng	49	Same			1917
Same	Lu Derun	50	Same			1914
Same	Zhu Zhaoming	35	Same			1915
Same	Zhou Jiedan	37	Same	Law institute		1914
Same	Zheng Yongtai	33	Same	Law institute		1914
Same	Lu Jiemin	24	Same	Elementary school		1919
Coroner	Jiang Ming	54	Same			
Probationary coroner	Zong Qi	41	Same			
Bailiff	Xiao Bingchuan	51	Same			1914
Same	Xuan Xianglong	58	Same			1914
Same	Pan Jiankuai	45	Same			1914
Same	Zhang Guobin	56	Same			1914
Judicial policeman	Liu Pengcheng	37	Same			1918
Same	Li Mingzhi	51	Same			1914
Same	Li Chuntian	37	Same			1914
Same	Liu Jingui	58	Same			1914
Same	Hua Bingjun	47	Same			1914
Same	Mao Kunshan	50	Same			1914
Same	Wang Canyun	42	Same			1914
Same	Mi Chunyang	40	Same			1918
Same	Hua Xingfu	39	Same			1915
Same	Fang Huanzhang	45	Same			1919

SOURCE: JGFD, RS-369.

Two facts should be noted here. First, the judicial staff in Jiangdu were all natives, except for the county magistrate, the trial officer, and one clerk (the last two were from the same county in Zhejiang). Second, under the county magistrate, the trial officer, and two clerks, the twenty-eight staff members were longtime employees, most of them since 1914, when county-level courts had been dismantled. These facts contrast sharply with the frequent turnover of county magistrates, who were outsiders to local society, and suggest that the county government jobs, even with a low pay, were coveted ones, not to be given up lightly, because they allowed jobholders to collect irregular fees from litigants. The county magistrate had to reckon with staff with local roots who were well entrenched in their places.

Besides the official staff on the county government payroll, each staff member had assistants or helpers, known as "deputies" (*daibiao*) or "unpaid workers" (*baiyi*), who relied completely on irregular fees to make a living. Hiring "unpaid workers" was illegal, but was widely practiced as late as the 1930s, despite repeated prohibitions by the JHC and the MJ. "Unpaid workers" were routinely given certain tasks, such as delivery of judicial documents or investigation of a crime scene, with which collecting irregular fees was associated.[33]

The jail overseer and guards were part of the county judicial staff. The position of overseer was an official one created by the Beiyang government. In the Qing era, the county jail had been run by a lowly official called a *dianshi* or *limu*. After the MJ issued regulations on prison staff qualifications in 1913, the head of the county jail was called a "jail overseer" and also supervised the county detention house. A majority of jail overseers in Jiangsu had some postsecondary education and/or legal training. Li Zhuxi, for example, a graduate from a normal university in Japan and a school of law and government in China, was an elementary school principal before becoming the overseer in Xinghua in 1913.[34] Wen Zheng graduated from the law department at a Japanese university and became the overseer in Yixing in 1919.[35] Ma Jun graduated from the Jiangnan Higher Academy in 1912 and was appointed the overseer in Chuansha in 1914 and transferred to Guanyun in 1917.[36]

Unlike the trial officer and the jail overseer, who were recommended by the county magistrate before their appointments and therefore more or less had to cooperate with the magistrate, personnel below these two officers were often permanent employees of the CGO, whom the county magistrate could not do without. Since they were natives with local roots and connections, they tended to cooperate with local power holders, rather than with the county magistrate, when conflicts arose between the two. They were infinitely resourceful in obstructing any attempts to eliminate irregularities and abuses in the county judicial process, upon which their incomes were dependent.

Theoretically, therefore, all county judicial personnel were agents of the state performing judicial functions, but in reality they were often elements of abuse and corruption in the county judicial process, undermining the state agenda. Even under the best of circumstances, the county magistrate was stuck in his sociopolitical environment without an ideal course of action. He could not succeed in performing his judicial duties without the service of his staff; but neither could he deliver justice in the full sense of the word, even if he wanted to, when his staff routinely perverted the process of "delivering justice."

The County Judicial Process

The Semi-Formalization of County Judicial Work

The central government's formalization agenda entailed administrative rules governing county judicial functions mandated by the Ministry of Justice, but the rules were widely ignored by county magistrates and trial officers. The most common lapse was in the area of the judicial paperwork required by the formalization of institutional operations. As late as 1931–1932, inspectors from the JHC found that in Wujiang and Gaoyou, case files that had accumulated for many years were not bound into books as required by the ministry. In Wujiang, more than 300 receipts for document delivery were not enclosed in their case files.[37] In Yixing, more than ¥2,800 in judicial fees was collected without using judicial stamps.[38] In Jintan, the trial transcript was missing from the file of a criminal case that was still pending. In Yangzhong, there was no record of judicial fees collected, and complaints written on plain paper sheets instead of official complaint forms were found in case files. Similar lapses abounded in many counties, and the JHC president found them unacceptable.[39] The findings in 1931–1932 were neither the first nor the last. In the mid-1930s, the JHC was still ordering all county magistrates to compile and send in truthful monthly reports on closed cases.[40]

If the lapses in paperwork only resulted in a mess in the CGO and incomplete data for the MJ, other lapses harmed litigants. It was found in Gaoyou in 1932 that when a case was accepted, a file was not always set up for it and the county magistrate or the trial officer often had no idea where the case was in the process. There was no chain of command and no accountability among county judicial clerks and record-keepers. A case might pass through the hands of seven or eight people, and when a superior inquired about it, no one could give an answer for weeks. In both the jail and the detention house, the procedures for registering incoming inmates with judicial documents were not followed, and there were no clear records of inmates. Some men were held in the detention house for more than a year without being processed, others were tried and sentenced but still held in the detention house instead of serving time in the jail, and still others who had served out their terms remained in the jail, which not only violated the law but also cost extra inmate rations.[41]

Clearly, the formalization agenda pursued by the MJ and the provincial judicial authorities was neither appreciated nor seriously implemented at the county level. County judicial personnel probably did not see why so much paperwork—an innovation in the county-level administration—was important and necessary. Sometimes, though, there were legitimate reasons why certain paperwork was not done. In 1921, when the JHP repeatedly ordered counties to compile and submit annual and monthly statistics of jails and detention houses as mandated by the MJ, Songjiang was among the counties that did not respond. Pressed by the JHP again, the jail overseer, Peng Xisheng, explained that due to frequent turnover of overseers (as many as six in 1920 alone) no systematic data had been preserved for him to work with. He had statistics only for April–October 1921. In a follow-up order, the JHP chief, Xu Shouheng, said that if the jail did not have complete data, the overseer should consult the data at the CGO, since both the county magistrate and the trial officer handled cases.[42] Xu's assumption that there would be duplicate data at the CGO and the jail was probably overoptimistic, however.

Irregular Charges and Bribery

When a litigant decided to bring a lawsuit to the CGO, it was a serious commitment—he or she would spend a lot of money and time along the way before the lawsuit could reach a conclusion. Corroborated by the archival sources and a book by Deng Changyao, a circuit administrator in Ningxia province who had served as magistrate in several counties in Hunan and Shaanxi provinces, published in 1925,[43] post-1949 memoirs describe how county judicial staff imposed irregular charges on litigants at every turn.[44] After first paying a legal scribe, who often had connections with county personnel, to draft a complaint, the litigant would pay a complaint-writing clerk at the CGO to get his or her complaint copied onto the official complaint form (not necessarily the ministry-issued one) and pay clerks and/or the trial officer to make sure the case was accepted. Then it was the turn of bailiffs or judicial policemen to take fees. Since there were no or little county funds to pay for travel expenses and meals for bailiffs or judicial policemen who delivered the summons to the defendant in a case, they would charge the receiver of the summons for their trouble in making the trip, and the amount was negotiated around a "going rate." The same applied to delivering the county magistrate's decision in a civil case, or a conviction and sentence paper in a criminal case, and other judicial documents. When the day of the hearing or trial came, both parties to the lawsuit would pay clerks to get ushered into the county magistrate's courtroom, or they would risk being reported as absent, which would mean indefinite delays, more deliveries of summonses, more payments, and more trips to the county seat. Both parties would try to pay the clerks who were present at the hearing or trial as interpreters for the county magistrate, who usually did not speak local dialect, to make sure they were not shortchanged by the clerks during the proceedings. In short, what had typically been practiced in Qing-era county yamen proceedings largely continued in the Republican era.[45]

During the trial, civil litigants would have to support themselves residing in a cheap hostel at the county seat, where they were hounded by legal scribes seeking business, while criminal defendants would be held in the county detention house. When the trial was over, if the losing party decided to appeal, a new round of payments would have to be made to move the appeal forward. If a criminal defendant was sentenced to a prison term, another round of payments to county jail guards and their helpers would begin (see Chapter 8).

As late as the early 1930s, inspectors from the JHC found that in Gaoyou, judicial staff would bring their relatives or personal friends into their offices as "interns," who sold information about lawsuits; in Liyang, judicial staff would, off the books, farm out their jobs, such as delivering judicial documents in the countryside, to private helpers, who could thus collect irregular fees; and judicial clerks and coroners also engaged in irregularities and abuses.[46] When litigants failed to pay judicial fees or claimed eligibility for the waiving of such fees, county judicial functionaries would be told to collect the fees or verify the financial conditions of the litigants claiming waivers. The functionaries would then go after the litigants and collect and pocket the payments, while reporting that they had failed to collect the fees.[47] Since the county magistrate relied on the service of county staff, he would tend to tolerate irregularities and corruption to some extent, reasoning that given the low pay of county functionaries, there was no way to eliminate these practices.

With irregularities and abuses accepted as the norm, a county magistrate who was determined to clean up such practices would be regarded as eccentric and face fierce resistance. In Lianshui, in the early 1920s, there were as many as twelve complaint-writing clerks and more than twenty judicial policemen who made a living by selling opposing parties illegal copies of complaints and collecting irregular fees, known by a variety of names, such as fees for ticket books (*piaoben*) (probably meaning summons tickets), fast delivery of complaints (*kuaizhuang*), super-fast delivery of complaints (*kuai kuaizhuang*), document services (*shuchai*), and courtroom services (*tangshi*). These categories may be considered a form of regularization and legitimization of the clerks' irregular practices. In 1925, the newly arrived county magistrate, Gao Meixian, undertook to reform the county judiciary, with the support of several members of the county assembly. He fired all twelve complaint-writing clerks and hired four middle-school graduates as replacements. On September 20, when Gao was out of town, the fired clerks and some judicial policemen gathered a crowd of over 100 and stormed the CGO. After severely beating two of the newly hired clerks, the mob went on to hunt down three county assemblymen in a restaurant and beat them up before being stopped and arrested by the county security force. After receiving petitions from local elites, including the townships association, the security force commanders, the agriculture association, the education association, the chamber of commerce, and the education bureau, the JHC sent an official to the county, where after an oral examination, he retained the four clerks hired by Gao and in addition hired twenty-four judicial policemen, thus ending the incident.[48] The violent outburst of the fired county clerks suggests how deeply entrenched in corruption they were, how outraged they were by Gao's actions, and how long the corrupt practices had been tolerated and accepted as normal by previous county magistrates. Gao's boldness was a rarity. Presumably, he took action because at least some local elites (assemblymen) wanted him to, for local reasons unknown to us.

Corruption of this kind and abuses by county judicial staff that did not involve the county magistrate directly were routine. If a county magistrate was prone to bribery, the amount of money involved would be larger and the way in which the bribery took place subtler. But sometimes when it came to a shakedown—squeezing the rich for payoffs—the process was not subtle at all. In 1928, the Suqian county magistrate, Dong Hancha, arrested Wang Bingjin, a wealthy man, on a trumped-up charge that he had colluded with bandits, keeping a frightened Wang in the filthy county jail until he coughed up ¥50,000.[49] Deng Changyao observed in 1925 that "if the county magistrate and the trial officer had selfish motives, the abuses committed by clerks under them would multiply ten times; and if the trial officer and judicial clerks socialized with local gentry and officials, there must have been bribery and miscarriage of justice."[50]

County Judicial Proceedings

How did the county magistrate or the trial officer try a case, supposing that no bribery and other abuses on his part were taking place? A 1928 government handbook, *Xianzhang xuzhi* (What County Magistrates Should Know), laid down the following sixteen rules to follow in performing judicial functions:

(1) Supervise the trial officer and close all backlogged cases in a timely way.

(2) Try cases as soon as they arrive and keep any necessary delays within legal limits.

(3) Investigate the crime scene in person in homicide and robbery cases.

(4) Use plain language to publicize judicial procedures.

(5) Try cases openly, unless under special circumstances and as permitted by the law.

(6) Pay attention to first-time testimonies.

(7) Respond quickly to litigation received.

(8) Note the time at which cases are registered.

(9) Take care of issuing and receiving summons.

(10) Personally assign policemen their duties and prevent them from farming them out.

(11) Set the standard fare for travel and prohibit irregular charges.

(12) Make sure the arrival of litigants at court is not manipulated by policemen.

(13) Be patient and impartial in trying cases.

(14) Do not allow torture in trials.

(15) Do not detain defendants arbitrarily, and allow bail where appropriate.

(16) Publish fines with the cases, and do not impose fines arbitrarily or for private benefit.[51]

These guidelines were similar in most aspects to those prescribed for magistrates under the Qing dynasty.[52] Reflecting the reform, however, some aspects were new, such as the prohibition of torture in trials, the role of the trial officer, the practice of release on bail, and the use of fines as punishment. Yet, the detailed admonitions on the county magistrate's behavior in performing judicial functions suggest that those problems were known to exist in county judicial processes.

Under the law on the county magistrate's judicial functions, when a lawsuit was brought to trial at the CGO, criminal defendants had no legal representation or defense. Civil litigants did not have lawyers either, but they could have relatives to serve as their surrogates (*daili ren*) under the Provisional Regulations on the County Magistrate Trying Lawsuits. In November 1920, the Wu county magistrate, Wen Shaoliang, asked the JHC whether having a surrogate in civil litigation was limited to a plaintiff, because a defendant would often evade showing up at trial by sending a surrogate instead, which slowed down the judicial process, causing case backlogs. The JHC made it clear that civil defendants were entitled to having surrogates to attend trial for them if they had legitimate reasons to be absent; and only when it was necessary to question a defendant did he have to appear at trial.[53] The rule ensured the rights of civil defendants, but also contributed to case backlogs, since defendants had motives to delay cases against them by not appearing at trials, and it was difficult to determine what would not be "legitimate" reasons for such absences.

The normal county trial proceeded as follows:

(1) The litigants stated their personal information and the cause of the litigation.

(2) The county magistrate questioned litigants and witnesses, if any.

(3) At a later date, the county magistrate announced a decision (*caijue*) in a civil case or a conviction and sentence (*panjue*) in a criminal case, which was written down as a document to be delivered to the homes of the civil litigants or the criminal defendant.[54]

(4) At that point, litigants or defendants stated whether they would appeal, which was recorded and signed—an appeal against a civil decision was called a "complaint" (*kanggao*) and one against a criminal conviction and sentence was called an "appeal" (*shanggao*).

That would be the end of the county trial. Stages 1 and 2, however, were what could make the case drag on for months and years, if a defendant or a key witness could not be located. Stage 4 was another place for the case to remain unclosed when one party or both parties wanted to appeal (see the next section). Throughout the process, the county magistrate or trial officer had absolute power and discretion to make a decision, issue a conviction, and impose sentences, per his understanding of the facts and the law, as did judges in a court. This discretional power was called the principle of free evaluation of evidence through inner conviction (*ziyou xinzheng zhuyi*).[55]

Of course, the county magistrate or trial officer often got the facts or the law, or both, wrong (as noted in Chapter 4 above, the rate of error in county trials was between 24.1 and 26.1 percent). When the proper procedures were followed, appeals and trial reviews saved many civil litigants and criminal defendants from being wrongfully penalized. A civil case about the ownership of a piece of land tried at the Chuansha CGO in 1926 was decided in favor of the defendant. The plaintiff appealed to the Shanghai DC, and the court upheld the decision of the county trial. The plaintiff further appealed to the JHC, and the court sent the case back to the DC for retrial. The retrial resulted in a decision in favor of the plaintiff, and the defendant lost his appeal to the JHC.[56] Similarly, a 1934 civil case about the ownership of a piece of land tried in Baoshan led to the prosecution of a witness by a procurator of the Shanghai DC for falsifying a private document (a deed). The court trial acquitted the defendant, and the procurator appealed against the acquittal to the JHC but lost his appeal there.[57] Even though it would be difficult to quantify, one gains an impression from the archives that the judicial system as a whole, from the semi-formal CGO to the formal courts at the district and provincial levels, largely worked as it was designed to do by the law, which should balance discussions of the problems that existed in the system.[58] Even at the county level, if the county magistrate or the trial officer followed the law and procedures, which they often did, the abuses and irregularities committed by county functionaries usually increased the litigation cost for litigants, but did not necessarily change the judicial outcome, which was largely determined by the merits of a case (in terms of the court decision, but not its enforcement, as will be seen below).

It often happened that when the county magistrate announced his decision in a case, the litigant or defendant did not state an intention to appeal, and when he or she later tried to appeal, the county magistrate had to reject the request under the law.[59] The litigant would try to petition the superior court by writing letters accusing the county magistrate or the trial officer of injustice, which would routinely result in investigations ordered by the JHC, consuming untold amounts of institutional resources. The county magistrate could not be blamed for ordinary citizens' ignorance of judicial procedures and for adhering to the procedural law, but it is doubtful that the magistrate made conscientious efforts to inform litigants and defendants of their rights in all cases.

Legal Culture at the County Level

Were Local People Overly Litigious?

Like their imperial predecessors, many county magistrates routinely complained that the people in their jurisdictions were extremely litigious, inclined to resort to civil lawsuits for the smallest disputes, and short-tempered and quick to get into physical scuffles that led to criminal lawsuits.[60] Such a discourse, along with citing widespread robbery and banditry, was a standard explanation or excuse for case backlogs at the CGO, for overcrowding in county jails, and for all the problems in county judicial processes. The county magistrate was not the only person who so complained. In Gourong, where the DC and the DP were established in August 1912 (before being dismantled in 1914), the chief procurator, Zhong Guansheng, a native of Gourong (this was before the rule of avoidance was established), spoke of his fellow natives as inclined to engage in fraud and deception and quick to quarrel and resort to lawsuits (*xiza shangqi, xishi jiansong*). "In the few days following the opening of the court and procuracy, half of the lawsuits filed at the court were frivolous. . . . When a person has a dispute, he blows his case out of proportion so that the other party will suffer from a long-

TABLE 6.2

Samples of the County-Level Monthly Caseload in Jiangsu, 1911–1937

Date	County	Civil closed	Civil unclosed	Criminal closed	Criminal unclosed	To be enforced	Total
1911.6	Jiangning	23	3	6	3		35
1913.8	Chuansha	26	10	6	1		43
1916.1	Danyang	29	14	31	33		107
1916.2	Danyang	3	33	28	20		84
1922.8	Wu		95		34	8	?
1924.1	Baoshan	15	25	28	15	9	92
1924.3	Nanhui	29	79	44	107	37	296
1924.5	Taicang	12	19	26	25	5	87
1927.8	Nanhui	18	46			24	?
1927.9	Songjiang	26	11	71	22		130
1931.8	Songjiang		46		8		?
1936.2	Tai	89	128	113	187	68	585

SOURCE: JGFD, TJ-12, 37, 307, 519, 555, 706, 724, 1115, 1472, 2164.

dragged-out lawsuit."[61] Such a view is echoed in county gazetteers and memoir literature.[62] The gazetteer of Yancheng noted that it was customary for local people to "pursue a dispute as small as a hair through lawsuits as large as mountains."[63] In short, that local people were very litigious was a widely shared perception in the official discourse in the Republican era.

Did the discourse reflect the reality? How true was the perception? If it was not true, how and from where did it arise? To answer these questions, we may examine the archives that enumerated cases typically processed each month. Here only random samples from the wealth of information are presented. Table 6.2 shows the monthly caseloads at several counties in 1911–1937 at various intervals. It may be noted that the number of unclosed cases increased relative to closed cases over the years.

A better handle on whether people were litigious than the numbers shown in Table 6.2 is perhaps to compare the frequency of lawsuits with the size of the populations of counties at a given point of time, as shown in Table 6.3. The number of lawsuits in the table is taken from a JHC document on judicial affairs in all counties where county magistrates adjudicated cases for the month of January 1925, and the population figures come from a separate source, where the data were collected in 1919.[64] Based on the information shown in the table, one may conclude that lawsuits were not unduly frequent in proportion to population

TABLE 6.3

The County Population–Litigation Ratio in Jiangsu, 1920s

County	M.	T.	Civil	Enforce	Criminal	Total	Closed	Unclosed	Population	Percent
Jiangpu	1	1	11 + 5	14 + 0	21 + 10	61	16	45	125,238	0.05
Danyang	1	1	49 + 2	13 + 0	15 + 10	89	13	76	424,271	0.02
Luhe	1	1	18 + 5	5 + 0	15 + 22	65	33	32	287,741	0.02
Gourong	1		16 + 0		38 + 10	64	4	60	205,570	0.03
Jintan	1		15 + 4	1 + 0	13 + 4	37	14	23	230,593	0.02
Lishui	1		6 + 1	3 + 0	10 + 4	24	10	14	144,690	0.02
Gaochun	1		0 + 1	2 + 0	5 + 5	13	4	9	175,560	0.01
Liyang	1	1	14 + 10	6 + 0	17 + 19	66	35	31	295,522	0.02
Yangzhong	1		12 + 2	1 + 0	35 + 9	59	19	40	110,453	0.05
Changshu	1	2	45 + 17	46 + 1	71 + 44	224	107	117	792,842	0.03
Wujing	1	2	35 + 5	11 + 4	45 + 50	150	83	67	698993	0.02
Wuxi	1	3							916,466	
Wujiang	1	1	17 + 3	42 + 0	55 + 15	132	62	70	535,565	0.02
Kunshan	1	1	11 + 1	7 + 2	11 + 9	41	12	29	233,263	0.02
Yixing	1	1	9 + 9	1 + 0	46 + 18	83	48	35	544,634	0.02
Jingjiang	1	1	54 + 13	31 + 2	52 + 19	171	50	121	356,691	0.05
Nantong	1	1	115 + 30	2 + 0	63 + 51	261	109	152	1,300,009	0.02
Rugao	1	2	90 + 42	38 + 12	95 + 87	364	203	161	1,190,377	0.03
Taixing	1	2	99 + 54	32 + 7	162 + 76	430	212	218	807,998	0.05
Jiangyin	1	1	20 + 8	1 + 0	23 + 12	64	13	51	666,060	0.01
Songjiang	1	1	26 + 0	18 + 0	55 + 11	110	52	58	408,752	0.03
Fengxian	1	1	20 + 18	7 + 0	71 + 14	130	62	68	211,193	0.06
Nanhui	1	2	29 + 45	51 + 3	83 + 47	258	126	132	451,969	0.06
Baoshan	1	1	20 + 2	11 + 1	21 + 11	66	26	40	343,305	0.02
Chongming	1	1	30 + 16	5 + 0	66 + 54	171	87	84	575,331	0.03
Waisha	1	1	58 + 21	18 + 1	116 + 48	262	158	104		
Haimen	1	1	58 + 28	13 + 2	74 + 27	202	54	148	563,452	0.04
Jinshan	1		6 + 1	1 + 0	29 + 8	45	29	16	154,002	0.03
Qingpu	1	1	47 + 1	1 + 0	58 + 3	110	2	108	268,549	0.04
Chuansha	1		1 + 7	5 + 1	19 + 16	49	18	31	110,854	0.04
Taicang	1	1	36 + 3	11 + 0	55 + 9	114	10	104	269,672	0.04
Jiading	1	1	27 + 4	15 + 1	70 + 11	128	16	112	235,857	0.05
Yancheng	1	1	114 + 13	25 + 0	281 + 29	462	219	243	912,054	0.05
Huaiyin	1	1	14 + 2		85 + 26	127	27	100	423,319	0.03
Jiangdu	1	2	82 + 24	25 + 6	266 + 77	480	186	294	1,479,605	0.03
Gaoyou	1	1	75 + 34	35 + 5	110 + 45	304	148	156	557,723	0.05
Xinghua	1	1	124 + 38	22 + 7	60 + 45	296	117	179	661,759	0.04
Baoying	1	1	26 + 9		13 + 19	67	42	25	410,137	0.02
Tai	1	2	49 + 43	45 + 2	88 + 51	278	107	171	950,073	0.03
Dongtai	1	1	126 + 18	9 + 0	49 + 24	226	49	177	1,130,726	0.02
Huai'an	1	2	53 + 30	3 + 0	166 + 76	328	180	148	654,960	0.05
Funing	1	1	42 + 8	7 + 1	182 + 19	259	32	227	1,021,484	0.03
Siyang	1	1	10 + 0		60 + 11	81	8	73	496,411	0.02
Lianshui	1	1	56 + 8		558 + 76	698	88	610	442,041	0.16
Yizheng	1	1	42 + 8	5 + 0	54 + 20	129	40	89	210,393	0.06
Tongshan	1	1	28 + 7		324 + 42	401	35	366	858,410	0.05
Donghai	1		35 + 4	1 + 0	121 + 14	175	60	115	493,749	0.04
Pei	1	1	9 + 9		28 + 29	75	38	37	274,985	0.03
Feng	1		18 + 10		83 + 15	126	21	105	291,023	0.04
Suqian	1		59 + 3		135 + 12	209	12	197	589,965	0.04
Suining	1	1	5 + 3		11 + 27	46	38	8	430,721	0.01
Guanyun	1	1	23 + 4	3 + 0	139 + 20	189	23	166	484,859	0.04
Ganyu	1	1	16 + 13		51 + 30	110	54	56	419,387	0.03
Xiao	1	1	15 + 0		60 + 2	77	9	68	428,565	0.02
Pi	1	1	25 + 2		113 + 23	163	22	141	511,447	0.03
Dangshan	1	1	5 + 1		32 + 11	49	17	32	213,568	0.02
Shuyang	1	1	42 + 6		357 + 50	455	45	410	470,069	0.10
TOTAL/%						9,853	3,304	6,549	28,452,905	0.04

(0.04 percent provincewide), even though there was an increase in lawsuits during the Republican era, as noted in Chapter 4.[65] Why, then, did county magistrates feel overwhelmed by litigation? The answer is that they had very limited resources to effectively and efficiently perform their judicial functions, which included confining and feeding defendants and convicts in the county detention house and county jail (see Chapter 8).

A significant fact about the statistics cited above is that there were more pending cases from previous months than cases received in a current month. It was those backlogged cases that frustrated county magistrates and, more important, judicial officials, who expected "results" from institutional operations. In fact, however, even the problem of case backlogs in the Republican era was favorably comparable with the imperial era. In 1807, when the Jiaqing emperor ordered all provinces to report case backlogs, Hunan province had 3,228 unclosed cases (with a population of 28.9 million), Fujian province, 2,977 (12 million), and Guangdong province, 2,107 (16 million).[66] Pushed by an energetic governor, Ting Richang, from June 1867 to January 1870 Jiangsu disposed of more than 17,700 cases, most of which were backlogs since 1864, a number that would translate into an annual average of 5,900 in 1864–1867.[67] In comparison, Jiangsu had 6,466 unclosed cases in 1925, when the total number of cases processed at all jurisdictions of the province in a year greatly exceeded the number in the imperial era. Nevertheless, case backlogs made judicial officials and county magistrates feel overwhelmed by litigation and think that the judiciary was not as effective and efficient as it was supposed to be. There was a great anxiety to eliminate case backlogs, but the problem never went away. The real question, then, is why so many cases remained open at the CGO, and, for that matter, at all the other courts as well.

Why Cases Remained Open

Various factors accounted for the situation where the majority of cases at the CGO in a given month were pending old cases, some of

SOURCES OF TABLE 6.3: JGFD, RS-303; JZN, 68–72.

NOTE: The columns after county names represent "county magistrate," "trial officers," "civil cases," "civil enforcement cases," "criminal cases," "total number of cases," "cases closed," "cases unclosed," "population," and "percentage." Under "civil," "enforce," and "criminal," the number before a plus sign indicates old cases and the number after shows cases accepted in the current month. The case numbers for Wuxi were missing in the source, so the computation of provincial case frequency excludes Wuxi's population.

which had been open for years. Both criminal and civil cases sometimes dragged on for no obvious reasons in the cases themselves, but because the county magistrate was either slothful or overwhelmed by his administrative and judicial duties. Other cases remained unclosed because civil defendants had no incentive to move their cases forward, but rather to do everything possible to block or delay cases against them. Still others, often criminal cases, could not be closed either because the defendant(s) remained at large, or witnesses were unavailable, or because the evidence was not sufficient to convict, but the defendants, as criminal suspects, had to be kept behind bars, and their cases remained open. Many cases could not be closed because the procedural norms and forms established by the reform allowed defendants and litigants to game the system to thwart their opponents at the expense of the judiciary's institutional effectiveness and efficiency.

One case in Lianshui involved members of a Zhang family vying for seventeen *mu* of land left by a branch of it that had no male descendant. The lawsuit and countersuit started in 1907, and not until 1914 was a decision reached, and in 1916, the losing party was still petitioning the JHC, alleging a conspiracy between the winning party and the witness in the case. According to the report by the county magistrate in response to a query from the JHC, the case, which had been decided long before the current magistrate's tenure, had dragged on for years because the parties had repeatedly failed to show up at trials, but kept filing briefs against each other.[68] In the county case record, then, the case was in the "unclosed" category.

A civil case could often drag on for years because one party to a dispute was able to manipulate the system to delay a decision in favor of the other party. Tao Liumen of Jiangning paid the required fees to obtain a piece of polder land along Lake Huang Tiandang from the Bureau of Polder Land (*shatian ju*), a government agency, in 1918. His ownership of the land was verified by both the CGO and the provincial government and certified by the Ministry of Finance, yet a certain Guo Dabang challenged his ownership in 1919. The resulting lawsuit went through first and second trials, which confirmed Tao's ownership of the land, but in May 1921, Guo managed, on appeal, to obtain an order from the Supreme Court that the Jiangning DC retry the case, and Guo requested the DC to conduct another survey of the land in dispute, even though such survey had been done twice in earlier trials. As of January 1922, the survey had not been conducted, and the case was therefore still pending. Complaining to the JHC about the DC's delay, Tao asked "Is this how the judicial institution that protects human rights operates?" The JHC ordered the Jiangning DC to deal with the case as swiftly as possible. Yet nothing had happened by May 1922, and Tao had to write to the JHC again, saying that as a citizen, he despaired of the recovery of judicial sovereignty (referring to an end to extraterritoriality) and the future of the judiciary, given the way the courts had handled his case.[69] Even such rhetoric did not help Tao, since whatever should be done had to be done by the district court or the county magistrate, not by the JHC. Although this case was first tried at the district court that happened to exist in Jiangning, the tactics used by a losing party to prevent the closure of a case resembled those in many cases tried in county offices.

A criminal case in Tai illustrates a different scenario. In July 1924, Huang Shengyou was found beaten and strangled to death at the age of sixty-nine. Strong circumstantial evidence pointed to Jing Yewen and Woman Zhang, a widow, as suspects. The suspected motive of the murder was that Zhang had had affairs first with Huang and then with Jing, and that Jing had killed Huang out of jealousy. Jing had been seen running in the direction of the victim's home on the night of the murder, after he had looked for but could not find Zhang, according to witnesses. A pair of woman's pants and a pair of man's pants that had been washed but were not dry yet, and on which bloodstains could be discerned, were found in Zhang's home. But since Jing and Zhang did not confess, and there was no eyewitness to the killing, the case remained open, and Jing and Zhang remained in custody as of April 1926. Magistrate Wang Shoujong wrote to the JHC explaining why the case was pending and asking for instructions. The court replied that the county should send the pants found in Zhang's home to forensic specialists for examination and should gather all the evidence and study it carefully. "It is not proper for the High Court and High Procuracy to tell you any specifics about how to do it," said the order.[70] Such situations, in their endless variations, were a major reason why many criminal cases dragged on without reaching a conclusion. In a sense, the procedural norms and forms established by the reform contributed to this. In the imperial era, the defendants in such a murder case would certainly have been tortured to get confessions from them, but torture had been prohibited by the reform since the New Policy years. Magistrate Wang could now at his discretion convict the suspects on the basis of the circumstantial evidence to get it over with, but the crime called for the death penalty, and the ensuing trial review by the High Court might send it back to him for retrial, in which event, he would have to deal with it all over again. At the same time, in cases of theft, robbery, and other violent crimes, to release an accused suspect would provoke local elites anxious about "unruly" elements among the poor. So the case remained unclosed, and the defendants in custody.

If a litigant could deliberately prevent a case from moving forward in order to frustrate his or her opponent, and the county magistrate could do little about it, much less could be done when the losing party to a civil dispute kept defaulting on his or her obligations under a court decision. This was the primary reason why many civil cases and civil enforcement cases were extremely difficult to close.

Jiang Bulan of Lianshui sued in 1909 to get back 176 *mu* of land that he had bought from Gu Guisheng, but that were seized by Tang Haoran under a false pretense supplied by Zhang Zhenbiao. Five years later, after two trials, Jiang won the case, and the district court ordered Tang to return the land and Zhang to hand over related documents. But Tang and Zhang refused to follow the court order. Jiang went to the JHC and the circuit administrator three times each to request an enforcement of the court decision. In response, eight orders were issued to the county magistrate to enforce the court decision, but to no avail. In May 1917, eight years after the initial lawsuit, Jiang wrote despairingly to the JHC urging action, saying: "I heard that law is very strict under the Republican government; but how come the world is still so pitch black, without sunlight!" After repeated requests from Jiang, now sixty-two, and repeated orders from the JHC president, the Lianshui county magistrate, Tang Shuji, finally revealed in October 1917 what the problem was. Gu Guizheng, the original owner of the land in question, lived in Huai'an, and Zhang Zhenbiao lived in Shuyang, and it was difficult to summon them to Lianshui. After Magistrate Tang wrote to the magistrates of Huai'an and Shuyang counties on the matter, Gu finally arrived, but the Shuyang county magistrate replied that Zhang was too old and sick to travel. At the time of his reporting, Magistrate Tang was asking whether Zhang Zhenbiao could send a surrogate to Lianshui.[71] In short, either because the Lianshui county magistrate did not make serious efforts at enforcement, or the practical problems he faced lay beyond his control, or a combination of both, Jiang Bulan was unable to get back his land eight years after his initial lawsuit and three years after his winning the case in court, and the case remained unclosed in the docket of the county magistrate. The case demonstrates the powerlessness of a winning litigant and the unhelpfulness of the county magistrate (and the judicial system as a whole) in the face of local connections and complex relationships among those involved in litigation.

In some cases, the losing party to a civil lawsuit was able simply to ignore civil decisions made by the county magistrate, or the magistrate did not seem to be interested in or capable of enforcing civil decisions. In 1927, the JHC decided in an appeal case from Donghai that Huang Gaoshu should pay Huang Shao'an ¥1,000, and the latter should return a piece of land to the former. For nearly two years after Huang Gaoshu paid his money, however, Huang Shao'an was able to evade returning the land and supplying the names of tenants who rented the land, despite Huang Gaoshu's repeated requests to the CGO for enforcement.[72] Similarly, Qian Gengqu of Yixing won a lawsuit against Zong Zhishan, who was ordered to pay a debt of ¥424 in March 1929 and lost his appeal in March 1930. By August 1931, however, Qian had still not seen his money. After issuing one summons, to which Zong did not respond, the CGO took no further action.[73] The county magistrates in those cases did not pursue enforcement, probably because they realized they did not have the wherewithal to do so and did not want to waste their time and energy in a futile exercise. Under the rules on civil enforcement (see Chapter 3), the county magistrate could have detained the losing litigants, but since they could hold them no more than three months under the rules, some magistrates chose not to bother at all, because they knew the detained litigants would just sit out the three months in jail, while being fed at the county's expense.

Another case reveals a different problem. In January 1920, Woman Lin of the Cheng family in Liyang wrote to the JHC that the judgment in her favor of a civil dispute had still not been enforced six months after the decision. But according to Magistrate Yang Yinqing, the decision had not been enforced because at each hearing for the enforcement, Woman Lin raised new demands that were not part of the judgment.[74] One has no way to know for certain whether the county magistrate was making an excuse for his failure to enforce the civil decision, but such behavior on the part of the winning litigant would seem plausible.

Some cases remained open for years simply because litigants kept appealing and then failing to show up at trials. A civil suit about inheritance of land in Chuansha started in late 1929 and did not end until

November 1936 after appeals at the Shanghai DC and the JHC. When it was finally decided by the JHC, both parties to the case were absent from the court.[75] The litigants may simply have given up or settled the case without notifying the court.

Trial Delays

Besides cases that could not be closed, there were cases simply waiting to be tried. Many criminal cases especially were not tried in a timely fashion in accordance with the criminal procedural law. In May 1930, JHC Inspector Chen Ludan reported that the detention house in Liyang held fourteen defendants whose cases remained unclosed. One had been arrested in 1928 and eight in 1929.[76] Similarly, in December 1933, the detention house in Chongming had held forty-three criminal defendants for more than three months, and eleven of them for more than a year. Eleven were having their cases reviewed or appealed, but the rest had yet to be tried.[77] All this violated the regulations. Although the sources do not say, the reasons for the trial delays in those cases could very well be the familiar ones—unavailability of witnesses and insufficient evidence for conviction.

Another important reason why cases were not tried in time was simply that the CGO did not possess sufficient resources to deal with an unusually large number of cases, as was the case in Gaoyou in the early 1930s. Gaoyou had a population of 600,000, and the people were said to be litigious. The poor harvests since the flood of 1931 resulted in an increase in civil lawsuits over debts, as well as criminal cases. Over 1,300 new cases were received in one year. Yet, under the judicial funding scheme, Gaoyou was classified as a second-grade county, with one trial officer, one clerk, and four record-keepers. The trial officer was to try criminal and civil cases, enforce civil decisions, reply to inquiries and complaints, write conviction and sentence documents, go to the countryside to investigate criminal and civil cases, and check all official communications on judicial affairs. No matter how hard he worked, the trial officer could at most dispose of eighty cases a month, and never as many as he received, which was why there were more than 500 backlogged cases at the CGO. Furthermore, because the people were economically hard pressed, it was especially difficult to enforce civil decisions, and the number of civil decisions waiting to be enforced reached more than 300. Although the JHC sent a temporary trial officer in May 1934 to help clear up backlogged cases, which resulted in disposing of over 300 cases, more than 100 backlogged cases remained, and still more civil decisions were to be enforced, while new cases were piling up again. On August 24, 1934, Magistrate Cao Boquan wrote to the JHC requesting appointment of an additional trial officer, one clerk, and two record-keepers as permanent positions. Not surprisingly, the JHC did not want to allocate additional funds for one particular county. President Lin Biao responded that the provincial budget had already been adopted and that Cao's request could not be considered for the time being.[78] The situation in Gaoyou was by no means atypical.

At this point, a general observation about county-level litigation in Republican Jiangsu may be offered. As the archival sources show, locals involved in civil lawsuits were usually people of some wealth (even if only very modest wealth) and were willing to invest time and money to pursue their cases. Really poor people had little property to dispute over (though they might be sued for debts if they were perceived to be able to pay), but they often ended up as criminal defendants for assault, kidnapping, theft, and robbery. Consequently, counties that had a relatively wealthier population on average, mostly located south of the Yangzi River (the Jiangnan region), saw more civil litigation, which tended to generate judicial revenue. Enforcement of civil decisions was difficult, but it was really a problem for the litigants involved and did not cost the CGO anything, even though the county magistrate's case record might suffer. On the other hand, counties that had a generally poorer population, mostly located north of the Yangzi River (the North China region), such as Gaoyou, cited above, tended to have more criminal cases, which generated little judicial revenue but cost much more in resources, especially for the incarceration of defendants and convicts. This was a crucial variable affecting how county judicial functions were performed and perceived.

In conclusion, the paradox of the judicial reform was that the expansion of the court system was supposed to increase the state's capacity to process lawsuits, which meant fewer case backlogs, but in reality the expansion of judicial functions invited increasingly more litigation than the system was able to handle adequately. As the judicial system became more accessible, people were more willing to go to court, believing that they would get justice, in predicaments to which they would previously just have resigned themselves. Moreover, the procedural norms and forms, including those with regard to appeals, made it easier for litigants and defendants to manipulate the system to delay the cases against them; and at the same time, the system lacked meaningful resources to enforce civil decisions, especially at the county level. In a sense, the perennial case backlogs did not necessarily mean the failure of the reform; rather, they were an indication of its success in establishing formal procedures, or due process. As we have seen, however, successful procedural formalization did not necessarily result in justice.

In the Republican era, the social environment of the county judiciary remained substantively what it had been in the imperial era. After the retrenchment of the court system in 1913–1914, the county magistrate remained surrounded by local elites, who had ways and means to influence the magistrate's judicial functions, and by county functionaries, who, having local roots, had every incentive and opportunity to commit abuses and irregularities as a matter of course. The new forms of institutional reach of the state on the county level were the trial officer, a statutory post that did not exist in every county, and the jail overseer. Officially appointed by the provincial judicial authorities, those two lowly officers were subject to the same kinds of local pressure as was the county magistrate to contravene the norms and forms mandated by the central government, even if they themselves were not corrupt in the first place.

While the social environment remained essentially the same, the reform tended to foster more and more litigation, including appeals and trial reviews. Given the social environment, the increase in lawsuits had at least two consequences. First, with limited resources, the county magistrate was confronted with an increasingly heavier caseload and many more unenforceable civil decisions, hence the case backlogs. Second, county-level functionaries were more likely to violate the forms and norms mandated by the central government and were offered more opportunities to squeeze civil litigants and criminal defendants, hence more abuses and irregularities. Not surprisingly, therefore, case backlogs and corruption were the two most frequently cited problems in the county judicial process in the Republican era.

CHAPTER 7

Power and Justice in Local Society

> Even when he succeeds in getting appointed to a district, the job of the magistrate is by no means an easy one. In the first place he must try and work with the staff at his Yamen, the majority of whom are local people and who are very jealous of their rights and privileges. He must endeavor to cultivate the friendship of the leaders of the local gentry, many of whom have axes of their own to grind, and who, taking advantage of the privileges now enjoyed by democracy, do not hesitate to impeach any magistrate who does not work in harmony with them.
>
> —Robert W. Swallow, *North China Herald* (Shanghai), September 11, 1935[1]

Except for the word "democracy" by which the writer may have meant the Republic, the statement quoted above well describes the forces in local society that countered and undermined the county magistrate's power. Scholarship on modern China has long established that from the late imperial through the Republican era, local elites, whose composition became more diverse (they no longer being limited to the traditional gentry, which also evolved), augmented their power and dominated local society.[2] This study will not alter that broad understanding. Yet, against the backdrop provided in the preceding chapter, a close examination of the forces at work in the county judicial process will yield important insights into specific forms of exercising power by various players in local society.

Did the state penetrate local society more deeply as a result of the creation of new judicial institutions at the provincial level (and, in some locales, also at the county level) that facilitated litigation? What influence did such institutional changes have on local power relationships at the county level and below? Who were empowered and who, if any, were adversely affected? How did local elites and nonelite people alike utilize the county judicial process through institutional, political, and social channels and resources, including discursive strategies, to advance or defend their respective interests? How did county judicial functions, on the one hand, and political, social, and cultural conditions in local society, on the other, shape and reshape each other in the course of the judicial reform? This chapter addresses these issues through an analysis of the respective roles of local gentry, chambers of commerce, legal scribes, and GMD cadres, all of whom figure prominently in county judicial archives. The cases examined below are illustrative, not exhaustive; they show patterns, not statistical data. However limited its results, judicial reform at the county level had an impact on local society, because it empowered certain social groups and complicated the power relations there, which in turn conditioned and complicated the delivery of justice that the reform promised.

Local Gentry and County Justice

Local Gentry and County Judicial Institutions, 1912

As we have seen, courts and procuracies were established in many counties in Jiangsu in 1911–1913, only to be abolished in 1913–1914. During the short period when those institutions existed, the relationship between them and local elites varied in different locales, all revealing an intense competition for power among local gentry who had a keen sense of who would gain what power in local society through the judicial reform. Three diverse cases follow.

The DC and the DP in Gourong began to operate on August 1, 1912. A week later, the DP chief, Zhong Guansheng, sent Governor Cheng Dequan a report complaining that the local people were given to frivolous lawsuits and informing the governor that he had issued a public warning against false accusations, on penalty of prosecution. Within a week, Zhong sent another report requesting permission to resign. The locals not only persisted in frivolous lawsuits, and were impervious to argument, but members of the local gentry walked right into the court to argue for parties in litigation or spread rumors outside. As a native of

Gourong, Zhong was one generation junior to most members of the local gentry. It would be illegal for him to accommodate their interference in judicial proceedings, but if he upheld judicial independence, there might be unrest, given the locals' ignorance of law. In sum, Zhong said, a Gourong native managing Gourong affairs created difficulties several times more than an outsider managing local affairs would. For the sake of Gourong's future, he should resign. Cheng Dequan responded that judicial independence was provided for by the Provisional Constitution, and if judicial officers abided by the law and adhered fearlessly to the principle, those who tried to interfere in judicial process would disappear. Cheng promised that while holding judicial officers to high standards, he would eagerly protect them as well and would not promote and demote them based on unsubstantiated local rumors. Cheng endorsed Zhong's public notice against frivolous lawsuits and asked him to continue his efforts.[3] What Cheng advised Zhong to do, of course, was easier said than done. That local gentry would try to interfere with the judicial process was to be expected, especially when the judicial officer was a local son. While reflecting Zhong's integrity and his intention to do right things, his plea pointed to the desirability of the rule of avoidance. Soon after the rule of avoidance was established in 1913, however, courts and procuracies at the county level were dismantled in 1913–1914. But the situation Zhong faced would continue to confront county magistrates who handled judicial affairs, even though they were outsiders to local society.

The second case demonstrates the power of local gentry despite formal judicial organs at the county level. In early 1912, Xu Tai of Taixing, who had served as a county runner for over thirty years, brought forty muskets from his native place in Manchuria to Tai, hoping to sell them to local militia groups. When his muskets were discovered by Wang Huifang, a member of the county assembly and the head of local militia, Xu was arrested for private possession of military weapons, tried at the DC, and sentenced to three years' imprisonment. Then an inmate who had lost money gambling inside the county jail falsely reported that Xu and others were conspiring to escape. Before the DC and the DP took action, the county assembly, pushed by Wang and two other members, resolved that Xu and four other inmates be executed. The district procurator had the execution carried out on August 18. When he received a petition from Xu's wife demanding justice for the wrongful execution of her husband, the acting governor, Zhuang Yunkuan, noted that in the Republican era, human rights should be respected, and that the execution without approval ran counter to the governor's intention to reform the judiciary and protect the people. Yet he did not pursue the matter any further and only told Xu's wife to go to the court to seek redress when the new procurator assumed the office.[4] It may be surmised that as a longtime county yamen runner, Xu Tai had probably offended Wang and others somewhere along the way, and Wang seized the opportunity to get rid of Xu in revenge. Whatever Wang's motive was, an intriguing question is how and why the procurator would follow the decision of the county assembly to execute five inmates on flimsy grounds (the word of an inmate), without any legal basis whatsoever. Limited information does not allow a definite answer, but one may infer that the procurator (possibly a native at this point in time) was somehow beholden to local gentry like Wang, who controlled the county assembly (and the militia) and used it as a legitimate vehicle to dominate local society. Such an event—a county assembly ordering the execution of five inmates and a DP carrying it out—indicated the power and brazenness of local gentry like Wang who were empowered by new institutions such as the county assembly. This episode helps contextualize local assemblies' attempts to control judicial institutions and appointments, discussed in Chapter 4.

Local gentry's interference in judicial matters was a time-honored practice, especially when it came to civil disputes and litigation; at times, local gentry even handled criminal matters, as the above case indicates. This did not always sit well with all judicial officers who operated the new judicial organs, however, especially those not beholden to local elites. The third case represents one of those occasions where conflicts arose between local gentry and the new judicial institutions. In early 1912, the DP in Taicang discovered a homicide case in Shuangfeng township that had been privately settled without being reported to the judiciary. In prosecuting the case, the DP learned that the victim's mother had reported the case to the township manager, Zhao Jinchuang. Acting on the information, the DP summoned Zhao for failing to report the homicide and for having the matter settled privately. Zhao did not respond until the second summons was served. At the pretrial hearing, Zhao was ordered to kneel down, but was allowed to go home on bail afterward. Within days, three members of the Township Assembly and four "citizens," who self-identified as one scholar and three merchants, submitted a petition on behalf of Zhao to the DP protesting against the

DP humiliating and abusing Zhao, an insult to the entire township. "Although township head was a minor position, it is the administrative institution of the township, and [Zhao] was elected by its citizens," they objected. In reality, of course, the head was not elected by all the citizens of the community; at best, he was selected (*tuiju*) by local elites in the name of an election. The petitioners argued that Zhao had no responsibility to report homicide to the judiciary; Zhao had committed no crimes; and there was no cause to summon Zhao and have him kneel down at the hearing. They wanted an explanation to assuage "the people's indignation."

The DP Chief Guo Xingji rejected the petition, citing judicial independence, but the petitioners refused to back off and sent a second petition a week later in the name of the Shuangfeng Township Assembly. They argued that when the homicide victim's mother went to Zhao to report her son's death, Zhao had told her to go to the judicial authorities, which ended his responsibility as township head and did not amount to allowing a private settlement. They again raised the issue of Zhao's reputation being ruined. Having had enough of the matter, Guo submitted the whole case to the acting governor, Zhuang Yunkuan, enclosing the two petitions and defending his having summoned Zhao and then ordered him to kneel down for disorderly behavior in the courtroom. Guo strongly opposed the assembly intervening in the DP's business, with a familiar rhetorical question: "If such illegal usurpation is to be tolerated, how can one imagine the future of justice?" In the meantime, having heard that Zhao was lobbying the governor's office, Guo wrote a personal letter to the head of the JD arguing the same point in his defense. The letter proved unnecessary, because Acting Governor Zhuang supported Guo: summoning Zhao and "disciplining" him to maintain courtroom order were within the authority of the DP and were justified in this case. If anything improper had been done to Zhao, it was up to Zhao to seek redress according to the law, and the township assembly had no authority to intervene.[5]

Behind this incident, there was probably some untold story—perhaps a running conflict between the DP and the local gentry in Taichang since the establishment of the DP. It appears that the DP used the homicide case to rough up Zhao and teach him a lesson. What Guo revealed in his report to Zhuan Yunkuan is suggestive. It was the opinion of Xu Yinjie, a procurator under Guo, that Zhao should be summoned for allowing the private settlement of a homicide case. Guo said that because

Xu and Zhao had known each other all along, he had presided over the hearing so that Xu could recuse himself from the proceedings. It seems likely that Xu masterminded the action against Zhao. What is significant is that the judicial officers used their institutionalized judicial power to deal with local gentry they found obnoxious, with a discourse of judicial independence, and that the latter used their institutional vehicle—the township assembly—to fight back, with a discourse of the township head representing the people.

The above cases point to a new type of local power struggle. The dominance of the local gentry, whose composition changed over time, had always existed in local society and was to be expected. What appeared in these cases were new forms of conflict, competition, and interaction between gentry and other elements in local society, including county-level judicial organs. The extension of the state institutions into local society in the form of courts and procuracies tended to reconfigure the local power structure. Judicial officers as state agents from outside local society encountered local power holders who were armed with new institutional resources, such as the local assembly, as well as discursive strategies. Although the judicial institutional formalization at the county level was cut short in 1913–1914, the provincial and district courts and procuracies that survived would continue to have new social and political implications for local gentry who sought local dominance.

Local Gentry and the County Magistrate in the 1920s

After county-level courts and procuracies were dismantled in 1913–1914, some local gentry must have felt a great relief. Now they had a much greater space and a freer hand to intervene in judicial matters, because they would not deal with independent judicial organs, but with the county magistrate, who relied on their cooperation for his administrative duties, just as in the imperial era. A case in Xiao, a county in northwestern Jiangsu, reveals how a county magistrate yielded to the power of local gentry in a civil dispute that involved criminal acts.

A widow, Woman Chen of the Zhang family, had arranged for the second of her two daughters, Aijie, to marry Sun Huaishan, a man in their village. However, her elder daughter's husband, Jiang Peilian, wanted to marry off Aijie in a faraway place, leaving him to inherit the entire Zhang family property. After consulting with the township manager, Hao Qizhen, Jiang arranged for a man named Zhang Wo to kidnap Aijie and sell her to Chen Shisheng, who lived in another township. Woman Chen reported this to the CGO, and Magistrate Liu Yanqi dispatched the police, who rescued Aijie. Chen Shisheng then sued Zhang Wo for failing to deliver the goods he had paid for (namely, Aijie), and at Hao Qizhen's suggestion, Jiang sold land and trees belonging to Woman Chen to pay off Chen Shisheng. When Woman Chen went with Aijie to the county seat to sue for the return of her property, Zhang Wo kidnapped them both (presumably having been informed in advance by Jiang of their movements), let Chen Shisheng rape Aijie, and kept her confined in Chen's home (presumably to get Chen to withdraw his lawsuit). When Woman Chen managed to escape and sued Hao Qizhen at the CGO, other gentry-managers lobbied the county magistrate on Hao's behalf. Magistrate Liu ruled that Jiang was to pay Women Chen the money obtained from selling her trees; the buyer of her land was to return it to her (Jiang having refunded what he had paid for it); and Hao Qizhen and another township manager, Hao Jingyun, were to choose a husband for Aijie, who had said at the trial that she did not want to marry Sun Huaishan.

Aijie was sold to Wang Shuangyin in another township soon afterward, and Hao Qizhen ordered the township militia to forcibly take her to Wang's home to complete the transaction. Not only did Woman Chen thus lose custody of her daughter, but those who had been ordered to return her land and the money from selling her trees defaulted. When she sued at the CGO again, the defendants Hao Qizhen, Zhang Wo, Jiang Peilian, and Zhang Jiechang (the middleman in the sale of Aijie to Wang Shuangyin) did not show up at the trial. Woman Chen then filed another complaint, and Magistrate Liu summoned only her and Jiang Peilian to the CGO. Liu ruled that Woman Chen should get 300,000 copper coins for her lost land and 70,000 coins for her lost trees; Jiang should return the remaining 14 *mu* of land to her; and the case of Aijie was dismissed. In a petition to the JHC in November 1924, Woman Chen stated that, being hard pressed financially, she had reluctantly accepted the 370,000 copper coins (she would rather have got back the land), and that Jiang had not returned the 14 *mu* of land. In the meantime, Sun Huaishan also petitioned the JHC, describing what had happened to his fiancée, Aijie, and holding the "evil gentry-manager" (*liedong*) Hao Qizhen responsible. Both Woman Chen and Sun Huaishan angrily asked in their petitions what law allowed the county magistrate to rule that Aijie's marriage should be handled by the township managers Hao Qizhen and Hao Jingyun.

In response to the JHC's inquiry, Magistrate Liu asserted that Woman Chen was senile and had been fooled by local ruffians into arranging the marriage of her daughter, a minor, to Sun Huaishan, who was nearly forty years old. There had never been a marriage contract, and at the county trial, Aijie had sworn that she would not marry Sun. He had therefore ruled that (1) Aijie should be in the custody of her elder sister; (2) the township manager Hao Qizhen and others should choose a good family for her to marry into; and (3) Woman Chen should not force Aijie to marry Sun. As for Woman Chen's land, after being returned by Jiang Peilian, it would serve to support her in her old age. Subsequently, when Hao Qizhen and Hao Jingyun reported that, in consultation with Aijie's elder sister and relatives, they had found a proper husband for Aijie—Wang Shuangyin, he (Liu) had approved the match. When Woman Chen sued again, Magistrate Liu had summoned Wang Shuangyin and Woman Chen to the CGO, and Wang had expressed his commitment to Aijie. As for Woman Chen's property, Jiang Peilian submitted to the county 370,000 copper coins and four deeds that Woman Chen had accepted and signed a receipt for.[6] Since there are no further documents on the case, it presumably ended there.

The case deserves analysis in several respects. (1) The county magistrate acted to prevent a marriage arranged by Woman Chen, yet what she did was legal under the law in 1924; at the same time, the magistrate facilitated the sale of a woman arranged by township managers, which was illegal.[7] At the end of the day, Aijie still did not have a say in her own marriage. She was kidnapped, raped, and finally sold to a stranger against her will. The only decision she was allowed to make was not to marry Sun Huaishan, and this was only because it suited Jiang Peilian's plan. (2) Township gentry-managers controlled the local militia, among other things, and did not hesitate to use it in such "community affairs." Their power was obviously recognized and reckoned with by the county magistrate, whose judicial power only served to legitimate whatever the gentry-managers wanted to do. (3) The magistrate lacked any means to enforce civil decisions, especially when the defaulting parties (Jiang Peilian here) were allied with local elites. (4) The magistrate did not mention, and the High Court did not pursue, Women Chen's assertion that Chen Shisheng had raped Aijie. Even if local custom allowed Chen Shisheng to rape a woman he had paid for, the act was still a crime under the law. The JHC probably neglected to pursue the cases against Chen because it did not believe everything Woman Chen said in her petition, or it knew that it would be difficult for the county magistrate to prosecute the case, or a combination thereof. In any case, such was the "justice" presided over by a county magistrate beholden to local gentry in the 1920s.

Local Gentry, the County Magistrate, and the High Procuracy in the 1920s

When they deemed it necessary, the gentry also reached beyond the local arena, interacting with provincial and central government agencies on judicial matters that affected their interests. In 1923, to reduce the inmate population and save money, the Ministry of Justice ordered all provincial prisons and county jails to review inmates' cases, and to parole those who had served half of their terms. On August 12, the magistrate of Dangshan county, Zhou Honggao, submitted a list of six inmates with their crimes, sentences, time served, and behavior in prison, as specified by the ministry. When the JHP received the list and forwarded it to the ministry, a petition signed by Zhang Zhenhuai, a "representative of citizens," reached the JHP chief, Zhou Yike. Zhang, a member of the local gentry in Dangshan, opposed the release of Ji Daowu, one of the six inmates to be paroled, who was serving time for gambling. According to Zhang, Ji Daowu's brother Ji Daosan was a well-known bandit who commanded more than 300 followers and had ravaged the region since 1912. Ji Daowu had engaged in banditry at different times but had escaped capture and prosecution until he was caught gambling in 1920. If released on parole, he would join his brother's bandit gang, and it would amount to "releasing a tiger into the mountain and allowing the beast to eat people." Zhou Yike's initial reaction was his handwritten note on the petition: "If [the inmate] was eligible to be released, he must not be held without cause, or the county may serve as guarantor." Nevertheless, he ordered Magistrate Zhou to investigate whether the inmate had repented and behaved well in prison, and whether there were other mitigating circumstances. Responding within two days, Magistrate Zhou only restated the information he had given earlier without answering Zhou Yike's questions. The county magistrate seems to have been more concerned about reducing inmate population than about the possibility of Ji's joining bandits. Zhou Yike had to ask again for a detailed report, while at the same time the ministry approved the parole of all six inmates in response to the brief forwarded by the JHP. Zhou Yike transmitted the ministry's response to the county magistrate, but put Ji Daowu's parole on hold, pending a report on Ji from the magistrate. Seeing no way around it, Magistrate Zhou finally sent in a report about Ji on September 18, confirming what Zhang had said about Ji and his bandit brother. Zhou Yike reported the case to the ministry, proposing to void Ji's parole. The ministry approved.[8]

This case sheds some light on the working of the judicial system and the role of local gentry in it. (1) Did Magistrate Zhou know that Ji Daowu's brother was a well-known bandit? If he did, apparently he did not consider it legally relevant to Ji's parole, which was correct under the regulations on parole and the ministry's directive; and he probably acted in spite of local gentry's opposition. But the local gentry obviously considered the fact a highly relevant argument against Ji's release and took vigorous action accordingly. In this case, the local gentry played the role of watchdog on county judicial functions and a source of information for the provincial judicial authorities. (2) The institutional rules required the JHP to take petitions from local gentry, or any parties, seriously (see Chapter 10). It therefore issued an order for the magistrate to report on the case. (3) Once Zhang Zhenhuai had forced the issue with the JHP and the latter had responded by insisting on a full report on Ji, the magistrate could no longer evade the issue but had to respond to the local gentry's concerns. At that point, he had no reason to take the risk of being held responsible for Ji's joining his bandit brother upon his release. He therefore agreed with Zhang's opinion. (4) In such matters, the ministry relied entirely on the opinions of the part of the system that processed local information—the JHP, in this case. In sum, the local gentry knew how the bureaucracy operated and had learned to use the institutional rules to address their concerns successfully. In contrast, the county magistrate was in a weaker position than his predecessors in the late imperial era, because local gentry could now appeal either to the provincial judicial institutions or to the provincial governor, or to both. In other words, an expansion of the state system by way of judicial institutions was not necessarily detrimental to the power and interests of local elites, and could be responsive to them. This was one more facet of the complexity in understanding the reach of the state.

The County Chamber of Commerce and Civil Disputes

One manifestation of the rise of local elites in the early Republican period was the increasingly larger role that local chambers of commerce played. Since the New Policy years, the state had expected such organizations to help in economic development and perform constructive social functions in the public arena. In January 1914, the MJ and Ministry of Industry and Commerce issued the Regulations on Commercial Dispute Arbitration Offices, which required chambers of commerce in the country to set up such offices, at their own expense, to arbitrate local commercial disputes.[9] After 1927, the regulations remained in force under the GMD government. For the state, this arbitration mechanism, as a supplement to the judicial formalization agenda, would not only help reduce the number of civil suits, but also promote local commerce and benefit the economy in general. The state's authorization officially empowered local elites' organizations and enhanced their status and legitimacy as "public" associations in local society. As the result, county-level and township-level chambers of commerce were active in resolving civil disputes during the period under study.

Actually, the 1914 Regulations only legitimized and regularized a social phenomenon that had already existed. The Suzhou Chamber of Commerce was founded in October 1905, and intervention in commercial disputes was one of its major functions. By December 1906, the chamber had arbitrated more than 70 civil-commercial disputes, and by August 1911, more than 320 disputes. In arbitrating commercial disputes, the chamber served as a mediator persuading disputants to compromise, not as an arbitrator passing judgment, and the proceedings were open and transparent. In the rare cases where one party committed egregious acts of fraud and the like, and refused to mend its ways, it would be expelled from membership in the chamber and face ostracism by the business community. The chamber enjoyed a high reputation for being impartial and effective in handling commercial disputes.[10]

Besides the high-profile chambers of commerce in Shanghai and Suzhou, those at the county seats and large market towns played a crucial role in mediating commercial disputes, and therefore an auxiliary role in the county judicial process. The Songjiang County Chamber of Commerce (SCCC), founded in 1906, is a case in point. One of the chamber's major functions was to mediate and arbitrate commercial disputes.[11] In August 1912, a native bank (money shop) lodged a complaint with the chamber against an apparel shop that had failed to honor a debt of more than ¥1,540, involving a third party as witness to the loan. After receiving written arguments from the three sides, each telling a different story, in March 1913, the chamber called the parties to a meeting to settle the dispute, which successfully ended the matter.[12] The bank went to the chamber rather than the CGO to recover the loan, because it wanted to avoid the cost of litigation, and also to avoid getting a bad name, since taking a borrower to the CGO would appear unforgiving and deter potential customers. The bottom line, however, was that the chamber commanded respect and reputation for being able to resolve a dispute fairly.

The SCCC's effectiveness was also shown in another case. In November 1912, a shoemaker wrote to the chamber stating that Yang Guiqing, an army battalion commander, should have paid ¥50 for shoes the army had ordered but had only paid ¥26; he had promised remit the balance later but never did. The SCCC director wrote to Yang's superior officer, Shen Baoyi, requesting assistance in obtaining the balance of ¥24 for the shoemaker. Shen responded positively, taking ¥24 from Yang's salary and sending it to the chamber director in January 1913.[13]

After the state authorized chambers of commerce to arbitrate commercial disputes in 1914, the SCCC continued to play its now formalized role. In 1923, the owner of a cotton towel factory in Songjiang tried to retrieve ¥36 from a bankrupt retail store in Pingwang town, Wujiang county. The factory owner requested the chamber to write to its counterpart in Pingwang so that he would get his money when the store was liquidated. The SCCC took action on his behalf, and the Pingwang Town Chamber of Commerce responded affirmatively.[14] The factory owner seems to have considered it more cost-effective and efficient to go through the SCCC than go to the CGO for litigation or communication with the chamber of commerce in Pingwang. The archives show that similar intervention by the SCCC on behalf of local merchants with its counterparts in other towns and counties was a routine affair, which means that chambers of commerce in other places functioned in the same way the SCCC did.[15]

Sometimes, one party to a dispute had already filed a lawsuit at the CGO, but still brought the matter to the chamber to reinforce the claim—the same strategy that litigants would use in a reverse scenario, that is, resorting to lawsuit in order to pressure the other party to accept mediation and settlement out of court.[16] Wei Xianglou invested ¥600 as a partner in a business with Mei Lanquan in 1917. Two years later, Wei decided to pull out of the business. With three witnesses present, his investment was calculated to be worth ¥400; and Mei agreed to return the money in four installments in four years, with a monthly interest of 0.012 percent. But Mei defaulted on the first payment in January 1920, and by 1923, when the four-year period was up, Mei had paid nothing. When Wei went to ask Mei for the money in July 1923, the latter physically assaulted him. Wei sued Mei at the CGO and also filed a complaint at the SCCC asking for an investigation into the matter.[17] This move was clearly designed to strengthen his lawsuit against Mei at the CGO, especially if the chamber's investigation were to produce evidence supporting his claims. Wei probably also wanted to make sure that the decision could be more easily enforced when the county magistrate ruled in his favor; it would be harder for Mei to defy the county magistrate's decision if he also faced the opinion of the chamber.

Another variation of this was for a disputant to resort first to litigation and only involve the chamber after losing the case in court. Even in such cases, the chamber tended to take action, and the county magistrate tended to defer to its opinion. In October 1920, Huang Yisun, a merchant in Wujin, sued Wu Zhongheng, Liu Qizeng, and Liu Guizheng of Songjiang in a dispute about how to distribute the dividend of a sugar firm, and Magistrate Zhu Shuyuan ruled in Huang's favor. The defendants, who were members or directors of the SCCC, thereupon asked it to intervene. The county magistrate agreed to hand over the case file to the chamber for discussion. Huang then petitioned the JHC that it order the magistrate to deliver the ruling and close the case according to the law. In response to the JHC's inquiry, Magistrate Zhu explained that the litigation was about how much of the dividend should be distributed and how much retained, and that he had sent the case to the chamber for an expert opinion, which did not violate any law. Denying that he had ruled on the case and held up the ruling, he said he was urging the chamber to report back.[18] Even if Zhu's story was true, the clout of the chamber with which the county magistrate reckoned is unmistakable.

A third variation was for commercial disputants to resort first to the chamber for a resolution of their disputes and, failing that, to file lawsuits with the CGO but continue negotiations mediated by the chamber. Litigating disputants thus worked on both tracks to ensure a satisfactory resolution, and the negotiation track tended to prevail. In 1930, a local bank sued Feng Hengfu at the CGO for defaulting on a loan of ¥698.80, after having failed to settle the dispute at the SCCC. Feng told the county magistrate that he had paid back the loan through the chamber's mediation and asked for the return of his debt documents. The bank countered that Feng had only paid ¥600, which did not cover all of the loan, let alone the interest as well. The magistrate then asked the chamber for a report. Cai Guangyao, the SCCC standing committee member who served as the mediator in the case, reported that Feng was willing to pay only ¥600, and the bank had insisted on the repayment of the entire loan, plus interest; but after Cai's repeated mediation, the bank had finally agreed to give up the balance and the interest. Cai was not sure who should pay the litigation fees, and he hoped the county magistrate would be able to persuade the two parties not to revive the litigation for such a small issue and urge the bank to return Feng's debt documents to close the matter.[19] In cases such as this, the chamber played a constructive role in local society, though it was an exercise of power.

Variations on the strategy of resorting to mediation and litigation either alternately or simultaneously for the resolution of a civil dispute were familiar in civil disputes in the late imperial era. The difference was that in the Republican era, the chamber of commerce was an officially sanctioned mediator and arbitrator, replacing unofficial local elite mediators, especially in commercial disputes. Whether a commercial dispute ended up in the CGO for litigation or in the chamber of commerce for arbitration was up to the parties involved. If a county magistrate was shrewd enough, he would know that the best course of action was to pass such cases to the chamber for resolution. This had at least two advantages: (1) it conserved the CGO's institutional resources, and (2) showing respect for the power of local elites in such matters would improve his chances of getting their cooperation in other matters, such as collecting taxes and soliciting donations.

The role of county-level chambers of commerce examined above was one way local elites exercised their power, which reinforces the point that the so-called local elites were not an undifferentiated group, but people of diverse social standings, especially in the early Republican era. It is unsurprising that the commercial interests represented by chambers of commerce such as the SCCC seem to have been more inclined to set certain rules and play by them, which converged with the principle of the rule of law, whereas those local elites who may be considered sociopolitical entrepreneurs tended to use their power self-interestedly in ways that contravened the law and the customary sense of fair play in local society. Among the various groups of local elites surrounding the CGO, the county magistrate was able to find at least one that was often helpful to him in respect to his judicial and administrative duties—the chamber of commerce. Beyond the issue of county judicial process, the role of chambers of commerce would also suggest that the state could achieve certain goals in local society, not through expanding institutional structures into the county level and below, but through legitimizing and regularizing the institutional power of certain groups among local elites with specific mandates and within specific functional fields—another example of this is the GMD initiative to enlist local elites in reforming county jails (see Chapter 8).

The Role of Legal Scribes

"There were no lawyers under the old system," a foreign commentator observed in 1925, "but there were scriveners who drew up petitions and sometimes interceded by indirect methods in behalf of litigants. These persons occupied a despised and low scale on the social order and some of this odium attached to the new bar."[20] The perception that lawyers might have been contaminated by the "odium" of scriveners in the old system was shared by many. In his 1914 opinion on judicial reform, Minister of Justice Liang Qichao proposed that lawyers' qualifications be reevaluated to weed out ethically and professionally unqualified practitioners who were indistinguishable from pettifoggers. The Political Council agreed and further suggested that lawyers who were found violating regulations be disciplined and those who broke the law prosecuted.[21] Here the term "pettifogger" or "litigation stick" (*songgun*) was a strongly pejorative one, but the line between a lawyer and a pettifogger (legal scribe) was not easy to draw in practice, beyond the license that the lawyer held.

The anxiety that lawyers would do what pettifoggers were perceived to be doing—inciting litigation—was echoed in government regulations on lawyers. The Ministry of Justice's 1915 Obligations of Lawyers stipulated that lawyers who incited litigation and fabricated facts should be disciplined, and its 1920 revision reminded lawyers that they should not deceive either a court or a client. The same language appears in the 1927 Regulations on Lawyers. Moreover, under Article 157 of the 1935 criminal code, anyone who incited litigation to make a profit was subject to punishment of up to one year's imprisonment or detention or a fine.[22]

None of the regulations and the provisions in the criminal code were enforceable, however, because the offenses were difficult to prove in court, especially that of "inciting litigation." Throughout the Republican era, there were sporadic efforts at getting rid of "pettifoggers," yet for want of a specific law to define and punish pettifoggers, such efforts never succeeded. Legal scribes remained a permanent feature of the social landscape, especially in counties where no courts existed, and lawyers could therefore not appear at county trials. A look at the drives against legal scribes reveals their indispensable role in the local power arena that was the county judicial process.

In May 1916, the magistrate of Yizheng county, Bai Shiyi, wrote to Governor Qi Yaolin, decrying the "evils of pettifoggers." Incited by pettifoggers, local people filed frivolous lawsuits and often renewed lawsuits after they had been settled through mediation at the CGO, Bai said. He wanted to eradicate pettifoggers but found no specific law enabling him to do so and asked for instructions. Qi referred Bai's query to the JHC for its opinions. In a directive for Bai and all county magistrates in the province, the JHC president, Cai Yuankang, wrote that there was indeed no specific law on pettifoggers, but many activities of such people fell under certain articles in the PNCC. Since the county magistrate was to act as procurator, he could investigate pettifoggers' activities and prosecute the offenses according to the law. "What the county magistrate said is not without points, but he failed to fully grasp the new criminal code," Cai concluded. The governor acknowledged Cai's directive and did not disagree in any way.[23]

The articles of the PNCC that Cai cited were Article 30 (to incite others to commit crimes), Article 178 (to destroy or fabricate evidence), Article 243 (to fabricate personal seals and documents to prove obligations or rights or to do so for others), Article 382 (to obtain property by extortion or fraud), and Article 383 (to betray the trust and harm the properties of a person while working on the person's behalf).[24] Yet, it would be very difficult for a procurator to prove in court that a "pettifogger" had actually committed those crimes, since "inciting" lawsuits would not necessarily, and typically did not, involve the acts named in the law. Cai's directive, in other words, only made it clear that being called a pettifogger for writing complaints was not a crime that could be prosecuted. Whether or not related to this development, the Yizheng county magistrate Bai would leave his post in August 1916, having been on the job for only six months.[25]

Attempts at legal actions against pettifoggers were put aside for ten years until a new drive was launched in 1926 by Governor Chen Taoyi and Warlord Sun Chuanfang, who was in control of Jiangsu at the time. In a joint order dated April 27 to the JHC, Chen and Sun said that pettifoggers profiting from inciting litigation among the people were utterly despicable and responsible for case backlogs that could never be disposed of. Since the Jiangsu provincial governor had ordered two years before that workhouses for vagrants be established to house local thugs and ruffians, deserted soldiers, fired policemen, and the like, the Chen-Sun order said, all county magistrates should apprehend pettifoggers and put them in workhouses incommunicado so that they were unable to incite litigation. The JHC was told to transmit the order to all county magistrates and all district courts, and it did so.[26] Although the legality of the order was questionable, the JHC officials did not choose to challenge Chen and Sun at this point, probably in part because the objective of reducing the judiciary's caseload by limiting pettifoggers' activities seemed to have merit. They were probably also waiting to see what, if anything, would come of the order.

The order signaled open season for hunting pettifoggers in some counties. One case reached the JHC and the JHP from Wu Peng, the county magistrate of Jiangyin, in early June 1926. Armed with the Chen-Sun order, Wu arrested Li Jianchu and Zheng Xueming, "the two most notorious pettifoggers" among many in the town. He asked whether he might just lock them up until a workhouse was established (he did not say when that would be). The JHC president, Zhu Xianwen, and the JHP chief, Zhou Yike, replied that the county magistrate should either take administrative action to send them to a workhouse or prosecute them according to the law if they had committed criminal offenses.[27] The unspoken message was that the county magistrate could not just detain the two men without due process.

In August 1926, Ruan Yuqi, the county magistrate of Taixing, telegraphed Chen Taoyi and Sun Chuanfang to report the arrest of Lu Junyan, an alleged pettifogger who had written complaints for several litigants, and asked for instructions on how to deal with him. Lu had been convicted of fabricating documents and other offenses in 1920 and 1921.

Such a person must not be allowed to go free, Ruan said, but because of lack of funds, the county had no workhouse. He asked whether the JHC might designate a workhouse in another county to confine Lu or whether he could hand Lu over to the county jail overseer for "education" for several years as a penalty. Chen and Sun referred Ruan's telegram to the JHC for a decision.

This case finally allowed provincial judicial officials an opportunity to state their legal position to Chen Daoyi and Sun Chuanfang. In their reply, Zhu Xianwen and Zhou Yike pointed out that if the pettifogger committed offenses under the criminal code, such as extorting money from litigants or inciting people to make false accusations, he should be punished under the law; if he only wrote complaints for litigants without breaking the law, the county magistrate could send him to a workhouse to learn a trade as an administrative action to stop incitation. If there was no workhouse in the county, the county magistrate might consult with a neighboring county about sending Lu to a workhouse.[28] Clearly, Zhu and Zhou would go along with an administrative action to stop a scribe from inciting litigation (they doubted that writing complaints per se was incitation), but they did not see any cause for criminal prosecution in such a case. Chen and Sun accepted their opinion and so instructed Magistrate Ruan.[29] Beyond the issue of pettifoggers, it appears that in the Beiyang era, the provincial government in Jiangsu, even in the person of Warlord Sun Chuanfang, deferred to the opinions of the JHC and the JHP on judicial issues. The latter were tactful but unyielding in insisting on the rule of law and in trying to rectify the actions of the provincial government that violated the principle.

But the hunt for pettifoggers was not over yet. In early October 1926, the county magistrate of Jiading, Qian Baohe, wrote to the JHC and the JHP saying that local gentry and police had reported to him that after losing his job as a policeman in Anting town, a certain Shou Jianyi had come to specialize in writing complaints for litigants by twisting truths and manipulating facts, even pretending to have government connections to peddle his trade. Qian had taken the trouble to look through past case files and had found several complaints written by Shou. When brought to the CGO, Shou admitted to writing complaints for relatives and friends. He claimed that he was still a probationary policeman, which Qian found false. Because there was no workhouse in Jiading, Qian asked whether Shou should be sent to the workhouse in Suzhou or just held as civil case detainee (*minshi guanshou ren*) in the county detention house. In an order issued to Qian, Zhu Xianwen and Zhou Yike repeated the message that writing complaints did not constitute criminal offense per se and did not fall under judicial purview. The county magistrate might exercise administrative authority to send Shou to a workhouse, but should not put him in the detention house as a civil case detainee.[30]

The strong sentiment among county magistrates against complaint-writing scribes or the so-called pettifoggers is easy to understand. Overburdened by an increasing workload and criticized for case backlogs, the county magistrate instinctively blamed "pettifoggers" for the mass of lawsuits filed at the CGO. In reality, of course, legal scribes were not the producers but the products of litigation. Complaint-writing scribes were able to survive and thrive at the county level during the Republican era due to several factors. (1) For many local people, scribes were the first stop on the way to file a lawsuit at the CGO, despite the Ministry of Justice's efforts to eliminate that literacy barrier by having complaint-writing clerks at all courts and county offices. (2) Lawyers were not allowed to practice in county trials and therefore were not readily available in counties without courts. (3) Whatever "pettifoggers" did was expected and accepted by litigants as part of the litigation process and its cost.

Ironically, however, the most important reason legal scribes flourished was the reform that made the judicial process more accessible to ordinary people and thus encouraged more lawsuits. With more and more people willing to resort to lawsuits to resolve disputes, demand for the service of legal scribes increased proportionally. Moreover, the formalization agenda of the reform brought forth ever more minute and detailed rules, procedures, and regulations in the judicial process, which made it ever more difficult for ordinary people, especially the illiterate, and those in places where courts did not exist and lawyers could not practice, to use the judicial system on their own. For such people, the assistance of a legal scribe was a must if they wanted to seek legal redress. The county magistrate might regard a legal scribe as a person of incitation and manipulation, but in fact a legal scribe often served those who needed him most—the poor, the illiterate, and the underprivileged—in the legal games they were forced to get involved in. The presence of complaint-writing scribes in the Republican era simply reflected that reality. In other words, legal scribes were indispensable for the judicial system to function as designed, even though officially they were never part of the design. The JHC refused to support prosecution of legal scribes for writing complaints because it knew they played a role in local society where judicial service was underdeveloped. Just like off-the-books functionaries at the CGO, legal scribes provided a service that ordinary litigants, and indeed the judicial system for that matter, needed. That is why they were neither officially recognized nor seriously proscribed, and were always able to make a living, albeit one with a bad name.

In this light, it is no wonder that one county trial officer, who had served in that capacity for over twenty years and came to prefer dealing with legal scribes to dealing with lawyers, went so far as to call the scribes "secretaries of the masses" (*dazhong shuji*) as late as 1935.[31] Similarly, a writer in 1931 called the "public scribe," who wrote letters as well as litigation complaints for the illiterate, one who "hears the joys and sorrows of the nation," saying that when a scribe was called as a witness, "the court, as a matter of fact, is often more inclined to accept the merits of the testimony of the impartial public scribe than the arguments of the lawyers in such cases."[32] Even though the writer may have been guilty of somewhat romanticizing the scribes, he captured the necessary role they played in daily social life and the judicial process in local society.

The Long Shadow of the Party

In the Nanjing decade, there was a particular dimension of local power struggle not seen before. As the GMD tried to penetrate local society by building institutions below the county level, some people would join the GMD to act as party cadres to gain legitimacy and power vis-à-vis other power-holders in the local arena. Feeling empowered by the doctrine of "ruling the country through the party" and the agenda of "partyizing" the judiciary, GMD organs and cadres frequently intervened in judicial matters and individual lawsuits. The historian Bradley Geisert has pointed out the demise of radicalism within the Guomindang in Jiangsu by 1929–1930, when the party apparatus in the province was reorganized and the more radical elements were purged.[33] But that does not seem to have been the case at the county level, or at least not in all counties. In some counties, the party affairs reorganization committees (PARC), which came into being precisely during the reorganization of

1929–1930, took it upon themselves to intervene in judicial matters and did so with the same revolutionary rhetoric as often seen in the mid-1920s, even though nationally such radical rhetoric had faded in GMD official discourse.

In June 1930, the Qingpu PARC wrote to the provincial PARC, accusing the trial officer Shen Yansheng of ignoring rule by the party and rejecting the committee's guidance in the name of judicial independence. The incident originated in a case of rent dispute between a tenant and a landlord. Gu Amei worked on 18 *mu* of land rented from Zhu Guanghua for 15 picul of grain a year. They had a dispute over the rent for 1926, and Zhu took the case to the County Bureau of Rent Collection. Gu paid ¥50 as extra rent for 1926 to the bureau as ordered, but Zhu did not get the money, because the county magistrate departed from his post without accounting for county funds. When Gu went to Zhu to pay the rent for 1927 and 1928, Zhu again raised the issue. Gu took the case to the county rent arbitration committee (RAC), which ruled that Gu should pay ¥162 for 1927–1928 rent, but that Zhu did not have a claim to extra rent for 1926. Zhu thereupon filed a civil lawsuit against Gu at the CGO. Under the Jiangsu Provisional Regulations on Rent Arbitration, if one party to a dispute did not accept the RAC's decision, that party should appeal to the provincial RAC. The county PARC therefore held that the CGO should not have accepted Zhu's lawsuit. Nevertheless, the trial officer Shen Yansheng tried the case and ruled that Gu should pay Zhu ¥170 for the new rent within three months.

Although the difference between Shen's ruling and the RAC's decision was only ¥8, the county PARC members were angry at Shen's disregard for the RAC's arbitration, and they adopted a resolution to take action. Because "Shen ignored peasant sufferings and the committee cannot but provide guidance from the party's standpoint," the PARC summoned him before it and gave him a lecture on the GMD's concerns about peasant sufferings and on the regulations on rent arbitration. Shen rejected the "guidance" by invoking judicial independence. Very much incensed, the committee charged, in its letter to the provincial PARC, that Shen had "failed to understand rule by the party, rejected the committee's guidance, abused power, and undermined the rent arbitration regulations. Nothing can be more in violation of this party's fundamental principle of supporting peasants." "Such an official cannot be tolerated by the party-state, nor accepted by the masses. To uphold the party's authority-credibility and to alleviate peasants' sufferings, this committee's 18th meeting decided to impeach [Shen]." It asked the provincial PARC to speak to the JHC so that Shen be fired immediately. To add to the weight of its charges, the committee also said that Shen did not care to attend various political activities that it sponsored, such as the Sun Yat-sen commemoration week, thus showing his contempt for the Guomindang .

When the JHC received the letter via the provincial PARC, the court promised that it would investigate the case. With unusual caution, the JHC president both sent a court clerk to Qingpu and ordered the county magistrate there to investigate and report on the matter. Both reported back that Shen was an upright person, about whom peasants had no complaints, and that the incident stemmed from a misunderstanding on his part. Shen had not known that the RAC had ruled on the rent dispute. As for Shen's failure to attend certain political activities, it was simply because he was too busy with his duty as trial officer.[34] It appears that the whole incident was a reaction from the county PARC members to Shen's perceived disregard or even contempt for their self-important political activities and their intervention in civil disputes.

The incident bears on several interesting points. First, whatever the intention and agenda of GMD leaders in Nanjing, at least some local party cadres would continue to engage in the discourse and activities informed by the GMD political rhetoric of an earlier time, for local and particularistic reasons, even after the demise of radicalism within the party at the national and provincial levels. That the rhetoric about supporting peasants was no longer fashionable at higher levels is demonstrated in the Liu Yusheng case noted elsewhere.[35]

Second, the GMD issued the rent arbitration regulations and set up the rent arbitration committee for the same reasons that it instituted labor dispute arbitration regulations and committees (and continued the policy of commercial arbitration by chambers of commerce). Those measures, part of the scheme for a corporate state, were designed to mediate and contain social conflicts and undercut sources of social unrest that were the breeding ground for the communist insurgence; they were also supposed to help reduce the burden of civil litigation on the judiciary. As the above story illustrates, however, such measures led to a blurring of boundaries between judicial and administrative resolutions of rent disputes and therefore between the judicial and administrative functions of the CGO and between the functions of the GMD organs and the CGO. By virtue of its self-appointed power to supervise the work of the rent arbitration committee (possibly staffed by party members), the county party organ had no difficulty challenging the authority of the trial officer or the county magistrate when a case was taken by the disputants from administrative mediation to judicial adjudication. Where the judiciary as a system was concerned, the situation also created unnecessary additional work for the JHC, which was obliged to respond to petitions and complaints from the provincial and county party organs. The net effect of those mediation mechanisms and communication channels between the provincial and county levels was to create additional tensions among various county-level institutions and increase the cost or waste of institutional resources. Whether or not the state's control of local society was served in the process is debatable.

Whatever their motivations and despite the waste of institutional resources as a result of their actions, county-level party organs' self-appointed role in monitoring the county judicial process sometimes resulted in exposing wrongdoings and disciplinary action being taken against the culprits. In July 1930, the Baoshan PARC reported to the provincial PARC the misconduct of the trial officer Zhang Wei in handling a criminal case. On May 15, four men were arrested for transporting 260 *liang* of opium. At a county trial, Zhang Wei had sentenced them each to eighteen months' imprisonment, suspended for two years, and fines of from ¥80 to ¥1,500. At a retrial a few days later, however, Zhang Wei reduced the highest fine from ¥1,500 to ¥900 and released a car that had been confiscated from them to the auto company that had rented it. The change in Zhang's ruling caused the county PARC to cry corruption. Besides the inconsistency of the two sentences, the circumstantial evidence cited was that Zhang had gone to Shanghai between the two trials, probably to negotiate a deal with the defendants' connections in the city. The committee further accused the trial officer of being frequently unfair in trying cases, from which "the people suffered without recourse." When the JHC ordered the Baoshan county magistrate, Qiu Mingjiu, to investigate, Qiu defended Zhang's overall record but admitted that he had erred in trying this case, giving the appearance of irregularities. Qiu proposed that since Zhang had already been transferred to Luhe, the case not be pursued further. But the JHC president ordered that Zhang be given a reprimand.[36] In another case, the GMD organ in Fengxian acted as moral police to report on a trial officer's extramarital affairs, which the cadres said had damaged the credibility of the judiciary. In response, the JHC launched three investigations, the last of which confirmed the alleged misconduct and led to disciplinary action against the trial officer, who had already left the post.[37]

The influence of the GMD agenda of partyizing the judiciary came in surprising shapes and forms. Although the JHC did not seem enthusiastic about pursuing whatever the party organs were pushing it to do in the name of political correctness, at least one minister of justice went out of his way to be politically correct, to a ludicrous degree. In Songjiang, a certain Wu Boyang owned a piece of land that was part of the foundation of the one-time outer city wall, where he planned in 1932 to build a house, which would block the store sign of an engraving shop owned by Gu Wenbao from view. To prevent Wu from building, Gu therefore proposed to the CGO that a Sun Yat-sen monument be erected on the land, which would make it public land. After three years of legal and administrative wrangling, the provincial government finally ruled that a monument might be built in a "Sun Yat-sen Park," not on the land in dispute. Gu thereupon proceeded to have a monument erected on Wu's land at his own expense. Although he was unable to stop Gu from doing this, Wu sued him at the Songjiang DC in June 1935 and won. Gu was ordered to remove the monument, and he subsequently lost appeals to the JHC and the SC. On August 18, the district court, at Wu's petition, enforced the decision and dismantled the monument, but kept the building materials so that the structure could be rebuilt in the projected park.

The matter was not over, however. Having exhausted legal recourse to get his way, Gu resorted to political maneuvering to retaliate against the court. In September 1936, Gu wrote to the MJ accusing the Songjiang DC personnel of destroying a Sun Yat-sen monument, though he admitted that he had lost the case in court. Minister of Justice Wang Yongbin, a political appointee with connections to the CC clique within the GMD,[38] notified the JHC that, even though the SC had decided that the disputed land belonged to Wu Boyang, a Sun Yat-sen monument should not be lightly demolished. In destroying the monument, the DC must have intended to insult the late Sun Yat-sen. "It is especially despicable that such a thing was done by a court," Wang declared, and he instructed the JHC to find and punish those responsible. The investigation, of course, only confirmed that the enforcement had been legally and properly carried out. Nevertheless, Wang refused to back off. He insisted that the probationary judge Yu Jian and the probationary clerk Li Qinghe, who had supervised the enforcement at the scene, be given two demerit points each. In early February 1937, the Songjiang DC president Yang Litang petitioned the JHC. Citing the hard work done by Yu Jian and Li Qinghe, Yang proposed that the good record of Yu Jian and Li Qinghe offset the demerits, taking into account that they were being blamed for what they had done in accordance with the court decisions and the provincial government's decision. The JHC president Lin Biao did not, however, choose to act on the proposal.[39] Clearly, Yang was protesting against the disciplinary action against Yu and Li, but the chilling effect of Minister Wang Yongbing's absurd arbitrariness was such that even the JHC president did not think the matter was worth a fight that might harm his personal career.

As the above cases demonstrate, the county judicial process was influenced by the GMD's ideology and party organization and the attendant political culture, and social actors were able and willing to access and manipulate the available political symbols and rhetoric, as well as social relationships, and maneuver between and among judicial, administrative, and political institutions. In this process, the rule of law and rule by the party stood in an inverse relationship to each other—the spirit of party rule prevailed at the expense of the rule of law, and vice versa.

A more serious and intractable type of situation engendered by GMD party-state occurred when a party organ and/or a county government took illegal or extralegal actions and refused to face the legal consequences. Shi Xiaozhang's was a typical case. Shi had formerly been a wealthy man in Dangshan. In 1927, on trumped-up charges (presumably those of the "local bully and evil gentry"), the county party headquarters and the CGO confiscated his properties—his residence in town and farmhouses in country, more than 4,000 *mu* of farmland, and cash, bonds, furniture, calligraphies, paintings, antiques, and rice, animals, farming tools, and so on worth tens of thousands of yuan. In the late 1920s, Shi petitioned the provincial government, the GMD center, and the NG for the return of his properties. The CGO and the party organ in Dangshan were ordered to return Shi's properties, but they simply ignored the orders. Shi then sued the two entities at the JHC, which designated the Jiangning DC to try the case in April 1932. However, the defendants refused to respond to summons, saying that they could not be responsible for what had been done by their predecessors. The Jiangning DC informed them that under the civil procedural law, they had to respond to the plaintiff and argue their case in court. But both the defendants insisted that they did not have any documents regarding what had happened five years before and could not argue their case in court. Frustrated, Wang Zhaopeng, the DC president, asked the JHC to intervene, and it communicated with the provincial government. The provincial government chairman, Gu Zhutong, and the CAD chief, Zhao Qilu, promised the JHC that they would instruct the CGO to comply with the court order. By March 1935, three years later, however, the CGO and party organ in Dangshan had still not complied, and Wang Zhaopeng found it necessary to urge the JHC to intervene again. In April 1935, Chen Guofu, the provincial government chairman who replaced Gu, again promised the JHC that the defendants would be ordered to appear in court.[40] The sources do not reveal whether the case was ever tried in court.

This case is instructive for an understanding of the complex relationship that existed among the court as the judicial field of the state system, the county government as the administrative field, and the GMD organization as the political wing of the state. As we have seen in other cases, when the county magistrate performed judicial functions, his office was an extension of the provincial judicial authorities, that is, part of the judicial system, and it had to deal with and negotiate possible interference from the county-level party organ as an adversary. But when the CGO itself was the defendant in litigation, it became an adversary of the judicial system, of which it was part in other circumstances. In this case, the Dangshan CGO did act like an adversary; and along with the co-defendant and the usual adversary, the county party headquarters, it played the worst possible role in confronting the judiciary, showing contempt for the court and obstructing justice. And they were able to ignore and resist the Jiangning DC order for more than three years and the orders from the provincial and central governments for more than five years. These facts defy any attempt at a facile conclusion about the reach of the state at the county level in the Republican era and during the Nanjing decade in particular, because it is difficult to define in the first place which of the three entities—judicial, administrative, and political—represented the state. One could argue that all three were components of the state, representing different, and often conflicting, functions and agendas of the state. No doubt, however, in this case, the function of the judicial system and the agenda of the judicial reform, both manifestations of modern state building, were ingloriously obstructed by the components of the same state system.

The case also speaks to the relationship between the county government and local elites. Earlier in this chapter, cases are made that the county magistrate usually tried to accommodate local elites and yielded to the local power structure. In this case, Shi Xiaozhang got a raw deal in the early 1930s because he never recovered from the blow dealt to him in 1927 and was no longer a person of wealth, power, and influence in local society thereafter. The CGO and the party organ could afford to abuse and ignore him. More important, any attempt to honor Shi's rights and to return his farmland and houses would have caused too many complications for the CGO to handle, because Shi's property had surely ended up in the hands of local elites who remained powerful and influential in the 1930s. Alternatively, any monetary compensation to Shi, which would have been a likely ruling by the court, might be well beyond the financial capacity of the CGO, given the tight county finances and other state-mandated priorities at the time (such as the anti-drug campaign). In a sense, the course of action that the Dangshan CGO and the party organ took—to evade the legal and financial consequences of the acts committed by their predecessors—was the only logical and sensible one from their perspective. This was also probably why the government and party authorities at the provincial and national levels allowed the two county-level entities to do so. An obvious lesson here, repeatedly seen, not only in twentieth-century China but in world history in general, is that the most egregious extralegal and illegal seizure of properties without compensation that could be inflicted upon a citizen was one by state agencies or public institutions in the name of the people and a revolution.

This chapter has examined four types of players involved in the county judicial process, each constituting an important dimension of the intersections and interactions among and between different institutions, entities, and mechanisms. These included formal institutions (courts, county government offices, GMD organs) and informal social networks (local elite connections, both vertical and horizontal), officially sanctioned social entities (chambers of commerce) and unofficially tolerated ones (legal scribes), and appointed county magistrates and trial officers performing their duties and self-appointed party cadres and gentry intervening in judicial affairs. The different roles of those elements in the county judicial process may be summarized as follows: (1) chambers of commerce, empowered by state sanction, were helpful to the county magistrate in performing judicial functions; (2) legal scribes were allowed to provide needed services to litigants and indirectly to the judiciary, including county judicial functions; (3) adapting to the changing conditions, local gentry resumed their time-honored role in negotiating and interfering with the county judicial process, especially in places where no courts existed; and (4) finally, in the Nanjing decade, GMD cadres emerged as local elites of a new type, who sought their own empowerment by taking it upon themselves to monitor and report on the performance of county judicial functions and became a meddlesome factor there. The judicial reform provided all these players with opportunities of empowerment that had different social and political significances in local settings, and the players' respective responses in turn helped shape the local results of the reform. By their participation or interference, they complicated the county judicial process in positive and negative ways. The stories told in this chapter thus illustrate the complex interactions between the logic of local practice and that of modern state building and their paradoxical consequences in the course of the judicial reform. But the story would not be complete without considering county jails and detention houses, to which we now turn.

CHAPTER 8

Prison Reform and County Jails

> There is no denying that county jails in Jiangsu province are substandard in facilities and incomplete in organization. To improve facilities, however, there must be funds earmarked for [the purpose]; and comprehensive supervision and flexible operation especially rely on sufficient funds. Jiangsu is where the [national] capital is located, with a dense residential population and frequent construction projects. The provincial treasury barely satisfies administrative operations and new judicial functions, while judicial revenue is as helpful as a cup of water for extinguishing the fire on a cartful of wood. Reforming old jails therefore cannot be put on agenda in a short period of time.
>
> —Zhu Shusheng, president of the Jiangsu High Court, 1937[1]

The judicial reform began with penal reform in the New Policy era, and penal reform required prison reform. From then on, prison reform was a major part of the judicial reform through the Nanjing decade. While the reform drive led to a few newly built provincial prisons where new regulations were implemented, conditions in county jails and detention houses remained deplorable. A lack of funding was often cited to account for the situation, as Zhu Shusheng did as late as 1937. That is no doubt an important reason, but one should not overlook sociological issues that lay beyond the financial strains at the county level. This chapter deals with those issues, as well as with finance, to explain how and why county penal institutions fell short of the reform goals.

Reform Goals and Reality in Counties

From the beginning, prisons and detention houses were conceived of as separate institutions in places where courts were installed, but such separation rarely existed in most counties where county magistrates handled judicial affairs. The county jail, located inside the CGO compound, held defendants as well as convicts. In some counties where detention houses did exist separately from jails, their conditions were as bad. Reports from counties in 1913 revealed that more than half of detention houses in the country held inmates beyond their capacities. Some housed several hundreds and others nearly 1,000. In those extremely crowded and squalid facilities, diseases spread and deaths occurred frequently. Minister of Justice Liang Qichao noted that "[before being convicted of any crimes] defendants already suffer more pains than sentenced convicts," and urged that defendants be released on bail or on their own recognizance. He spoke of the proper treatment of defendants as a matter of due process that "concerns the judicial reform in the short run and the protection of human rights in the long run."[2]

In March 1913, the MJ issued its Directive No. 67, listing eight items by which county jails would be measured and on which counties should make reports: (1) If a county did not have a detention house and used the jail to hold defendants, the defendants should be strictly separated from convicts, and (2) they should be treated according to the Regulations on Detention Houses. (3) County jails should have both single cells and communal cells. (4) Inmates confined in communal cells should be classified and separated according to their crimes and punishments. (5) County jails should establish workshops depending on their revenues, and (6) have sickrooms. (7) Jails with little air and light and with high humidity should be rebuilt as much as possible. (8) The jail overseer and other staff should reside within the jail to perform their duties.[3] The directive was an attempt at formalizing county jails, but it also conceded to the reality by allowing much leeway. The key concession was that counties did not have to separate jails and detention houses. Some of the items on this wish list—single cells, sickrooms, and workshops—were in the realm of fantasy in view of actual conditions in counties.

The directive solicited few responses from provinces, and the MJ had to issue multiple directives to all provincial HC and HP, urging them to get reports from county jails under their jurisdictions, again to no avail.[4] It turned out that many counties did not receive Directive No. 67.[5] The establishment and then the abolition of the OPJI in 1913 and the Second Revolution the same year disrupted the channels of communications between the provincial judicial institutions and the CGO (the only such breakdown within the judicial system prior to 1937). But when communications were restored, the Jiangsu HP still had difficulty getting responses from county jails on the matter. By October 1914, only seventeen counties (out of sixty) had sent in reports on jail conditions and their improvements.[6] Chief Procurator Xu Shengjin was forced to issue another scolding order demanding compliance from the other counties.[7]

Jail overseers were reluctant to report on the conditions in jails because the eight-item standards that the MJ used to measure county jails were so removed from the reality that overseers did not know where to start the improvement or how to report on it. In a report submitted on December 20, 1914, the overseer in Yixing neither followed the eight-heading format provided by the MJ nor enclosed a required drawing of the jail. He simply described the jail as being too small and overcrowded to separate inmates, let alone having single cells, a sickroom, and a workshop. Inasmuch as he had asked in vain for funds for remodeling the jail upon assuming his duties six months before, he hoped the JHP chief would understand his difficulties.[8] The report from Gourong was similar. The overseer stated that the jail was unable to implement the standards because of the poor conditions there. Separating convicts and defendants and having single cells were impossible, because the jail consisted of rented residential houses, which were small and crowded. It was equally difficult to set up a workshop in the jail given the lack of space and funds. The overseer had also asked for funds to build a sickroom in the jail before but had been turned down.[9]

Another county that had failed to report earlier defended itself on more startling grounds—it did not have a jail. According to the county magistrate, the jail in Luhe had not had many inmates, and it had therefore been closed down by the order of the former JHP chief in November 1913. Thereafter convicts were held in the detention house.[10] If the report was true, the former JHP chief had ignored the regulations on jails and detention houses, but probably for practical reasons—financial conditions in that county.

The reports from the counties that responded formally to the MJ directive revealed the lamentable conditions in county jails. In Yancheng, the jail had a capacity for 90, but it actually held over 130 people, both convicts and defendants. The overseer promised that efforts would be made to separate convicts and defendants, reserve one room as a sickroom, improve sanitary conditions, and build more rooms, including a workshop, "when funds were available."[11]

As the archives suggest again, in the Beiyang era, the line of communications and the chain of command within the judicial system actually ran from Beijing through the provincial level down to counties, even where county magistrates performed judicial functions. The provincial and county institutions responded to the central government initiatives as much as financially feasible. Where reform initiatives in institutional formalization failed to be implemented in counties, it was not because counties willfully resisted such initiatives, but because the financial and material resources there did not match the ambitious goals of the reform. As for procedural formalization, noncompliance with it had to do with the social context and local practices.

On the part of the central government, the formalization agenda marched ahead as determinedly as ever, at least on paper. In 1919, the MJ issued Regulations on County Jails and Detention Houses to separate the two kinds of institutions at the county level.[12] In effect, the regulations were held up as long-term goals to be achieved when possible and, more important, as public relations documents to be used to show foreign powers that China was moving toward judicial modernity. The conditions on the ground in both kinds of institutions in counties remained below the prescribed standards during the Republican era.

Coping with Problems in County Jails

Most of the problems encountered in county jails were long-standing issues inherited from earlier times, such as overcrowding and unsanitary conditions, but some were new issues, ironically, arising from judicial reform, such as separating convicts and defendants and making inmates work behind bars, which required additional space and resources. The agenda of institutional formalization demanded conformity to nationwide standards, and anything less was a problem. Despite the efforts made, however, most problems turned out to be persistent.

Female Prisoners

Female inmates were relatively few in the prison system, but their presence put additional demands on prisons, especially ill-equipped county jails and detention houses. We saw in Chapter 3 how the issue troubled the Jiangsu First Prison (JFP) in the mid-1930s. As for county jails, the regulations of 1919 stipulated that male and female inmates were to be strictly separated. In reality, however, female quarters in county jails and detention houses were virtually nonexistent, which meant noncompliance and more opportunities for abuses. Recognizing the reality, in February 1920, the MJ ordered that counties near a provincial new prison send their female inmates to that prison.[13] New prisons were few and far in between, however, so the order was irrelevant to most counties.

Some county jails were so small and dilapidated that they did not have space to house female inmates at all. In 1923, inspection of the jail in Jiangpu determined that its structure was not suitable and that it should be remodeled to include female quarters.[14] This did not happen. The facility for female inmates (both defendants and convicts) was a small roadside residential house without a yard, away from the jail itself. The isolated "female jail" caused management and security problems for the overseer (in 1925, a female inmate escaped). In late December 1926, the overseer requested permission to use over ¥200 originally designated for setting up a prison workshop to build two thatched rooms behind the jail as his family lodging, so that his bedroom inside the jail could be used as a female cell. This did not happen either. In February 1927, the overseer wrote to the JHP chief, Zhou Yike, reporting that with the Shangdong Army (*lujun*) massed in and around Jiangpu, soldiers frequented the outer facility for women to "have fun" (*youwan*), which contravened the prison rules; but if one tried to confront the soldiers, violence might occur. He demanded an urgent solution. Zhou suggested that female inmates be sent to the JFP. The overseer replied that the three female inmates were defendants awaiting trial, and that it would be inconvenient to send them away and then bring them back to be tried. Zhou then ordered the Jiangpu county magistrate to dispose of the cases quickly and send any convicted female inmates to the JFP.[15] Needless to say, the remolding of the jail never took place.

Prison Work in County Jails

Informed by Western models and traditional ideals, the MJ envisioned inmates working behind bars as part of a reformed prison system. The prison regulations of 1913 provided that inmates should work from seven to ten hours every day, and that the types of work should depend on the inmate's age, the crime committed, prison term, skills, former occupation, and ability to establish a livelihood after imprisonment. The income from the prison work belonged to the national treasury, but the inmate would receive a bonus that was no more than 30 percent of the prevailing wages for ordinary workers in the same trade, which would be withheld until the inmate was released.[16] In 1915, a national meeting on prison reform suggested trades that could be followed behind bars, such as manufacturing stationery for judicial institutions.[17] The MJ reached an agreement with the MF to exempt transit taxes on products of prison work for three years, starting in August 1915.[18] The 1920 Regulations on Prison Work provided detailed rules on how prison work should be organized.[19]

Institutionalizing prison work had very limited results. New prisons largely complied with the regulations.[20] But most county jails did not have prison work programs at all. In October 1915, the Jiangsu governor approved a proposal from the JHC, the JHP, and the FD that only new prisons and ten financially stronger counties should get funds to build workshops for prison work.[21] The plan did not materialize. Reports in 1919 from counties in Jiangsu show that even some of the ten counties, such as Wujin and Tai, did not have inmates working in jails. In fact, most county jails badly needed funds to expand prison space or repair prison structures to house inmates properly before they could do anything about prison work.[22]

In May 1928, the MJ in Beijing issued the Measures of Prison Work in Old Jails, to be first tested in Jiangsu, Zhejiang, and Anhui provinces, which were actually under GMD control by then. The GMD government continued the same policy. In 1930, the MJ in Nanjing expanded the practice by making prison inmates work outside the prison, and it reissued the Regulations on Prison Work in 1932.[23] By and large, however, prison work remained a rare practice in county jails in the Nanjing decade. Only a few counties, such as Chongming and Yixing, had set up workshops for inmates by 1932 and 1933.[24] In 1934, while 60–70 percent of inmates in new prisons in Jiangsu worked inside prison walls, only 20–30 percent of inmates in county jails did.[25] The issue of prison work shows again that whenever national initiatives involved financial investments, they were difficult to carry out at the county level.

Deaths in County Jails

In the Republican prison system, inmate deaths were common. The 1913 Prison Regulations and Provisional Detention House Regulations provided that when a death occurred in those institutions, the head of the institution should report it to the district procurator, who should come to the scene to examine the body and certify the death. In November 1913, after the retrenchment of courts in counties, the Wujiang county magistrate made an inquiry to the provincial governor on how to handle such a case in counties where the county magistrate handled judicial affairs. Governor Han Guojun referred the inquiry to the JHC, which in turn referred it to the JHP, but there was no response.[26] Without clear instructions, county magistrates would act in the spirit of the Prison Regulations and, in lieu of a district procurator, verify an inmate's death and, along with the jail overseer and a physician, sign a death certificate, which was sent in duplicate to the JHP. The latter did not raise any questions over the practice.[27]

In March 1915, Governor Qi Yaolin, who was authorized to supervise the provincial judiciary, raised the issue and asked the JHC to devise a uniform rule for counties to verify inmate deaths. To an inquiry from the JHC, the MJ replied in May 1915 that the county magistrate should act as procurator to verify inmate deaths, but to be prudent, the death of anyone convicted of a capital crime should still be jointly verified by the county magistrate and another magistrate from a neighboring county.[28] Joint verification was designed to prevent unauthorized execution of those sentenced to death. In fact, in 1914, at least one county magistrate in Guangxi province was disciplined for executing an inmate without approval and then making a false report that the inmate had died of illness.[29] In the 1920s, county magistrates often reported the deaths of convicts who had been sentenced to death for robbery, but the provincial authorities usually did not pursue such cases any further (see Chapter 9).[30]

Overcrowding

Along with case backlogs, overcrowding in the prison system, including county jails, was one of the most intractable problems that frustrated reformers. With regard to overcrowding in detention houses, the MJ repeatedly urged procuracies and courts to process cases quickly to cut the number of defendants under detention. As for the overcrowding in new prisons and county jails, the PNCC offered a partial solution in parole,[31] the procedures for which were set out in detail in the 1913 Parole Management Regulations.[32]

Yet parole did little to alleviate overcrowding in penal institutions. In 1920, the problem was such that the MJ's Regulations on Releasing Prisoners on Bail stated explicitly that when the number of inmates in new prisons and county jails exceeded capacity, they could be released. Inmates serving terms of between two months and five years could be released on bail (*baoshi*) if they had served more than half of their terms and met certain conditions. Prisoners incarcerated for certain serious crimes were not eligible.[33]

Overcrowding in county jails decreased in the late 1920s but had rebounded by the mid 1930s (see Chapters 3 and 5). In July 1934, the JHC asked the Civil Affairs Department to find out why the number of inmates in the jails at Pi, Yixing, and Donghai had risen so dramatically.[34] The responses from the county magistrates were revealing. In Yixing, out of the 126 defendants in the detention house, 99 were drug offenders waiting to be tried by military organs. In Pi, because people were quick to resort to lawsuits and losing parties would make false accusations against the trial officer, four trial officers and three commissioners processing case backlogs succeeded one another in the county within five months of the county magistrate taking the office. Each turnover interrupted case processing. Under previous county magistrates, subcounty district security forces would arrest and then release criminals on bail to pocket the bail money. The county magistrate prohibited the practice, which resulted in more defendants under detention. Pi was adjacent to Shandong province, from which bandits would slip into the county, and the arrest of bandits further increased the number of inmates in the detention house. The county magistrate had discovered that the county police office was illegally holding 48 defendants, and he had them transferred to the detention house, thus adding to the number there. The county GMD headquarters arrested several dozen counterrevolutionaries each month. All these factors led to the rise in the number of inmates in the county.

Similarly, in Donghai, the county magistrate transferred defendants previously held in the police office to the detention house. Besides, the subprovincial district chief, the subprovincial district security force, and the tax police were all headquartered in Donghai, with their jurisdictions over five counties. All bandits, robbers, salt smugglers, and drug offenders arrested in the five counties were held in the Donghai detention house. Although the county magistrate and the trial officer worked hard and had processed more than fifty cases of robbery and banditry, the convicted still had to be held in the detention house while their cases were going through trial reviews or appeals.[35] Clearly, there was a large gap between the demand for more prison space and the availability of such space, which was beyond the county magistrate's control. The situation was especially aggravated in Donghai where different law enforcement agencies were headquartered, with no additional prison space to go with them.

In 1935, the JHC surveyed county jails to see whether cells had been added in the past five years and, if so, how many. In six counties, additions had been made by rearranging existing facilities. In Taicang, for example, two rooms for a workshop and a guard bedroom had been converted to cells, increasing the number of cells to 34, with a capacity for 140 inmates. Only in Fengxian and Jinshan had new cells been added (eight and two cells respectively), which were paid for with donations from the local elite.[36]

The overcrowding caused by the anti-drug campaign of the mid 1930s impacted county jails as well. In fact, it was a nationwide phenomenon. In August 1936, the MJ circulated a document showing that Anyang county in Henan province rented residential houses to hold drug offenders when inmates in the county detention house reached 757, where the designed capacity was for 280. The MJ asked all counties in all provinces to use civilian housing to deal with the overcrowding caused by the anti-drug campaign.[37] Zhu Shusheng, acting president of the JHC, responded that there were more than 100,000 opium smokers in Jiangsu, and that each county arrested hundreds at a time. Although twenty-eight counties had allocated increased space to incarcerate drug offenders (the total additions would accommodate 3,730 inmates), there was a constant shortage of space. The difficulty in seeking additional space was that public facilities were already occupied by government institutions, while civilian residences rarely had a capacity for 200–300 people. Zhu indicated that the JHC was consulting with the provincial government to find ways to address the problem.[38]

The provincial government was not helpful, however. In February 1937, Zhu sent a long letter to the head of the provincial government, Chen Guofu, pleading for help with the inadequate funding and overcrowding in Jiangsu's prison system. Many county jail overseers in the province complained to the JHC about the difficulty of obtaining funds for inmate rations, especially in jails that also held convicted robbers and bandits. That was why appointed overseers were reluctant to take their offices, and those who did take office, facing an impossible task, quickly resigned or asked to be transferred to other jobs. As for overcrowding, when inmates were held beyond capacity, security and management became difficult to handle, let alone sanitation, moral instruction, prison work, and other matters.[39]

To solve the problems, Zhu made two requests: (1) that administrative agencies find facilities to house convicted drug offenders and robbers/bandits tried under martial law so that overseers could focus on reforming jails gradually. Zhu attempted here to dissociate the judiciary and the prison system from the prisoners tried by the military and security apparatus. (2) That until such time as administrative agencies found facilities for convicts tried under martial law, the subcounty district security headquarters and county governments use the provincial appropriation to advance a monthly sum to county jails to cover the rations of the said prisoners and the wages of guards. Any remainder of the sum would be accounted for after the actual expenses had occurred.[40]

Chen Guofu did not respond until March 31, 1937, a month later, when he rejected Zhu's requests. Rations for robbers, bandits, and drug offenders should be paid for in the first place out of general county funds and the revenue from the anti-opium campaign, and then by additional funds. The provincial appropriation should not be used for that purpose. With regard to overcrowding in county jails, Chen claimed that nineteen counties in the province with large numbers of drug offenders had asked to set up temporary detention facilities or workhouses to confine those offenders separately. Other counties could take the same measure to ease overcrowding.[41] In Jiangsu, actually, twenty-eight counties had set up temporary facilities to house drug offenders, but the piecemeal additions were simply not enough, and no more such additions could be found, of which Chen Guofu pretended he was unaware. In short, county jails faced a lack of space, yet no solution or help was forthcoming from anywhere. The provincial government was determined to defend the interests of the provincial administrative institutions at the expense of the judiciary, including county-level judicial functions.

Prisoner Escapes

Escapes took place more frequently at county jails than in new prisons, although three juvenile inmates managed to escape from an institution as modern as the Beijing Prison in 1913.[42] Less than secure facilities and horrendous conditions in county jails were conducive to escapes. Minister of Justice Zhang Zhongxiang admitted as much in 1914, but he stressed that if the head of a facility properly supervised the guards, inmates would not have chances to escape.[43]

Various orders from the MJ had little effect in preventing prisoner escapes, but they placed the county magistrate and the jail overseer in a difficult situation. They were denied extra funds to hire more guards or remodel county jails and detention houses, and they were ordered not to overuse shackles, handcuffs, iron collars, and chains on inmates, to make confinement conditions humane. But when inmates escaped, they faced disciplinary action for negligence. When Miao Wengui arrived in Tongshan as jail overseer, he found that inmates were routinely chained and locked together at night, which made it impossible for them to turn their bodies when sleeping. He abolished the practice; but as the result, some inmates escaped, and he was disciplined for negligence.[44] Under those circumstances the logical course of action for county magistrates, jail overseers, and guards was to systematically use restraining devices on inmates, despite the MJ orders.

Disciplinary actions against county magistrates and overseers for prisoner escapes were institutionalized in the Beiyang era. To this end, the provincial governments in Heilongjiang and Hunan originated a policy of reducing the county magistrate's salary by a given percentage and using the money to repair the prison, which ironically indicated that the disrepair of jails was to blame for escapes.[45] The initiatives in Heilongjiang and Hunan inspired the MJ and the Ministry of the Interior, which issued regulations to that effect in January 1917. Based on the scheme developed in Hunan, the rules reduced one month of the county magistrate's salary to one-third for the escape of a prisoner sentenced to death or a life term, and 20 percent for a prisoner serving 3–15 years. If the magistrate was able to recapture the fugitive within three months, the deduction would be refunded; if he was unable to recapture any fugitive sentenced to death or a life term within specified time limits, he faced further disciplinary action under the 1913 Regulations on Disciplining County Magistrates.[46]

In January 1918, Regulations on Disciplining Civil Servants replaced the 1913 Regulations on Disciplining County Magistrates. When the county magistrate was disciplined for prisoner escape, he faced penalties ranging from a reduction in salary to demotion to removal from office. Salary reduction (10–25 percent) would last for from one to twelve months; demotion for one year, and removal from office for two to six years.[47] In 1914–1919, the High Commission for Disciplining Civil Servants took action for prisoner escapes against county magistrates, among whom were those of Jinshan, Gourong, Liyang, Yizheng, and Jiangyin in Jiangsu, and penalties ranged from suspension from office for four years to reduction of salary by a quarter for six months.[48]

In 1913–1918, while county magistrates were penalized by various disciplinary actions for prison escapes, jail overseers were routinely fired for the same cause.[49] After 1918, more jail overseers than county magistrates were disciplined for prisoner escapes by the Ordinary Commission for Disciplining Civil Servants. Between 1922 and 1927, no fewer than twenty-nine jail overseers in Jiangsu were disciplined by dismissal, suspension, demotion, reduction of salary, and recording of demerits.[50] The disciplinary penalties for jail overseers meant that they were now treated as civil servants, another step toward institutional formalization.

Some examples will illustrate how the disciplinary mechanism worked regarding county personnel. In June 1917, a jail inmate escaped from Taichang. With permission from the MJ and the provincial governor, the JHP duly took disciplinary action. The county magistrate suffered a 20 percent deduction of one-month's salary, and the overseer lost his job.[51] In March 1918, two defendants escaped from the detention house in Chongming, and only one of them was recaptured. Since the uncaptured fugitive was suspected of crimes entailing a prison term of three years, the county magistrate's salary was reduced by 10 percent for one month, and the overseer was given two demerit points and suffered a reduction of 10 percent of one month's salary. In another case, the county magistrate of Haimen was able to recapture a fugitive three months and eight days after the escape, but his request for a refund of the money deducted from his salary was denied by the MJ. In Liyang, when an inmate escaped on February 23, 1918, Magistrate Qiu lost 20 percent of one month's salary and the jail overseer was fired. When the fugitive was recaptured over three months later, Qiu requested a refund, stating that a detective had caught the fugitive in Jiangning on May 21 but, owing to another mission, could not bring the fugitive back to Liyang until June 5, thus putting the date of the recapture within three months of the escape. The truthfulness of Qiu's statement may be suspect, but he was granted the refund.[52] These examples show that with the coordination between the JHP and the MJ, disciplinary actions against county officials were seriously enforced—another indication of the reach of the central government at the county level in the Beiyang era.

Irregularities and Inmate Subculture

According to Zhu Gemin, a jail overseer in several counties in Jiangsu during 1921–1944, prison staff often engaged in some illegal practices. They overreported operating costs and embezzled prison work revenue and—most commonly—inmates' rations, which was done by reducing quantities, adulterating rice with cheaper peas, buying rice at a lower price than was accounted for, reporting more inmates than the actual numbers, and so forth. If relatively well-to-do prisoners made payments, they were allowed to eat the meals their families cooked and sent into jail, in which case jail staff would profit both from the payment and from the inmate rations thus saved.[53]

The irregularities and abuses in county jails often went hand in hand with an inmate subculture where the strong preyed on the weak. Hardened criminals serving long or life terms were the meanest in abusing new inmates. County jail staff tended to use those predatory prisoners to manage the jail and control the inmate population. A variety of names were used to designate such prisoners' special status, from the traditional term "dragon head" (*longtou*) to Republican-era equivalents such as "inside guard" (*neikanshou*) or "deputy" (*daibiao*). When new inmates arrived, the dragon head would demand payment or some other form of submission and subject those who could not pay to mistreatment and physical abuse, from forcing them to sleep next to the toilet pot to taking away their rations to beating them up. Those practices were repeatedly prohibited, but they continued to exist in many places. Apparently, jail staff regarded the inmate subculture, not only as conducive to their making personal gains, but also a useful and cost-effective mechanism to manage county jails, given the overall conditions there. Thus "peace and order" in jail were maintained on the basis of inequality and injustice among inmates.

In late 1922, in response to a petition from several citizens in Jingjiang, the JHP chief Xu Shouheng ordered the Wu DP to investigate the management of the jail in that county. After interviewing a former county clerk and some inmates in the jail, District Procurator Sun Yuan found the allegations to be true. The former clerk said that whenever new inmates arrived in the jail, they had to pay some money. Old inmates would share 20 percent of it, the guard at the gate, the clerk, and the head guard would get 10 percent each, and the remaining 50 percent would go to the CGO (the office received from ¥20 to ¥80 from this source each month).[54] The custom dated back to the Qing era and had never been abolished. The inmates testified that the overseer would sell certain inmates pieces of printed cloth for ¥2.40 each. Those who bought such "badges" were called "inside guards." They got newly arrived prisoners to pay to get their shackles removed and reported bad behavior by other inmates to the overseer, in return for which they were not chained and yoked together by the neck every night. Prison inmates were immoral, Sun Yuan observed in his report, and even if they were treated equally, the strong might bully the weak to extort money. Inasmuch as some inmates were given titles and power over other inmates, the alleged extortion probably did exist. The so-called inside guard was a "dragon head" by another name, in violation of the standing prohibition of the Ministry of Justice.

Sun Yuan also found that out of ninety-one male inmates, only five did not have shackles on them. Other inmates said that except for one who was blind, the four men had paid money to have their shackles removed. The four men insisted that they had earned the treatment by providing services to the jail or were unshackled because of illness. One of the four had been convicted of robbery and escape and was serving ten years. Yet this inmate was not only free of shackles but also was free to go out in the morning and return in the evening in the name of buying daily supplies for the jail. In this case, Sun observed, the jail was no longer a place for punishing crime, but a lodging house. He also noted that the practice of chaining and yoking inmates together by the neck at night to prevent escape violated prison regulations and should be abolished. The gross abuses and irregularities in Jingjiang shocked the JHP chief and led to the dismissal of the overseer.[55] It is doubtful, however, that much changed in the jail, given what we know of the conditions there.

It was not uncommon for inmates to be allowed to go in and out of the jail freely. Zhu Gemin found similar situations in Rugao, Huaiyin, and Jiangpu, where he was sent as jail overseer. In Jiangpu, because the jail was so cramped and dilapidated, inmates were free to go out and return at night, using the jail as a lodging place.[56] Some county jails strangely still had a so-called familial message chamber (*jiaxin fang*), where in the Qing era, the wives of convicts awaiting execution had been allowed to stay with their husbands to get pregnant, but it was now taken by stronger inmates for private use, such as meeting family members and engaging prostitutes. Zhu Gemin personally found such facilities in Rugao, Huaiyin, and Pi and ordered their demolition.[57] In such places, the penal reform's goal of incarceration as punishment by deprivation of freedom was all but lost.

The kind of irregularities described above existed throughout the period under study. Robert William Swallow, a British Baptist missionary and longtime China resident, wrote in 1937: "I know of one [county] prison where it is said that you can obtain anything you want, even singsong girls, so long as you have funds at your disposal. Another prison was dominated by a man who was serving a life sentence and not only did he gamble with the other prisoners but employed a secretary to keep his accounts. His autocratic rule was ended when some of the other prisoners filed a petition against him because he kept back their daily food allowance in order to compel them to pay their debts."[58] Even if a "dragon head" was brought down by inmates' petitions occasionally, it did not change the inmate subculture or eliminate the everyday irregularities and abuses.

Another type of irregularity was the use of inmates for private services outside the jail by the jail staff. This became quite common in the 1930s, and the JHP issued orders in 1935 strictly prohibiting taking inmates out of jails for private services or having inmates post bail to work outside prison. Some twenty-two counties reported to the JHP that no such thing existed in their jails.[59] If the reports are to be believed, the practice probably existed in over twenty other counties.

In the final analysis, despite all the prison regulations and reform initiatives, the law of the jungle operated in the prison system, especially in county jails, where unscrupulous jail staff preyed on all inmates, while resourceful and predatory inmates curried favor with, or won the "respect" of, jail staff and then preyed on other inmates with impunity. Many abuses and irregularities, such as those associated with an inmate subculture, did not necessarily result from the shortage of judicial funding, but from the inescapable psychological and sociological factors in the harsh environment of penal confinement. With successful formalization, such irregularities and abuses might have been reduced to a minimum, but lack of resources prevented the formalization agenda from being implemented at the county level. As a result, irregularities and abuses continued in the penal system and were often accepted by inmates and jail staff alike as a matter of course, or as part of the penalty for inmates.

Human Relations and County Jail Politics

Local Elites and County Jails

The county jail was not a closed system, independent of the wider social environment. In fact, how county jails and detention houses were managed was an important matter to local society in more than one way. Prisons held criminal elements that could constitute a threat to local peace and order if they broke out or were released improperly. Local elites in particular had a stake in the proper maintenance of the county jail and detention house in their locale. For that reason, the state sought the cooperation of local elites in reforming county jails. Two specific approaches of the state should be discussed here: One was to solicit donations from local elites for repairing and remodeling jails, and the other, in the Nanjing decade, was to organize, and involve local elites in, county-level semi-official organizations for improving county jails and detention houses.

Since the lack of funding prevented the prison reform from moving forward, the state called for soliciting donations from local elites. When the MJ asked county jails to report on the status of their improvement in 1921, one of the things the ministry wanted to know was whether funds could be raised or donations collected to repair jails and set up workshops. Most counties found it difficult to raise funds or solicit donations locally. The Yangzhong county magistrate reported that since his was a barren region with a poor population, the county was devoid of rich families, generous gentry, and public-minded persons, and it was difficult to solicit donations. When the Provincial Assembly decided to establish workshops in all county jails in 1920, the county magistrate invited local gentry to a meeting at which he explained the benefits of such a workshop and asked gentry to help raise funds and collect donations. But the gentry responded that they were unable to help in this way because the local people were too poor. The Suqian county magistrate told a similar story, while the Ganyu county magistrate donated ¥200 of his own money to start a workshop in the county jail when he could not get any donations from local people.[60] Not surprisingly, the counties that reported their inability to get donations were mostly in the poorer northern part of the province.

The only county that gave a positive report in 1921 was Wujin, a relatively wealthier locale in Jiangnan. In 1918, a former county magistrate donated his own money and asked the jail overseer to do the same. They also solicited donations from merchants and peasants and eventually raised ¥1,191 to remodel the county jail. Besides repairing existing communal cells and other facilities, the remodeling added nineteen single cells, two communal cells for women, two sickrooms, one mortuary room, one office, and fourteen rooms for workshops. The sitting county magistrate used ¥40 left over from the remodeling project and loaned ¥100 from the budget, plus ¥200 the overseer borrowed elsewhere, to get a workshop going.[61] Such a bright spot was rare in Jiangsu, however.

The donations from local elites to the prison reform came sporadically. In early 1933, a "citizen Yuan Shenchuan" (so identified) simply walked into the Zhengjiang DC to offer ¥22 for inmates (¥0.20 each) held in the court detention house and ¥70 for those in the Zhengjiang Prison to celebrate the Chinese New Year.[62] Although some routine reports from jail overseers mention that local gentry would donate money for prisons to buy fans and straw mats for inmates in summer and/or cotton coats and quilts in winter, it is also possible that occasional donations, especially in small sums, went unreported.

In the 1930s, efforts to solicit donations from local elites continued as part of the routine work of the CGO. In May 1930, when the JHC's

Inspector Chen Ludan visited Liyang, he and Magistrate Zheng invited the head of the local chamber of commerce and four wealthy merchants to a meeting and solicited donations for remodeling the county jail. The chamber pledged ¥1,000, and the four merchants also jointly pledged ¥1,000. Magistrate Zheng said that he would ask Huang Jinrong, one of the well-known leaders of the underworld in Shanghai, who was a personal friend of his, for donations. In his report to the JHC, Chen Ludan opined that the donations from the chamber of commerce and from Huang Jinrong were probably more reliable (than the merchants' pledges).[63] The officials had perhaps learned from experience that personal donations could not be counted on for prison reform.

Involving local elites in semi-official institutions to improve county jails was a more successful approach. Such initiatives began in October 1931, when the MJ issued Provisional Regulations on Committees for Improving County Jails and Detention Houses. The ex-officio members of the committee in each county included the county magistrate, the trial officer, the jail overseer, section chiefs of the county government, and representatives of the local chamber of commerce and local agricultural association. The ex-officio members recommended local elites (*qiying shuoshi*) and GMD cadres as volunteer members, though the number of volunteer members could not be more than half that of the ex-officio ones. The issues the committee addressed at its biweekly meetings included (1) moral education and prison work, (2) investigating cases of parole and release on bail, (3) repair of facilities and budget, (4) soliciting donations, and so forth.[64] The initiative signaled the state's efforts to reach local society through co-opting local elites.

How did such committees actually operate and interact with local society? The Committee for Improving County Jail (CICJ) in Songjiang was set up in late 1931. Two local leaders—the director of the Songjiang County Chamber of Commerce and the head of the semi-official Workhouse for Vagrants—served on the committee. By January 1932, the CICJ convened its third meeting, and the county magistrate issued a formal order asking the chamber of commerce director to attend the meeting and prepare a written report on his inspection of the county jail and detention house.[65] During its existence, the CICJ devoted most of its attention to the financial side of improving the county jail and detention house. At a meeting held on January 26, 1932, it was reported that the jail was holding 157 male and 15 female inmates, plus 9 male and 7 female inmates in transit (*jiya fan*). It was decided that a guard booth outside the jail should be built at an estimated cost of ¥16, provided by the county government. The CICJ also resolved that the county government should find money to buy additional restraining instruments for the jail. At a meeting held on February 27, 1932, at the county magistrate's suggestion, the CICJ resolved to stop having prisoners work manufacturing imitation money for death rituals (*mingqian*), because it promoted superstition. But at the next meeting, the CICJ decided to let them continue doing so for the time being, because to switch to weaving would require an investment of ¥648 in equipment.[66] In April 1936, the CICJ resolved to solicit donations in its name and to seek public bids for procurement of inmate ration rice. At another meeting that month, the CICJ discussed how to reduce inmate population, because at the time, 60–70 percent of inmates were drug offenders; it resolved, among other things, that the county's winter shelter should be repaired to house drug offenders, and that those accused of opium smoking but who were not addicts be released without bail.[67]

The meeting records of the CICJ show that the committee's function was to build consensus between local elites and county officials regarding how to spend the limited resources on reforming the county penal institutions and to generate support and donations from local society. Although the gains for the jail and detention house seem to have been limited in this particular case, by officially involving local elites in prison reform affairs, the CICJ helped prevent potential conflicts between the county government and local elites over managing county penal institutions, while enhancing and legitimating the public role of those elites in local society—a win-win arrangement. This little-known exercise in the Nanjing decade constituted an interesting dimension of the state's expansion into local society and the state-society interaction.

The County Magistrate and the Jail Overseer

The MJ repeatedly reminded the provincial authorities and the county magistrate that the overseer was an arm of the provincial judicial institutions, not the magistrate's personal assistant, to be installed and replaced at his pleasure. Although under the relevant regulations, the overseer was appointed and dismissed by the HP, in real life, the overseer had to be on good terms with the county magistrate in order for him to do his job, no matter how he intended to run the jail. The following is a case of the county magistrate shielding a corrupt jail overseer.

In March 1916, several "citizens" (so signed) in Yixing accused the overseer Chen Yunfa of corruption, charging that he embezzled inmate rations, demanded payments from new inmates (those who could not afford were physically abused), and allowed strong and tough inmates to prey on the weak. Because the county magistrate, Zhong Xing, did not care how the jail was run (saying that the inmates were bad people and deserved their treatment), and because Chen was well connected with other functionaries in the CGO, including the police and the security force, he was free to abuse inmates, who did not dare to speak up.

Although the allegation implicated the Yixing county magistrate, the JHP chief Wang Shurong issued an order, with a copy of the petition, to Magistrate Zhong and asked him to verify the facts and make a report. The archives do not contain a reply from Zhong. Nothing seems to have changed at the county jail, which led to an uprising. On the morning of September 2, 1916, when guards opened the cells, inmates attacked them with rocks, wooden sticks, and scissors. One guard was killed, and another was tied up, Chen Yunfa was seriously injured, and sixteen inmates escaped. The county magistrate ordered the closing of city gates and led a hunt for the escapees. Thirteen escapees were caught, and three were reportedly drowned while crossing a river.

Magistrate Zhong telegraphed the JHC and the JHP, as well as the provincial governor, asking for instructions, especially whether an official from a neighboring county should be appointed to verify the incident, which was a standard procedure in the event of prison breakout. The JHC and the JHP ordered interrogation and severe punishment of the escapees according to the law, but did not order verification by an official from a neighboring county. It was the governor who followed the procedure and appointed the county magistrate of Wuxi to go to Yixing and verify the incident. Within a month, Magistrate Zhong reported that four of the captured escapees had been executed under the criminal code and the Law on Punishing Robbers and Bandits (for more on which, see Chapter 9), with the approval of the provincial governor and provincial military governor.

No inquiry was made into why the breakout took place and whether it had to do with Chen's misconduct—such an inquiry would probably have found Chief Procurator Wang guilty of failing to pursue the issue raised by the earlier petition from local people. In the wake of the incident, Chen Yunfa requested to be transferred to another county for medical reasons. The JHC and the JHP ordered that Chen and the overseer in Jiangdu switch their posts.[68] Jiangdu was not a place better served by medical facilities than Yixing. Clearly, both Chen himself and Wang understood that Chen was no longer an appropriate person to be in charge of the jail in Yixing. In all likelihood, it was the negligence of Zhong and Wang that allowed the tragedy to happen and the corrupt jail overseer to get away with his misdeeds. This case demonstrates that the effect of any established rules and procedures depended on whether those in charge of operating and enforcing them did so properly. It also explains why in most cases, the authorities launched investigations in response to petitions from local people against judicial misconduct (see Chapter 10).

Overseers, Guards, and Local Power Holders

The jail overseer had to be careful, not only with the county magistrate, but also with other power holders in the county government and local society. Local power holders, disgruntled guards, and mistreated inmates, in combination or individually, would and did accuse the overseer of wrongdoing to wreck his job. Such events often unfolded in a confusing pattern, but provided illuminating cases of how the power game of local politics was played in the course of the reform.

In September 1931, a letter signed by "all inmates" reached the JHC from Lishui, accusing the jail overseer Liu Chuankai of severely beating up a female inmate. The JHC president, Lin Biao, ordered the county magistrate, Xie Zheng, to investigate and report on the incident. After finding that a female inmate had been beaten but not severely, Xie did not take further action. Five months later, the JHC received another letter signed by "all inmates" from Lishui. This time, Liu was accused of more wrongdoing, including embezzling inmate rations. Lin Biao ordered another investigation. Before the order arrived, Xie Zheng had already been forced to take action due to the intervention of the GMD ward executive committee, which also received the accusations against Liu. The party committee resolved to "refer the case to the county government to investigate and vigorously deal with the matter." The investigation by the CICJ, apparently urged by the party committee, also found some wrongdoing at the jail, though it was vague about the details. Faced with these actions, Xie Zheng suspended Liu and reported the action to the JHC.

Meanwhile, Liu wrote a letter to Lin Biao in his own defense, saying that he devoted himself to his job and did not engage in socializing among local officials. But the local custom in Lishui was for newly appointed officials to treat other county officials to a banquet so as to ward off trouble in the future, even if he did something illegal. Liu had offended local people by not socializing. Yang Yushu of the GMD ward executive committee spread the word that Liu did not respect him, indicating that Yang had a grudge against Liu. As it happened, a cunning inmate named Dong Laosi often violated the rules in the jail. Once, Liu had had Dong handcuffed for an hour as a warning. In retaliation, Dong, claiming to speak in the name of all the inmates, had made the accusations against Liu to the GMD committee (and to the JHC as well, of which Liu was unaware). Yang Yushu jumped at the opportunity and went to the jail to ask inmates whether their rations had been severely reduced. Dong arranged for the other inmates to confirm this. The party committee then asked the county magistrate to discipline Liu. Liu stated in the letter that he had been wrongfully suspended, and that the JHC should send someone to investigate to get the truth. Lin Biao, however, had no interest in getting involved in local politics. He simply recalled Liu to the province (to be appointed elsewhere) and assigned a new overseer to Lishui.[69] Thus one pattern did not change from the 1920s to the 1930s: rather than intervene in local politics when a conflict arose between a jail overseer and a county magistrate or other county officials or local elites, the provincial judicial authorities would simply remove the person in trouble and appoint a replacement.

Tao Shouhe, the new jail overseer appointed to Lishui, fared no better than Liu Chuankai, because he too offended the local power networks from the beginning, and because he failed to stamp out misconduct of his subordinates in running the jail. Within two months of Tao's appointment, Chen Xuewen and Xie Yinghan, inmates in the county jail, alleged in a letter to the JHC that Tao embezzled inmate rations and extorted money from inmates, among other things. Lin Biao ordered Xie Zheng to verify this and report on the matter. In deference to the party cadre Yang Yushu, who was now also sitting on the CICJ, Xie turned the case over to Yang. Yang and two other members of the CICJ reported the following from their investigation:

(1) Tao had arrived in Lishui with seven or eight jail guards and fired all the former jail guards except one.

(2) The head guard, Liang Ji, and a guard named Zhu Gui, who were Tao's confidants, had tried to extort money from Chen Xuewen. Liang had offered to have Chen released on bail for ¥8, which Chen could not

afford. Zhu promised to have shackles removed from Chen for ¥8. Chen paid ¥4, but the shackles were not removed. Later, Zhu returned ¥3 and a small pack of opium in lieu of ¥1 to Chen . Angry and frustrated, Chen attempted suicide. Liang had since gone on leave and disappeared.

(3) Tao allowed his wife to go around the jail freely as a patrolling guard.

(4) Tao had reduced the wages of guards to pay his wife's wage.

(5) Tao embezzled inmate rations by using a lighter-weight steelyard to weigh rice for inmates.

Xie signed the report on June 22 and requested the JHC that Tao be fired.[70]

The MJ also received allegations against Tao and ordered the JHC chief procurator, Wang Simo, to investigate. Wang accepted and forwarded Xie Zheng's report to the MJ, proposing that Tao be prosecuted at the Jiangning DC under Article 100 of the Law on Organizing Courts. At the same time, the JHC president, Lin Biao, ordered Zhou Xiang, the trial officer in Gourong, to conduct another investigation in Lishui and report within three days.

Zhou's investigation partially corroborated Yang's report, signed by Xie Zheng, but it also exposed the falsehoods contained in that report:

(1) Liang Ji had once told Chen Xuewen that for ¥8, he would ask Tao to release Chen on bail. When the incident came to light in late May, Liang had resigned, and Tao had appointed his wife to take over as the acting head guard.

(2) The case of the guard Zhu Gui extorting money from Chen Xuewen had been tried and closed at the CGO on June 21; that of inmate Zhang Yuzhen extorting money from another inmate, Sun Jingsong, was tried on April 2; and that of the inmate Zhang Chengtong injuring Sun Jingsong was tried on April 20. Tao said he had not been aware of those incidents beforehand.

(3) As a patrolling guard, Tao's wife had a wage of ¥8, which was raised to ¥14 after Tao made her the acting head guard, but her wage was not paid at the expense of other guards' wages.

(4) The steelyard used at the jail was standard. The CGO secretary said that some inmates from the jail who cleared weeds at the CGO ground complained about rations. But the cook at the jail claimed that each inmate was given 20 *liang* of cooked rice every day, and one catty (*jin*) of salt and 10 *liang* of vegetable oil were used in cooking.[71]

(5) The jail had a physician, and there was a record book showing how much medicine was bought from a drugstore whenever there was a sick inmate.

(6) Chen Xuewen and Xie Yinghan told Zhou that they had never written any petition against Tao.

Yet the investigation by Zhou Xiang did not cause the JHC to reverse the decision to prosecute Tao Shouhe, Liang Ji, and Zhu Gui. Lin Biao sent Zhou Xiang's report to the chief procurator Wang Simo for reference in prosecuting the case.[72]

It seems clear that someone engineered the matter in the name of the two inmates. The main grievance against Tao was probably his firing former jail guards and replacing them with his own men and even his wife, which deprived locals of their coveted jobs, who perhaps had connections with or might have been given those jobs as favors by Yang Yushu and other local power holders. Tao's behavior not only violated the customary sense of fair play in local society with regard to economic opportunities (his wife's "high" pay was an outrage to those who had lost their ¥8 jobs), but also destabilized the power structure that Yang and his ilk maintained. That was why the latter seized on any slight misconduct by Tao and his subordinates to bring him down. If they did not have enough evidence, they would make sensational accusations anyway, as they probably knew the pattern of the JHC responses to local accusations. Despite the weak and inconclusive evidence against Tao, the JHC was prepared to prosecute the accused overseer and his underlings. The response illustrates the drive on the part of the JHC to stamp out abuses in the prison system and its reliance upon local power structure to operate county penal institutions with some semblance of justice. Local power holders learned to use the higher authorities' intent to clean up irregularities in county penal institutions to their own advantage in local politics, without expecting an actual cleaning up of irregularities rooted in the social environment of which the local power structure was part.

The Jail Overseer's Perspective

For a balanced view of what transpired in the Republican-era county jails, it is useful to take look at the perspective of the jail overseer. The above-mentioned cases already show how jail overseers would tell their side of the stories. Their stories may be taken with a grain of salt, just as accusations against them should be. But the overall sociopolitical environment and the financial situation in which county jails and detention houses operated give one a certain understanding of the difficulties with which jail overseers worked and of the reasons for abuses and irregularities. To get a better picture, some direct testimonies from jail overseers are presented below.

Zhu Gemin, the former jail overseer mentioned earlier, summarized the life of prison staff in the following terms. With low salaries, no one among prison personnel at county jails (and new prisons too) could be completely above corruption. Some had moral scruples and tried to be as honest as possible, but others lined their pockets at every opportunity; and some of the latter had the bad luck to get caught and punished. Many jail overseers faced an impossible situation: they were restrained by superiors, countered by local elites, frustrated by troublemaking guards, resisted by inmates, hampered by a shortage of funds, and confronted by emergencies such as escapes and riots. "One could neither stay nor leave, the pain of which cannot be described by words," Zhu said in a memoir written in his old age in the late 1980s.[73] He does not seem to have had any motive to exaggerate or misrepresent his experiences, and what he said is largely corroborated by the archival sources.

In May 1937, toward the end of the period this book covers, a document entitled "The Jail Overseers' Lament," signed by "Jail overseers in provinces and counties in the country," reached the MJ. It was a petition that complained about the conditions under which the jail overseer worked and asked for redress. Obviously, this was a self-serving document, but because it was written by jail overseers from their perspectives and driven by their grievances, it is worth a full reading:

> The authorities do not think highly of the job of the jail overseer, but the overseer directly supervises important inmates such as political prisoners and communist bandits and therefore indirectly helps maintain the security of the state and society. Counties outside provincial capitals typically have only a few dilapidated jail cells to hold most of the important prisoners. The overseer has to shoulder his responsibilities twenty-four hours a day without a peaceful night's sleep. The overseer has to take care of all duties from paper work to daily routines, unlike judges, procurators, and trial officers, whose responsibilities end when they step out of their offices. Neither are old jails like new prisons, which have more staff, more funds, and division of labor. The overseer has responsi-

bilities similar to those of judges, procurators, trial officers, and governors of new prisons, but his monthly salary is less than that of a head guard in a new prison. Nothing is more unbalanced and less fair in one's rights and duties provided by the Constitution.

The monthly salary of the overseer is ¥24 in Jiangxi province, ¥34–40 in Hunan, and ¥40–50 in Henan, Anhui, and Jiangsu. At a time when the price of everything is going up, it is hard to make ends meet, let alone take care of one's family. One was able to get by during the warlord period, when living expenses were low and there were not many taxes and surcharges. Now living expenses are increasing every day. With the income tax, the aviation fee,[74] the printed matter fees, subscriptions to the provincial government bulletin and all kinds of judicial and penal journals, and local temporary levies and surcharges, which add up to six or seven types, the living standards of the overseer are far worse than in the warlord period. Although the government has frequently proposed improving county jails recently, it has never mentioned improving the treatment of the overseer and paying jail guards more to prevent corruption, while every care is taken with regard to the treatment of inmates. It seems that the overseer is restricted by dictates, whereas wicked prisoners deserve more compassion.

What one hates most is that whenever the county magistrate or the trial officer is replaced, the overseer has to accept whoever is recommended by the new county magistrate or trial officer to be jail guards, whether there are openings or not. If the overseer resists, the delivery of inmate ration funds is delayed or fault is found with him on various pretexts. Since the higher authorities do not try to get the truth, the overseer is dismissed at best or criminally prosecuted at worst. As for the persons recommended by the county magistrate or the trial officer, if they were competent, that would be more acceptable; but under close inspection, those people are either the county magistrate's relatives or former underlings, and mostly illiterate. They not only do not fulfill their duties but also commit irregularities and make trouble. If the overseer strictly prohibits their wrongdoing, they rely on their patron to resist, speaking ill of the overseer to the county government on the one hand and conspiring with inmates to make false accusations against the overseer [on the other]. Whenever the higher authorities order the county government to investigate, if the overseer is able to play along with the county government office, he may keep his position, even though he has made mistakes. Otherwise, the county government office takes the opportunity to make trouble and the overseer has his rice bowl broken instantly [i.e., loses his job] and even receives criminal punishment. It is most disheartening to ponder why he deserves such treatment and who makes him suffer.

There are highly talented men working as jail overseers in all provinces and counties. They only lower themselves to serve as jail overseers because of circumstances and lack of support. Powerful people know the overseer's weakness and use it as a way to push him around. Given his low salary, the overseer lacks a long-term commitment to his job. Furthermore, the guards who are recommended by the county government and the trial officer are irresponsible and unmindful of what is right. As a result, inmates break out of jail and disrupt societal peace, and the overseer has no merits in managing the jail to speak of.

The overseer handles inmates' ration. Inmates know the grain price perfectly well, but they just want to eat as much as possible, and the higher authorities only want to save money. The overseer, when facing the shortage of funds, is forced to use the inmate ration fund to cover other expenses. Without knowing the overseer's difficulties, inmates are often quick to accuse the overseer of embezzlement, and when everyone says so, gold turns into nothing. No matter how transparently and publicly the inmate ration is accounted for, the overseer can never escape giving offense. Oh, the responsibility of the jail overseer! Oh, the circumstances of the jail overseer! Oh, the life of the jail overseer![75]

The writing speaks for itself, and one cannot but conclude that this was a reasonable analysis of the jail overseer's situation. The evidence presented in this book corroborates most of what these jail overseers had to say.

County penal institutions—jails and detention houses—were part of the county judiciary, and the examination of those institutions and the way they operated in the Republican era adds to a more complete understanding of what the judicial reform was able to achieve and failed to achieve at the county level and why. Obviously, where the prison reform fell short of the goals, it was because (1) the formalization agenda pushed by the central government was not accompanied by the financial resources needed to carry it out in counties, and (2) there was a wide gap between the institutions and procedures that the reform was to establish and the socioeconomic and sociocultural context of the local society in which the CGO had to operate. The two problems aggravated each other. This chapter suggests that a lack of control by the central government was not the main reason for the problems that existed in county penal institutions, at least in Jiangsu. As a matter of fact, a largely unbroken line of communication and a chain of command within the judicial system and in matters of prison management ran from the national capital down to the county level. The periodic inspections and reports, the investigations into county jails in response to complaints from various parties, and the disciplinary actions taken against county magistrates and jail overseers for prison escapes or misconduct all indicate quite effective institutional mechanisms of communications and control. Unlike the process of trials and appeals and enforcement of civil decisions, which were far more difficult to execute under established norms and far easier to subvert, the management of penal institutions was relatively straightforward and material resource–based, and the mechanisms of communications and control therefore worked better in comparison. It should also be noted that the GMD experiment of establishing committees for improving county jails represented a successful attempt, albeit with limited results, at reaching and working with local elites at the county level for the good of both the state and local society. What the state was unable to control and change without sufficient resources was the local sociopolitical environment and the power structure embedded in it. That was where the prison reform encountered the greatest obstacles and where it was undermined.

PART IV

Between Formalization and Informal Practices

CHAPTER 9

"Quick Justice": Punishing Robbers and Bandits

> It will be remembered that at the end of 1927 the Nanking Government, recognizing the gravity of the situation in their territory due to the increase in crime and especially crimes of violence, enacted a "Law for the Suppression of Robbery and Brigandage." . . . It is no exaggeration to say that the interpretations attached to the new law by the judicial authorities [the Supreme Court] at Nanking have altogether emasculated the law and constitute a direct encouragement to those gentry [*sic*] who live by robbery, murder and kidnapping.[1] We sympathize with the law-abiding citizens whose property and security is thus jeopardized. Imprisonment has absolutely no terrors for robbers, murderers and kidnappers, whose activities, momentarily damped, perhaps, by the Bandit Law, may be expected to revive again with full force.
>
> —*North China Herald* (Shanghai), February 18, 1928[2]

While the judicial reform was unfolding as an effort at formalizing institutions and practices, paradoxically, certain informal practices were consistently maintained and regularized from the New Policy decade through the Nanjing decade. Part IV deals with two such practices that temporally continued throughout the period under study, involving policies, actions, and interactions all the way from the central government through the provincial authorities to the county magistrate and local people. This chapter focuses on the harsh manner by which offenders of violent crimes such as robbers and bandits were punished without due process. The practice was "informal" in the sense that, enabled by a special law, it allowed trial and execution of robbers and bandits outside the formal court system and without the normal appeal process and death penalty review provided for by the criminal code and criminal procedural law.

To a large degree, the way robbers and bandits were harshly punished outside the formal judicial system and criminal proceedings reflected a constant tension between officials in the judicial field and those in the administrative field. Since such a tension can also be seen in historical contexts other than early-twentieth-century China, some underlying reasons for the tension specific to China at that time should be made explicit here. In the larger historical perspective, three factors combined to account for the said tension and the evolution of the criminal category "robbers/bandits" and the punishment of the offenders. First and foremost, widespread robbery and banditry was a fact of life in late imperial and Republican China, primarily but not exclusively because of pervasive rural poverty. Faced with that reality, administrative officials and military commanders at the provincial and county levels demanded that summary execution of "robbers/bandits" be an option. In contrast to legally minded judicial officials who were not responsible for maintaining local public security, provincial governors, county magistrates, and local military commanders had to combat violent crimes and maintain law and order in their jurisdictions. Those officials saw quick justice and harsh punishment as the most immediately effective tools.

Second, the newly enacted criminal code and procedural law and the newly established judicial system had paradoxical consequences. Judicial officials, especially at the national and provincial levels, tended to insist on the formal judicial procedures, but where those procedures were followed, they tended to make the judiciary seem ineffective and inefficient. Administrative officials and military commanders were thus more inclined to resort to quick justice.

Third, because the judicial reform did not reach the goal of establishing formal courts in all of China's counties, county magistrates were in charge of trying criminal and civil cases in most places. This situation made it conceptually more acceptable for administrative officials in the central government to grant county magistrates (and local military commanders) the power to execute violent offenders outside the formal judicial system and criminal proceedings; and it also made it institutionally easier for local officials to carry out summary executions as they saw fit, despite the efforts by judicial officials to limit the practice. In short, to understand the practice this chapter addresses, it must be kept in mind that nationwide establishment of a formal court system was still only half complete.

The Genesis of the Bandit Law

Dealing with Bandits in the Late Qing Era

Under Qing law, capital cases went through an elaborate review process at the levels of the prefecture, province, and central government. Death sentences had to be approved by the Board of Punishment (BP), the Court of Judicial Review (Dalisi), and the Censorate (Ducha yuan), before being finally confirmed by the emperor. Defendants condemned to death at the end of the procedures were classified into one of two categories—either they were executed immediately (*lijue*), usually done with those who had committed treason or some other unpardonable crime, or they were held in jail for their cases to be reviewed (*jianhou*) at the Autumn Assizes (Qiushen), as usually occurred with other kinds of crimes. In the latter category, about 10 percent would be judged to deserve execution; the rest would receive lesser punishments or be left for the following year's assizes. Even those assigned to immediate execution were actually held for three days before the sentence could be carried out.[3]

At the same time, however, Qing law granted military commanders the power to carry out summary execution, or execution on the spot (*jiudi zhengfa*), of any rebels or robbers who took up arms fighting government forces or resisting arrest. "Execution on the spot" actually meant an execution carried out after the death sentence was approved by provincial authorities, but without a normal trial and review of the death sentence. In Qing law the term "rebels" (*panfan*) referred to those who attempted to overthrow the state (*moufan*) or harm the imperial family (*dani*), while a "thief" (*qiedao, qiezei*) or "robber" (*qiangdao, dao*) was someone who would steal or plunder. These all fell into the legal category of "rebel/robber/thief" (*daozei*).[4]

A new development in the mid nineteenth century had lasting effects. In 1853, during the Taiping Rebellion (1851–1864), the Qing imperial court officially authorized provinces to carry out summary execution of "local bandits" (*tufei*) who were taking advantage of the authorities' preoccupation with "rebels" (*nifei*). Not only was summary execution widely practiced, but it continued long after the rebellion was over. Provincial and local officials would often bend the rule and summarily execute types of offenders other than rebels and bandits. In 1908, Lin Shaonian, the governor of Henan, even asked the imperial court to permit the immediate execution of rebels associated with religious sects (*huifei*), members of secret societies, and robbers without the advance approval of provincial authorities.[5] Although the request was rejected, it may be safely assumed that such summary sentences had been carried out in the country without imperial approval. Governor Lin was simply trying to get the practice officially approved.

Some high officials questioned the practice of summary execution being routinely applied, not only to rebels, but also to other offenders, conveniently labeled "bandits" or "robbers." In 1881, the Imperial Censors Hu Longxun and Chen Qitai were among the critics, and the BP ordered provinces to return to the death penalty review process—but to no avail, because provincial governors and governors-general argued that such executions were necessary to ensure public security.[6] In 1898, Imperial Censor Wu Weibin proposed to the throne that except in the eastern provinces and when bandits resisted government forces as rebels (*panni*), a situation in which summary execution could be justified, normal robbery cases should be sent to superior authorities for review, as the statute stipulated. But this memorial was buried for over ten years. Not until February 1909, when the judicial reform was under way, did the imperial court refer the memorial to the ML for an opinion. The ministry fully supported Wu's proposal in a written opinion. With imperial approval, the opinion was then issued as a directive to the provinces.[7]

The new policy did not go unchallenged. Citing rampant banditry in their provinces, Shen Bingkun, governor-general of Yunnan and Guizhou, and Yuan Shuxun, governor-general of Guangdong and Guangxi, requested imperial permission to continue summary executions. Told by the throne to respond to the two memorials, the ML refuted Shen's and Yuan's arguments and rejected their requests on two main grounds. First, judicial process had to be uniform in the country, or the future of constitutional government would be endangered. Second, moral cultivation and economic nourishment (*jiaoyang*) rather than harsh punishment (*xingwei*) was the right way to deal with banditry. "If robbers were everywhere, as Shen Bingkun claimed, was it not in spite of summary execution practice heretofore?" asked the ML rhetorically.[8]

The Commission for Studying Constitutional Government (CSCG) under Prince Yi-kuang fully supported the position of the ML on this issue. In a separate response to a memorial from Xi-liang, governor-general of the eastern provinces, in April 1911, the CSCG insisted on the ML order that summary execution should be applied *only* to bandits acting like rebels. The commission pointedly noted that even a criminal (*zuiren*) who resisted arrest was different from someone openly resisting government forces (an act that would constitute rebellion) and should be dealt with according to normal trial procedures.[9] The progressive position taken by the CSCG exemplifies the reform efforts spearheaded by reform-minded officials at the time. But the debate on this particular issue in the New Policy decade led to no resolution before the Qing regime was replaced by the Republic in January 1912.

Defining Bandits in the Early Republic

The Provisional New Criminal Code (PNCC) enacted in March 1912 introduced a new legal approach to capital crimes and the death penalty review process: capital punishment was to be reviewed by the MJ; execution was to be carried out by hanging, within prisons instead of in public places; and insane people and pregnant women were not to be executed (an exemption that had also existed under Qing law). But it was not immediately clear whether summary execution of rebels, bandits, and robbers was prohibited by the PNCC: that is, whether those offenders should be executed on the spot without trial by the regular court and without the review provided by the law. The uncertainty was due partly to the precedent of summary execution of such offenders and partly to the absence of a criminal category of "bandits" in the PNCC. The key question was what constituted acts of banditry and robbery that deserved punishment as severe as acts of rebellion.

The issue came to the fore in April 1912, when the Heilongjiang Department of Justice (HDJ) (Tifa si) made an inquiry to Governor Song Xiaolian on how to apply the PNCC to robbery cases (*dao'an*). Song in turn asked President Yuan Shikai for instructions. On May 2, Yuan replied that if the guilt of captured bandits (*fei*) was proven by solid evidence as well as confessions, they should be punished with military procedures (*junfa congshi*) so as to deter hardened criminals—here "military procedures" was a euphemism for execution on the spot. Notably, Yuan Shikai turned out to be the person who first tried to nail down the meaning of *fei* as a legal category of criminals, since the word did not exist in Qing law or in the PNCC.

In a telegram to the MJ, the HDJ called Yuan's order into question, pointing out that the PNCC contained the word *dao* (robber) but not *fei*, and that Yuan's instructions on the special procedure to punish bandits, outside the PNCC's articles on robbers, avoided appearing to change the law by administrative order and showed the president's great concern for security and his skill in balancing the law and practical needs. It is anyone's guess whether the last observation expressed satire or admiration. The telegram did reason, however, that in dealing with robbery cases in the province, offenders had interchangeably been called *mazei* (mounted thieves), *hufei* (bearded bandits), or *qiangdao* (robbers). Now that only bandits were dealt with through military procedures, leaving the prosecution of robbers to be handled under the PNCC, to avoid friction between the military and the administrative (and judicial) organs that would otherwise arise, there was a need for clear definitions of what constituted bandits and robbers.[10]

On June 17, 1912, Minister of Justice Wang Chonghui replied to the HDJ with a ministerial directive sent to all provinces. Article 36 of the Provisional Constitution gave the president the power to declare martial law, Wang said, and therefore, under the constitution, the only way for the president to punish special crimes outside the ordinary law was to apply military procedures in a declared martial law area. Obviously, Wang was trying to limit the applicability of summary execution. Furthermore, Wang defined "bandits" to interpret Yuan's May 2 order as follows: those who committed serious crimes that harmed public security, whether directly or indirectly, when and where martial law was in force, were called bandits and were to be punished through military procedures, whereas ordinary robbers should be prosecuted and tried by judicial organs according to the PNCC. The two situations should never be confused. Wang noted emphatically: "In the former Qing era, there was such a practice as 'execution on the spot' whereby people were killed at will, without trial, without restriction, and without record. Nothing damaged the law and ravaged the people more than that. No actions to restore the old practice in the name of military procedures should be tolerated in the Republican era."[11]

Here Wang tried his best to narrow the definition of *fei*, making it a temporary category applicable only at the times and places where martial law was in force, so that regular judicial institutions could prosecute and try cases of robbery according to the PNCC everywhere else.

Just as also happened in the New Policy decade, the MJ directive met with resistance from provincial administrative officials. In Fengtian province, under Governor Zhao Erxun, robbery cases had been handled by the administrative officials under military procedures since the 1911 Revolution. When Wang Chonghui's June 17 directive arrived, the Fengtian HC and HP pointed out the contradiction between the directive and his province's practice to Zhao, who responded that punishment of bandits needed to be severe, because the province was infested with "bearded bandits" (*hufei*), and the newly enacted PNCC did not deter such lawless elements, because it was more lenient than the old Qing law. Zhao said that his earlier instructions—to follow military procedures and punish on the spot those who committed capital crimes under the PNCC—were both compatible with the PNCC and locally appropriate. He further argued that even such executions were undertaken only when evidence of the bandits' guilt was absolutely solid and after their cases had been reviewed by superior officials, a practice far from what the minister of justice decried as killing people at will and without restriction. Apparently unwilling to accept the governor's response, however, the HC and HP turned to the MJ for instructions.[12]

The ministry, now under Xu Shiying, defended its position. Xu argued that Chapter 32 of the PNCC addressed the crime of robbery, which was a purely criminal and not a military matter. The punishment of robbers should be determined by trial, and only the trial officer had the power to impose the death penalty, following proper procedures for carrying out an execution. The fact that the public security situation was worse in Fengtian than in other provinces had no relevance to the law. The essence of any legislation lay in its permanence and uniform effectiveness throughout the country; a law should not be changed by an administrative order and allowed to vary to suit the needs of one time and one place.[13]

The 1914 Law on Punishing Robbers and Bandits

Although the MJ's legal position was logically unassailable, its reasoning failed to prevent summary executions of "robbers" and "bandits" by administrative officials and military commanders in many provinces. The situation led to one of the proposals that Minister of Justice Liang Qichao put forward in February 1914. In view of the proliferation of banditry, which the court system had not helped stop, Liang said, some criminals should be dealt with outside it, but other forms of interference in judicial proceedings should be strictly prohibited so that administrative officials and the people would be happy and the court system would be left alone.[14] Liang thus took a step back from the ministry's earlier position on the issue, because he saw the inevitability of administrative and military officials executing robbers and bandits and hoped to separate robbery/banditry cases from other criminal cases, which might be protected from the interference of nonjudicial officials.

Whatever Liang's motives, the Political Council appointed by Yuan Shikai to review policies agreed with his proposal. The council suggested that in provinces where banditry was rampant and where martial law was in force, extraordinary temporary methods should be taken to deal with bandits who used firearms and committed capital crimes. Doubtful cases could be referred to the provincial high court, and annual reports on banditry cases should be submitted to the MJ. No other interference by administrative officials in judicial process should be tolerated, thereby ensuring the law's credibility and authority.[15] Note that the council's position was actually similar to Wang Chonghui's in June 1912—"temporary methods" might be put in effect for a specific place and time period (that is, where martial law was declared), which differed from Liang's complete retreat on the issue. But that fine point was ignored. In July 1914, the State Council issued its Regulations on Punishing Robbers and Bandits (Chengzhi daofei tiaoli), and five months later, these were codified as the Law on Punishing Robbers and Bandits (LPRB) (Chengzhi daofei fa), which was to be permanently applicable throughout the country, not just in certain areas and time periods where martial law was in force.

The LPRB, for the first time in Chinese legal history, combined the words *dao* and *fei* to create a new and special category of crimes that were to be punished with draconian harshness. It mandated the death penalty for the following offenses: armed robbery in the home or on the road by a group of three or more; piracy at sea; rape during a robbery; homicide or injury to at least two victims during a robbery; arson; storming a prison or other public facility with a group of one hundred or more; carrying explosives; and being sect members (*huifei*), military deserters (*taobing*), bandits (*hufei*), or mounted thieves (*mazei*). The law allowed county magistrates or military commanders to execute such robbers and bandits as defined by the law after reporting the cases to and getting permission for the execution from a provincial governor or superior military officer. Legal counsel and defense was excluded, since lawyers could only appear at formal courts, not at trials conducted by country magistrates or by military officers. High courts would receive annual reports of how many people were executed in such cases in their provinces and forward the information to the MJ.[16] In short, judicial institutions had no control over such cases at all, and their only role was to collect statistics of the executions.

When the initial version of the LPRB as "regulations" was issued in July 1914, the MJ clarified that where district courts existed, the law was to be applied by the courts, not by county magistrates.[17] Given that most of China's more than 1,700 counties had no courts, the stipulation could have little effect in limiting the possible excesses resulting from the law. Moreover, the Implementing Rules of the Law on Punishing Robbers and Bandits issued in December 1914 further weakened the supervisory role of provincial authorities in cases processed under the LPRB. The rules allowed a county magistrate who believed that a swift execution was imperative for local security to execute an offender charged under the law after requesting permission from the provincial governor by sending a telegram summarizing the case, rather than the entire case file.[18]

The MJ soon discovered problems in the implementation of the LPRB. Many county magistrates stretched the law and applied it to offenses that it did not cover; moreover, county magistrates often sent a brief telegram asking for permission to execute offenders charged under the law without providing sufficient information for the provincial governor to exercise oversight. The MJ obtained Yuan Shikai's endorsement for a ministerial directive demanding that all jurisdictions in the country correct those abuses.[19] Yet the ministry still found seven years later that county magistrates and military commanders frequently sent telegrams requesting permission under the LPRB to perform executions that were not always justified by local security situations.[20]

In short, the LPRB created a separate category of crimes outside the existing criminal code and allowed summary execution of the offenders outside the regular judicial institutions and procedures. The military had always had leeway to execute people as "rebels" and "bandits," but the LPRB of 1914 institutionalized the practice and threw the door wide open for county magistrates as well as military commanders to use and abuse this power. The high courts' after-the-fact annual reports on executions were not designed to limit the excesses of county magistrates and military commanders. The MJ knew there were abuses, but the law gave it little leverage to intervene.[21]

The 1927 Provisional Regulations on Punishing Robbers and Bandits

In August 1927, the newly established GMD government issued a directive to the effect that the substantive and procedural laws of the Beiyang government still temporarily applied. This immediately brought up the issue of whether the LPRB was applicable in criminal cases. In October 1927, Xu Mo, the county magistrate of Dantu, Jiangsu, wrote to the Jiangsu Provincial Justice Department (JPJD), asking whether the LPRB was still in force. At the same time, Duan Jie, the county magistrate of Lianshui, pleaded adamantly with the JPJD for the authority to execute bandits on the spot, as permitted by the LPRB. According to Duan, banditry prevented people from paying taxes and merchants from traveling; he described bandits as eluding government forces and destroying local peace and order. Moreover, those arrested were difficult to convict of capital crimes under the criminal code. As a result, the county jail was overcrowded, while banditry continued to plague the county. To deter it, Duan wanted the power to execute individuals positively identified as bandits by local security forces or other locals and to report such cases after execution. In other words, this Republican-era county magistrate wished for the same power sought by the Qing official Lin Shaonian in 1908. Chen Hexian, the former law professor who headed the JPJD, was unable to bring himself to ignore the criminal code and criminal procedural law, and he rejected both requests and warned all county magistrates in the province to adhere to the PNCC.[22]

As was seen in Chapter 3, in 1928, the GMD government unveiled and put into effect a complete formal criminal code that replaced the PNCC, along with a new version of the criminal procedural law. The 1928 criminal code was revised again in 1935. Though in both versions, the new criminal code was indeed progressive and more in tune with Western models, the code (and the criminal procedure law) would not suffice for the GMD party-state to deal with issues of law and order, contrary to what Chen Hexian thought. Besides instituting special laws and special courts designed to suppress political offenses, Nanjing resorted to harsh special laws to punish common criminals.

In November 1927, Nanjing issued the Provisional Regulations on Punishing Robbers and Bandits (PRPRB) (Chengzhi daofei zanxing tiaoli), or "Bandit Law," as foreigners called it, which revived the LPRB of 1914. The law made sixteen kinds of offenses capital crimes (up from nine under the LPRB), but the provincial HC was to refer such cases to the provincial government for review before the execution could be carried out. Under the regulations, the sentence could be imposed either by a court or by a county magistrate in charge of judicial affairs. If military personnel were the offenders, they would be tried and executed by their commanding officer after the sentence had been approved by the unit's highest-ranking commander.[23] Although the law was putatively set to expire after six months, it was in fact renewed every six months for the duration of the Nanjing decade.

The PRPRB deprived criminal defendants of the legal protection offered by the new criminal code and procedural law. Legal scholars at the time criticized the law for blatantly violating judicial independence and due process in three ways: (1) it gave county magistrates and military officers, who had no legal training, the power to impose the death penalty; (2) it allowed the provincial government to approve death sentences and to send officials to retry doubtful cases, thereby giving judicial powers to administrative officials; and (3) it denied those sentenced to death—the heaviest possible penalty, which was irreversible—the right to appeal that the criminal code guaranteed defendants sentenced to imprisonment or other lesser punishments, thus violating their human rights.[24]

Ironically, the *North China Herald*, a British newsweekly published in Shanghai, which often criticized the arbitrariness and cruelty of Chinese judicial practices when defending extraterritoriality, lamented that because it failed to impose the death penalty for *all* offenses under the Bandit Law, the law was not draconian enough to deter criminals who threatened the property and safety of "the middle and upper classes of the Chinese residents of the [International] Settlement [in Shanghai] and the surrounding districts." Under the PRPRB, "persons gathering together to commit armed robbery" would be sentenced to death. The Supreme Court interpreted "persons gathering together" (*juzhong*) as four or more people. Ruling in a robbery case per the interpretation, the Provisional Court in Shanghai's International Settlement did not impose the death penalty on three defendants convicted of eleven charges of violent crime, which caused the *Herald* to protest. Indeed, the SC's interpretation may be considered an effort to limit the applicability of the Bandit Law, consistent with the attitude of judicial officers in the Republican era. Judging that the SC had erred in the direction of being too lenient and thus "emasculated the law," the editor of the *Herald* argued that anything short of the death penalty would have no deterrent effect on violent criminals. "Imprisonment has absolutely no terrors for robbers, murderers and kidnappers, whose activities, momentarily damped, perhaps, by the Bandit Law, may be expected to revive again with full force."[25] Obviously, the *Herald*'s usual criticism of Chinese law and judicial practices, with its rhetoric about the rule of law, judicial independence, and due process, yielded here to practical concerns about the peace and security of the International Settlement. With encouragement such as this, the GMD government would not view the PRPRB as potentially impeding its efforts to abolish extraterritoriality.

The Evolution of a Criminal Category

Looking back at the origins and the development over time of the Bandit Law (both the 1914 and 1927 versions), we see the evolution of a legal category of crimes or criminals, that is, the category of "bandits" (*fei*). As noted above, in the late Qing era, the word *fei* initially referred to all lawless and marginal elements in society who might have committed violent acts, whether against civilians or officials, the poor or the rich. In Qing official communications, the word was often part of compound terms such as "local bandits" (*tufei*), "sect bandits" (*huifei*), "bearded bandits" (*hufei*), but it also encompassed other types such as "mounted thieves" and "roaming fighters" (*youyong*), meaning military deserters. Conceptually, such offenders might have come to include both "rebels" (*panni* or *nizei*) and "robbers and thieves" (*dao, zei*), covered by the category *daozei* in Qing law. However, the word *fei* and the types of offenders it referred to did not exist as a legal category of crimes or criminals in the Qing criminal code (the Law and Substatutes of the Great Qing and the draft criminal code of 1910). Nevertheless, local officials and military commanders viewed those offenders as dangerous and needing to be swiftly suppressed—hence the practice of summary execution and its approval by the Qing court.

After Yuan Shikai defined *fei* as a type of criminals punishable by summary execution, the LPRB of 1914 combined it with *dao* to form a new legal category of crimes and criminals, *daofei*, mandating the death penalty for such offenses. Within this novel but ill-defined category, "bandits," "robbers," and "rebels" were conflated, equated, and indistinguishable. Its very vagueness was useful to local administrative officials and military commanders—now any and all lawless activities that local officials regarded as a threat to the peace and order in their jurisdictions could be easily covered by the category, and any and all marginal social elements (robbers, bandits, rebels, members of religious sects and martial arts societies, "subversives" of any kind, and anyone who resisted arrest) could be called "bandits" and executed as such. Not insignificantly, the subsequent official communications about this category ensured that the word *fei* would enter legal parlance and political discourse in Republican China, where "collusion with bandits" (*tongfei*) was a frightening and indeed deadly accusation. Bandits came to be understood as gangs of marauding killers who were morally despicable and deserving of the death penalty—hence the references to "communist bandits" (*gongfei*) by the GMD and to "Chiang bandits" (*jiangfei*) by the CCP.

By the time that the GMD inherited or revived the LPRB in the form of the PRPRB in 1927, the legal category of "robbers and bandits" continued vaguely to cover rebels and subversives. Among the sixteen capital offenses under the law—described in traditional literary style rather than precise legal language—were "gathering in mountains and marshes to resist government forces" (*xiaoju shanze kangju guanbing*) and "instigating people to harm public security and launch an uprising" (*shanhuo renxin raohai gong'an erqi baodong*). But at the same time, in concept if not necessarily in practice, true rebels and subversives (that is, political opponents of the regime) were now classified as political criminals in separate categories under other special laws outside the criminal code (see also Chapter 3). In practice, however, political opponents or rebels could conveniently be called bandits and dealt with under the PRPRB, especially after "communist bandits" came into widespread use, and vice versa—common criminals or marginal social elements could summarily be executed as "communists."[26] Since both the category of robbers/bandits and that of political criminals were punished under special laws outside the regular judicial system and criminal proceedings, they became interchangeable.

Both the Beiyang government and the GMD government also enacted other special laws to address common crimes. In the Nanjing decade, for example, the Regulations on Punishing Kidnappers (Chengzhi bangfei tiaoli) were enacted in November 1928, even though the PRPRB already covered the offense of "kidnapping for ransom." Under the regulations, anyone guilty of abduction for ransom would be sentenced to death, as would anyone who assisted kidnappers in committing this crime. County magistrates and members of local police and security forces who failed to act against kidnappers would be charged as sheltering kidnappers, and those who failed to apprehend kidnappers within a month would be dismissed from their posts.[27] This law was abolished in May 1932, along with several other special laws.[28] But new special laws were enacted thereafter, including the 1935 Provisional Regulations on Punishing Crimes of Harming National Currency and the 1936 Provisional Regulations on Opium Prohibition and Punishment, Provisional Regulations on Narcotics Prohibition and Punishment, and Provisional Regulations on Punishing Custom Duties Evasion. Nevertheless, because of its vagueness and resulting loose application by local officials, the single legal instrument most damaging to the rule of law, judicial independence, and due process was the Bandit Law.

Punishing Robbers and Bandits in Jiangsu

County Magistrates and Punishment of Bandits

A county magistrate might well have conscientiously sought to perform his judicial functions with care and caution. But because of his institutional locus in the state system, he was more inclined than judges in a formal court to punish violent offenders with summary execution. Responsible for local peace and security, he would want to deter violent crimes in his jurisdiction; when such crimes did occur, he would want to dispose of the defendants quickly to clear his docket and make room in the county jail, as the Lianshui county magistrate, Duan Jie, explained to the JPJD in 1927. As the following cases show, county magistrates were motivated to execute alleged or convicted robbers even before the LPRB of 1914 was enacted.

In December 1911, the county magistrate of Chongming sent a report on a homicide case to Governor Cheng Dequan. A certain Dong Ruicu had tried to borrow money from the wife of the Yang family; when rebuffed, he had killed the woman in trying to take the money by force. A county trial convicted Dong of robbery and murder. The magistrate asked for permission to execute Dong in accordance with Qing law.

Cheng's veto was accompanied by a lengthy explanation. Since the Provincial Assembly had resolved to apply the draft new criminal code of 1910 in November 1911 (see Chapter 2), he noted, it was improper to apply the old Qing law.

Cheng made additional legal points. First, even under the Qing law, only armed robbers openly resisting government forces in the fashion of rebels would be executed on the spot. Dong was just a common criminal, and his case did not fall into that category. Second, according to the procedural law, conviction was final only after the period of appeal was over. Even under the Qing law, a sentence of execution on the spot had to be reported to the provincial authorities and the truthfulness of the charge reexamined by a provincial official before it could be carried out. Such executions "had never been as easy and callous" as the magistrate's request implied. Third, the conviction of Zhu Kaolang, a co-defendant in the case, was invalid. As the testimonies at the trial had shown, Zhu had done no more than talk with Dong about borrowing money; he had waited outside the house of the Yang family and knew nothing of Dong's actions inside. "Under the principle of criminal law, establishing the crime committed requires that three conditions be met: (1) intention; (2) action; and (3) consequence." Zhu's intention was to borrow money, which was legitimate, and he did not participate in the action of robbing and killing the woman. He was therefore not responsible for her death (the consequence). Cheng told the county magistrate to reexamine the case accordingly.[29]

Cheng went a step further. He issued a general directive on December 17, 1911, to the JHP, along with his comments on the Dong case: "[Conviction and sentence in] a criminal case must go through the period of appeal before being carried out. Litigation procedural laws containing such provisions are quite common in civilized countries. Although judicial organizations in our country are still in the budding stage, legal principles must be followed by all, to adhere to the procedures of multilevel trials and to respect human rights." He demanded that judicial officers fully understand his instructions on the Dong case and that all courts in the province report their cases to their superior institutions once a month.[30]

Yet not all county magistrates seemed to know or care about the changes in the death penalty review procedures contained in the draft criminal code of 1910 that had been in force in Jiangsu since November 1911. On January 4, 1912, two homes were robbed—one in Yuanming village and the other in Wang village, Kunshan county. Acting on gossip, on that same day, Magistrate Fang Huan led the merchant corps to apprehend three men involved in the Yuanming robbery. The following day, another five men were arrested for the other robbery. The victims identified the suspects and named other robbers still at large. On January 16, Fang Huan sent a telegram to the governor's office asking for permission to execute the first three men as bandit leaders.

As Cheng Dequan was away from the post of governor from January to April 1912, the request was received by the acting governor, Zhuang Yunkuan, who granted the permission by a telegram on January 17. The three men were executed the next day (within two weeks of the crime's commission). When Fang Huan informed Zhuang of the execution and his plan to imprison the other five men for ten years, Zhuang replied that as long as he did not violate judicial principles, the county magistrate might improvise ways to jail those men.[31] Here both the county magistrate and the acting governor ignored the Provincial Assembly's decision to apply the 1910 draft criminal code as well as Cheng Dequan's earlier directive. They simply followed the Qing practice of punishing robbers and rebels with summary execution.

By the time Cheng Dequan was formally appointed to the governorship in April 1912, the draft criminal code of 1910 had been enacted as the PNCC. On May 14, 1912, Cheng informed all county magistrates that whereas it had been expedient for provincial governments to approve death sentences before the central government was established, now that all the ministries were in place, Article 40 of the PNCC—providing that death sentences be approved by the MJ—ought to be followed, and files of all capital cases should be sent in duplicate to the JHP for forwarding to the MJ.[32]

In at least one case, the directive fell on deaf ears. On January 15, 1912, in Zhujiagou, Huaiyin, four men raided a Buddhist temple. One stayed outside as lookout while the other three scaled the wall and broke into the temple. Before getting away with some plunder, they tortured the magistrate monk and one of the temple helpers to find out where the valuables were. Informed of the crime the next day by the local headman and the chief monk, Magistrate Xu Zhonglin ordered the local garrison force to hunt down the robbers. Three were captured, but the ringleader remained at large. At a county trial, the three men admitted to their crime. Sun Rongxia and Xia Sanluzi had been inside the temple when the robbery took place, and Yao Dianyun had been outside. Applying the articles in the Qing law on robbery committed with a firearm and on ordinary robbery, respectively, Xu sentenced Sun and Xia to death, with the execution to occur immediately, and Yao to twelve years in prison. With the approval of a regional military commander (*jiangbei hujun shi*), Xu had Sun and Xia beheaded on August 11, 1912, even though the PNCC specified that execution should be by hanging. Only after the men were dead did Xu report the whole case to Cheng Dequan.

Cheng's response was to issue an order scolding Xu. He repeated that at a time of military conflict, before the north and the south were unified, death sentences carried out with the approval of a superior official had been expedient; but with a national government in place for several months, the country's judicial affairs should now be directed and supervised by the MJ. "It was extremely callous of the county magistrate to have never reported the case to the ministry." After President Yuan had issued the order to enact the PNCC, "it was extremely ludicrous that the county magistrate was still applying Qing law, which had been discarded." Cheng instructed Xu to follow Article 40 of the PNCC and to report capital cases to the MJ, warning him not to overstep his authority at will.[33] Xu Zhonglin and other county magistrates either did not know or deliberately did not follow the death penalty review procedures provided by the PNCC. In any case, it was in their institutional and personal interests to have common criminals—robbers—executed as "robbers/bandits."

The record of Cheng's legal thinking and actions is highlighted here to show that not all administrative officials were inclined to resort to the summary execution of violent criminals, and that Cheng did support the rule of law, judicial independence, and due process. His deference to the authority of the MJ in following the death penalty review procedures once again serves to balance the prevailing impression in the scholarship on Republican China that provincial-level officials were always at odds with the central government, and that centralized state authority did not make itself felt at the provincial level. But an official like Cheng Dequan who did not favor "quick justice" may have been rare, and even Cheng's authority and order failed to deter county magistrates. Ironically, Cheng's deference to the MJ in reviewing capital cases was undercut by the ministry's retreat on the issue. After the LPRB was enacted in 1914, summary executions would only become more widespread and more frequent.

The Law on Punishing Robbers and Bandits and Miscarriage of Justice

Aside from personal motivations, after 1914, every county magistrate functioned within a legal and institutional framework—the absence of a formal court in most counties and the existence of the Bandit Law—that enabled him to apply the Bandit Law more frequently than was warranted. No statistical evidence is easily available to help us to determine what percentage of all county magistrates in Jiangsu or in the country acted excessively or improperly in summary execution of robber/bandits.[34] But the frequent official communications on the issue from the Ministry of Justice (which certainly had relevant statistics, since it received reports on such cases) suggest, and the case files available to this study seem to corroborate, that county magistrates could, and many did, easily circumvent due process by resorting to the rather sweeping and permissive Bandit Law in dealing with common robberies.

Thus, in practice, the legal and social consequences of the Bandit Law were not only unduly harsh punishment for certain common crimes but also rough handling of robbery cases by county magistrates and local military commanders, even when the guilt of the accused was still in question. That the law denied offenders the right to appeal and sidestepped the death penalty review procedures made wrongful prosecution and execution more likely. As the historian Phil Billingsley has shown, banditry was a real social pathology in Republican China; but the county magistrate, the military, and the local gentry were not always motivated, in their calculation of self-interest, to suppress real bandits, especially those who were relatively strong.[35] The men, and sometimes women, arrested and executed under the Bandit Law were often either destitute rural people who carried out robberies, kidnappings, and other crimes, or just innocent peasants who had been wrongfully accused. The following two cases illustrate how, under the Bandit Law, abuses and miscarriage of justice could happen in the hands of a county magistrate (or a local military commander).

Case one: On April 18, 1924, a telegram arrived at the JHC from Chen Zhixian, a peasant in Pi county, saying that he was wrongfully accused of being a bandit and had been tortured into confessing. Chen asked the court to intervene. The court ordered the Pi county magistrate, Xu Shaoxiu, to handle the case according to the law and report on it as soon as possible, but Xu did not respond. On May 8, Chen sent a second telegram, desperately pleading with the JHC to have his case moved to another jurisdiction to save him from being victimized by a conspiracy. The court issued another order to Magistrate Xu, asking for a copy of the entire case file. Xu kept silent until June 18. Without sending the case file, Xu simply notified the JHC that Chen's case had been tried under Article 1 of the LPRB and been reported to the provincial military and civil governors; the provincial government had sent an official to participate in the trial, and the case was now closed.[36] In other words, Chen had been executed. While we may never know the truth about Chen's guilt or innocence, the county magistrate's behavior is suspicious, since he obviously prevented the JHC from looking into the case. The LPRB authorized his actions, as long as he reported the case to the provincial governors, and under the law the high court was powerless to intervene in such cases to save lives.

Case two: In January 1924, the JHP received a petition written in the name of all the inmates at the Guanyun County Jail stating that a local garrison commander, Yu Zhenzhong, had forced confessions out of four inmates by having them tortured. One of the four was Cao Qingsheng. Zhou Yike, the JHP chief, asked Magistrate Peng Shiqi for a report, but did not get a response. On February 21, 1924, Cao Qingsheng's uncle Cao Tinghua sent a telegram to the JHP claiming that his nephew had been tortured to death by Yu Zhenzhong, who was now trying to cover up the truth. Prompted by Cao Tinghua's telegram, Zhou took three actions. (1) He issued another order to Peng, asking for a truthful report and criticizing him for allowing Yu to take inmates from the county jail rather than handling the case himself. (2) He ordered the Donghai county magistrate, Wang Jue, to go to Guanyun and investigate the case. And (3) he sent a memo to the provincial governor informing him of these events.

On February 28, Wang Jue sent back a report. Cao Qingsheng had been arrested after a suspect in a case of robbery and arson, in which six lives had been lost, had fingered him. When delivering Cao to the county jail, Yu claimed that Cao was injured because he had resisted arrest and physically struggled. An autopsy showed that Cao had sustained injuries to his lower back, legs, and ankles.[37] Yu's story contradicted what Cao's loved ones claimed, but Wang was unable to determine whether Cao had been injured during the arrest or was tortured after it, because Magistrate Peng had failed to make note of any injuries when

Cao was brought to the county jail.[38] Wang's report seemed to say that Yu had not taken Cao from the county jail; it was Yu who had arrested Cao (and then tortured him) before handing him over to the county jail.

For reasons unknown, Wang did not seem to do his job thoroughly. He made no effort to interview the soldiers who arrested Cao to find out whether Cao had resisted arrest and, if he had, what kind of injuries he had sustained, and whether they matched the autopsy record. As for Peng, he never sent a report to Zhou Yike about the case, despite receiving no fewer than five orders from Zhou and additional inquiries from the provincial government, the MJ, and the GP in Beijing, all in response to Cao Tinghua's multiple petitions to them.[39] Apparently, no disciplinary action was taken against the garrison commander, who had allegedly caused Cao Qingsheng's wrongful death, or against the county magistrate, who had defied the orders of Zhou and other higher authorities.

One may conclude that the LPRB provided county magistrates and local military commanders with sufficient protection to defy the orders and deflect pressures from the higher authorities, especially judicial officials. The inquiries from the provincial government were part of the routine responses to petitions and did not necessarily reflect the concern of the provincial governor over the fate of accused robbers/bandits in particular cases. The inquiries from the GP, the MJ, and the JHP reflected concerns over judicial procedures or the legality of a county magistrate's actions, but their intervention was ultimately ineffectual, given the legal and institutional framework in which county magistrates (and local military commanders) functioned—these officials could claim that executing "robbers and bandits" under the LPRB was part of their administrative rather than judicial functions and that they were therefore not accountable to the judicial authorities.

The Untimely Deaths of Convicted Robber/Bandits

The same institutional logic can be seen in another scenario of the miscarriage of justice in robbery/banditry cases, that is, when men convicted under the LPRB died under suspicious circumstances before their death sentences were approved by the provincial authorities. As noted in Chapter 8, in 1915, the MJ had mandated verifying the deaths of inmates in custody, but county magistrates did not always follow the rule, especially in cases of those convicted under the LPRB. In November 1921, in Pi county, a robber named Ji Yixin was wounded while resisting arrest. At his trial, he admitted to robbing and injuring a victim and was thus sentenced to death under the LPRB. Ji reportedly died of his wounds while awaiting confirmation of his sentence by the provincial and military governors. Magistrate Li Shiliang stated in his report to the JHC that he had verified the death and questioned the physician, the guards, and other inmates in the jail to make sure there had been no foul play. He had then had the body buried. Li had neither asked for verification of Ji's death by an official from another jurisdiction nor filled out a death certificate, and the JHC brought these facts to the attention of the provincial governor. The governor held that Magistrate Li was negligent and had the case reported to the JHP. Chief Procurator Xu Shouheng opined that since Li had verified that no foul play was involved, there was no need to have another official open the coffin to examine the dead body; but Li was given a warning for negligence—failing to follow the rule laid down in the MJ directive of 1915.[40]

Although it was not the first or only case, Magistrate Li's behavior prompted the JHP to issue a directive to all county magistrates in the province, reiterating the rule about verifying deaths in county jails. The directive noted that convicts sentenced to death frequently died in jail before the approval of their sentences, and that while most county magistrates followed the rule in asking for additional verification of those deaths by an official from another jurisdiction, some county magistrates did not. It emphasized that magistrates in counties far from the provincial capital could ask the magistrate of a neighboring county to verify the untimely deaths of convicts who had been sentenced to death.[41] Because of lax enforcement, some county magistrates did not take the said rule seriously. In November 1922, the Rugao county magistrate reported that two robbers sentenced to death and awaiting execution had died in the county jail within a span of three days. He claimed to have ascertained that there had been no foul play, after which he had had the two bodies buried. The JHP repeated its earlier response—the county magistrate was told to follow the rule in the future, but no investigation was ordered.[42] In January 1923, a similar case was reported from Shuyang, where a robber sentenced to death under the LPRB died in custody.[43] The JHP does not seem to have actively investigated the untimely deaths of offenders convicted under the LPRB, because the law did not allow the provincial judicial institutions to intervene in such cases to begin with.

The GMD Provincial Government and the Provisional Regulations on Punishing Robbers and Bandits

As we have seen, in the Beiyang era, provincial judicial institutions had little power to intervene in cases processed under the LPRB, since the law permitted the county magistrate to bypass the HC and HP completely and communicate directly with the provincial governor. Under the 1927 PRPRB, the HC reviewed death sentences in cases prosecuted under the law (after the HP was abolished in 1928) and the provincial government approved or disapproved such sentences. That the provincial government as an administrative body had the final say in capital cases was again at odds with the principle of judicial independence. Moreover, HC opinions in reviewing capital cases prosecuted under the PRPRB were not always respected by the provincial government; and the procedure was no guarantee against arbitrary execution made possible by the law.

In August 1928, the Pi county magistrate, Lu Xianglin, sent a report on a robbery case to the provincial government, without a formal document attesting conviction and sentence as required by the PRPRB, and asked for permission to execute the offender. According to Lu, over the years, a certain Liu Xue'an had participated in several robberies and kidnappings. In December 1922, Liu was among more than 100 men who had kidnapped a family for a ransom of ¥12,500, killing two people in the process. In July 1927, Liu was among nine people who had robbed a family and kidnapped the man's wife and two sons for a ransom of ¥1,500. Saying that he was afraid of detaining Liu for too long (because the prisoner might escape), Lu requested permission to execute Liu in accordance with the PRPRB. In an official written opinion, the JHC president, Zhang Jundu, found that several facts were not clarified in the case and that the county magistrate had violated the rule by not preparing a conviction and sentence document as prescribed by the law. Reviewing the case and Zhang's opinion, the Provincial Government Commission (PGC) decided that the case should be retried and that the magistrate should be reprimanded for his failure to supply documentation despite the provincial government's express instructions.[44] JHC oversight was thus able to prevent an arbitrary execution, though the defendant might still receive a death sentence at his retrial.

In October 1928, the Dangshan county magistrate, Pan Qi, sent the JHC a capital case that had earlier been sent back for retrial. Two defendants, Liu Po and Zhang Qingyun, had been sentenced to death for robbery and kidnapping for ransom. The JHC once again expressed disagreement with case's outcome. Liu Po was among more than ten people who had robbed a family and kidnapped a nineteen-year-old woman for a ransom of ¥70, which was paid by the family. Although Liu admitted that he had been at the scene, the retrial did not establish what he had gained from the robbery and precisely how he was involved. Sentencing him to death was therefore arbitrary. Liu also confessed that in 1924, he had followed a bandit for three or four months and participated in looting three villages, but the CGO did not investigate what had taken place on those occasions. The second defendant, Zhang Qingyun, confessed to guiding others to rob several places, but the retrial did not establish who had been robbed and whether extortion or kidnapping had been involved. Nevertheless, the county magistrate convicted Zhang of committing robbery with firearms and kidnapping for ransom and imposed two death sentences on him. That result was improper, the opinion concluded, and the case should be sent back for another retrial. When the case reached the PGC, however, Liu Po's death sentence was approved; only Zhang Qingyun was to be retried.[45]

In June 1929, the Provincial Water Public Security Force arrested He Shuqing, a young man of twenty-one from Jining, Shandong province, inside a temple at Liu'an, Gaoyou county, and rescued a kidnapped nine-year-old boy who was being held there. At a county trial, He confessed that he had been invited to help three other men kidnap the boy; he also admitted to having participated in an earlier kidnapping of a six-year-old boy and to having received ¥12 from the ransom. The victim of the recent kidnapping—the nine-year-old boy—and his father positively identified He at the trial, but none of those affected by the first kidnapping were present. He Shuqing was sentenced to death for two counts of kidnapping for ransom under Article 2 of the PRPRB and Articles 9 and 42 of the criminal code. In an opinion signed by President Lin Biao, the JHC found discrepancies between the victim's testimonies and He's confession about the date of the recent kidnapping, and noted that the identity of the earlier victims was uncertain. The court recommended a retrial to get all the facts. But the PGC resolved to approve the death sentence.[46]

The examples cited above show that under the 1927 PRPRB, the sole judicial institution that had a role to play in punishing robbers and bandits was a provincial high court, but its role was not sufficient to prevent excesses in legally sanctioned summary executions. The records of the Jiangsu PGC meetings show that in the 1930s, death sentences imposed under the PRPRB that were reviewed by the PGC were routinely authorized without much discussion. Only two of the death penalties in robbery/banditry cases considered at twenty-eight Jiangsu PGC meetings between October 24, 1933, and February 13, 1934, were set aside for further investigation; all the others were approved.[47] Once a county magistrate had applied the PRPRB and imposed a death sentence, the PGC tended not to reverse it, even if the opinion of the HC differed. The PGC seems to have used a much lower legal standard than the JHC in considering the appropriateness of a death sentence in robbery/banditry cases. In the Dangshan case described above, for instance, the PGC was apparently satisfied that Liu Po's participation in one kidnapping warranted his death sentence; it regarded reviewing his role in the crime and his actions pertaining to earlier crimes as irrelevant. Had those cases been tried in formal courts, there conceivably would have been fewer convictions and death sentences, and perhaps more lives would have been spared. Of course, the intent of the PRPRB was exactly to circumvent the court system and allow the county magistrate a freer hand in dealing with violent crimes committed by robbers and bandits. Such freedom was possible precisely because about two-thirds to three-quarters of the counties in the province, and indeed the country, lacked formal courts. Thus the failure to establish formal courts in all counties made it both desirable (in county magistrates' eyes) and possible (within the existing institutional settings) to punish a special category of common criminals harshly, outside the criminal code and procedural law.

Although the Bandit Law (both the LPRB and the PRPRB) allowed county magistrates and local military commanders to carry out summary executions of robbers and bandits outside the regular judicial system and procedures, it did not follow that all robbery and banditry suspects were summarily executed—in fact, most common criminals were sent to jail. Because many offenders committed crimes other than those specified in the Bandit Law, the law could not be applied to them. And when the guilt of some of those accused of the offenses covered by the Bandit Law could not be established to the satisfaction of a county magistrate or a military commander, they remained under detention as suspects, contributing to the case backlogs in the CGO and to the overcrowding in county jails and detention houses. On the other hand, at least to a degree, the pressure to clear case backlogs and reduce the inmate population in county jails and detention houses might have persuaded some county magistrates to convict and execute robbery/banditry suspects on less than sufficient evidence.

This chapter has examined why and how a special category of crimes or criminals—bandits (and robbers)—was gradually conceptualized, legally defined, and harshly punished outside the formal judicial institutions and procedures from the late Qing era through the Nanjing decade. As we have seen, the Bandit Law was partly rooted in the Qing legal-judicial practice of executing bandits on the spot, which was revived by Yuan Shikai's definition of "bandits" as a criminal category, established by the 1914 LPRB, and finally taken over by the GMD government in the 1927 PRPRB. Under this law, certain common criminals were dealt with at the expense of due process, even though the judicial reform had enshrined the rule of law and judicial independence in the recently enacted criminal code and criminal procedural law.

That Nanjing chose to renew the PRPRB periodically as "provisional regulations," rather than making it a formal permanent law, suggests that GMD officials were aware that in circumventing due process, the law did not square with the principles of the rule of law and judicial independence that had guided the judicial reform since the New Policy decade, which the GMD professed to uphold. In other words, the informal way in which robbers/bandits were harshly and sometimes arbitrarily punished was considered a tolerable expediency that was imposed on the state by the circumstances, something to be abandoned at an opportune time. Of course, for the GMD government, the time never seemed opportune. Ironically, the elaborate rules produced by judicial reform made the local officials responsible for public security increasingly impatient, further inclining them to the ad hoc execution of violent offenders. They simply saw this as a more efficient and effective way of dealing with crime than the mandated formal procedures promulgated from above. And judicial officials who were mindful of rules and procedures seem to have resigned themselves to this reality.

CHAPTER 10

The Praxis of Petition and the Economy of False Accusation

> Most people involved in litigation are cunning. To vent their anger when they cannot win their lawsuits, they blame the officers who tried their cases. That is why there are often allegations against local officials. Irresponsible attacks [on officials] damage the creditability of public servants and hinder their performance of their official duties. This malicious practice should not be encouraged!
>
> —Wujiang County Magistrate Xu Youchuan to the High Court president, 1935[1]

Judicial reform institutionalized the appeal process for civil and criminal cases tried at all courts (and trial review for criminal cases tried at the CGO). Litigants did use formalized procedures to appeal to higher courts when they felt their cases had been unfairly judged or wrongfully prosecuted, and those juridical channels would reach the higher levels of the state system. At the same time, a critical institutional mechanism widely used by people dealing with, or working within, the judicial system was simply to write a petition, in the form of a letter (sometimes on an official complaint form) to higher authorities, both judicial and administrative. Although noted at different points in earlier chapters, this practice deserves consideration in a separate chapter in the context of a larger issue—how the practice reflected the successes and failures of the institutional and procedural formalization in the judicial system.

The practice of writing petitions on judicial matters was legally informal, in the sense that the successive Republican governments never enacted any laws or issued any regulations on petition-writing and on responding to petitions on judicial matters and individual lawsuits. Since petitions were submitted outside formal juridical channels, they were not part of judicial procedures; but they addressed judicial matters and individual cases that petitioners believed were not handled properly by the judicial system. Yet petitioning was always accepted as legitimate, and the way in which officials responded to petitions became regularized into routines or standard operating procedures that were followed consistently in the Republican era, indicating that neither ordinary people nor the state trusted the formal judicial institutions and procedures. In a sense, therefore, the degree to which petitioning was practiced by litigants and nonlitigants reflected the degree to which the formal judicial institutions and procedures failed to function to the satisfaction of litigants and even people who were not involved in lawsuits. But there was also something else to it. A closer look at petition-writing and official responses to petitions reveals, not only how the informal practice was utilized and regularized by the state as a governmental tool, but also, and no less significantly, how actors in local society used the state system and its bureaucratic logic for their own purposes and to their own advantage in lawsuits or in local power struggles. The combined effect of those efforts was simultaneously to supplement and complicate the judicial functions of the state. In presenting the various scenarios of the practice, this chapter sheds additional light on how and where the judicial system created by the reform did and did not work. A demonstration of the way in which petitions were handled by various state institutions also opens up another layer of the interwoven institutional relationships and complex interactions between the judicial and administrative fields and their respective and overlapping hierarchies within the state system.

Petition-Writing as Praxis

Neither the process of writing petitions about judicial matters nor that of responding to them was ever prescribed by law in the late Qing and Republican periods.[2] Yet petitioning by ordinary people was a time-honored praxis, dating back to the imperial era, when officials were openly encouraged to submit secret memorials and filing a lawsuit was essentially a matter of a plaintiff writing an accusing letter on an official form (or a scribe doing so on his or her behalf). In the Republican era, formal procedures for filing lawsuits on official complaint forms for a fee were established, but the practice of writing petitions outside these formal judicial procedures continued and proliferated. Besides riding on a time-honored tradition, the practice was further legitimized and justified by the public and official discourses about the Republican state system, which was supposed to be responsive to "the people's opinions" (*minyi*) and protective of "the people's rights" (*renmin quanli*).

In addition to the ideological rationale, the central and provincial government authorities felt compelled to respond to petitioners for important practical reasons. First, with the agenda of modern state building, and for the sake of the effectiveness and legitimacy of the state, the government had strong motivations to attempt to minimize misconduct and corruption among officials and functionaries at all levels, and particularly the lower levels, and to remedy wrongs committed against ordinary citizens and punish wrongdoers. Second, petitions constituted a useful source of information, otherwise unavailable, on what was going on at the lower levels of the state system and in local society—such information was a relatively effective control mechanism over lower-level officials by their superiors—quite literally, knowledge was power.[3] This was why the provincial and national authorities never wanted to close off this source of information provided by petitions. In the spirit of judicial independence, the governor of Jiangsu, Cheng Dequan, scolded some local elite organizations for interfering in judicial appointments with petitions and told various individual petitioners to take their cases to formal judicial institutions, but he never categorically rejected the act of petitioning per se. It appears that the Republican governments expected that there would be problems in the judiciary, some of them caused by judicial officers and functionaries, ranging from corruption to professional incompetence, which could be exposed by petitions and then remedied by official responses from the higher levels of the state system.

By the early Republican years, the manner in which administrative and judicial officials responded to petitions had been regularized by precedent into certain bureaucratic routines. There was a steady increase in the number of petitions between 1912 and 1937, reflecting the rise in the number of lawsuits, which entailed ever more investigation and paperwork, consuming untold institutional resources. Just as case backlogs in the judiciary resulted in part from reforms that encouraged the use of the formal judicial system by ordinary citizens, the increase in informal petitioning was at least in part due to the legitimization of such petitions by regular official responses to them.

Petitions came from a variety of sources: litigants (and their relatives), prison and detention house inmates (and their relatives), local elites, prison and jail guards, and local GMD organs. Litigants usually petitioned the authorities because they felt judges or county magistrates had failed to handle their cases properly or fairly, and because the formal appeal procedure was of no help, in situations such as when they had been detained without trial or their appeals had been rejected or they had been convicted of crimes they had not committed and had lost appeals. They also petitioned while their cases were going through the appeal procedures, simply to increase the odds that their side of the story would be heard by the proper authorities, and that they would not be disadvantaged by their opponents through extralegal channels or means. Prison inmates petitioned to complain about their mistreatment by corrupt prison officers and/or guards. Local elites petitioned to intervene in particular cases or to expose perceived misconduct by judicial officers, including jail overseers. Local politics was usually involved when county personnel or local GMD organs petitioned, and one side would try to have disciplinary action taken by the higher authorities against the other. Petitions from litigants and jail inmates were often written by scribes, but some badly composed and poorly handwritten petitions in the archives were apparently written by litigants and jail inmates themselves who were unable to hire scribes or get more literate relatives to write for them.

Petitioners mostly wrote to the Ministry of Justice, the JHC (and the JHP in the Beiyang period), the provincial governor, and during the Nanjing decade also to the Control Council, the National Government, and the GMD Center. Since, no matter whether an administrative or judicial entity received them, all petitions that concerned lawsuits or judicial procedures or judicial administration were eventually referred to the relevant high court (and the high procuracy), those provincial judicial institutions were the agencies responsible for investigating alleged wrongs and taking action accordingly.

Based on case records in the archives, the regularized routine institutional mechanism in responding to petitions alleging misconduct at counties and district courts may be summarized as follows:

(1) When a jail overseer, trial officer, or other member of the county government staff was accused of corruption or mishandling cases, the county magistrate was to investigate and report.

(2) When a county magistrate was allegedly involved in wrongdoing or mishandling cases, the magistrate of a neighboring county was to investigate and report.

(3) When the alleged misconduct or corruption was serious (for example, the unlawful death of a detainee), a court clerk from a district court or the high court was to be sent to the county to investigate, sometimes in addition to an investigation by the magistrate of a neighboring county.

(4) If judicial officers at district courts, branch district, or branch high courts (and their procuracies) were accused of misdeeds, the high court was to send a court clerk to investigate.

In short, when judicial misconduct at the county level was alleged by a petition or petitions, the county magistrate, as adjudicating officer, was under the scrutiny and authority of the provincial judicial institutions, besides being under the provincial government in his capacity as an administrative official. Once again, the fact that most county magistrates also performed judicial functions resulted in the overlapping authorities of the administrative and judicial fields within the state system.

Under the same standard operating procedures, the outcomes of petitions varied depending on the merits of individual cases. The scenarios of petitions and their results fall into four categories: (1) after investigation, accused officials or personnel were found guilty of wrongdoing, and legal or disciplinary actions followed; (2) accused judicial officers were found guilty of errors in judicial procedures and were disciplined; (3) petitions were set aside or rejected for lack of merit (falsehood, illegality, or frivolousness); and (4) accusations against judicial personnel or county magistrates were determined to be false after investigation.

Based on the archival sources alone, it is often difficult to know whether a county magistrate covered up the misconduct of the trial officer or the jail overseer under him whom he was supposed to investigate, or for that matter whether a district court president did so for his subordinates. Both the petitioner(s) and the accused often dramatized or exaggerated the truth, and the arguments are often one-sided. However, the internal evidence sometimes allows one to judge the relative merits of allegations and of ensuing investigations.[4]

To understand the phenomenon this chapter addresses, it should be borne in mind that there was some tolerance of deviation from the established norms and forms. It was actually up to the county magistrate or other local officials to determine the exact scope of the tolerance. Based on his familiarity with the social environment in which the system (and he himself) functioned, he could choose to ignore certain irregularities as acceptable and inevitable; or he could choose to try to rein in those behaviors as unacceptable and punishable acts. And there was also a gap between the perspective of the county magistrate and that of ordinary citizens and litigants, which explains certain complaints on the part of the latter. The cases presented below show how local actors, including judicial personnel, used the institutional mechanism and bureaucratic routines either to fight perceived misdeeds and injustice or to advance and defend their own interests, concretely illustrating a range of issues that prompted petitioners to act. These cases also shed additional light on how and in what kind of social environment the judiciary operated and interacted with the administrative field within the state system.

Official Misconduct

In March 1915, during an inspection tour of Songjiang, Governor Qi Yaolin came upon a local resident, Jiang Zhao, who handed in a petition requesting the governor's intervention in a case in which his father, Jiang Xian, had been wrongfully accused and detained without trial for three months. Qi had heard of the case before and asked the Huhai circuit administrator to investigate. After receiving Jiang's petition, Qi instructed the JHC that the local officials involved in the case were to be suspended immediately and handed over, along with other parties to the case, to the Shanghai DC for trial, and that the guilty should be severely punished.

The ensuing investigation and trial at the court found as follows. On November 4, 1914, Shen Chengzhao and Sun Jianxiang, respectively, the Songjiang commissioners of opium prohibition and self-government, had arrived at the home of a wealthy merchant in Hougang town, Wang Wangyun, to ask him to buy government bonds in the amount of ¥200 at 6 percent interest. Probably suspecting that he would never see his money again, Wang would only agree to buy bonds for ¥50. Angry at Wang's "stinginess," Shen and Sun then got a police chief, Sun Fu, to have Wang's home searched by three policemen for opium, some two ounces of which were found. Threatened with severe punishment for the drug offense, and with a merchant friend, Pan Xingqing, acting as middleman, Wang agreed to buy bonds for ¥200, in addition to negotiating a payment of ¥500 to bribe Shen to drop the drug charge. Jiang Xian, Wang's rent collector, delivered the money to Shen on a boat he traveled on. To cover up the bribery, however, Shen announced unexpectedly that Wang would have to face the drug charge at the CGO after all (Shen perhaps calculated that Wang would not dare reveal his having bribed him, a crime in itself). At the county trial, the county magistrate fined Wang ¥120 for the drug offense, and Sun Fu paid the fine on Wang's behalf out of the ¥500 Wang had given Shen. Of the remaining ¥380, ¥200 went into Shen's pocket and Sun Fu took ¥180. Wang still had to buy bonds in the amount of ¥176. The whole affair caused Wang to fall ill for more than a month. Unable to get over the matter, Wang sued Jiang Xian at the CGO for embezzling the ¥500 that Jiang had delivered to Shen. Because CGO personnel were implicated, the county magistrate delayed the trial and eventually requested the transfer of the case to the Shanghai DC (before the transfer took place, the trial delay caused Jiang Zhao to petition Governor Qi Yaolin). On May 26, 1915, the court sentenced Wang Wangyun to ten days' detention, and Pan Xingqing and Jiang Xian to five days' detention each for bribery. Shen Chengzhao was given a prison term of three and a half years, plus forfeiture for life of the rights to vote and to hold public office, and Sun Jiaxing and Sun Fu were each sentenced to three years' imprisonment for swindling. The JHC duly reported the results of the case to Qi Yaolin, as instructed.[5]

This case speaks to several points of historical significance. First, county-level positions created as the result of the New Policy reforms, such as those of opium prohibition commissioner, self-government commissioner, and police chief, enabled their holders to abuse their powers by squeezing money from citizens. Second, these officials would squeeze a local elite figure like Wang without qualms, because unlike the county magistrate, they were not responsible for basic county government functions, such as tax collection, that would require the cooperation of local elites. In other words, these low-level officials acted in a completely selfish manner, even against the interests of the county magistrate. Third, Wang sought revenge, not by directly suing the abusers, whom he was guilty of bribing, but by suing Jiang Xian, who would have to finger the abusers in order to clear himself (even though the bribery would come to light in the end). That is to say, Wang knew how to use the judicial process. Fourth, the informal practice of petitioning allowed Jiang Zhao to rescue his father from detention without trial and to move the case to formal criminal proceedings in a regular court for a fair trial. In this instance, the petitioning mechanism and the administrative and judicial institutions worked together, which resulted in exposing and punishing the wrongdoers.

A second case involved judicial personnel. In October 1918, Zheng Dongcheng, a merchant in Huaiyin, lodged a lawsuit at the CGO against Hu Bingxu, a probationary judge of the First Branch High Court (FBHC), for adultery with his concubine, and against Zhang Baokang, a judge of the same court, for arranging the affair. Concurrently, Zheng sent petitions to the JHC and the MJ for fear that the county magistrate and the FBHC would be unable to do justice, given that the case involved judges at the court that handled appeals from county trials in Huaiyin. The JHC issued a secret order for Qiu Zaiyuan, the supervising judge at the FBHC, to investigate the case, and separately sent Shi Chuanjiu, a JHC clerk, to Huaiyin to conduct a covert investigation. Both investigators concluded that despite his denial, Hu had most likely had an affair with Zheng's concubine. At the same time, Zhang Baokang was found to have frequented a local prostitute where Zheng's concubine and Hu met. While the case was still under trial at the county, the JHC took action based on the investigations. After reporting to the MJ, the JHC fired Hu Bingxu, who was still subject to legal penalty pending the outcome of the trial, and suspended Zhang Baokang for "violating the code of conduct for officials," pending further action by the Committee on Disciplining Judicial Officers. Judge Qiu Zaiyuan was given a warning for failing to supervise his subordinates in the court.[6] Again, the petitioning mechanism worked in this case for the petitioner and the state system.

A third case involved county jail staff. In April 1937, the JHC received petitions from two Wujiang local men, Gu Yunming and Sun Tiezheng, and from inmates in the county detention house accusing Sun Zhongxiang, the chief, and Wu Wanjiang, a cook, of abuses (extorting money from inmates, embezzling from the inmate ration fund, and molesting female inmates and women visiting their loved ones held in the facility). The JHC ordered the Wujiang county magistrate to investigate. The magistrate reported that the allegations about embezzlement and extortion could not be substantiated, but that one water carrier working for the detention house did claim that he had witnessed the cook molesting a woman visiting her father jailed there. The JHC thereupon ordered that the cook be fired immediately.[7] This case illustrates that the JHC would not tolerate wrongdoing even by a lowly cook at a county detention house, and that such wrongdoing might not have been brought to light without the petitioning mechanism.

These cases point to a pattern—county-level officials, judicial officers, and county jail staff were disciplined, not for juridical misconduct, but for social behavior considered immoral or criminal. The key phrase the JHC and the MJ used in justifying disciplinary action in such cases was "to enforce the code of conduct for officials" (*yisu guanzhen*). The phrase was also frequently cited by petitioners to reinforce their allegations, as was the phrase "to uphold the authority and credibility of the judiciary." Such rhetoric did carry weight, as the perception and expectation among both high officials and local people, consistent with the traditional Confucian admonition, were that to be entrusted to administer justice fairly and impartially, officials, especially judicial officers and personnel, should be morally superior people. In the above cases, the official discourse and the institutional mechanism of responding to petitions converged to produce the results.

If immoral personal misconduct among judicial personnel was not tolerated, neither were juridical misdeeds. The judicial authorities did not hesitate to punish those found to have committed juridical misconduct alleged by petitions. In late 1922, the jail overseer in Jingjiang was accused by local citizens of taking bribes to bend the law; and when an investigation ordered by the JHP and conducted by the chief of the Wu DP uncovered a variety of irregularities, the jail overseer was fired.[8] It appears that the provincial judicial officials were public-minded and fair-minded in that they would punish county judicial personnel more severely for deliberate abuses or personal immorality than for unexpected mishaps on the job such as prisoner escape. Petition-writing was particularly useful in uncovering and punishing the former kinds of problems, which would otherwise more easily have gone undetected by the higher authorities.

Procedural Errors

One type of petition from litigants was about judicial personnel mishandling lawsuits, often in the form of procedural errors. Because such errors went against the formalization agenda, the judicial authorities had no tolerance for them, especially in courts and procuracies. In April and May 1922, Woman Wang wrote to the JHC and the MJ complaining about the way the Jiangning DC had mishandled her lawsuit. The court bailiff had delivered a summons meant for her to a hotel in Jiangning where she used to stay, instead of to her home address, and the document was not signed by the court clerk who issued it. The JHC took this seemingly minor breach of the rules seriously. Although the clerk argued that the woman had told him to send court documents to the hotel, whose owner would (and did) receive them on her behalf, the JHC president held that the clerk had violated procedure on both counts—failing to sign the document and failing to send it to the litigant's home address, and the clerk was fired.[9]

In July 1934, Qian Jianhou of Wujiang petitioned the MJ, reporting that the county magistrate refused to return bail money of ¥300 that he had paid prior to trial. The JHC ordered the county magistrate to comply with the law. The latter returned the money, but not the three years and five months' worth of interest on it, violating the Regulations on Safekeeping Litigation Deposits. It took another petition by Qian to the JHC and another order from the court to get the county magistrate to comply.[10] The magistrate may have had trouble coming up with the money, which might have been used by him as "shifting payment" (see Chapter 5). It would have been difficult or impossible, short of lengthy and costly litigation, for Qian Jianhou to recover his money, had the informal mechanism of petitioning not been available.

In December 1935, the MJ received a petition from Sheng Shichun of Songjiang, who was involved in a lawsuit over an inheritance. The trial at the Songjiang DC resulted in a decision to have a local bank collect rent from the properties of both parties, but on his appeal, the JHC overruled the decision and ordered a retrial. Sheng found, however, that on instructions from the DC, the bank continued to collect the rent regardless of the JHC order, and he requested the MJ to investigate and stop the illegal action by the DC. At the inquiry from the JHC, the DC argued that because the case file had not been returned to it from the JHC, it could not retry the case, but had to enforce the decision of the first trial, and that the rent collected would be held by the bank and eventually given to the winning party in the case. The JHC president responded that it was wrong to enforce a decision that had already been voided by the HC, and that the DC should cease the enforcement immediately. The MJ was duly informed of the result.[11]

The above cases should suffice to show that the national and provincial judicial authorities were committed to the norms and forms established by the reform and were keen to enforce them when it was discovered that they had been breached. At the same time, petitioning also worked for litigants in many cases where juridical errors committed by courts would not otherwise have been corrected. The frequency of such cases turning up in the archives indicates two things: first, it was difficult to establish norms and forms in the judicial process and have them followed all the time and everywhere within the entire judicial system; and, second, with a commitment to institutional and procedural formalization, the MJ and the JHC made consistent efforts to enforce judicial procedures by expending institutional resources to intervene in cases where procedural errors had been reported or uncovered. It was in the context of the formalization agenda, and the difficulty of achieving it completely, that the informal practice of petitioning functioned as a useful tool for both the state and litigants. Paradoxically, the informal practice of petitioning played an important role in helping inform the higher authorities of breaches of the formal rules and procedures, and therefore in enforcing them.

Petitions Rejected for Lack of Merit

Complaints about the failure of the judicial system to deliver justice should not necessarily be taken at face value, however. The archival sources reveal that many petitions were sent to the authorities for wrong reasons: litigants failed to understand the procedural laws, and when their lawsuits were rejected for technicalities—nonconformity to the formal procedures—they felt cheated by the system.

In March 1915, Huang Jinkui of Wuxi wrote to the provincial governor accusing the Shanghai DP of illegally rejecting his lawsuits. Huang turned out to have filed a lawsuit against a certain Hua Ayong at the Wuxi county office for seducing his concubine Wang Sibao and sued Wang herself at the Shanghai DP for fleeing his house (the suit had no legal merit as a criminal case). His lawsuits had been rejected because Wang's actions were a civil matter and could not be litigated at the DP. Huang had also sued one Tao Rongsheng for marrying Wang Sibao as his legal wife, a case Huang did not have the competence to bring under the PNCC.[12] Huang was simply using any and all avenues he could think of to get his concubine back, and petitioning the provincial governor was just one more to try.

In another case, Cao Jingrong petitioned the JHC in 1919 because he believed the Shanghai DC had wrongfully enforced a civil decision. Cao had paid a deposit of ¥80 to Woman Shen of the Jiang family to rent a house, which shortly thereafter came under dispute in an inheritance lawsuit between Woman Shen and Woman Chen, also of the Jiang family. The DC ruled in favor of Woman Chen and enforced the decision. The problem for Cao was that he wanted the deposit he had paid Shen to offset four months' rent, but Woman Chen would not credit the deposit, since she had not received it. The JHC informed Cao that he had no competence in the inheritance lawsuit and its enforcement and that he would have to take up the issue with Woman Chen or sue her separately (the court seemed to reason that the deposit was paid for renting the house and that Women Chen as its new owner should acknowledge the deposit).[13] Cao had lost his deposit through no fault of his own, and either he did not know how to get it back through formal litigation or he was trying to do so more cheaply and efficiently by writing a petition.

A more complicated case shows the great lengths to which litigants would go in trying to change the results of judicial proceedings. In April 1935, a disturbing petition reached the MJ via the National Government Civil Servant Office. It came from the Hunan Native Association in Shanghai (HNAS) and had been transmitted by He Jian, the Hunan provincial government chairman. The petition said that when a group of refugees fleeing the drought in Hunan arrived in Qingpu, Jiangsu, they had been attacked by peasants of Maodian village, and fifty-two of them had been killed. The petitioners demanded justice for the victims and punishment of the culprits. The JHC ordered the Qingpu county magistrate, Qian Jiaxiang, to handle the case according to the law and report the results as soon as possible. When Qian did not respond, the JHC president issued two more orders, on June 4 and July 27, urging him to act. On August 7, Qian finally submitted a conviction and sentence document on the case.

The incident had taken place in February 1935. According to a report in *Shen Bao* (Shanghai News), about 1,000 Hunan refugees had arrived in Qingpu, asking the county government for help. The latter had explained the local economic difficulties and arranged for them to leave the county. On February 12, however, about 300 refugees had reentered the county and arrived at Maodian village on Dianshan Lake, begging for food. The villagers gave them some food, but the refugees had not left. A family in the village happened to be having a wedding that day. The refugees stormed the wedding banquet, and the frightened wedding guests ran away. The refugees, after eating up the food on the tables, proceeded to loot the family's house, and then went on to rob other families. After the initial shock, the outraged villagers regrouped and fought back. Outnumbered, the refugees began to flee the village, which was surrounded by the lake on three sides, and many of them jumped into the icy water in panic and drowned.[14] Based on the facts, the county trial had acquitted several defendants of murder charges, since the local peasants had been trying to fight off the looting refugees, and most of the victims had drowned in the lake and had not been killed directly by the villagers.[15]

The JHC forwarded the document to the MJ, which was satisfied. But the HNAS was not. It petitioned the Judicial Council and the Control Council in October, accusing the Qingpu county magistrate, Qian Jiaxiang, and the trial officer, Shen Yuankai, of taking bribes to let the guilty go free. The petitioners enclosed a photograph of the dead bodies of the victims and, ironically, a copy of the settlement agreement signed on March 4 between the head of the Qingpu County Second Ward and five refugee representatives. Under the agreement, the county would provide ¥300 each for the families of the victims whose bodies had not been found, ¥150 each for those whose bodies had been recovered from the lake, ¥3,000 for funeral expenses, and ¥500 for the remaining refugees to travel back home. The Qingpu CGO had, in fact, committed a large amount of money (an unexpected extra expenditure in the context of tight county finance) trying to settle the matter. The councils transmitted the petition to the JHC, which replied that the plaintiff and defendants were appealing the first trial result, and that the requests in the petition were the same as the grounds of the appeal. If there had been anything improper in the first trial, it would be corrected in the second trial.[16] Apparently, large-scale networking by the HNAS, which reached as high as the Hunan provincial government, and even the national capital, backed up the petitions. The HNAS did not believe that the Qingpu county magistrate or even the JHC would do justice in the case. For the Hunanese and the HNAS, some people had to be executed for the deaths of the fifty-two refugees for justice to be done, no matter under what circumstances the tragedy had occurred. But the law did not agree, and their petitions failed.

In addition to the above types, there were petitions from criminal defendants claiming innocence. In such cases, the authorities tended to accept an explanation from the judicial officer who had handled the case. In September 1925, Zhang Jimin of Fengxian petitioned the JHC claiming that the county magistrate had wrongfully detained him. The magistrate replied that Zhang Jimin had been detained because he was suspected of a criminal act. The story was that Lu Shengyang, a tenant of Zhang Liangang's, had been unable to pay rent for several years, and the land—totaling three *mu*—had therefore been taken back by Zhang and rented to Xu Xuegeng. In August, incited by Zhang Jimin, Lu had forcibly taken more than 300 catties of cotton from the field now tilled by Xu. For doing so, both Lu Shengyang and Zhang Jimin were arrested. Although Zhang Jimin contended in the petition that Xu had no evidence to prove that he incited Lu, the JHC believed the county magistrate, but told him to try the case as quickly as possible.[17] Presumably, the JHC held that criminal defendants would routinely claim innocence and whether Zhang was guilty or not would be proven in court. The only issue that mattered was that the defendant should be tried within a legal time limit. This was largely the pattern of how the higher authorities dealt with petitions from criminal defendants claiming innocence.

The Political Economy of False Accusation

The last category of petitions—false accusation—deserves separate consideration. False accusations could and did exist in any state and judicial system. As Philip Huang notes, false accusations are frequently found in the litigation records of the Qing dynasty.[18] Melissa Macauley characterizes false accusation as "the stock-in-trade" of legal scribes, a way for common people to gain judicial access, and a legal defense strategy.[19] What was different here is that false accusations were made, not in the context of lawsuits, but as petitions outside the judicial process. In the Republican era, the unofficial legitimization of petition-writing and regularization of official responses to petitions as an informal practice led to an unintended but inevitable consequence—the abuse of petitions in the form of false accusations, which otherwise would have existed anyway but probably on fewer occasions.

The PNCC provided punishment for making false accusations, as did Qing law, but this applied only when a person made a false accusation in a formal lawsuit. Writing a letter to the higher administrative and judicial authorities was not a formal lawsuit but an informal complaint or exposé, and therefore no legal penalty could be applied. Indeed, there was never a case where anyone was prosecuted for making false accusations in a petition. That is to say, false accusations proliferated in the Republican era precisely because petitioning was an *informal* act, as opposed to lawsuits handled by the judiciary as judicial proceedings, which were much more formalized than in the imperial era. This fact, along with regularized official responses to *all* petitions, simply encouraged making false accusations, behavior not easily distinguishable from truthful exposure through petitions of juridical errors and unlawful wrongdoing. The Republican state seems to have accepted that there would be false accusations among petitions, and that the resources wasted in responding to false accusations was part of the cost of employing petitioning as a monitoring mechanism.

After the regular official responses to petitions became public knowledge, petitioners were more inclined to make false or exaggerated accusations through petitions against their personal enemies, usually those who had some kind of judicial advantage or power over them. In a petitioner's calculations, making a false accusation was a low-cost or no-cost endeavor—the petitioner would lose nothing, except perhaps the expense of hiring a legal scribe, and might be well repaid by getting revenge. Thus, as petitions multiplied over the period under study, so did false accusations among them.

Of the eighty or so petitions sampled by this study, 25–30 percent fall into the category where allegations of official misconduct and/or juridical injustice were determined to be false after investigation. Some cases appeared to be obviously false accusations, and others were of a dubious nature, especially when an allegation against a trial officer or a jail overseer was investigated by his immediate superior, the county magistrate. The following cases will illustrate a spectrum of allegations, from obviously false to possibly false, showing the motivations, calculations, and patterns of making false accusations.

Charges Against Courts and County Offices

In September 1917, Yao Qinglan petitioned the MJ saying that the JHC had illegally accepted the appeal of Woman Han, who was Yao's opponent in a civil lawsuit. As it turned out, Han had asked to submit her appeal to the JHC in Suzhou on the last day of the appeal period (the twentieth day from the decision of the second trial), because she would have missed the appeal deadline if she had had to travel back to the Shanghai DC, where the second trial took place, to declare her appeal. The JHC explained that it had accepted the appeal simply out of consideration for the litigant, which did not violate the spirit of the procedural law, and the ministry agreed.[20] This episode shows that, while intending to adhere to formalized rules and procedures, the JHC was flexible enough to act in the spirit of the procedural law, and that the litigant, Yao Qinglan (or his lawyer), was quite alert to the letter of the procedural law in trying to make an issue out of the court's action on technical grounds.

In September 1919, several Songjiang petitioners, who designated themselves as "citizens," wrote to the JHC accusing the county clerk of charging excessive complaint and copying fees. In response to an inquiry from the JHC, the county magistrate replied that it was a misunderstanding. (1) At the going exchange rate between silver yuan (¥) and copper coins, the standard fee for copying documents was 100 characters for ¥0.112, which equaled 152 small copper coins (*wen*), but small copper coins were rare in circulation, and litigants usually paid with copper yuan (*tongyuan*), which were rounded to the nearest whole number. Thus litigants would pay 15 copper yuan (less than 152 wen) for 100 characters, 30 copper yuan (less than 304 wen) for 200 characters, and 46 copper yuan (more than 456 wen) for 300 characters, while expecting to pay 45 copper yuan for 300 characters because they had paid 30 copper yuan for 200 characters, not realizing the rounding used. (2) When the CGO sold out of criminal complaint forms, and a new supply had not yet arrived, the CGO would sell criminal appeal forms as substitute so as to move cases forward; and when the latter also ran out, the office would accept handwritten complaints but charge copying fees and complaint fees, in the expectation that the handwritten complaints would be copied onto official complaint forms when the latter became available. Litigants failed to understand why those fees should be charged when handwritten complaints had already been accepted.[21]

The county magistrate's explanation sounds reasonable; but on the first point, considering what the petitioners said—they were charged 16 copper yuan for 100 characters, 31 for 200 characters, and so forth, it appears that the county clerk always rounded up, never down, to whole numbers, thus overcharging litigants. But when the magistrate defended the clerk, the JHC took what he said at face value and did not pursue the issue any further. For the JHC president, his job was done in responding to petitions—there was a reasonable answer to his inquiry, which could be filed away along with the petition.

Trial Officers and Their Accusers

The majority of petitions targeted county trial officers or jail overseers. The pattern reveals the multifaceted circumstances under which the county judiciary operated. In September 1925, Governor Chen Taoyi transmitted a petition by several "citizens" in Fengxian to the JHC that accused the trial officer Qian Jiang of abusing power, being corrupt, and socializing with evil gentry-managers (*liedong*). Several civil lawsuits were cited as examples of miscarriages of justice under Qian. The JHC dispatched Shen Baoyuan, a former trial officer of Chongming, to investigate. Shen asked a lot of questions of people in the streets about judicial practices in the county and Qian's behavior before showing up at the county office to examine the files of the cases mentioned in the petition. Shen found that the allegations were groundless and that the petitioners used pseudonyms, but that Qian might have socialized with various township managers (*xiangdong*) when he performed administrative duties on behalf of the county magistrate, which gave the appearance of corruption and "probably gave rise to this case." The trial officer would assume some of the county magistrate's duties, Shen reported, in part because he was posted in the old county seat, 20 *li* east of Nanqiao town, where the CGO had been located since 1912. During the Qing era, a deputy of the county magistrate (*xianzuo*) had been stationed in Nanqiao. In the Republican era, out of tradition and convenience, the county magistrate used the trial officer as a deputy in administrative as well as judicial affairs, even though their locations had been switched around. In response to Shen's report, the JHC ordered that the Fengxian county magistrate not have the trial officer perform administrative duties, and that the latter focus on his judicial duties.[22] Thus, exposing no wrongdoing, the false accusation ironically led to the discovery of a division of labor that made practical sense in the county, and probably was not what the accusers wanted to change, but was in violation of the rules and regulations on the duties of the county magistrate and the trial officer.

Five years later, in December 1930, four "representatives of all the people" from the same Fengxian county petitioned the MJ to the effect that the trial officer Huang Xingquan failed to process lawsuits in a timely fashion, causing great suffering among litigants. The JHC president issued orders for the trial officer of Nanhui, a neighboring county, to investigate, and for the Fengxian county magistrate, Sun Qingchen, to make a separate report, but only Sun's report is in the archives. Sun cleared Huang of any wrongdoing, but noted a long-standing rivalry for judicial attention between people in the old county seat and those in Nanqiao. The popular consensus was that the trial officer should be stationed in the old county seat, but Huang had stayed in Nanqiao for some time in order to handle many banditry cases there, which perhaps disturbed some pettifoggers in the old county seat (since Huang's absence impeded their businesses), prompting them to act against Huang. Based on the report, the JHC closed the case and notified the ministry.[23] Notably, this time around, the JHC did not raise the issue of the obvious division of labor between the county magistrate and the trial officer. This might mean that the court did not want to be too involved in certain local arrangements that violated the rules but did no harm. The case actually reveals that local people in the old county seat of Fengxian wanted the trial officer to be there for their convenience, probably in administrative as well as judicial matters, despite the JHC order five years before.

In December 1934, Dai Zupei of Wujiang petitioned the JHC and the Control Council separately. According to Dai, when he had filed a criminal lawsuit against Yang Ruikun for illegally taking over his property, the trial officer Zhou Xiang had held that the case was valid and had ordered Yang to pay bail of ¥500. At the second hearing, Zhou had suddenly refused to proceed with the case, however, saying that Dai should file a civil lawsuit, and forced Dai to sign a document to withdraw the criminal lawsuit. Dai believed that Zhou had changed his position because he had been bribed by the defendant. Dai alleged that it was a pattern that Zhou would demand that a defendant pay a large sum of money as bail and then set aside the case for months to signal the defendant to bribe him. When ordered to investigate and report on the case, Magistrate Xu Youchuan defended Zhou. At the first hearing, Xu said, the facts were not clear and witnesses had yet to be called, which was why the defendant had been ordered to post bail.

At the second hearing, it became clear that the case was a civil matter, and Zhou had therefore persuaded the two parties to settle the dispute, and Dai had signed to withdraw his lawsuit. Dai's present petition was exaggerated and fabricated, apparently because he had changed his mind and was trying to reinstate the lawsuit. Six months later, in May 1935, Zhou Xiang was again accused of taking bribes and shielding the guilty in a homicide case in Wujiang, and the county magistrate again defended Zhou to the JHC, saying that there was no evidence of wrongdoing.[24] One is unable to determine from the archival sources whether the magistrate was shielding a crooked trial officer or the latter was falsely accused by disgruntled litigants, or the truth lay somewhere in between.

There was a pattern, however, of litigants or defendants trying to take down the trial officer who handled their cases, for legitimate or illegitimate reasons, by petitioning the higher judicial and administrative authorities. In a sense, however successful the reform had been, the judiciary would not and could not have satisfied the expectations of all litigants and nonlitigants. People petitioned because the authorities routinely ordered investigations into alleged mishandling of cases, which might put some pressure on judicial officers handling their cases. Philip Huang has argued that during the Qing era, litigants often resorted to official lawsuits simply to put pressure on the opposing parties to settle disputes in a "third realm" between official adjudication and societal mediation.[25] Here we see a pattern where litigants engaged in civil lawsuits or charged with criminal offenses would resort to writing petitions to the higher authorities to put pressure on adjudicating judicial officers. Of course, writing letters to higher officials alleging injustice by local officials had been a routine practice in the Qing era.[26] In the Republican era, however, there was a court system and a separation between the judiciary and the administrative bureaucracies at the provincial level and, to a degree, at the county level. Petitioners could write to the judicial as well as administrative authorities at higher levels while pursuing their cases at the county office or the court. The development of the judicial system provided more venues for local actors to engage the state in pursuit of their interests. In this sense, paradoxically again, judicial formalization encouraged informal practices.

The County Magistrate and His Enemies

Along with trial officers, county magistrates were often accused by petitioners of wrongdoing, and again such allegations might be entirely false or partly true or true. One example of ambiguity in a case due to limited information in the sources is as follows. In December 1936, Xing Zhengguo of Shuyang complained to the Control Council that he had been detained on trumped-up charges by the county government for more than five months. The JHC told the FBHC president, Sheng Shibie, to investigate. Sheng only asked the Shuyang county magistrate to send up the case files. The files showed that Xing had been issued a criminal summons on January 6, 1935, for inciting litigation arising from a case of gambling and assault in which he had not been involved, but he did not respond to the summons. Sheng concluded that Xing's allegations were groundless.[27] One scenario that Sheng did not consider, or did not care to consider, was that Xing might have been taken into custody after failing to respond to the summons, and that his detention did not enter the case files precisely because he was detained without trial—what his petition was complaining about. As noted earlier, judicial officials tended not to take petitions from criminal defendants seriously.

From cases of obvious false accusations against county magistrates, it is clear that the county magistrate could easily make enemies whether he wanted to do something right or to do nothing. Jiao Kui of Kunshan had formerly been a tax collector, in the capacity of "village secretary," and was notorious for using all kinds of pretexts to line his own pockets. In 1927, the Nanxingdu Township Assembly decided to fire him as tax collector and reported the decision to Magistrate Liu Zheng. To find new leverage and enrich himself, Jiao thereupon set up a Kunshan County Branch of the National Anti-Drug Association, riding the tide of the anti-opium movement. In the capacity of the branch head, Jiao accused Xu Fuchun, a police officer who had been on the job for more than ten years, of opium-smoking, and then wrote to the Jiangsu Provincial Justice Department (JPJD) accusing Magistrate Liu of sheltering Xu. Liu was able to ward off the accusation and called Jiao a local pest (*difang zhidu*).[28] But the case shows how resourceful such a "local bully" could be: Jiao was able to take advantage of the political situation, game the system, and become a power player with whom the county magistrate had to reckon.

In contrast, an outsider to local society like the trial officer was less able to harm a county magistrate. The new regulations provided that the trial officer be appointed by the HC, rather than nominated by the county magistrate. As a result, the magistrate and the trial officer might not get along. In March 1927, the JHC appointed Zhou Guangyong as the trial officer of Pi. Zhou's behavior bothered Magistrate Shen Zhen on several counts. Zhou arrived in the county sixteen days late; he bragged about his position to solicit personal favors; he flew into a rage when Shen corrected his writing of judicial documents; he falsely claimed to be a relative of the local military commander; in trying one case, he let go five witnesses whom he had earlier ordered to testify at trial; and, finally, when Zhou was told to quit the job and leave the county by the local military commander, who had learned about the claims of this fake relative, he was found to have about ¥800 with him after being on the job for less than two months, with a monthly salary of ¥80. After leaving, however, it was Zhou who petitioned the JPJD and accused Shen of mishandling lawsuits. The JPJD did find two cases in which Shen's rulings were incorrect, but Shen was able to make the case against Zhou stick. Zhou was not disciplined only because he was no longer on the job.[29] However, if he did not succeed in making his false accusation against Shen stick, he did not lose anything by it either.

Prison Officers Accused

Not surprisingly, a large number of petitions alleged various irregularities and abuses in provincial prisons, county jails, and detention houses at both levels. While many were legitimate complaints, others were false accusations targeting prison officers. In June 1921, a group of seven gentry-elders and four commercial shops in Chaohejing, Shanghai county, where the Jiangsu Second Prison was located, petitioned the MJ. Their major stated concern was that the new governor of the prison did not discipline the guards he had brought with him, who often went out in groups of seven to ten, making scenes in the streets and the market and causing disturbances. The elders also reported rumors that inmates were deprived of their morning gruel and were tortured and otherwise mistreated. They were worried that inmates might be driven to riot.

Minister of Justice Dong Kang ordered the JHP to verify the matter. The chief procurator in turn ordered the Shanghai DP chief, Wang

Yijian, to investigate. Wang found that the prison had formerly had sixty-four guards, and the new prison governor, Wu Tang, had hired an additional twenty, but did not bring any with him. Wu had fired eight guards for gambling and wandering around. The previous prison governor had provided morning gruel in place of cooked rice to save inmate rations. Since it was not consistent with the Regulations on Prison, Wu had had the gruel replaced with cooked dry rice. Wu denied that there was torture in the prison, but admitted that one inmate was punished for frequently making trouble.

In his report to the JHP, Wang Yijian concluded that the guards who were disturbing the local people were probably those Wu had fired. Wang did not consider it torture to apply corporal punishment to a few unruly inmates as a warning to others, especially in view of the fact that prisoner escapes had once taken place at the prison under a former prison governor with lax rules.[30] In this case, the local elites did not seem to have a motivation to make false accusations against Wu, but their petition was full of false information. Ironically, the investigation, which was the routine response to a petition, resulted in a positive evaluation of Wu's job performance.

County jail overseers were far more frequent targets of accusations than the governors of provincial prisons. The conditions in county jails were much worse than in newly built or remodeled provincial prisons; and the culture in the CGO tended to spawn corrupt practices. Although this might explain complaints arising from real grievances, false accusations against jail overseers often arose from petty local politics, mostly competition for scarce resources or jobs such as that of jail guard, for example.

In April 1930, three jail inmates in Zhengjiang accused the overseer, Xia Ding'en, of extorting money from inmates, smoking opium confiscated from inmates, having female inmates cook his meals, eating in the female cells, and embezzling inmate rations. Ordered to investigate, the county magistrate reported to the JHC that after his arrival at the jail, Xia had been able to rectify certain irregularities that had existed before, and that none of the allegations against him could be proven; moreover, two of the names signed on the petition were fictitious. Someone was determined to bring down Xia Ding'en, however. Another letter signed by "inmates" and dated June 11, 1930, accused Xia and the head guard, Han Zhiming, of gambling, smoking opium, and having sex with female inmates. This time, the JHC ordered the Zhengjiang DC to investigate. The court clerk Wu Gang quizzed two inmates of the jail who happened to be at the Zhengjiang DC in connection with a separate case, and the inmates responded that they had not witnessed anything Xia was accused of. On June 24, Wu quietly went into the jail in Zhengjiang, where he did not see any gambling or opium-smoking either. Wu separately interviewed three inmates (one female), who all said good things about Xia and Han. Finally, in a conversation with Wu, Xia Ding'en said that since his arrival, he had fired more than 100 guards, and that he surmised that the petition might be their work. In his report to the DC president, Wu concurred.

When the Zhengjiang DC president Wang Yongzhong sent up the report on July 3, a third petition arrived at the JHC. This one, signed "Citizen Fang Bo et al.," alleged that Xia Ding'en had formerly been a jail overseer in Huai'an, where he had been convicted of embezzling inmate rations and had served over a year in prison before being released on parole. Not knowing Xia's bad record, the JHC had appointed him at Zhengjiang. Xia mistreated inmates, embezzled inmate rations, and had taken a bribe of ¥180 to remove the shackles from an inmate. The letter requested Xia's removal and punishment. When ordered to investigate, the Zhengjiang DC sent another clerk, Dong Guozhang, to conduct a covert investigation. Dong interviewed three inmates separately, and no one corroborated the allegations. He talked to the inmate whose shackles had been removed, who said that they had been taken off because he was sick. He had voluntarily donated ¥200 for the jail to raise the floor in twenty-six cells. The money had been sent directly to the construction office by a member of his family, and the overseer had never laid hands on it. Dong finally met Xia. The latter told the same story and again surmised that the accusations had been made by fired former guards.[31] The persistence of former guards in writing accusing petitions against Xia is striking, indicating how deeply they resented Xia's firing them and cutting off their sources of income, both legitimate and illegitimate.

The pattern repeated itself in Zhengjiang in 1932. A letter signed "All the inmates at Zhengjiang county jail " reached the JHC in February, accusing the jail overseer Lu Ying of embezzling inmate rations, appointing personal friends, allowing opium-smoking in the jail, and pocketing charitable donations. The accusations were so serious that the immediate reaction of the Penitentiary Section official who first read the letter was to propose the outright dismissal and prosecution of Lu. The official's reaction would explain why those who made accusations wanted to exaggerate their cases as much as possible. But the JHC president Lin Biao overruled the proposal and ordered the Zhengjiang county magistrate, Zhang Peng, to investigate. As it turned out, the accusations against Lu, which were repeatedly sent to no fewer than three different government agencies and to a merchant who had donated money to the prison, were false; and the accusers were fired guards.[32] One is again struck by the persistence and resourcefulness of the accusers, in proportion to which the institutional resources wasted in responding to false accusations were considerable.

More ambiguous cases (in terms of the truth) also abound in the archives. In September 1931, a letter in the name of the people of Jintan accused the jail overseer Lü Jiajun of taking ¥600 from an inmate named Jiang Huizhao to release him on parole. Within ten days, another letter, signed by nine people claiming to be relatives of the inmates in the Jintan jail, made further accusations: Lü had ingratiated himself with the county magistrate and fooled various governmental agencies, while neglecting the sanitation in the jail; he embezzled jail funds; and he demanded money from inmates who were eligible for parole to copy court documents concerning their cases. The letter alleged that whenever members of the Committee for Improving County Jail (CICJ) visited the jail, Lü was always at the side of the visitors, so that inmates did not dare to speak up. It asked the JHC to send investigators to interview inmates privately. The JHC ordered the Jintan county magistrate, Qu Huan, to verify the allegations. Qu questioned six inmates separately at the CGO. None of them claimed that the overseer had demanded bribes. Qu then went to the jail, where one inmate stated that he had had to pay ¥3 as copying fee for parole, but Qu dismissed the testimony, since it contradicted what the inmate had earlier said at the CGO. "There are 87 convicts in the jail," Qu said. "Jiang's one-sided words cannot be trusted." Moreover, Qu could not find the signers of the second letter. He asked two CICJ members to investigate further, and the latter did not find any wrongdoing either. Qu concluded that the accusations were false.[33]

This case is typical of a recurring pattern: a petition alleged that the overseer engaged in corruption, presumably tolerated by the county magistrate, but the latter was usually ordered to investigate the overseer. It is difficult to ascertain whether the county magistrate impartially investigated or actually covered up the overseer's wrongdoing. The truth may well lie somewhere in between. That is, the overseer might have committed some commonplace irregularities, which the county magistrate knew about, but in the latter's judgment, they were not serious enough to warrant action and were inevitable anyway, no matter who was the overseer. At the same time, because the irregularities were not serious enough, whoever wrote a petition would have to exaggerate the case to get the attention of the higher authorities, which would further turn off the magistrate. Given the way in which responses to petitions were regularized, however, if the magistrate intentionally covered up serious corruption and abuses, he could be accused of such; and when the magistrate was accused of misconduct, someone from another jurisdiction would be sent to investigate and the magistrate would have much less chance to clear himself. This potential scenario would probably have been a sufficient deterrent to prevent most county magistrates from covering up serious corruption and abuses in county jails and detention houses.

Besides disgruntled former employees who had lost jobs for misconduct, personal dislikes could also engender false accusations. In 1936, an inspector from the JHC found some irregular procedures in procuring inmate rations at the Danyang county jail, but did not consider that the jail overseer, Li Zhanchun, had committed embezzlement. However, the county office accountant, Xu Peizong, seized the opportunity to send a petition to the High Court, alleging that based on Xu's auditing of accounts at the county jail, Li had embezzled funds. Based on the petition alone, probably because it was from an accountant, the JHC ordered the Zhengjiang DC to prosecute Li, but the court found no cause to prosecute and dropped the case. Judging from Li's self-defense in his letter to the JHC, it appears that the whole matter originated in personal dislikes between Li, who had been transferred to the position from Guanyun in May 1935, and Xu, who assumed his office in February 1936.[34]

What is remarkable about these cases is that the judicial authorities at the national and provincial levels treated all petitions, including those that turned out to be false accusations, with equal weight; and even when a same person was accused by one petition after another, the authorities responded to each and every petition and repeatedly ordered investigations. It seems that the authorities would rather spend resources to investigate to find the allegations to be false than allow wrongdoing in the judicial system to go unpunished. In all the cases sampled for this study, only one petition from an inmate was dismissed without investigation. It was against an officer at Jiangsu Third Prison, and although the petitioner used a formal criminal complaint form instead of a letter to make the accusation, the JHC chief procurator was of the opinion that the inmate was trying to get even with the prison officer for punishing his bad behavior in prison.[35] On the other hand, at least one investigation was ordered, not because of petitions from below, but because the JHC president had read a report in a newspaper that money had been extorted from an inmate, who had been mistreated by two other inmates at the Wu DC Detention House. Even though the ensuing investigation found no misconduct on the part of the guards, the JHC ordered the staff there be reprimanded for failing to prevent such incidents.[36]

The overall picture that emerges from the archival sources is that the provincial judicial authorities were vigilant against wrongdoing and made strenuous efforts at reducing, if not eliminating, abuses and irregularities in the judiciary, including the prison system, especially at the county level. It is in the larger context of this never-ending endeavor that the regularization of official responses to the informal practice of petitioning took place, because it helped keep a constant check on the health of the system, where the institutional and procedural formalization could not.

The special law on punishing robbers and bandits and the regularization of responses to petitions were anomalies in the formalization scheme of the Republican state. Unlike some other problems in the judicial reform discussed in earlier chapters, these anomalies did not result from financial constraints; if anything, responses to petitions actually cost large amounts of institutional resources—man-hours, in particular—that could have been spent on clearing up case backlogs, for example. The two anomalies were born of historical conditions. On the one hand, most administrative officials at the provincial and county levels considered harsh measures and quick justice necessary to combat the widespread robbery and banditry stemming from rural poverty, an approach reminiscent of the subsequent "strike hard" campaigns in the People's Republic of China.[37] On the other hand, accepting and responding to (and thus encouraging) petitions from people from all walks of life was sanctioned both by tradition and by the discourse on the Republican government being responsive to the people's voices. It also proved useful as a mechanism enabling the higher authorities to learn what was going on in local society and at the lower levels of the state system. That is why although writing petitions and responding to them was never prescribed and formalized by law, the handling of petitions was in effect regularized into routines and standard operating procedures.

In terms of their impact on defendants and litigants, the punishment of robbers and bandits outside the formal judicial institutions may be viewed as neglecting the rights of the accused, and the responses to petitions outside the formal judicial procedures as accommodating the desire of litigants and citizens seeking justice. These practices represented two opposing aspects of Republican juridical operations that remained informal but were regularized to a degree as routine functions of the state system. As the state consciously used them to supplement the perceived inadequacies of formal judicial functions, these practices constituted a significant dimension of the central question this book has examined—how justice was delivered when judicial institutions and procedures were still in a transition toward modernity through formalization.

Conclusion

> Few foreigners or Chinese either realize the difficulties that have faced the Chinese courts the past 14 years. To install and operate a new and strange system displacing a system thousands of years old would be a huge feat under the best of circumstances. When it is considered that these courts have managed to work at all in the face of unsympathetic if not hostile military factions our admiration for those judges who have stood the test must go up. The judges as well as the court subordinates are paid very poor salaries and charges of corruption have been rather frequent. This should not blind us, however, to the merits of those faithful ones who have striven so desperately to build up the court system and extend it throughout the country. Now that the nucleus of capable men is enlarging through experience on the bench and at the bar more success may be expected in the next 14 years.
>
> —N. F. Allman, *North China Herald* (Shanghai), October 17, 1925[1]

Writing in 1925, N. F. Allman, a well-known American lawyer in Shanghai, who would later serve as a member of the Shanghai Municipal Council of the International Settlement, was no doubt overoptimistic about the next fourteen years of China's judicial reform, but he was surely fair-minded in noting the achievements of the reform under difficult conditions. Indeed, while stories of unjust proceedings presided over by county magistrates were often told in the pages of the *North China Herald*, reports from its correspondents around the country also appeared commenting positively, like Allman, on the conduct of new Chinese courts. Again in 1925, a correspondent reported a case at the

JHC where a foreigner's Chinese servant was prosecuted for theft but was acquitted for lack of evidence. "In a British or an American court, he might have or might not have been convicted: but the case seemed to be handled in a very just and very legal manner." The correspondent also noted that a land dispute between a foreign Christian mission and a Chinese litigant had been adjudicated in favor the mission, and "no one, so far, can claim there has been anything illegal or unfair in the methods used, or procedure followed."[2] A report filed from Guangdong province in 1928 spoke of the Chinese judiciary in the following terms: "Less and less is heard about 'graft' or squeeze in the local courts with the passing of time. It cannot be gainsaid that in this direction there has been a marked improvement. As a consequence, the courts have got a better name, and have been frequented more and more by the general public." The Chinese Supreme Court "has been making an excellent record for itself, and is the one real safeguard of the entire legal system in China to-day. A pity it is that more attention is not paid to improving the personnel of the lower courts."[3] Both the positive and negative reports on the Chinese judiciary in the *Herald* reflected the fact that China's judicial system was in a transition from traditional laws and judicial practices to modern replacements informed by Western models, a transition characterized by institutional and procedural formalization. In this transition, the county judicial process was the place where deviations from the norms and forms tended to occur most frequently, but by no means on a wholesale scale everywhere. To properly grasp and assess China's judicial reform in the early twentieth century, its multiple contexts are summarized here to conclude this study.

Contemporary international power relations constituted the first historical context. The comments and observations of the *North China Herald* and the *China Weekly Review* quoted throughout this book highlight the international setting in which China's judicial reform unfolded, and the external pressures for results, of which Chinese reformers were constantly reminded, as the condition for an end to extraterritoriality. This external spur to the reform cannot be overemphasized—it explains the motivations and the evaluation standards of the reform. On the one hand, it conditioned what Chinese reformers took as the model for reform and explains why they did not seriously, for the most part, consider such issues as substantive justice versus formal justice or the suitability of Western models to the Chinese social environment at the local level. On the other hand, it conditioned how the reform's outcome was measured by foreign observers and Chinese reformers alike.

China's national, provincial, and local conditions, and the perspectives and behaviors of the Chinese situated at those different levels of the state system and in local society, which are the central concerns of this book, were the second context. At the national level, guided by the rule of law, judicial independence, and due process, the reform was designed to achieve judicial modernity as legal, institutional, and procedural formalization and its performance. In a fundamental sense, that agenda was predicated upon a rejection of the traditional notion of a minimalist state and embracing a modernizing state that was expanding its functions and the required expenditures.

The motivation to achieve judicial modernity as part of a modern nation-state proved to be strong enough to generate a sustained momentum for the reform throughout the 1901–1937 period. At the same time, the externally compelled, as opposed to internally generated, transformation of legal conceptualization and judicial institutions and procedures was confronted with two historically conditioned problems. One was the financial costs of the formalization agenda, which kept rising as the reform invited more and more societal demand for the judicial services of the state; and the other was the disjunction between the reform goals mandated by the central government and the political, economic, and sociocultural conditions in local society that were inhospitable to those goals. The two problems aggravated each other.

The first problem constituted the context in which we have seen the relationships and interactions between (1) the judicial and administrative fields of the state system, (2) the central and the provincial governments, (3) the provincial judicial and administrative institutions, (4) the provincial authorities and county governments, and (5) all of the above and local society, in the course of the reform. To capture all these relationships and interactions, the key words are "negotiations" and "compromises"—at the expense of judicial modernity. The decision to dismantle courts at the county level in 1913–1914, for instance, was forced by financial necessity, even though the central government could always be criticized for setting wrong priorities, and the practical effect of the retrenchment was that it seriously undermined the formalization agenda that foreign powers demanded and Chinese reformers wished to achieve.

One kind of negotiations and compromises was routinely manifested in communications within the judicial system, and the state system as a whole. The initiatives for reform issued from the central government were driven by a vision of a modern judiciary, but to county officials, the initiatives appeared very much out of touch with the local conditions those officials dealt with on a daily basis. To resist policies that were perceived as unrealistic, local officials engaged in a contest over what that reality was through paperwork—the tools the central government used to communicate the reform agenda—by pointing out local conditions inhospitable to the reform initiatives. This way, many reform initiatives were watered down even before being implemented at the county level, and they were further subverted and undermined by deviations from the norms and forms that the initiatives aimed to establish.

The reform initiatives mandated by the central government often appeared utterly unreasonable, not only to county officials, but also to local people. Could it be easily justified to Chinese peasants that criminal convicts should live in new prisons with better amenities than many law-abiding poor peasants could ever afford in their rural villages? Why would county jail guards from local society care about improving confinement conditions for presumed bad guys in jail while they did not see a raise in their wages? Or, if peasants protested against taxes collected for new schools in the New Policy era, why would they support new prisons being built at their expense?[4] That is where the disjunction between the national and the local originated and where the deviations from institutional and procedural norms and forms took place.

Deviations from officially mandated norms and forms, especially at the county level, were officially considered irregularities and abuses, but such behaviors were survival strategies or power struggles on the part of local actors situated in their social context. As long as the social environment did not change substantially, such behavior would persist, with its own logic. Irregularities and abuses were therefore routinely criticized and sometimes disciplined, but, for the most part, they were routinely tolerated, because they were deemed unavoidable, given local conditions, which included the mentality of local people (both county-level agents of the state and local residents involved in litigation). Ultimately, whatever came out of the reform at county government offices, at formal judicial institutions, and in national and provincial-level government offices was the net result of those negotiations and compromises. This context sheds the most significant light on the outcomes of the reform.

The fact that judicial modernity was only one aspect of making China a modern nation-state is a third context in which to assess the reform. In other words, when the reform was unfolding during 1901–1937, the Chinese state also engaged in other modernization projects with similar mixtures of successes and failures, though similar problems often manifested themselves in different ways. At least some aspects of what is shown in this book were also seen in the results of other modernization projects in the Republican era, especially during the Nanjing decade. Christian Henriot's study of Shanghai municipal government and Julia Strauss's study of GMD state building provide important parallels.[5] Henriot credits Chinese municipal officials in Shanghai with having pushed a vision of modernization, based both on Western models and on traditional Chinese social organizations, with which they consciously allied themselves, endowing them with new missions.[6] Here one is reminded of the state-sanctioned role that local chambers of commerce played in mediation and arbitration of commercial disputes in the Beiyang era and the Nanjing decade and the GMD efforts to involve local elites in reforming county jails with semi-official organizations. But local society in Shanghai was also beholden to tradition in the way it reacted to the policies and programs of the new government; "even among the foreign-educated elites the element of continuity outweighed any factors tending toward a break with the past," Henriot notes.[7] Finally, however, the first obstacle the municipal government faced was a shortage of resources. None of this is surprising, given how local society interacted with the judicial reform with its own logic and dynamics. Similarly, Strauss's findings about the Ministries of Foreign Affairs and of Finance offer parallel cases to the Ministry of Justice in the Republican era. Viewed in this context, the successes and failures of the judicial reform were at least on a par with those of other modernization projects, but it was an even more complicated task and was undertaken under what were probably even more difficult conditions. What the reform accomplished and why it failed where it did can thus be better appreciated.

Comparison of the judicial reform in the early twentieth century with the similar reform in the late twentieth century is also illuminating. China's international position has certainly changed from the earlier era (extraterritoriality and foreign concessions no longer exist, for example), but the external pressure to conform to Western-defined international standards in judicial process in order to be accepted as a modern nation and as an equal member of international society has hardly diminished. That is to say, the post-Mao Chinese judicial reform has continued to strive for goals similar to those pursued in the early twentieth century—legal, institutional, and procedural formalization. Similar (and different) problems and difficulties have also persisted. Among the issues that arise are (1) judicial independence—the relationship between the judiciary and the CCP, (2) violations of established rules and procedures at the lower levels of the state system, (3) severe punishment of certain crimes, (4) corruption among judicial officers and personnel, which is far more rampant than in the earlier period, and (5) the financial costs of the reform project (which is the least critical issue in comparison with the other problems and with the Republican era).[8] To conclude, in view of the problems and issues that have been plaguing judicial reform in post-Mao China, one is inclined to give the reform in 1901–1937 a higher mark. Conversely, an understanding of the reform in 1901–1937 compels one to look at the post-Mao judicial reform and its results in a more historically informed manner, and with lower expectations.

Reference Matter

Notes

Introduction

1. FP, 1932/6/5: 3–4; quotation marks from the original. Shi Lianfang (1910–1971) was a section chief in the Ministry of the Interior (MRD, 698).

2. Botsman, 2005, 8.

3. Botsman, 2005, 8.

4. Xiaoqun Xu, 1997.

5. On the Qing phenomenon, see Macauley, 1998.

6. Arguably, next to taxation, the courts were the second most important arena where ordinary citizens had to deal with the state system frequently, and where local power structures interacted with state agents.

7. The term "the reach of the state" is borrowed from Vivienne Shue (1988), who uses the notion to explore ways to conceptualize and analyze the Chinese polity under Mao and after. The issues that she tackles are surprisingly relevant to the concerns of this book. In a summary of her aims that would equally describe what I am attempting to explain about Republican China with regard to the judicial reform, Shue writes: "In essence, these are essays about how to think about the Chinese state: about its complex structures, roles, and capacities; about its interrelations with Chinese society as a whole and with rural social organization in particular; and most especially about the process of its evolution, the patterns of change we can discern not only in its forms and functions but also in its most fundamental ethos" (1). In this book, by "the reach of the state," I mean first of all the reach of the central government into the provincial and county levels within the state system, and secondly, the reach of the state, including its provincial and county level agencies, into local society. Incidentally, the need for a better understanding of the Republican state system is seen in Shue's skipping over the Republican period in her historical survey of China's state making in comparison with European history (see her chap. 3).

8. The scholarship on the Chinese Republican state has not fully captured

the complexity of the state system. For a recent overview of the Republican state, see Myers, 2000.

9. On the Qing practice of secret memorials, see Bartlett.

10. Giddens, 42. Giddens makes the comments in his analysis of "the reflexivity of modernity," the gist of which is that official statistics continuously enter into the social universe that the information is taken from and used to account for. He has more to say about its implications. I note only the technical aspect of the phenomenon here.

11. JGFD, JZ-268.

12. JGFD, JZ-505.

13. ZFZ, 1933/1: 80.

14. ZFZ, 1933/1: 83–86.

15. ZG, 1915, no. 1069; no. 1240.

16. ZG, 1915, no. 1069.

17. ZFZ, 1937/2/1, 9.

18. ZFZ, 1936/2/1, 3–6; 1936/10/1, 10–11.

19. Xu, 2001, 83–106; Xiao-Planes, 2001; Thompson, 1995.

20. Esherick and Rankin, 1990; Xin Zhang, 2000.

21. JGFD, BG-130.

22. Macauley, 1998.

23. Duara, 1987; Strauss, 1998.

24. Ocko, 1983; Huang, 1996; Macauley, 1998.

25. Mendelsohn, 1981.

Chapter 1: Western Models and Chinese Practices

1. Translation from Reynolds, 1993, 202–203. The ambiguity of the edict (the reference to "Her Majesty" and "we") may be explained briefly: from September 1898 to November 1908, Empress Dowager Ci Xi was in control of the imperial power and the Guangxu emperor was under house arrest. The memorials from officials were formally addressed to both the empress dowager and the emperor, maintaining the fiction that the emperor was still in power. When both Ci Xi and Guangxu died in late 1908, the Xuantong emperor (1908–1911) was a two-year-old boy. Imperial family members exercised power as regents in the name of the emperor, and memorials from officials were formally addressed to the emperor only. To avoid getting into the specifics of imperial palace politics at that time, which do not concern this book, the term "the imperial court" is used to refer to the imperial decision-making power, no matter who was in control, during 1901–1911.

2. The English-language literature on the New Policy and its ramifications includes Cameron, 1963; Reynolds, 1993; Bastid, 1988; Borthwick, 1983; Thompson, 1995; and Xiao-Planes, 2001. New Policy judicial reform has not been adequately studied: Cameron gives it four pages (171–175); Reynolds touches on it briefly in two short chapters (161–192); Dikötter (2002) has a chapter on the beginning of prison reform in the New Policy decade; Meijer, 1950, remains a classic on the reform of Chinese criminal law in the late Qing era but does not cover other aspects of the judicial reform.

3. MacMurray, 1973, 351, 414, 431.

4. CWR, 1922/8/19, 450; Meijer, 1950, 13, 64–65; Cameron, 1963, 171, 173; Reynolds, 1993, 181.

5. Yang Honglie, 1930, 886; Meijer, 1950, 10.

6. ZLD, QS, 2: 384.

7. ZLD, QS, 2: 246; Pomerantz-Zhang, 1992; Xu, 1997.

8. QCLDS, 849–851; Meijer, 1950, 42–43.

9. Bays, 1970.

10. Li Renkai, 2005, 121–166.

11. Svensson, 2002, 98–100. Svensson concludes that the concept did not enter the Chinese political lexicon until after 1898 (84–85).

12. DZ, 1907, no. 8.

13. QCLDS, 840.

14. Goldman and Lee, 2002, 17–29; Duara, 1995, 170–174; Karl, 2003, 33–38; 119–120.

15. QCLDS, 879.

16. QCLDS, 876.

17. Reynolds, 1993, 111–127.

18. Li Guilian, 1998, 9–36; Svensson, 2002, 78; cf. Liu, 2004, chap. 4.

19. Yu Jiang, 2001.

20. Cheng Liaoyuan, 2002.

21. QCLDS, 834.

22. Meijer, 1950, 25–26.

23. DFD, *juan* 10, 1–4; Meijer, 1950, 22–24.

24. DFD, *juan* 10, 1–4; Meijer, 1950, 22–24.

25. Meijer, 1950, 32.

26. Jerome Bourgon has argued that the move to abolish those cruel punishments was not entirely Western-inspired, but had been pushed by Chinese reformers for a long time (Bourgon, 2003). He is right on this particular issue, but the judicial reform as a whole, beyond the abolition of the three cruel punishments, was largely informed by Western models.

27. DFD, *juan* 3, 1–2; DZ, 1904, no. 6; Meijer, 1950, 24–25.

28. DZ, 1904, no. 6.

29. DL, 47–61, 82–84; Shen Zhiqi, 1715, 42–53; Meijer, 1950, 21.

30. DFD, *juan* 3, 16–17; DZ, 1904, no. 6.

31. Zhang Jinfan, 1994, 460–497.

32. Pär Cassel has argued that this kind of "legal pluralism" of the Qing provided the immediate precedents for extraterritoriality that was set up in the mid-nineteenth century to accommodate Westerners' demands (Cassel, 2003).

33. DFD, *juan* 3, 10–11.

34. DFD, *juan* 3, 2–10; DZ, 1908, no. 6.

35. QCLDS, 839.

36. In the Qing judicial practice, an act that was not expressly proscribed by the law could still be considered an offense and punished by applying analogous articles in the law.

37. *Qingshi gao*, "Xingfa Zhi"; QCLDS, 845–849; DFD, *juan* 11; see also Meijer, 1950, 66–76.

38. Matsuda Emiko, 1995; Meijer, 1950, 79–96.

39. QCLDS, 854–857, 858–862, 867–872, 887–889; ZGB, no. 284, 8/11/1908;

also see Yang Honglie, 1930, 894; Meng, 1931, 256; Meijer, 1950, 43–44, 79–93; Pan Nianzhi et al., 1992, 214–220.

40. QCLDS, 857–858.
41. ZGB, no. 284, 8/11/1908; no. 345, 10/11/1908.
42. QCLDS, 870–872.
43. QCLDS, 865–866.
44. Meijer, 1950, 96.
45. Meijer, 1950, 109–112; Pan Nianzhi et al., 1992, 227–228.
46. ZGB, no. 1182, 1911/2/16.
47. QCLDS, 890–891.
48. QCLDS, 851–854.
49. ZGB, no. 242, 1908/6/30.
50. QCLDS, 879–880.
51. QCLDS, 857.
52. QCLDS, 855.
53. Huang, 1996.
54. DZ, 1907, no. 12.
55. QCLDS, 835–836, 850.
56. During 1903–1908, the Qing government worked on drafting a number of commercial laws, which were conceived separately from both the criminal and civil codes with which the Qing officials were wrestling.
57. DZ, 1907, no. 3.
58. DZ, 1907, no. 3.
59. DZ, 1908, "Occasional Supplement," 27–31.
60. QCLDS, 843–844.
61. DFD, *juan* 4, 1–15; ZGB, no. 826, 1910/2/18.
62. ZGB, no. 46, 1907/12/10; no. 48, 1907/12/12.
63. ZGB, no. 666, 1909/9/4; DFD, *juan* 7: 12–14; Meijer, 1950, 44; Yang Honglie, 1930, 919.
64. Brunnert and Hagelstrom, 1912, 346–347.
65. DZ, 1907, no. 8.
66. ZGB, no. 533, 1909/4/24.
67. CY, 1913, 396–397; Chang, 1926, 172.
68. ZGB, no. 826, 1910/2/18.
69. DFD, *juan* 6, 1–3.
70. DZ, 1908, no. 4.
71. DZ, 1904, no. 6.
72. DZ, 1905, no. 8.
73. DZ, 1905, no. 8, 123–127.
74. On the requirement for confession under Qing law, see Harrison, 1964; Connor, 2000.
75. ZGB, no. 1194, 1911/2/28. In the Republican era, torture continued to take place in county trials (see, e.g., NCH, 1917/3/31, 674; 1924/4/26, 127).
76. DFD, *juan* 11, 1–15.
77. Pan Nianzhi et al., 1992, 211–214.
78. ZGB, no. 338, 1908/10/4; Meijer, 1950, 43–44; Zhang Jinfan, 1994, 714.
79. Zhang Jinfan, 1994, 714–715.
80. ZGB, no. 826, 1910/2/18.
81. ZGB, no. 1182, 1911/2/16.
82. Zhang Jinfan, 1994, 272–292; Bodde and Morris, 1973, 113–122, 131–143.
83. DZ, 1904, no. 6.
84. See DL, *juan* 36.
85. DZ, 1904, no. 6.
86. QCLDS, 831–833.
87. DZ, 1908, no. 12.
88. ZGB, no. 848, 1910/3/12; DZ, 1910, no. 4.

89. NYT, 1910/9/11, 5; 1910/10/2, 4.
90. Fabu, 1910; Geng Wentian, 1933, 47–48; Xue Meiqing et al., 1986, 194–195.
91. Shimada, 1977. On Ogawa's role in Japanese penal reform, see Botsman, 2005, 194–200.
92. The reformers would eventually use *kanshou suo* for detention house and *jianyu* for prison. In this book, I use "prison" for a provincial prison for convicts, and "county jail" for a county-level facility for convicts, usually an old jail house called *xian jiujian* in the Republican era.
93. Xue Meiqing et al., 1986, 204–210.
94. Shimada, 1977.

Chapter 2: Judicial Modernity as Performance of Formality

1. NCH, 1912/10/5, 31–32.
2. Yang Youjiong, 1937, 28; Pan Nianzhi et al., 1992, 305.
3. Technically, the draft criminal code was never put into effect prior to 1912.
4. Yang Honglie, 1930, 1032–1035.
5. JGFD, GZ-1.
6. Svensson, 2002, 111–112.
7. ZG, no. 12, 1912/5/12.
8. JGFD, GZ-1.
9. Qian Shifu, 1984, 158–159.
10. Yang Honglie, 1930, 1039–1094; CWR, 1923/3/3, 12–16.
11. CWR, "New China Edition," 1928/10/10, 105.
12. By official account, in July 1912, the MJ had a general office and three departments, with a staff of no more than seventy-two (ZG, 1912, no. 86).
13. Geng Wentian, 1933, 27–29; Qian Shifu, 1991; MZN; MRD.
14. MR, 1918/10 /26, 300.
15. Nathan, 1976, 72–74; cf. MZN.
16. Strauss, 1998.
17. MR, 1918/9/14, 53.
18. NCH, 1923/1/20, 200.
19. FP, 1923/7/1, 3.
20. ZG, 1912, no. 219.
21. ZG, 1912, no. 219.
22. ZG, 1914, no. 720.
23. ZG, 1914, no. 720.
24. ZG, 1912, no. 121; MRD.
25. JGFD, RS-98.
26. DFD, *juan* 4, 11, 13; Qian Shifu, 1984, 371–372, 374–376.
27. Meng, 1931, 258.
28. ZG, 1912, no. 125; no. 142.
29. ZG, 1914, no. 720. An Institute of Judicial Studies was established in October 1914 for judicial officers who had been selected by tests but not appointed yet (ZG, 1914, no. 882).
30. JGFD, RS-352.
31. ZG, 1912, no. 229; ZGFH, no. 36, 9–11.
32. JGFD, RS-98; ZG, 1913, no. 240.
33. ZGFH, no. 36, 11.
34. ZG, no. 301, 1913/3/9.
35. ZGFH, no. 36, 4.
36. ZG, 1915, no. 961.
37. ZGFH, no. 36, 3–4.
38. JGFD, GZ-75.
39. ZG, 1913, no. 371.
40. ZG, 1913, no. 301.

41. JGFD, JG-6.
42. JGFD, JG-6.
43. JGFD, BG-64.
44. JGFD, RS-6.
45. ZG, 1914, no. 720.
46. ZG, 1914, no. 720; no. 740.
47. ZG, 1915, no. 1053.
48. Chang, 1926, 172–173; FP, no. 244, 1–2; CWR, 1931/1/10, 214.
49. Yang Honglie, 1930, 1100–1101.
50. ZG, 1914, no. 687; ZMFD, 5555–5557.
51. ZG, 1914, no. 687.
52. CWR, 1931/1/10, 235; ZG, 1917, no. 469; ZMXFD, 1127–1128; Qian Shifu, 1984, 377–378.
53. Chang, 1926, 172–173.
54. ZG, 1913, no. 597.
55. ZG, 1914, no. 648.
56. ZG, 1914, no. 610.
57. ZG, 1914, no. 621.
58. ZG, 1914, no. 648.
59. JGFD, GZ-75.
60. JGFD, LS-1.
61. ZG, 1916, no. 281.
62. JGFD, LS-33; *Shi Bao*, 1918/9/16. 5; ZG, 1918, no. 942.
63. JGFD, GZ-69; ZG, 1918, no. 981.
64. JGFD, LS-33; *Shi Bao*, 1918/10/28, 5.
65. FP, 1927/1/16, 18.
66. JGFD, LS-25; LS-39.
67. ZG, 1912, no. 114. For more on the Beijing Model Prison, see Dikötter, 2002.
68. ZG, 1913, no. 423.
69. ZG, 1916, no. 353.
70. Dikötter, 2002.
71. Chang, 1926, 177–178; Dikötter, 2002.
72. ZG, 1913, no. 67; ZG, 1913, no. 570; MJFX, 1–10.
73. ZG, 1913, no. 597.
74. ZG, 1913, no. 308.
75. ZG, 1917, no. 365; ZG, 1919, no. 1231; ZG, 1921, no. 1942; JGFD, JZ-357.
76. ZG, 1922, no. 2337; JGFD, BG-359; JGFD, JZ-1106; BG-83, 84, 85, 412, 414.
77. ZG, 1921, no. 1942.
78. ZG, 1912, no. 19.
79. Xu, 2001, 41.
80. JGFD, RS-159; ZG, 1914, no. 705.
81. ZG, 1914, no. 722.
82. JGFD, RS-159.
83. ZG, 1921, no. 1969.
84. JGFD, RS-301.
85. In 1922, the MJ ordered all courts to collect fees for delivery of documents by enforcement measures (ZG, 1922, no. 2299).
86. ZG, 1913, no. 544.
87. ZG, 1927, no. 4101.
88. ZG, 1927, no. 4139.
89. For more on regulation of lawyers, see Connor, 1994; Xu, 2001, 107–128.
90. JGFD, LS-30, LS-33; ZG, 1915, no. 1167.
91. JGFD, LS-30.
92. JGFD, LS-39.

93. Xu, 2001, 51–52.
94. ZG, 1913, no. 280.
95. JGFD, LS-24.
96. JGFD, LS-47.
97. JGFD, LS-47; JGFD, LS-57.
98. ZG, 1912, no. 45; Yang Honglie, 1930, 1126.
99. ZG, 1912, no. 58.
100. ZG, 1912, no. 33.
101. ZG, 1913, no. 554.
102. ZG, 1915, no. 1084.
103. ZG, 1917, no. 460.
104. ZG, 1914, no. 720.
105. ZG, 1915, no. 974.
106. ZG, 1918, no. 851.
107. ZG, 1927, no. 4044.
108. ZG, 1927, no. 4066.
109. JGFD, TJ-16.
110. JGFD, JZ-20.
111. ZG, 1915, no. 1240.
112. JGFD, JZ-20.
113. ZG, 1914, no. 690.
114. CWR, 1931/1/10, 214.
115. ZG, 1920, no. 1712.
116. ZG, 1922, no. 2121.
117. ZG, 1927, no. 4986.
118. ZG, 1914, no. 720.
119. ZG, 1920, no. 1701.
120. Ocko, 1983; Huang, 1996; Macauley, 1998.
121. ZG, 1914/1/30.
122. ZG, 1921, no. 1903.
123. ZG, 1921, no. 1932.
124. ZG, 1921, no. 1965.
125. Huang, 1996, 140–141, 146–151.
126. Buoye, 2000, 197–218.
127. ZG, 1913, no. 298.
128. ZG, 1913, no. 439.
129. ZG, 1913, no. 488.
130. ZG, 1913, no. 544.
131. ZG, 1920, no. 1614; ZG, 1921, no. 1933.
132. ZG, 1921, no. 1930.
133. ZG, 1927, no. 4091.
134. Na Silu, 1982, 169–172.
135. Yang Honglie, 1930, 930–931.
136. ZG, 1912, no. 104; Yang Honglie, 1930, 1095.
137. JGFD, GZ-1; Yang Honglie, 1930, 1095–1096.
138. ZG, 1913, no. 390.
139. ZG, 1914, no. 777.
140. ZG, 1918, no. 811; Yang Honglie, 1930, 1096; Meng, 1931, 257–258; Geng Wentian, 1933, 10–11.
141. ZG, 1918, no. 811.
142. DFD, *juan* 7: 7–8; Yang Honglie, 1930, 1093–1094.
143. ZG, 1920, no. 1874.
144. ZG, 1914, no. 944.

Chapter 3: Justice Under the Party-State

1. CWR, 1929/10/26, 310.
2. For CCP judicial practices, see Lötveit, 1973, 106–144; Butler, 1983; Michael, 1962; Leng, 1967; Cohen, 1968, 483–506; 1969; Liao Kuangsheng, 1983; Leng and Chiu, 1985; Ladany, 1992, 52–70; Lubman, 1999; Peerenboom, 2002.
3. MR, 1919/11/22, 506–507; Yu, 1966, 97; MRD, 703.
4. FP, 1926/9/19, 7.
5. FP, 1927/1/16, 17.
6. FP, 1927/6/13, 7–9; NCH, 1927/7/9, 48; MRD, 703.

7. FP, 1927/4/24: 15.
8. FP, 1927/4/17, 8.
9. JGFD, GZ-114; NCH, 1933/4/5, 2.
10. FP, 1927/4/24, 13.
11. JGFD, GZ-114; FP, 1927/6/13, 7; 1927/6/20, 14–16.
12. FP, 1927/6/20, 14.
13. FP, 1927/8/7, 6.
14. *Shi Bao*, 1929/2/22, 4; MFJ, 5: 203.
15. SG, 1929/3/9, back cover; 1929/3/30, 1.
16. SG, 1935/3/25, 1–3. On GMD control and regulation of the legal profession, see Xu, 2001, 121–128, 249–251, 254–287.
17. JGFD, GZ-144.
18. SFXG, 66.
19. FZ, 1936/12/2, 2; TFYCR, 23.
20. Sifayuan, 1936, 6.
21. Strauss, 1998.
22. Xu, 2001, 235–236.
23. CWR, 1921/11/5, 448; NCH, 1927/5/21, 330; MRD, 1520.
24. NCDN, 1927/5/17, 12; NCH, 1927/5/21, 330.
25. NCDN, 1927/5/19, 6.
26. CWR, 1927/10/22, 216; NCH, 1927/10/22, 144.
27. NCH, 1928/8/11, 234.
28. NCH, 1929/8/10, 218; He Shizhen, n.d., 282–294.
29. Xu, 2001, 237–239.
30. FP, 1927/8/7, 6.
31. FP, 1929/4/28, 19–22.
32. ZFZ, 1930/9, 1–12.
33. CWR, 1928/10/10, 105.
34. MRD, 543–544.
35. ZFZ, 1934/11–12, 1–27.
36. ZFZ, 1934/11–12, 7–9.
37. ZFZ, 1934/11–12, 23.
38. FP, 1929/4/21, 39, 40.
39. JGFD, BG-650.
40. FP, 1927/5/20, 17–18.
41. JGFD, BG-650.
42. GZG, 1927, no. 12.
43. "Local bullies and evil gentry" in the Republican era "represented the remnant of the lower rural elite of imperial days, marooned by the closing of traditional mobility channels, relatively unsuccessful in adapting to the requirements of the times, and with deteriorating social links to the higher elites of the cities," Philip Kuhn writes (1975, 293).
44. Geisert, 2001.
45. GZG, 1927, no. 12.
46. CWR, 1928/10/10, 106, 108.
47. Kuhn, 1975, 288–293.
48. CWR, 1928/10/10, 108.
49. Geng Wentian, 1933, 35.
50. NCH, 1930/4/15, 94; ZFZ, 1934/7, 18–19; ZFZ, 1937/2, 41–42.
51. NCH, 1932/11/30, 334.
52. Geng Wentian, 1933, 108.
53. GZG, 1929, no. 343.
54. ZMFD, 5549–5550.
55. JGFD, TJ-1713.
56. JGFD, BG-1203.
57. Xue Meiqing et al., 1986, 266–269, 290–309; Dikötter, 2002, 280–294.
58. CWR, 1928/10/10, 76; FP, 1929/4/21: 38.
59. Liang, 1928a, 61; "Judicial Administration in China" (1930), 435; MFJ, 6: 238–239; Escarra, 1936, 294–297.

60. MFJ, 11: 299–400.
61. FP, 1929/4/28: 38–39; Meng, 1931, 281.
62. Liang, 1928a, 61–62.
63. MR, 1918/9/14, 56.
64. NCH, 1935/7/3, 15; Escarra, 1936, 300.
65. CWR, 1935/7/6, 181; Escarra, 1936, 301–316.
66. Escarra, 1936, 316.
67. "Judicial Administration in China" (1930), 435–436; ZMXFD, 115–122, 143–170.
68. Bernhardt, 1999; Huang, 2001.
69. Meng, 1931, 281. Judges in Nationalist China "did not call on the authority of custom in adjudicating a case. They generally took great care to cite codified law," Philip Huang writes (2001, 66).
70. Meng, 1931, 282.
71. CWR, 1931/2/14, 390.
72. FP, 1929/4/28: 39.
73. CWR, 1930/8/9, 390; MFJ, 14: 462–465.
74. FP, 1929/5/15: 37–38.
75. MZN.
76. FP, 1933/2/ 19: 38.
77. CWR, 1933/8/12, 463; NCH, 1934/5/30, 308.
78. SN, 1936, D122–123.
79. CWR, 1933/7/29, 356; 1933/8/12, 463.
80. Geng Wentian, 1933, 33.
81. ZFZ, 1934/1: 150–151.
82. FP, 1924/6/29: 45; 1924/9/21: 1–5; Liang, 1928b, 106.
83. NCH, 1927/5/28, 375.
84. Liang, 1928b, 106; ZMXFD, 1112–1113.
85. MFJ, 1: 54–55; Geng Wentian, 1933, 12.
86. DFZ 9, no. 5 (1930/10); FP, 1930/2/23: 1–8; ZFZ, 1937/2: 1–9; FXZ, 1937/1: 1–55, 116–124; 1937/2: 8–13.
87. NCH, 1928/12/8, 385.
88. Meng, 1929, 310.
89. "Judicial Administration in China" (1930), 433.
90. Xu Mao, 1992, 259.
91. Sifayuan, 1934, 2; NCH, 1935/7/3, 2; Yang, 1937, 39–40.
92. FP, 1929/5/29: 37–38. Another source cited 231 new courts in July 1927–February 1929 (Meng, 1931, 283).
93. Sifayuan, 1934, 25.
94. ZFZ, 1937/2: 252–253.
95. FP, 1927/8/21, 8–9.
96. ZFZ, 1935/10: 73; Sifayuan, 1934, 25; 1936, 41.
97. ZFZ, 1935/12: 140; ZFZ, 1936/12: 130.
98. Sifayuan, 1936, 41–71; TFYCR, 22; ZFZ, 1936/10: 6.
99. Liang, 1928b, 108.
100. Sifayuan, 1934, 6.

101. SG, 1936/4/18, 1–2; FZ, 1936/4/22; XS, 1, 8 (1936): 179–181.
102. SG, 1936/7/7, 1–4; 1936/10/10, 2–3; FZ, 1936/7/8.
103. ZFZ, 1936/10: 6.
104. Sifayuan, 1936, 8.
105. Sifayuan, 1936, 41–71.
106. ZFZ, 1937/2: 253.
107. JGFD, LS–172.
108. Xu, 2001, 112–113.
109. JGFD, LS–140.
110. Geng Wentian, 1933, 12.
111. SG, 1936/7/7, 4–6.
112. FP, 1929/5/15: 35–36.
113. JGFD, TJ-1421.
114. ZFZ, 1933/1: 86–87.
115. Xu, 2001, 121–128.
116. Sifayuan, 1936, 35–38.
117. Wu Xueyi, 1941, 20.
118. Wu Xueyi, 1941, 43.
119. Sifayuan, 1935b, 66.
120. ZFZ, 1937/2: 255–256.
121. MDWH, 1–1.
122. SG, 1932/1/2, 15.
123. FZ, 1933/9/20.
124. FZ, 1932/2/24.
125. FZ, 1932/2/24.
126. Wu Xueyi, 1941, 51.
127. JGFD, GZ-225.
128. JGFD, GZ-225.
129. Wu Xueyi, 1941, 52.
130. MJFX, 226–228.
131. "Judicial Administration in China" (1930), 433–434; Meng, 1931, 282.
132. ZFZ, 1937/2: 254–256.
133. CWR, 1936/6/13, 72–73; MJFX, 34–35.
134. MJFX, 275; ZFZ, 1936/10: 8.
135. Xue Meiqing et al., 1986, 278.
136. MJFX, 285–288; ZFZ, 1936/10: 9.
137. MJFX, 269–270.
138. Sifayuan, 1938.
139. Xue Meiqing et al., 1986, 259.
140. CWR, 1931/2/14, 388.
141. On the anti-drug campaign, see Su Zhiliang and Zhao Changqing, 1998, 268–276, 301–306; Slack, 2001, 104–110; Dikötter et al., 2004, 127–130.
142. Su Zhiliang and Zhao Changqing, 1998, 1550–1551, 1554–1555.
143. JGFD, GZ-31.
144. JGFD, GZ-31.
145. JGFD, JZ-1424.
146. JGFD, JZ-1424.
147. JGFD, JZ-1424.
148. MDWH, 2–324.
149. Su Zhiliang and Zhao Changqing, 1998; Slack, 2001.

Chapter 4: Provincial Institutions and Judicial Reform in Jiangsu

1. CWR, 1922/8/19, 451.
2. A major exception was that during 1925–1927, when Sun Yat-sen's NG existed in Guangdong, the courts there stopped following orders from the MJ in Beijing, but even then they continued to apply the PNCC, as did the courts elsewhere.
3. Zhang Hua et al., 1990, 39.
4. Zhang Hua et al., 1990, 32–35. Other sources put the date of separating Jiangnan into Jiangsu and Anhui in 1667 (Shi Yangcheng, 1946, 49; JTDC, "Yange," 6).

5. Zhang Hua et al., 1990, 47.
6. Geisert, 2001, 8–14.
7. Geisert, 2001, 11–12; Huang, 1990, 21–42; Ocko, 1983, 21–29.
8. Zhang Hua et al., 1990, 32–51.
9. Shi Yangcheng, 1946, 55.
10. Cao Yulian, 1994, 4–8.
11. Zhao Ruheng, 1935, 13.
12. Zhao Ruheng, 1935, 7–14; Cao Yulian, 1994, 14–35.
13. Zhao Ruheng, 1935, 6.
14. Zhao Ruheng, 1935, 20–23.
15. Zhao Ruheng, 1935, 35–36.
16. Kuhn, 1975, 284–287.
17. Hu Ciwei, 1948, 3, 48–87.
18. Zhao Ruheng, 1935, 36.
19. DZ, 1907, no. 8.
20. QCLDS, 843.
21. QCLDS, 862–864.
22. ZGB, 1910, no. 1112.
23. Qi Gengsheng, 1989, 133.
24. JGFD, RS-4.
25. JGFD, TJ-7.
26. JGFD, RS-8; RS-10.
27. JGFD, RS-10.
28. Cheng Dequan was on leave from January 1, 1912, until April 13, 1912, when he was officially appointed as the governor (MZN, 243).
29. JGFD, RS-2.
30. JGFD, JG-6.
31. JGFD, GZ-11.
32. JGFD, RS-7.
33. JGFD, RS-12.
34. JGFD, RS-12.
35. JGFD, RS-9.
36. JGFD, RS-6.
37. For more on "dian," see Zelin, 1986; Huang, 2001, 72–78.
38. JGFD, RS-12.
39. JGFD, RS-6.
40. The offices of preparation for judicial institutions were a revival of the New Policy–era offices for organizing courts (*shenpanting choubeichu*), set up in 1907 under the provincial judicial commissioner (Brunnert and Hagelstrom, 1912, 347–348).
41. JGFD, RS-98; ZG, 1913, no. 258.
42. ZG, 1913, nos. 501, 507, 512, 513.
43. ZG, 1914, no. 735.
44. ZG, 1914, no. 754.
45. ZG, 1914, no. 735.
46. ZG, 1914, no. 774.
47. JGFD, RS-132.
48. ZG, 1914, no. 751.
49. SD, 1049-23 (2); ZG, 1917, no. 464.
50. JGFD, RS-140.
51. JGFD, GZ-114.
52. MDWH, 1–4.
53. FJ, 64.
54. FJ, 65.
55. JGFD, JG-1.
56. Qi Gengsheng, 1989, 133.
57. Printed sources mention the establishment of these courts in December 1911 (e.g., JZN, 270), but a report dated June 1911 from the Provincial Capital No. 1 CFI turned up in the archives (JGFD, TJ-12). Jiangning (the city of Nanjing) was the provincial capital of Jiangsu at the time.
58. JZN, 270.
59. ZGB, 1910, no. 826.
60. JGFD, JG-1.
61. JGFD, JG-1.

62. JGFD, GZ-1.
63. JZN, 270–271; Qi Gengsheng, 1989, 134; Zhao Ruheng, 1935, 221.
64. MSX, *juan* 2.
65. JGFD, RS-6.
66. ZG, 1915, no. 1053.
67. Qi Gengsheng, 1989, 134–135; Zhao Ruheng, 1935, 221.
68. JGFD, BG-61.
69. Qi Gengsheng, 1989, 135; Cao Yulian, 1994, 133–143.
70. Qi Gengsheng, 1989, 135.
71. JZN, 271–272; Qi Gengsheng, 1989, 135–136. According to these sources, the Dantu DC was restored in January 1923, but a piece of archival evidence shows a small amount of judicial revenue at the Dantu DC for 1922 (see Table 5.4 in Chapter 5), which means that the court was probably set up in late 1922.
72. KSJ, 31; JZN, 18.
73. JZN, 18.
74. KSJ, 31–32; JZN, 18.
75. Sifayuan, 1931, 4; Zhao Ruheng, 1935, 222.
76. Xu, 2001, 235–240. The Second Branch HC and the Third Branch HC in Shanghai's foreign concessions were virtually semi-independent. The archives show that generic directives sent from the JHC to branch high courts and district courts usually did not go to them.
77. Sifayuan, 1934, 3.
78. Sifayuan, 1934, 3; Zhao Ruheng, 1935, 222.
79. ZFZ, 1935/10: 71.
80. Qi Gengsheng, 1989, 142–143.
81. JGFD, RS-254.
82. The difference between the disposal rate at courts and at CGO is revealing (discussed in Chapter 6).
83. ZFZ, 1935/10: 71.
84. JGFD, JZ-961.
85. JGFD, JG-38.
86. JGFD, BG-1164.
87. JGFD, JZ-7.
88. KSJ, 106–116; JZN, 309–310.
89. NTWZ, 16–19.
90. JGFD, JZ-1038.
91. KSJ, 106–116; JZN, 309–310.
92. JZN, 313–318.
93. JZN, 311–312.
94. Sifayuan, 1931, 84–85.
95. Sifayuan, 1935, 7–8, 26.
96. JGFD, JZ-1508.
97. ZFZ, 1935/10: 72.
98. The Jiangsu Institute of Repentance in Suzhou, set up in 1931, held 74 inmates in August 1932 (Zhao Ruheng, 1935, 229).
99. MDWH, 2–646.
100. MDWH, 2–121.

Chapter 5: Judicial Finance: Nation, Province, and County

1. ZFZ, 1933/1: 79.
2. Huang, 2001, 43.
3. Duara, 1987.
4. Rawski, 1989, 13–27.

5. Bastid, 1985, 74.
6. On financial decentralization in the Qing, see Bastid, 1985.
7. Hickey, 1991; Van de Ven, 1996, 482.
8. Esherick, 1976, 113–120; Kuhn, 1979, 120–121; Prazniak, 1999.
9. Zhou Yumin, 2000, 397–400.
10. Li, 1922, 72–75; Van de Ven, 1996, 482–284.
11. Strauss, 1998, 112–113; Dong Mengxiong, 2000, 89; Sun Yugang, 2003, 362.
12. ZG, 1913, no. 298; no. 301.
13. Dong Mengxiong, 2000, 89–91. Van de Ven, 1996, 846, puts the date in 1916.
14. ZG, 1916, no. 298, *fulu* (appendix).
15. ZG, 1916, no. 298, *fulu* (appendix).
16. Jia Shiyi, 1917, 119.
17. SD, 1049–2841; ZG, 1914, no. 1053.
18. JGFD, RS-98; ZG, 1913, no. 357.
19. ZG, 1920, no. 1587.
20. ZG, 1921, no. 1832.
21. JGFD, GZ-55.
22. JGFD, GZ-55.
23. ZG, 1914, no. 739
24. ZG, 1914, no. 797.
25. ZG, 1916, no. 298, *fulu* (appendix).
26. ZG, 1920, no. 1547.
27. ZG, 1920, no. 1571.
28. ZGB, 1911, no. 1159; DZ, vol. 8, no. 1.
29. JGFD, RS-2.
30. JGFD, GZ-1.
31. JGFD, JG-13.
32. JGFD, JZ-368.
33. JGFD, JZ-368; ZG, 1916, no. 69.
34. JGFD, 39–1310.
35. MDWH, 2–1340.
36. JGFD, GZ-90.
37. The number is slightly different from the archival source cited above.
38. KSJ, 352–361.
39. KSJ, 363–376.
40. ZG, 1914, no. 720.
41. ZG, 1925, no. 3410.
42. JGFD, GZ-125.
43. Chen Guofu, 1983.
44. Sifayuan, 1936, 80.
45. JGFD, TJ-1418.
46. Jia Ziyi, 1936, 53.
47. JGFD, TJ-1418.
48. Kuhn, 1979, 121–123; Duara, 1987, 147.
49. Peng Yuxin, 1948, 3.
50. KSJ, 585–586.
51. After county level courts were dismantled in 1914, other offices of the county government expanded in the 1920s–1930s. More resources were spent on salaries of personnel than actual functions. As Duara (1987) observes, "so great was the pressure to develop the façade of modern government that administrative redundancy, exacerbating the shortage of available resources, was the result."
52. The "façade of modern government" Duara (1987) refers to was the formalization agenda in fields other than the judiciary.

53. In the provincial budget for 1917–1919, a first-grade county would get judicial fund of ¥434 a month.

54. In May–July 1914, for instance, Songjiang collected an average of monthly litigation fees of ¥165.3 (JGFD, TJ-47).

55. JGFD, TJ-326.

56. JGFD, TJ-47.

57. KSJ, 361–362.

58. MDWH, 2–1448.

59. MDWH, 2–1448.

60. MDWH, 2–1448.

61. MDWH, 2–1447.

62. Peng Yuxin, 1948, 4–5.

63. Chen Guofu, 1983, *caizheng* (finance) 5.

64. Chen Guofu, 1983, *caizheng* (finance) 543.

65. ZFZ, 1935/10: 72.

66. JGFD, JZ-1372.

67. MDWH, 2–1511.

68. For the month of July 1931, for instance, the new Songjiang CC collected ¥683.60 of judicial revenue, including ¥227.87 in surcharges (JGFD, TJ-1485).

69. Ni Yaokui, n.d., 268.

70. JGFD, BG-991.

71. MDWH, 2–1085; JGFD, TJ-1920.

72. On the Qing practice, see Na Silu, 1982, 176–179.

73. JGFD, JZ-1024.

74. JGFD, JZ-1024.

75. JGFD, JZ-1024.

76. JGFD, BG-84, 85, 412, 427, 428; JZ-1106.

77. JGFD, GZ-97.

78. JGFD, GZ-97.

79. JGFD, JZ-1403.

80. JGFD, BG-908.

81. JGFD, JZ-1403.

82. JGFD, JZ-54.

83. JGFD, JZ-54.

84. JGFD, JZ-69.

85. JGFD, JZ-523.

86. Miao Wengui, 1963, 23–24.

87. JGFD, JZ-28.

88. They occurred in Shuyang in May 1914 and in Songjiang in 1924, for example (JGFD, JZ-72; JZ-586).

89. Xu, 2001, 61–62.

90. JGFD, JZ-368.

91. JGFD, JZ-309.

92. JGFD, BG-359. The inmate ration in new prisons was raised to ¥0.10 per person-day (Miao Wengui, 1963, 31).

93. JGFD, BG-412, 428.

94. JGFD, JZ-586.

95. MDWH, 2–1504.

96. MDWH, 2–104.

97. JGFD, GZ-169.

98. JGFD, BG-733; JZ-1279; JZ-1286.

99. JGFD, BG-733.

100. JGFD, BG-733; JZ-1279; JZ-1286; JZ-1279; JZ-1403.

101. SD, 7–4739.

102. JGFD, JZ-1013.

103. JGFD, JZ-1344.

104. JGFD, JZ-1344.

105. JGFD, JZ-1213; JZ-1344.

106. MDWH, 2–1222.

107. ZFZ, 1933/1: 79, 88–89. Take an example in another province: the

Longxi DC in Fujian province should have received a monthly fund of ¥6,100, approved by the JC, but the provincial treasury would only give ¥1,300; the court was operating with ¥3,400 a month, of which ¥2,100 came from surcharges on various miscellaneous taxes (ZFZ, 1933/1: 91).

108. Zhu Gemin, 1989, 185.
109. Ni Yaokui, n.d., 279.
110. Ni Yaokui, n.d., 279.

Chapter 6: The Social Context of County Judicial Functions

1. NCH, 1917/11/3, 267. The italics and Chinese characters are in the original.
2. Esherick, 1976; Wong, 1977; Prazniak, 1999.
3. JGFD, RS-2.
4. JGFD, RS-2.
5. JGFD, JG-2.
6. JGFD, JG-2.
7. JGFD, JG-6.
8. JGFD, JG-2.
9. JZN, 36.
10. ZG, 1913, no. 569.
11. MFJ, 14: 48–54; Cheng Fang, 1939, 133–134.
12. JZN, 33–34.
13. MSX, *juan* 2.
14. DTWZ, 78–79.
15. TWZJ, 20, 23.
16. JTWZ, 23–25; YXWZ, 24–28; HAWZ, 97–99; JYWZ, 32–35; JC, 23–24; RW, 123–129; WZJ, 180–181; FWZ, 152–153; TWZJ, 19–25; JWZX, 27–28; TWZ, 9–10.
17. JZN, 35–44.
18. Esherick and Rankin, 1990, 3.
19. MSX, *juan* 2.
20. For conflicts between the CGO and GMD cadres, see Geisert, 2001.
21. PWZ, 114–115.
22. SQWZ, 47–50.
23. Wang Chengzhi, 1929, 50.
24. JGFD, BG-844.
25. CWR, 1936/9/19, 90.
26. E.g., in 1918, a county magistrate of Shucheng, Anhui province, was dismissed and barred from office for six years for arresting, torturing, and convicting several men in violation of laws and procedures; and 1919, a county magistrate of Dangshan, Jiangsu province, was dismissed and barred from office for four years for failing to ascertain the facts in a murder case (ZG, 1918, no. 793; 1919, no. 1163).
27. ZG, 1919, no. 1218.
28. KSJ, 45.
29. JDFC, sec. 6, 15–17; KSJ, 45–46.
30. KSJ, 46; Wei Li and Li Xin, 1989, 103.
31. JDFC, sec. 6, 16.
32. Wei Li and Li Xin, 1989, 106–107.
33. JGFD, BG-844.
34. JGFD, RS-139.
35. JGFD, JZ-384.
36. JGFD, JZ-384.
37. JGFD, BG-991; JZ-1441.
38. JGFD, BG-908.
39. JGFD, BG-844.
40. JGFD, BG-1164.
41. JGFD, JZ-1441.
42. JGFD, JZ-467.

43. Deng Changyao, 1925.
44. E.g., WZJ, 12: 49–50; FNWZ, 1: 77–79; SYWZ, 4: 96–99; YCWZ, 4: 162–165; SQWZ, 3: 29; JJWZ, 3: 38.
45. Reed, 2000; Na Silu, 1982, 63.
46. JGFD, BG-823, 991; JZ-1441.
47. JGFD, JZ-1441.
48. JGFD, RS-423.
49. SQWZ, 4: 44–46.
50. Deng Changyao, 1925.
51. XX, 75–76.
52. Huang, 1996, 203–218.
53. JGFD, JZ-329.
54. In 1914, to speed up disposal of cases, the MJ allowed county magistrates to announce decisions in minor civil cases orally (ZG, 1914, no. 918).
55. The term *ziyou xinzheng* came from Japanese, in which it was a translation of the French term "la conviction intime" (*Zhongguo dabaike quanshu–faxue* [Chinese encyclopedia–law], 835).
56. CXD, 34-1-759.
57. BXD, 43-1-425, 426.
58. This cannot be quantified due to a lack of complete case records for the country or a given province in a given period.
59. BXD, 43-1-18.
60. A statistics book compiled by the Jiangsu Provincial Government in 1930 contained the data from all counties submitted by county magistrates. Fourteen magistrates listed "very litigious" (*jiansong, haosong*) as characteristic of local people's habits and customs in their counties (JTDC, *hukou* (households), 66–67).
61. JGFD, RS-6.
62. JJWZ, 3: 37–38; YWZX, 4: 165.
63. YWZX, 4: 165.
64. JGFD, RS-303; JZN, 68–72.
65. Arguing for a different point, Philip Huang reaches the same conclusion for the Qing time. He also compares the Qing time and the Republican era, showing the increase in lawsuits in the latter period, but the number was still quite low. He further compares the number in the PRC with that in the United States, again showing the former to be much lower. Huang, 1996, 173–179.
66. Macauley, 1998, 66, 67.
67. Ocko, 1983, 82.
68. JGFD, JZ-8.
69. JGFD, JZ-496.
70. JGFD, BG-546.
71. JGFD, JZ-8.
72. JGFD, BG-796.
73. JGFD, BG-898.
74. JGFD, BG-130.
75. CXD, 34-1-820.
76. JGFD, BG-823.
77. JGFD, JZ-1286.
78. JGFD, BG-1164.

Chapter 7: Power and Justice in Local Society

1. NCH, 1935/9/11, 418.
2. Esherick and Rankin, 1990; Rowe, 1984; 1989; Strand, 1989.
3. JGFD, RS-6.
4. JGFD, BG-66.
5. JGFD, BG-52.
6. JGFD, JZ-715.
7. Qing law provided for marriage to be conducted by grandparents and

parents (DL, 204). The Republic did not have a law to change that until the civil code of 1929–30, which provided that a marriage agreement should be made by the man and the woman themselves (ZMXFD, 57).

8. JGFD, JZ-624.
9. ZG, 1914, no. 622.
10. Ma Min, 1993, 201–214.
11. SX, 480.
12. SXD, 3-1-2555.
13. SXD, 3-1-2555.
14. SXD, 3-1-2584.
15. SXD, 3-1-2584.
16. Huang, 1996.
17. SXD, 3-1-2584.
18. JGFD, BG-298.
19. SXD, 3-1-2594.
20. NCH, 1925/10/17, 129.
21. ZG, 1914, no. 720.
22. Xu Jiali, 1998, 115–117.
23. JGFD, GZ-42.
24. JGFD, GZ-42; Yang Honglie, 1930, 1107, 1132, 1143, 1163.
25. JZN, 42.
26. JGFD, RS-441.
27. JGFD, RS-441.
28. JGFD, RS-441.
29. JGFD, RS-441.
30. JGFD, RS-441.
31. JGFD, BG-1197.
32. CWR, 1931/8/15, 427.
33. Geisert, 2001.
34. JGFD, BG-863.
35. Xu, 2001, 184–185.
36. JGFD, BG-863.
37. JGFD, BG-863.
38. WZJ, 465–467.
39. JGFD, BG-1221.
40. JGFD, BG-1052.

Chapter 8: Prison Reform and County Jails

1. MDWH, 2–121.
2. ZG, 1913, no. 567.
3. ZG, 1913, no. 308.
4. ZG, 1913, no. 300, 451, 531.
5. JGFD, JZ-80.
6. JGFD, JZ-83.
7. JGFD, JZ-80.
8. JGFD, JZ-80.
9. JGFD, JZ-83.
10. JGFD, JZ-80.
11. JGFD, JZ-83.
12. ZG, 1919, no. 1173.
13. ZG, 1920, no. 1431.
14. JGFD, BG-427.
15. JGFD, JZ, 926.
16. ZG, 1913, no. 570.
17. MJFX, 399–400.
18. ZG, 1915, no. 1187.
19. ZG, 1920, no. 1502.
20. Dikötter, 2002, 105–107. Prison work was often financially unprofitable (Miao Wengui, 1963, 25).
21. JGFD, JZ-49.
22. JGFD, JZ-357.
23. MJFX, 407–408, 411–423.
24. JGFD, BG-908; JZ-1286.
25. JGFD, JZ-1347.
26. JGFD, JZ-42.
27. JGFD, JZ-76.
28. JGFD, JZ-42.
29. ZG, 1914, no. 933.
30. JGFD, JZ-42.
31. Yang Honglie, 1930, 1114.
32. ZG, 1913, no. 282.
33. ZG, 1920, no. 1729.
34. JGFD, BG-1164.
35. JGFD, BG-1164.
36. MDWH, 2–210.
37. JGFD, JZ-1408.
38. JGFD, JZ-1408.
39. JGFD, JZ-1508.
40. JGFD, JZ-1508.
41. JGFD, JZ-1508.
42. ZG, 1913, no. 446.

43. ZG, 1914, no. 720.
44. Miao Wengui, 1963, 23.
45. ZG, 1916, no. 109.
46. JGFD, JZ-268; ZG, 1917, no. 366; MJFX, 187.
47. ZG, 1918, no. 715.
48. ZG, 1915, no. 1050; 1051; 1917, no. 426; no. 504; 1919, no. 1061.
49. JGFD, JZ-307, 320.
50. ZG.
51. JGFD, JZ-307.
52. JGFD, JZ-320.
53. Zhu Gemin, 1989, 188–189.
54. This was one source of the unreported revenues at the CGO that the provincial authorities suspected to exist (see Chapter 5).
55. JGFD, RS-348.
56. Zhu Gemin, 1989, 191–92.
57. Zhu Gemin, 1989, 192.
58. NCH, 1937/9/11, 418.
59. JGFD, JZ-1417.
60. JGFD, JZ-357.
61. JGFD, JZ-357.
62. JGFD, JZ-1145.
63. JGFD, BG-823.
64. MJFX, 359–60.
65. SXD, 3-1-2618.
66. SXD, 3-1-2618.
67. SXD, 3-1-2547.
68. JGFD, JZ-329.
69. JGFD, JZ-1181.
70. JGFD, JZ-1181.
71. 16 *liang* would make one *jin*.
72. JGFD, JZ-1181.
73. Zhu Gemin, 1989, 187.
74. The "aviation fee" (*hangkong fei*) was a levy collected for building a Chinese air force.
75. JGFD, JZ-1408.

Chapter 9: "Quick Justice": Punishing Robbers and Bandits

1. Calling robbers, murderers, and kidnappers "gentry" was meant to be sarcastic.
2. NCH, 1928/2/18, 250.
3. Shen Zhiqi, 1049; Bodde and Morris, 131–143; Zhang Jinfan, 1994, 549–564; Na Silu, 1982, 219–216.
4. DL, *juan* 23, 24, and 25.
5. ZGB, no. 172, 1908/4/21.
6. QSG, "Xingfa zhi er."
7. ZGB, no. 802, 1910/1/18.
8. ZGB, no. 802, 1910/1/18.
9. QCLDS, 902.
10. ZG, 1912, no. 48.
11. ZG, 1912, no. 48.
12. ZG, 1912, no. 109.
13. ZG, 1912, no. 109.
14. ZG, 1914, no. 720.
15. ZG, 1914, no. 720.
16. ZG, 1914, no. 775; no. 931.
17. ZG, 1914, no. 795.
18. ZG, 1914, no. 931. The LPRB caused much confusion among officials as to the applicability of the law and related procedures (ZG, 1914, nos. 795, 802, 868; 1915, nos. 1006, 1013; Van der Valk, 1949, 47–52).
19. JGFD, GZ-40; ZG, 1914, no. 884.
20. ZG, 1921, no. 1882.
21. In 1922, the MJ issued an order to repeal the LPRB and then reinstated it in 1923 after opposition from the governors of several provinces (Yang Honglie, 1930, 1054–1055).

22. JGFD, BG-652.
23. ZMXFD, 1247–48.
24. FP, 1933/2/5: 1–4; 1934/4: 25–29.
25. NCH, 1928/2/18, 250.
26. For a comparison, the Japanese authorities in Taiwan after 1895 used the Bandit Punishment Ordinance to execute rebels resisting Japanese colonial rule (Botsman, 2005, 206–207).
27. MFJ, 1: 419–420.
28. FP, 1932/6/5: 4–5; JQ, 2: 517–518.
29. JGFD, GZ-1.
30. JGFD, GZ-1.
31. JGFD, BG-49.
32. JGFD, GZ-1.
33. JGFD, JZ-7.
34. As noted in Chapter 4, three district courts in Jiangsu processed 2,302 criminal and civil appeal cases from fifty-seven counties, and in 591 (25.7 percent) of those cases, the decisions made by county magistrates were voided or changed. One wonders whether the error rate in prosecutions and executions by county magistrates of robber-bandits under the LPRB was similar.
35. Billingsley, 1988.
36. JGFD, JZ-715.
37. The so-called autopsy means a visual inspection of the surface of the body, without medical equipment or examination of internal organs, tissues, etc., being involved.
38. JGFD, JZ-749.
39. JGFD, JZ-749.
40. JGFD, JZ-42.
41. JGFD, JZ-42.
42. JGFD, JZ-42.
43. JGFD, JZ-42.
44. JGFD, JZ-1044.
45. JGFD, JZ-1044.
46. JGFD, BG-848.
47. MDWH, 1–4.

Chapter 10: The Praxis of Petition and the Economy of False Accusation

1. JGFD, BG-1166.
2. Petitions discussed here should not be confused with complaints against actions of the government at the Administrative Court, for which rules were issued by the NG in March 1930 (NCH, 1930/3/18, 425).
3. Organizational theory posits that information asymmetry—in which the agent (or the subordinate) has more information than the principal (or the superior)—tends to foster more corruption and irregularities (see, e.g., Kiser and Tong, 1992).
4. On this point, see also Reed, 2000, xvi–xviii; Macauley, 1998, 15–17.
5. JGFD, RS-172.
6. JGFD, RS-253.
7. JGFD, BG-1288.
8. JGFD, RS-382.
9. JGFD, JZ-496.
10. JGFD, BG-1166.
11. JGFD, BG-1285.
12. JGFD, RS-181.
13. JGFD, JZ-382.
14. *Shen Bao*, 1935/2/24, 7.
15. JGFD, BG-1108.
16. JGFD, BG-1108.

17. JGFD, BG-508.
18. Huang, 1996, 99–100, 159–163.
19. Macauley, 1998, 140–142.
20. JGFD, JZ-382.
21. JGFD, JZ-382.
22. JGFD, BG-508.
23. JGFD, BG-863.
24. JGFD, BG-1166.
25. Huang, 1996.
26. Ocko, 1983.
27. JGFD, BG-1061.
28. JGFD, RS-414.
29. JGFD, RS-467.
30. JGFD, JZ, 312.
31. JGFD, JZ-1145.
32. JGFD, JZ-1145.
33. JGFD, JZ-1181.
34. JGFD, BG-1263.
35. JGFD, JZ-696.
36. JGFD, JZ-1146.
37. Tanner, 1999.

Conclusion

1. NCH, 1925/10/17, 129.
2. NCH, 1925/12/12, 476.
3. NCH, 1928/12/22, 475.
4. On peasants' protest against the New Policy projects, see Prazniak, 1999.
5. Henriot, 1993; Strauss, 1998.
6. Henriot, 1993, 234.
7. Henriot, 1993, 232.
8. More substantive discussion of the post-Mao legal-judicial reform is impossible here, and readers are referred to Peerenboom, 2002; Lubman, 1999.

References

Archival Sources

BXD—Baoshan xianzhengfu dang'an (Archives of the Baoshan County Government). Baoshan District Archives, Baoshan, Shanghai.

CXD—Chuansha xianzhengfu dang'an (Archives of the Chuansha County Government). Pudong New District Archives, Pudong, Shanghai.

JGFD—Jiangsu gaodeng fayuan dang'an (Archives of the Jiangsu High Court). Jiangsu Provincial Archives, Nanjing. One group of the files (category number 1047–41) is divided by subcategories. In my citations, the category number is omitted and subcategories are used, followed by file numbers: RS = *renshi* (personnel); GZ = *guizhang* (regulations); JZ = *jianzheng* (prison administration), TJ = *tongji* (statistics), JG = *jigou* (institutions), BG = *baogao* (report), and LS = *lüshi* (lawyers). Other category numbers, such as 1047–35, 1047–38, are simply followed by file numbers.

MDWH—Minguo dang'an wenjian huiji (A collection of archival documents of the Republic). Jiangsu Provincial Archives, Nanjing. This group of files, cataloged after 1998, is identified by category number 1054. Subcategory 1 is *zhengwu* (political affairs), and 2 is *sifa* (judiciary). In my citations, "1054" is omitted, and "MDWH, 1" or "MDWH, 2" is used, followed by file numbers.

SD—Sifabu dang'an (Archives of the Ministry of Justice). Number Two Historical Archives, Nanjing.

SXD—Songjiang xianzhengfu dang'an (Archives of the Songjiang County Government). Songjiang District Archives, Songjiang, Shanghai.

Printed Primary Sources

Cao Yulian. 1994. *Minguo Jiangsu quanli jiguan shilue* (A brief history of the government institutions in Republican Jiangsu). Nanjing: Jiangsu wenshi ziliao bianjibu.

Chang, Yao-tseng. 1926. "The Present Conditions of the Chinese Judiciary and Its Future." *Chinese Social and Political Science Review* 10, 1 (Jan.): 163–182.

Chen Guofu. 1983. *Jiangsu shengzheng shuyao* (An essential summary of the Jiangsu provincial government). Taipei: Wenhai chubanshe.

Cheng Fang. 1939. *Zhongguo xianzheng gailun* (A general treatise on county government in China). Shanghai: Shangwu yinshuguan.

Commission on Extraterritoriality. 1923. *Laws, Ordinances, Regulations and Rules Relating to the Judicial Administration of the Republic of China*. Peking. Reprint, Taipei: Chengwen chubanshe, 1971.

CWR—*China Weekly Review*. Shanghai, 1922–1937.

CWZJ—*Changshu wenshi ziliao jichun* (A collection of sources on history and culture of Changshu). No. 10 (July 1983).

CY, 1913—*The China Yearbook, 1913*. Shanghai: North China Herald, Ltd.

CY, 1923—*The China Yearbook, 1923*. H. G. W. Woodhead, ed. The Tientsin Press, Ltd.

Deng Changyao. 1925. *Xianshu zhi baibi* (One hundred abuses at county offices). Guihuacheng: Longqingzai.

DFD—*Daqing fagui daquan* (A complete collection of laws of the Great Qing). Beijing: Zhengxueshe, 1909.

DFZ—*Dongwu faxue zazhi* (Journal of the Soochow University Law School). Shanghai.

DL—*Daqing lüli* (The law and substatutes of Great Qing). Beijing: Falü chubanshe, 1999.

DTWZ—*Dantu wenshi ziliao* (Sources on the culture and history of Dantu). No. 3 (August 1986).

DZ—*Dongfang zazhi* (Eastern miscellanies). 1904–1911.

Escarra, Jean. 1936. *Le droit chinois: Conception et évolution, institutions législatives et judiciaires, science et enseignement*. Peking: H. Vetch; Paris: Recueil Sirey. Translated by Gertrude R. Brown for the Works Progress Administration under the title *Chinese Law: Conception and Evolution, Legislative and Judicial Institutions, Science and Teaching*, W.P. 2799, University of Washington, Seattle (Cambridge, Mass.: Harvard Law School, 1961).

Fabu. 1910. *Zhoupai fumei Dibaci Wanguo Jianyu Gailianhui huiyuan baogaoshu* (A report by delegates attending the Eighth International Prison Reform Conference in America).

FJ—*Faling jiyao* (A collection of important laws and ordinances). Zhengjiang: Jiangsu sheng minzheng ting, 1930.

FNWZ—*Funing wenshi ziliao* (Sources on the culture and history of Funing). No. 1 (October 1984).

FP—*Falü pinglun* (Law Review). Beijing, 1923–1937.

FWZ—*Fengxian wenshi ziliao* (Sources on the culture and history of Feng county). No. 7 (March 1988).

FXZ—*Faxue zazhi* (Law Journal). Shanghai, 1931–1937.

FZ—*Faling zhoukan* (Weekly Review of Laws and Ordinances). Shanghai, 1930–1937.

Geng Wentian. 1933. *Zhongguo zhi sifa* (China's judiciary). Shanghai: Minzhi shujü.

GZG—*Guomin zhengfu gongbao* (National Government Bulletin). Nanjing. 1927–1937.

HAWZ—*Huai'an wenshi ziliao* (Sources on the culture and history of Huai'an).

He Shizhen. No date. "Ji Shanghai gonggong zujie linshi fayuan" (on Provisional Court of the International Settlement in Shanghai), JWZJ, "Zhengzhijuan" (Volume on politics), 282–294.

Hu Ciwei. 1948. *Minguo xianzhi shi* (A history of county system in the Republic). Shanghai: Dadong shuju.

JC—*Jiangning chunqiu* (Spring and autumn of Jiangning). No. 4 (June 1986).

JDFC—*Jiangsusheng danxing faling chubian* (First compilation of provincial laws and ordinances in Jiangsu). Jiangsu shengzhang gongshu gongbaochu, 1924.

Jia Dehuai. 1941. *Minguo caizheng jianshi* (A brief history of finance of the Republic). Shanghai: Shangwu yinshuguan.

Jia Shiyi. 1917. *Minguo caizheng shi* (A history of finance of the Republic). Shanghai: Shangwu yinshuguan.

Jia Ziyi. 1936. *Jiangsu shenghui jiyao* (Essential information on the Jiangsu provincial capital). Zhengjiang: Jiangnan yinshuguan.

Jiangsu. Zhengjiang: Jiangsusheng zhengfu, 1928.

JJWZ—*Jingjiang wenshi ziliao* (Sources on the culture and history of Jingjiang).

JQ—*Juzheng quanji* (Complete works of Ju Zheng). 3 Vols. Chen Sanjing and Ju Mi, eds. Taipei: Institute of Modern History, Academia Sinica, 1999.

JTDC—*Jiangsusheng tongji dagang chubian* (The first compilation of outline statistics of Jiangsu province). Zhengjiang: Jiangsusheng mishuchu, 1930.

JTWZ—*Jintan wenshi ziliao* (Sources on the culture and history of Jintan). No. 7 (Dec. 1989).

"Judicial Administration in China." 1930. *Chinese Social and Political Science Review* 14, 4 (Oct.): 425–437.

JWZ—*Jiangsu wenshi ziliao* (Sources on the history and culture of Jiangsu).

JWZJ—*Jiangsu wenshi ziliao jicui* (The best collection of sources on the culture and history of Jiangsu).

JWZX—*Jiangdu wenshi ziliao xuanbian* (Selection of sources on the culture and history of Jiangdu). No.3 (May 1986).

JYWZ—*Jiangyin wenshi ziliao* (Sources on the culture and history of Jiangyin). No. 1 (Feb. 1983).

JZN—*Jiangsu zhengzhi nianjian: Shiyi nianfen* (Jiangsu political yearbook for 1922). Nanjing: Jiangsu shengzhang gongshu tongjichu, 1924.

KSJ—*Kaocha sifa ji* (A record of investigation of the judiciary). Beijing: Faquan taolun weiyuanhui, 1924.

Liang, Yunli [Liang, Yueng-li]. 1928a. "The New Criminal Code." CWR 46, 2 (Sept. 8): 61–62.

———. 1928b. "Judicial Reform Under the Nationalist Government." CWR, New China ed. (Oct. 10): 105–108.

Liu Zaojia. 1930. *Jiangsu renwen dili* (Human geography of Jiangsu). Shanghai: Dadong shujü.

Meng, C. Y. W [Meng Changyong]. 1929. "Judicial Reform During the Period of Political Tutelage." CWR 50, 8 (Oct. 26): 310–312.

———. 1931. "Modern Judicial Reform in China." CWR 55, 6 (Jan. 10): 214, 235–237; 55, 7 (Jan. 17): 256–258; 55, 8 (Jan. 24): 281–283.

MFJ—*Minguo fagui jikan* (A collection of laws of the Republic of China). Shanghai: Minzhi shuju, 1929–1930.

Miao Wengui. 1963. "Guomindang tongzhi shiqi de yuzheng (Prison administration in the Guomindang period)." In *Shanghai wenshi ziliao chungao huibian* (A collection of preserved manuscripts of sources on the culture and history of Shanghai), 12: 17–33. Shanghai: Shanghai guji chubanshe, 2001.

MJFX—*Minguo jianyu fagui Xuanbian* (A selection of prison laws and regulations of the Republic). Beijing: Zhongguo shudian, 1990.

Minguo renwu zhuan (Biographies of the Republic). Vols. 1–9. Beijing: Zhonghua shujü, 1978–1997.

MSX—*Minguo Shanghai xianzhi* (Shanghai county gazetteer of the Republic). 1935.

MR—*Millard's Review*. Shanghai, 1917–1922.

MRD—*Minguo renwu dacidian* (A comprehensive dictionary of people of the Republic). Shijiazhuang: Hebei renmin chubanshe, 1991.

MZN—*Minguo zhiguan nianbiao* (Chronological tables of officeholders of the Republican period). Beijing: Zhonghua shujü, 1995.

NCH—*North China Herald*. Shanghai, 1912–1937.

NCDN—*North China Daily News*. Shanghai, 1927.

Ni Yaokui. No date. "Jiangsu jiu sifa jie suoji" (Reminiscences of the old judicial circles in Jiangsu), JWZJ. "Zhengzhi juan" (Volume on politics), 268-281.

NTWZ—*Nantong wenshi ziliao* (Sources on the culture and history of Nantong). No. 17 (n.d.).

NYT—*New York Times*. 1910.

PWZ—*Peixian wenshi ziliao* (Sources on the culture and history of Pei county). No. 7 (1991/12).

QCLDS—*Qingmo choubei lixian dang'an shiliao* (Archival sources on the preparation for constitutional government in the late Qing). Beijing: Zhonghua shujü, 1979.

Qi Gengsheng. 1989. "Zhonghua minguo shiqi Jiangsu shenpan jigou kaolue (A brief study of the trial organs in Jiangsu during the Republic of China period)." *Jiangsu wenshi ziliao*, no. 33: 133–147.

Qian Shifu. 1984. *Beiyang zhengfu shiqide zhengzhi zhidu* (The political system of the Beiyang government period). Beijing: Zhonghua shujü.

———. 1991. *Beiyang zhengfu zhiguan nianbiao* (A chronological table of the Beiyang government officeholders). Shanghai: Huadong shifan daxue chubanshe.

QSG—*Qingshi gao* (Draft history of the Qing). "Xingfa Zhi" (Book on punishments).N.p.: Lianhe shudian, 1942.

RW—*Rugao wenshi* (Culture and history of Rugao). No. 1 (Sept. 1985).

SFXG—*Sifayuan Faguan Xunliansuo Gailan* (An overview of the Judicial Council Training Institute for Judges). Nanjing, 1935.

SG—*Sifa gongbao* (Judicial Bulletin). 1929–1932; 1934–1937.
Shen Bao (Shanghai News).
Shen Zhiqi, 1715. *Daqing lü jizhu* (Collected annotations to the Great Qing law). Reprint, Beijing: Falü chubanshe, 1998.
Sifayuan. 1931. *Minguo shiba nian sifa tongji* (Judicial statistics for the eighteenth year of the Republic [1929]). Nanjing.
———. 1934. *Sifayuan gongzuo baogao* (Work report of the Judicial Council). Nanjing.
———. 1935a. *Quanguo sifa huiyi huibian* (A collection of proceedings of the national judicial conference). Nanjing.
———. 1935b. *Sifayuan Faguan Xunliansuo Gailan* (An overview of Judicial Council Training Institute for Judges).
———. 1936. *Ershisan niandu sifa tongji* (Judicial statistics for the twenty-third year [1934]). Nanjing.
———. 1938a. *Sifayuan Zuijin Gongzuo Gaikuang* (An overview of recent work of the Judicial Council). Chongqing.
———. 1938b. *Ershiwu Niandu Sifa Tongji* (Judicial statistics for the twenty-fifth year [1936]). Chongqing.
Shanghai Nianjian (Shanghai Yearbook). 1934; 1936.
Shi Bao (Eastern Times).
Shi Yangcheng. 1946. *Zhongguo sheng xingzheng zhidu* (The provincial administrative system in China). Shanghai: Shangwu yinshuguan.
SN—*Shenbao Nianjian* (Yearbook of the Shanghai News). Shanghai, 1933; 1936.
SQWZ—*Suqian wenshi ziliao* (Sources on the culture and history of Suqian). No. 2 (Dec. 1983).
SX—*Songjiang Xianzhi* (Songjiang county gazetteer). Shanghai: Shanghai renmin chubanshe, 1991.
SXG—*Sifa Xingzheng Gongbao* (Judicial Administration Bulletin). 1932.
SYWZ—*Siyang wenshi ziliao* (Sources on the culture and history of Siyang). No. 4 (Dec. 1986).
SYG—*Sifa Yuan Gongbao* (Judicial Council Bulletin). 1932–1934.
TSWZ—*Tongshan wenshi ziliao* (Sources on the culture and history of Tongshan). No. 10 (July 1990).
TFYCR—*Twenty-Five Years of the Chinese Republic*. 1937. Nanjing: International Relations Committee.
TWZ—*Tongshan Wenshi Ziliao* (Sources on the culture and history of Tongshan). No. 10 (July 1990).
TWZJ—*Taicang Wenshi Ziliao Jicun* (A collection of sources on the culture and history of Taicang). No. 2 (Dec. 1984).
Van der Valk, M. H. 1968. *Interpretations of the Supreme Court at Peking, Years 1915–1916: Translations, Notes and Introduction*. Batavia: University of Indonesia, 1949; reprint, Taipei: Ch'eng-wen Publishing Co.
Wan Deyi. 1931. *Zhongguo sifa zhidu yibie* (A glance at China's judicial system). N.p.: Zhejiang faxue yuanjiuhui.
Wang Chengzhi. 1929. *Zhongguo sifa wenti* (China's judicial problem). Shanghai: Sanmin shudian.

Wang, Chonghui. 1917. "Law Reform in China." *Chinese Social and Political Science Review* 2, 2 (June): 13–21.
Wei Li, and Li Xin. 1989. "Zhonghua Minguo Shiqi Jiangsu Shenpan Dashiji (A chronicle of major trials in Jiangsu during the Republic of China)." JWZ, no. 33.
Wu Xueyi. 1941. *Sifa jianshe yu sifa rencai* (Judicial construction and judicial personnel). Chongqing: Guomin tushushe.
Wu Zhaoxin. 1937. *Zhongguo suishou shi* (A history of Chinese taxation). Shanghai: Shangwu yinshuguan.
WZJ—*Wenshi ziliao jicun* (A collection of sources on culture and history). No. 12 (Dec. 1985).
WZX—*Wenshi ziliao xuanbian* (Selection of sources on culture and history).
XS—*Xiandai sifa* (Modern Judiciary). 1935–1937.
XX—*Xianzhang xuzhi* (What County Magistrates Should Know). Nanjing: Guomin zhengfu neizhengbu, 1928.
Yang Honglie. 1930. *Zhongguo falü fada shi* (A history of the development of Chinese law). Shanghai: Shanghai shudian.
Yang Youjiong. 1937. "Zhongguo sifa zhidu zhi zhongde guancha" (A historical overview of Chinese judicial system). *Zhonghua faxue zazhi* (Journal of Chinese Legal Studies), new ed., 1, 5–6 (Feb.): 19–46.
Yao Gonghe. 1917. *Shanghai xianhua* (Leisured talk about Shanghai). Shanghai: Shangwu yinshuguan.
YWZX—*Yancheng wenshi ziliao xuanji* (A selection of sources on the culture and history of Yancheng). No. 4 (June 1986).
YXWZ—*Yixing wenshi ziliao* (Sources on the culture and history of Yixing). No. 6 (Feb. 1984).
ZFZ—*Zhonghua faxue zazhi* (Journal of Chinese Legal Studies). 1930–1937.
ZG—*Zhengfu gongbao* (Government Bulletin). 1912–1927.
ZGB—*Zhengzhi Guanbao* (Official Gazetteer of Political Affairs). 1906–1911.
ZGFH—*Zhengfu gongbao fenlei huibian* (Government Bulletin compiled in categories).
Zhang Jinfan. 1994. *Qingchao fazhi shi* (A history of the Qing legal system). Beijing: Falü chubanshe.
Zhao Ruheng. 1935. *Jiangsu shengjian* (An overview of Jiangsu province). Shanghai: Xinzhongguo jianshe xuehui.
Zhou Zuyi. 1986. "Xu Qian nianpu" (A biographic chronicle of Xu Qian). WZX, vol. 30, (Dec. 1986): 158–173.
ZJWZ—*Zhengjiang wenshi ziliao* (Sources on the culture and history of Zhengjiang). No. 8, 1984.
ZMFD—*Zhonghua minguo fagui daquan* (A complete compilation of the laws and regulations of the Republic of China). Shanghai: Shangwu yinshuguan, 1936.
ZMXFD—*Zhonghua minguo xianxing fagui daquan* (A complete compilation of current laws and regulations of the Republic of China). Shanghai: Shangwu yinshuguan, 1934.

Secondary Works

Bartlett, Beatrice S. 1991. *Monarchs and Ministers: The Grand Council in Mid-Ch'ing China, 1723–1820*. Berkeley: U. of California Pr.

Bastid, Marianne. 1988. *Educational Reform in Early-Twentieth-Century China*. Ann Arbor: Center for Chinese Studies, U. of Michigan.

———. 1985. "The Structure of the Financial Institutions of the State in the Late Qing." In S. R. Schram, ed., *The Scope of State Power in China*. New York: St. Martin's Pr.

Bays, Daniel H. 1978. *China Enters the Twentieth Century: Chang Chih-tung and the Issues of the New Age, 1895–1909*. Ann Arbor: U. of Michigan Pr.

———. 1970. "The Nature of Provincial Political Authority in Late Ch'ing Times: Chang Chih-Tung in Canton, 1884–1889." *Modern Asian Studies* 4, 4: 325–347.

Bernhardt, Kathryn. 1992. *Rents, Taxes, and Peasant Resistance: The Lower Yangzi Region, 1840–1950*. Stanford: Stanford UP.

———. 1999. *Women and Property in China, 960–1949*. Stanford: Stanford UP.

Billingsley, Phil. 1988. *Bandits in Republican China*. Stanford, Calif.: Stanford UP.

Borthwick, Sally. 1983. *Education and Social Change in China*. Stanford: Hoover Institute Pr.

Bourgon, Jerome. 2003. "Abolishing 'Cruel Punishments': A Reappraisal of the Chinese Roots and Long-term Efficiency of the Xinzheng Legal Reform." *Modern Asian Studies* 37, 3: 851–862.

Bodde, Derk, and Clarence Morris. 1973. *Law in Imperial China*. Philadelphia: U. of Pennsylvania Pr.

Botsman, Daniel V. 2005. *Punishment and Power in the Making of Modern Japan*. Princeton: Princeton UP.

Brunnert, H. S., and V. V. Hagelstrom. 1912. *Present Day Political Organization of China*. Trans. from the Russian with the authors' sanction by A. Beltchenko and E. E. Moran. Shanghai: Kelly & Walsh.

Buoye, Thomas M. 2000. *Manslaughter, Markets, and Moral Economy: Violent Disputes over Property Rights in Eighteen-Century China*. Cambridge: Cambridge UP.

Butler, W. E. 1983. *The Legal System of the Chinese Soviet Republic, 1931–1934*. Dobbs Ferry, N.Y.: Transnational Publishers.

Cameron, Meribeth E. 1963. *The Reform Movement in China, 1898–1912*. New York: Octagon Books.

Cassel, Pär. 2003. "Excavating Extraterritoriality: The 'Judicial Sub-perfect' as a Prototype for the Mixed Court in Shanghai." *Late Imperial China* 24, 2 (Dec.): 156–182.

Cheng Liaoyuan. 2002. "Qingmo de fazhi huayu" (The discourse on rule of law in the late Qing). *Zhongxi falü chuantong* (Chinese and Western Legal Traditions). No. 2. Beijing: Zhongguo zhengfa daxue chubanshe. 250–271.

Cohen, Jerome Alan. 1968. *The Criminal Process in the People's Republic of China, 1949–1963*. Cambridge, Mass.: Harvard UP.

———. 1969. "The Chinese Communist Party and 'Judicial Independence': 1949–1959." *Harvard Law Review* 82, 5: 967–1006.

Connor, Alison W. 1994. "Lawyers and the Legal Profession during the Republican Period." In Kathryn Bernhardt and Philip Huang, eds., *Civil Law in Qing and Republican China*. Stanford: Stanford UP.

———. 2000. "True Confession? Chinese Confessions Then and Now." In Karen G. Turner et al., eds., *The Limits of the Rule of Law in China*. Seattle: U. of Washington Pr.

Dikötter, Frank. 2002. *Crime, Punishment and the Prison in Modern China*. New York: Columbia UP.

Dikötter, Frank, Lars Laamann, and Zhou Xun. 2004. *Narcotic Culture: A History of Drugs in China*. Chicago: U. of Chicago Pr.

Dong Mengxiong. 2000. *Zhongguo jindai caizheng shi* (A history of modern Chinese finance). Kunming: Yunnan daxue chubanshe.

Duara, Prasenjit. 1987. "State Involution: A Study of Local Finance in North China, 1911–1935." *Comparative Study in Society and History*, 132–161.

———. 1995. *Rescuing History from the Nation: Questioning Narratives of Modern China*. Chicago: U. of Chicago Pr.

Esherick, Joseph W. 1976. *Reform and Revolution in China*. Berkeley: U. of California Pr.

Esherick, Joseph W., and Mary B. Rankin. 1990. *Chinese Local Elites and Patterns of Dominance*. Berkeley: U. of California Pr.

Fishel, Wesley R. 1952. *The End of Extraterritoriality in China*. Berkeley: U. of California Pr.

Geisert, Bradley K. 2001. *Radicalism and Its Demise: The Chinese Nationalist Party, Factionalism, and Local Elites in Jiangsu Province, 1924–1931*. Ann Arbor: Center for Chinese Studies, U. of Michigan.

Giddens, Anthony. 1990. *The Consequences of Modernity*. Stanford: Stanford UP.

Goldman, Merle, and Leo Ou-fan Lee. 2002. *An Intellectual History of Modern China*. Cambridge: Cambridge UP.

Harrison, Judy Feldman. 1964. "Wrongful Treatment of Prisoners: A Case of Ch'ing Legal Practice." *Journal of Asian Studies* 23, 2 (Feb.): 227–244.

Henriot, Christian. 1993. *Shanghai, 1927-1937: Municipal Power, Locality, and Modernization*. Translated by Noël Castelino. Berkeley: U. of California Pr. Originally published as *Shanghai, 1927-1937: Élites locales et modernisation dans la Chine nationaliste* (Paris: Éd. de l'École des hautes études en sciences sociales, 1991).

Hickey, Paul C. 1991. "Fee-Taking, Salary Reform, and the Structure of State Power in Late Qing China, 1909–1911." *Modern China* 17, 3 (July): 389–417.

Huang, Philip C. C. 1990. *The Peasant Family and Rural Development in the Yangzi Delta, 1350–1988*. Stanford: Stanford UP.

———. 1996. *Civil Justice in China: Representation and Practice in the Qing*. Stanford: Stanford UP.

———. 2001. *Code, Custom, and Legal Practice: The Qing and the Republic Compared*. Stanford: Stanford UP.

Karl, Rebecca. 2003. *Staging the World: Chinese Nationalism at the Turn of the Twentieth Century*. Durham, N.C.: Duke UP.

Kiser, Edgar, and Xiaoxi Tong. 1992. "Determinants of the Amount and Type of Corruption in State Fiscal Bureaucracies: An Analysis of Late Imperial China." *Comparative Political Studies* 25, 3 (Oct.): 300–331.

Komesar, Neil K. 2001. *Law's Limits: The Rule of Law and the Supply and Demand of Rights*. Cambridge: Cambridge UP.

Kuhn, Philip A. 1975. "Local Self-Government Under the Republic: Problems of Control, Autonomy, and Mobilization." In Frederick Wakeman Jr. and Carolyn Grant, eds., *Conflict and Control in Late Imperial China*. Berkeley: U. of California Pr.

———. 1979. "Local Taxation and Finance in Republican China." In Susan Mann Jones, ed. *Proceedings of the HEH Modern China Project, 1977–1978: Political Leadership and Social Change at the Local Level in China from 1850 to the Present*, 100–136. Chicago: U. of Chicago.

———. 2002. *Origins of the Modern Chinese State*. Stanford: Stanford UP. Originally published as *Les origines de l'état chinois moderne* (Paris: Éd. de l'École des hautes études en sciences sociales, 1999).

Ladany, Laszlo. 1992. *Law and Legality in China*. London: Hurst & Co.

Leng, Shao-chuan. 1967. *Justice in Communist China*. Dobbs Ferry, N.Y.: Oceana Publications.

Leng, Shao-chuan, and Hung-dah Chiu. 1985. *Criminal Justice in Post-Mao China*. Albany: State U. of New York Pr.

Li, Chuan Shih. 1922. *Central and Local Finance in China: A Study of the Fiscal Relations between the Central, the Provincial, and the Local Governments*. New York: Columbia UP.

Li Guilian. 1998. *Ershi siji de Zhongguo faxue* (Chinese legal studies in the twentieth century). Beijing: Beijing daxue chubanshe.

Li Renkai. 2005. *Zhang Zhidong mufu* (The Staff of Zhang Zhidong). Beijing: Zhongguo guangbo dianshi chubanshe.

Liao Kuangsheng. 1983. "'Independent Administration of Justice' and the PRC Legal System." *Chinese Law and Government* 16, 2–3: 123–152.

Liu, Lydia H. 2004. *The Clash of Empires: The Invention of China in Modern World Making*. Cambridge, Mass.: Harvard UP.

Lötveit, Trygve. 1973. *Chinese Communism 1931–1934: Experience in Civil Government*. Lund: Studentlitteratur.

Lubman, Stanley B. 1999. *Bird in a Cage: Legal Reform in China After Mao*. Stanford, Calif.: Stanford UP.

Lu Manping and Jia Xiuyan. 1992. *Minguo jiage shi* (A history of prices in Republican China). Beijing: Zhongguo wujia chubanshe.

Ma Min and Zhu Ying. 1993. *Chuantong yu jindai de erchong bianzhou: Wanqing Suzhou changhui ge'an yanjiu* (Duel variations of tradition and modernity: The case study of the Suzhou Chamber of Commerce). Chengdu: Bashu shushe.

Macauley, Melissa. 1998. *Social Power and Legal Culture: Litigation Masters in Late Imperial China*. Stanford: Stanford UP.

MacKinnon, Stephen R. 1980. *Power and Politics in Late Imperial China: Yuan Shikai in Beijing and Tianjin, 1901–1908*. Berkeley: U. of California Pr.

MacMurray, John V. A., ed. 1973. *Treaties and Agreements with and Concerning China, 1894–1919*. New York: Howard Fertig.

Matsuda Emiko, 1995. "Shinmatsu reihou sogi shoko" (A brief examination of the debate on propriety and law in late Qing). *Hougaku Ronsou* (Treatises on Legal Study) 2: 48–67; 5: 113–124.

Meijer, Marinus J. 1950. *The Introduction of Modern Criminal Law in China*. Batavia, Indonesia: De Unie. Reprinted Arlington, Va.: University Publications of America, 1976.

Mendelsohn, Oliver. 1981. "The Pathology of the Indian Legal System." *Modern Asian Studies* 15, 4: 823–863.

Michael, Franz. 1962. "The Role of Law in Traditional, Nationalist and Communist China." *China Quarterly*, no. 9: 124–148.

Myers, Ramon H. 2000. "The Chinese State During the Republican Era." In David Shambaugh, ed., *The Modern Chinese State*, 42–72. Cambridge: Cambridge UP.

Na Silu. 1982. *Qingdai zhouxian yamen shenpan zhidu* (The trial system at the county yamen in the Qing era). Taipei: Wenshize chubanshe.

Nathan, Andrew J. 1976. *Peking Politics, 1918–1923*. Berkeley: U. of California Pr.

Ocko, Jonathan K. 1983. *Bureaucratic Reform in Provincial China: Ting Jih-ch'ang in Restoration Kiangsu, 1867–1870*. Cambridge, Mass.: Harvard UP.

———. 1988. "I'll Take It All the Way to Beijing: Capital Appeals in the Qing." *Journal of Asian Studies* 47, 2 (May): 291–315.

Pan Nianzhi et al. 1992. *Zhongguo jindai falu sixiang shi* (A history of legal theories in modern China). Shanghai: Shehui kexue chubanshe.

Peerenboom, Randall. 2002. *China's Long March Toward Rule of Law*. Cambridge: Cambridge UP.

Peng Yuxin. 1948. *Xian difang caizheng* (Local finance in counties). Shanghai: Shangwu yinshuguan.

Pomerantz-Zhang, Linda. 1992. *Wu Tingfang (1842–1922): Reform and Modernization in Modern Chinese History*. Hong Kong: Hong Kong UP.

Prazniak, Roxann. 1999. *Of Camel Kings and Other Things: Rural Rebels Against Modernity in Late Qing China*. Lanham, Md.: Rowman & Littlefield.

Rawski, Thomas G. 1989. *Economic Growth in Prewar China*. Berkeley: U. of California Pr.

Reed, Bradly W. 2000. *Talons and Teeth: County Clerks and Runners in the Qing Dynasty*. Stanford: Stanford UP.

Reynolds, Douglas R. 1993. *China, 1898–1912: The Xinzheng Revolution and Japan*. Cambridge, Mass.: Harvard UP.

Rowe, William T. 1984. *Hankow: Commerce and Society in a Chinese City, 1796–1889*. Stanford: Stanford UP.

———. 1989. *Hankow: Conflict and Community in a Chinese City, 1796–1895*. Stanford: Stanford UP.

Shimada Masao. 1977. "Sinmatsu no gokusei kaikaku to Ogawa Shigejiro" (The reform of the prison system in the late Qing and Ogawa Shigejiro). In *Tezuka Yutaka kyoju taishoku kinen ronbunshu—Meiji hoseishi-seijishi no shomondai* (Professor Tezuka Yutaka retirement memorial collection of articles—Issues of the Meiji legal history and political history). Tokyo: Keio tsushinsho.

Shue, Vivienne. 1988. *The Reach of the State: Sketches of the Chinese Body Politic.* Stanford: Stanford UP.

Slack, Edward R., Jr. 2001. *Opium, State, and Society: China's Narco-Economy and the Guomindang, 1924–1937*. Honolulu: U. of Hawaii Pr.

Strand, David. 1989. *Rickshaw Beijing: City People and Politics in the 1920s*. Berkeley: U. of California Pr.

Strauss, Julia C. 1998. *Strong Institutions in Weak Polities: State Building in Republican China, 1927–1940*. Oxford: Oxford UP.

Su Zhiliang and Zhao Changqing. 1998. *Jingdu quanshu* (A comprehensive history of drug prohibition [in China]). Beijing: Zhongguo minzhu fazhi chubanshe.

Sun Yugang. 2003. *Zhongguo caizheng shi* (A history of Chinese finance). Beijing: Zhongguo shehui kexue chubanshe.

Svensson, Marina. 2002. *Debating Human Rights in China: A Conceptual and Political History*. Lanham, Md.: Rowman & Littlefield.

Tanner, Harold M. 1999. *Strike Hard! Anti-Crime Campaigns and Chinese Criminal Justice, 1979–1985*. Ithaca, N.Y.: Cornell UP.

Thompson, Roger R. 1995. *China's Local Councils in the Age of Constitutional Reform, 1898–1911*. Cambridge, Mass.: Council on E. Asian Studies, Harvard U.

Tien, Hung-mao. 1972. *Government and Politics in Kuomintang China, 1927–1937*. Stanford: Stanford UP.

Van de Ven, Hans J. 1996. "Public Finance and the Rise of Warlordism." *Modern Asian Studies* 30, 4: 829–868.

Van der Valk, M. H. 1949. *Interpretations of the Supreme Court at Peking, Years 1915–1916: Translations, Notes and Introduction*. Batavia: U. of Indonesia; reprint, Taipei: Ch'eng-wen Publishing Co., 1968.

Wong, Young-Tsu. 1977. "Popular Unrest and the 1911 Revolution in Jiangsu." *Modern China* 3, no. 3: 321–344.

Xi Ping et al. 1991. *Minguo shehui daguan* (An overview of society in the Republic of China). Fuzhou: Fujiang renmin chubanshe.

Xiao-Planes, Xiaohong. 2001. *Éducation et politique en Chine: Le rôle des élites du Jiangsu, 1905-1914*. Paris: Éd. de l'École des hautes études en sciences sociales.

Xu Jiali. 1998. *Zhonghua minguo lüshi zhidu shi* (A history of the lawyer system in the Republic of China). Beijing: Zhongguo zhengfa daxue chubanshe.

Xu Mao. 1992. *Zhonghua minguo zhengzhi zhidu shi* (A history of the political institutions of the Republic of China). Shanghai: Shanghai renmin chubanshe.

Xu, Xiaoqun. 1997. "The Fate of Judicial Independence in Republican China, 1912–1937." *China Quarterly*, no. 149: 1–28.

———. 2001. *Chinese Professionals and the Republican State: The Rise of Professional Associations in Shanghai, 1912–1937*. New York: Cambridge UP.

Xue Meiqing et al. 1986. *Zhongguo jianyu shi* (A history of Chinese prisons). Beijing: Qunzhong chubanshe.

Yu, George T. 1966. *Party Politics in Republican China: The Kuomintang, 1912–1924*. Berkeley: U. of California Pr.

Yu Jiang. 2001. "Jindai Zhongguo faxue yuci de xingcheng yu fazhan" (The formation and development of legal terminology in modern China). *Zhongxi falü chuangtong* (Chinese and Western Legal Traditions), no. 1. Beijing: Zhongguo zhengfa daxue chubanshe. 24–66.

Zelin, Madeleine. 1986. "The Rights of Tenants in Mid-Qing Sichuan: A Study of Land-Related Lawsuits in the Baxian Archives." *Journal of Asian Studies* 45, 3: 499–527.

Zhang Hua et al. 1990. *Qingdai Jiangsu shigai* (A brief history of Jiangsu in the Qing era). Nanjing: Nanjing daxue chubanshe.

Zhang, Xin. 2000. *Social Transformation in Modern China*. New York: Cambridge UP.

Zhao Xiaohua. 2001. *Wanqing songyu zhidu de shehui kaocha* (A social study of the litigation system in late Qing). Beijing: Zhongguo renmin daxue chubanshe.

Zhou Yumin. 2000. *Wanqing caizheng yu shehui bianqian* (Late Qing finance and social change). Shanghai: Shanghai renmin chubanshe.

Zhu Gemin. 1989. "Jiu jianyu neimu" (Inside information on the old jails). *Shanghai Wenshi Ziliao Xuanji*, no. 63. Shanghai: Shanghai renmin chubanshe.

ZLD, QS—*Zhongguo lishi dacidian* (A complete dictionary of Chinese history). "Qing Shi" (Qing history). Shanghai: Shanghai cishu chubanshe, 1992.

Glossary

ancha si 按察司
bagong 拔贡
baiyi 白役
banguan 班馆
bangshen yuan 帮审员
banfa 办法
banpo 伴婆
bao 保
baohu renquan 保护人权
baolan cisong 包揽词讼
baoshi 保释
biansu 辩诉
bifu 比附
caijue 裁决
caizheng ting 财政厅
chaidai 差代
chengfa li 承发吏
chengfashi 惩罚室
chengshen yuan 承审员
chengzhi bangfei tiaoli 惩治绑匪条例
chengzhi daofei fa 惩治盗匪法
chengzhi daofei tiaoli 惩治盗匪条例
chengzhi daofei zanxing tiaoli 惩治盗匪暂行条例
chi 笞
choubei yuan 筹备员
cizi 刺字
chuji fayuan 初级法院
chuji shenpan ting 初级审判厅
chuji jiancha ting 初级检察厅
daibiao 代表
daili ren 代理人
daizang ju 代葬局
daizhi suo 待质所
Dali yuan 大理院
dalisi 大理寺
danghua sifa 党化司法
dangyi 党义
dangzhi 党治
dani 大逆
dao 盗
dao 道
dao'an 盗案
daozei 盗贼
daoyin 道尹
Daqing lüli 大清律例
Daqing xianxing xinglü 大清现行刑律
dazhong shuji 大众书记
dian 典
dianshi 典史
dianyu si 典狱司
dianyu zhang 典狱长
dibao 地保
difang caizheng 地方财政
difang fayuan 地方法院
difang ligun 地方劣棍

difang shenpanting 地方审判厅
difan zhidu 地方之蠹
difang yubei fei 地方预备费
digun 地棍
donggun 董棍
dongxi geguo 东西各国
ducha yuan 督察院
dujun 督军
dusi 都司
fabu 法部
faguan yangcheng suo 法官养成所
falü bianzhuan guan 法律编撰馆
falü yi danghua 法律宜党化
fanxingyuan 反省院
faquan 法权
fayuan 法院
fei 匪
fenze 分则
fupan 复判
gaodeng fayuan 高等法院
gaodeng fayuan fenyuan 高等法院分院
gaodeng shenpanting 高等审判厅
geguo 各国
gongfei 共匪
gongli 公理
gongmin 公民
gongquan 公权
gongshe bianhuren 公设辩护人
gongsheng 贡生
gongshi 工食
guandian 官店
guanmei 官媒
guanyu yuan 管狱员
guoshui ting 国税厅
hangkong fei 航空费
haosong 好讼
hejie 和解
houbu 候补
hufei 鬍匪
huibi 回避
huifei 会匪
jianchayuan 监察院
jiancha zhang 检察长
jianhou 监候
jiangbei hujun shi 江北护军使
jiangfei 蒋匪
Jiangsu sheng fanxingyuan 江苏省反省院
Jiangsu sheng sifa ting 江苏省司法厅
jiansong 健讼
jianyan li 检验吏
jianyu 监狱
jianyu guizhe 监狱规则
jianyu tongji 监狱统计
jiao 绞
jiao 缴
jiaoyang 教养
jiaxin fang 家信房
jie 结
jijin fan 寄禁犯
jinshi 进士
jinyan zongjian 禁烟总监
jilu 记录
jin 斤
jingchang suiru 经常岁入
jinzu 禁卒
jiudi zhengfa 就地正法
jiufa 旧法
jiulü 旧律
jiya fan 寄押犯
juliu 拘留
juliu chang 拘留场
jun 郡
jun 军
junfa congshi 军法从事
junren jianyu 军人监狱
juzhong 聚众
kanggao 抗告
kanshou 看守
kanshou suo 看守所
kanshou zhang 看守长
kuai kuaizhuang 快快状
kuaizhuang 快状
laotou 牢头
li 里
liang 两
lianzuo 连坐
liedong 劣董
liedong songgun 劣董讼棍
lijiao 礼教
lijue 立决
ling 领

lingchi 凌迟
lixue guan 礼学馆
liu 流
liuzhi suo 留置所
longtou 龙头
luandang 乱党
lujun 鲁军
luren 掳人
lushi 戮尸
lushi 录事
lushu 录书
mazei 马贼
minben 民本
minjun guangfu 民军光复
minshi guanshou 民事管收
minshi guanshou ren 民事管收人
minshi jianyi anjian 民事简易案件
minzheng zhang 民政长
mingqian 冥钱
minyi 民意
moufan 谋反
neijian 内监
neikanshou 内看守
nifei 逆匪
nuo dian 挪垫
panfan 叛犯
panjue 判决
panni 叛逆
piaoben 票本
pingzheng yuan 平政院
qian 遣
qiangdao 强盗
qiedao 窃盗
qiezei 窃贼
qingyi bao 清议报
qiying shuoshi 耆英硕士
qiuliang 囚粮
qu 区
qu xingzheng yuan 区行政员
quandong 权董
renge 人格
renmin quanli 人民权利
renmin zhi quanli 人民之权利
renquan 人权
shanggao 上告
shangsu 上诉
shanhuo renxin raohai gong'an erqi baodong 煽惑人心扰害公安而起暴动
shanzhuang yuan 缮状员
shatian ju 沙田局
shehuihua 社会化
shendong 绅董
shenji chu 审计处
shenji fenchu 审计分处
shenjian suo 审检所
shengzhang 省长
shenpan ting 审判厅
shenpanting choubeichu 审判厅筹备处
shenpan zhang 审判长
shidangbu 市党部
shijie geguo 世界各国
shipu 食铺
shixiang lianhehui 市乡联合会
shoushu 收赎
shuchai 书差
shuiwai shouru 税外收入
shuji guan 书记官
shuji yuan 书记员
si 死
sifa choubei chu 司法筹备处
sifa dangrenhua 司法党人化
sifa dangyihua 司法党义化
sifa jiangxi suo 司法讲习所
sifa jingcha 司法警察
sifa tongji 司法统计
sifa yuan 司法院
songgun 讼棍
su 诉
tangshi 堂事
taobing 逃兵
tifa si 提法司
tingcheng 厅丞
tingli 庭吏
tingzhang 厅长
tongfei 通匪
tongpan 通判
tongyuan 铜元
tongzhi 同知
tuhao lieshen 土豪劣绅
tumu wenming 徒慕文明
tuxing 徒刑
tu 徒

tufei 土匪
tuiju 推举
waijian 外监
wanguo 万国
weidong 圩董
weiren 委任
wen 文
wenguan chengjie tiaoli 文官惩戒条例
wude shufu gongci 务得输服供词
xian 县
xian 限
xiandai shi zhi guojia 现代式之国家
xian fayuan 县法院
xian jiujian 县旧监
xian sifa chu 县司法处
xian sifa gongshu 县司法公署
xianzhang gongfei 县长公费
xiang 乡
xiangqing 乡情
xiang yanju 乡谳局
xiangzhang 乡长
xianzuo 县佐
xianzheng biancha guan 宪政编查馆
xiaoju shanze kangju guanbing 啸聚山泽抗拒官兵
xiaoshou 枭首
xinfa 新法
xinfeng 薪俸
xinlü 新律
xinzhi 新制
xing'an huilan 刑案汇览
xingshi jianyi ting 刑事简易庭
xingwei 刑威
xingzheng fayuan 行政法院
xingzheng yuan 行政院
xinzheng 新政
xiuding falü guan 修订法律馆
xiza shangqi, xishi jiansong 喜诈尚欺, 喜事健讼
xuexi 学习
xun'an shi 巡按使
xunfu 巡抚
xunjian 巡检
yanjiu dangyi 研究党义
yanglian 养廉
yidang zhiguo 以党治国
yingjie yuanjia wucheng 应解原价五成
yisu guanzhen 以肃官箴
yixue guan 译学馆
youguai 诱拐
youmin digun 游民地棍
youwan 游玩
youyong 游勇
yueding bianhuren 约定辩护人
yueyu 越狱
zanxing fangeming zhizui fa 暂行反革命治罪法
zanxing xinxinglü 暂行新刑律
zhan 斩
zhang 杖
zheshu 折赎
zhen 镇
zhengxian 政宪
zhili zhou 直隶州
zhong'an 重案
zhongyang caizheng 中央财政
zhongyang fazhi weiyuanhui 中央法制委员会
zhou 州
zhuangzhi 状纸
zhuanshen yuan 专审员
ziyi ju 谘议局
ziyou xinzheng zhuyi 自由心证主义
zizheng yuan 资政院
zizhi yihui 自治议会
zuigao fayuan 最高法院
zuiren 罪人

Index

CPSIA information can be obtained
at www.ICGtesting.com
Printed in the USA
BVHW03*1627021018
528933BV00035B/315/P

9 780804 755863